KARL JASPERS'S PHILOSOPHY

Expositions & Interpretations

KARL JASPERS'S PHILOSOPHY

Expositions & Interpretations

EDITED BY
KURT SALAMUN & GREGORY J. WALTERS

HB
Humanity
Books

an imprint of Prometheus Books
59 John Glenn Drive, Amherst, New York 14228–2119

Published 2008 by Humanity Books, an imprint of Prometheus Books

Inquiries should be addressed to
Prometheus Books
59 John Glenn Drive
Amherst, New York 14228–2119
VOICE: 716–691–0133, ext. 210
FAX: 716–633–0137
WWW.PROMETHEUSBOOKS.COM

12 5 4 3

Library of Congress Cataloging-in-Publication Data

Karl Jaspers's philosophy : exposition and interpretations / edited by Kurt Salamun and Gregory J. Walters.

p. cm.

Includes bibliographical references (p.) and indexes.

ISBN 978–1–59102–375–3 (hardcover : alk. paper)

1. 1. Jaspers, Karl, 1883–1969. I. Salamun, Kurt. II. Walters, Gregory J., 1956–.

B3279.J34K2947 2006
193—dc22

200502704

Printed in the United States on acid-free paper

CONTENTS

II. WORLD HISTORY OF PHILOSOPHY, WORLD PHILOSOPHY, AND POLITICS

III. FREEDOM AND WILL, PHILOSOPHIC FAITH, AND METAPHYSICS

VI. COMMUNICATION WITH ASIAN THOUGHT

LEGEND OF ABBREVIATIONS

AB *Die Atombombe und die Zukunft des Menschen: Politisches Bewusstsein unserer Zeit.* 4th edition (Munich: R. Piper, 1960 [1958]).

AP *Allgemeine Psychopathologie*, 9. unveränderte Auflage (Berlin/Heidelberg/New York: Springer-Verlag, 1973).

BPW *Karl Jaspers: Basic Philosophical Writings, Selections*, edited and translated by Edith Ehrlich, Leonard H. Ehrlich, and George Pepper (Atlantic Highlands, NJ: Humanities Press, 1994).

FE *Die Frage der Entmythologisierung* (Munich: Piper & Co., 1954).

FM *The Future of Mankind*, translated by E. B. Ashton (Chicago: University of Chicago Press, 1961).

GP 1 *The Great Philosophers 1: The Foundations*; *The Paradigmatic Individuals: Socrates, Buddha, Confucius, Jesus*; *The Seminal Founders of Philosophical Thought: Plato, Augustine, Kant*, edited by H. Arendt, translated by R. Manheim (New York: Harcourt, Brace & World, 1962).

GP 2 *The Great Philosophers 2: The Original Thinkers*: *Anaximander, Heraclitus, Parmenides, Plotinus, Anselm, Nicholas of Cusa, Spinoza, Lao-Tzu, Nagajuna*, edited by H. Arendt, translated by R. Manheim (New York: Harcourt Brace & World, 1966).

GP 3 *The Great Philosophers 3: The Great Philosophers*: *Xenophanes, Democritus, Empedocles, Bruno, Epicurus, Boehme, Schelling, Leibniz, Aristotle, Hegel*, edited by Michael Ermarth and Leonard H. Ehrlich, translated by Edith Ehrlich and Leonard H. Ehrlich (New York: Harcourt Brace, 1993).

GP 4 — *The Great Philosophers 4: The Disturbers: Descartes, Pascal, Lessing, Kierkegaard, Nietzsche—Philosophers in Other Realms: Einstein, Weber, Marx*, edited by Michael Ermarth and Leonard H. Ehrlich, translated by Edith Ehrlich and Leonard H. Ehrlich (New York, San Diego, London: Harcourt Brace, 1994).

GPsy — *Karl Jaspers: General Psychopathology*, Vols. I, II, translated by J. Hoenig and Marian W. Hamilton (Baltimore and London: The Johns Hopkins University Press, 1997).

GrPh — *Die grossen Philosophen* (Munich: R. Piper, 1957).

GrPh/N1,N2 — *Die grossen Philosophen: Nachlass 1: Darstellungen und Fragmente; Nachlass 2: Fragmente, Anmerkungen, Inventar.* Hrsg. von Hans Saner (Munich, Zurich: R. Piper, 1981).

GSZ — *Die geistige Situation der Zeit.* (Berlin: de Gruyter, 1931.–13. Aufl. 1979).

HS — *Hoffnung und Sorge: Schriften zur deutschen Politik, 1945–1965* (Munich: R. Piper, 1965).

IU — *The Idea of the University*, edited by Karl W. Deutsch, preface by Robert Ulich, translated by Harold A. T. Reiche and H. F. Vanderschmidt (Boston: Beacon Press, 1959).

MC — *Myth and Christianity: An Inquiry into the Possibility of Religion without Myth*, translated by Norbert Gutermann (New York: Noonday Press, 1964).

MMA — *Man in the Modern Age*, translated by Eden and Cedar Paul (London: Routledge and Kegan Paul, 1966).

OGH — *The Origin and Goal of History*, translated by Michael Bullock (New Haven, CT: Yale University Press, 1953).

P 1,2,3 — *Philosophie*, 3 vols. (Berlin & Heidelberg: Springer, 1973 [1932]).

PA — *Philosophische Autobiographie* (Munich: R. Piper, 1977).

PAE "Philosophical Autobiography," in *The Philosophy of Karl Jaspers*, P. A. Schilpp, ed., pp. 1–94, The Library of Living Philosophers, 2nd Augmented Edition with section on Heidegger [75/1–75/16] (Lasalle, IL: Open Court, 1981).

PE *Philosophy of Existence*, translated by Richard F. Grabau (Philadelphia: University of Pennsylvania Press, 1971).

PFR *Philosophical Faith and Revelation,* translated by E. B. Ashton (New York: Harper & Row, 1967 [German, 1962]).

PGO *Der Philosophische Glaube angesichts der Offenbarung* (München: Piper & Co., 1962).

PH1,2,3 *Philosophy*, 3 vols, translated by E. B. Ashton (Chicago and London: University of Chicago Press, 1969).

PSP *The Perennial Scope of Philosophy,* translated by Ralph Manheim (New York: Philosophical Library, 1949).

PSW *Psychologie der Weltanschauungen* (Berlin: Springer, 1971, 6th edition [1919]).

PW *Philosophy and the World: Selected Essays and Letters*, translated by E. B. Ashton (Chicago: Regnery, 1963).

RA *Rechenschaft und Ausblick. Reden und Aufsätze* (München: Piper, 1951.–2. Aufl. 1958).

RE *Reason and Existence*, translated by William Earle (New York: Noonday Press, 1955).

QGG The Question of German Guilt, translated by E. B. Ashton (New York: Capricorn Books, 1961).

TE *Three Essays: Leonardo, Descartes, Max Weber*, translated by Ralph Manheim (New York: Harcourt, Brace and World, 1964).

TNE *Tragedy Is Not Enough*, translated by Harald A. T. Reiche, Harry T. Moore, and Karl W. Deutsch (Boston: Beacon Press, 1952).

VdW *Von der Wahrheit* (Munich: R. Piper 1947).

VUZG *Vom Ursprung und Ziel der Geschichte* (Zurich: Artemis Verlag, 1949).

WP *Weltgeschichte der Philosophie. Einleitung*, edited by Hans Saner (Munich: Piper, 1982).

WW *Way to Wisdom*, translated by Ralph Manheim (London: Gollancz, and New Haven: Yale University Press, 1951).

ACKNOWLEDGMENTS

We wish to acknowledge our thanks to Ms. Evelin Maierhuber, chief librarian at the Institut für Philosophie, Karl-Franzens Universität, Graz, Austria, for unflagging technical assistance with preparation of the manuscript in its early stage. Thanks also go to Dr. Harald Stelzer who prepared the much needed and updated Jaspers bibliography. A very special debt of gratitude is due to Dr. Edith Ehrlich for her professional and philosophically acute English translations of the original and substantive German essays by Professors Knauss, Saner, and Cesana. Ms. Ann O'Hear provided invaluable expertise and assistance from the very outset of the initial submission of the manuscript, right up to the contract and production stage. We also gratefully acknowledge the publishing and translation subventions provided by the Austrian Karl Jaspers Society/*Österreichische Karl Jaspers Gesellschaft*, Graz, Austria, the Karl Jaspers *Stiftung*, Basel, Switzerland, and Saint Paul University / Université Saint-Paul, Ottawa, Canada.

The idea behind this volume—to prepare a contemporary and international collection of expositions and interpretations of Karl Jaspers's basic philosophical ideas that would be useful to undergraduate and graduate students, Jaspers researchers, and nonacademic philosophers—was conceived in conjunction with the XXth World Congress of Philosophy in 1998. Without the patience and cooperation of all the contributors, this volume would not have come into existence. To each of them, we express our heartfelt appreciation.

Finally, we wish to thank Steven L. Mitchell, editor-in-chief of Prometheus Books and its scholarly imprint Humanity Books. He understands well that Karl Jaspers is an original and seminal thinker whose works are rich in depth, vast in scope, far-ranging and complex, and distributed over a large corpus of writings. In an age where the commodification of information has transformed scholarly publishing, in general, and continental philosophy, in particular, we are grateful to him for taking on the work of this project directly. His philosophical commitment to the importance of Jaspers's philosophy, precisely as a challenge to the loving struggle for communication across cultures in our present historical situation, is greatly appreciated.

INTRODUCTION

Karl Jaspers is generally known as one of the two great German "existentialists,"[1] along with Martin Heidegger. Jaspers's philosophical thinking encompasses such a vast range of philosophical disciplines and problems that it is more accurate to describe him as one of the greatest European philosophers and humanists of the twentieth century.

His philosophical ideas and ethical impulses are highly relevant for reflection in the twenty-first century. Jaspers was born in Oldenburg, Germany, in 1883, and studied law at the universities of Heidelberg and Munich. He then changed to the study of medicine at the universities of Berlin, Göttingen, and Heidelberg, graduating from the University of Heidelberg in 1909. After a successful academic career in Heidelberg, which was interrupted during the Nazi period in Germany, he accepted a professorship at the University of Basel in Switzerland in 1948, and died there in 1969. Four important biographical facts help us understand the key influences on Jaspers's thinking.

First, Jaspers did not begin his academic career as a professional philosopher. He first studied medicine and wrote his doctoral thesis on the psychological problem of "homesickness and crime" with *Heimweh und Verbrechen* (1909). He worked for several years as a voluntary research assistant at the Heidelberg psychiatric hospital before becoming a professor of psychology at the university in 1916. It was not until 1920 that he became a professor in philosophy there. Jaspers's professions as a psychiatrist and psychologist provided him with many subtle insights into psychological phenomena, which influenced the development of his later existential philosophy. This was published in his three-volume, magnum opus, *Philosophie* (*Philosophy*) in 1932.

Nevertheless, Jaspers's first major book was a study in the methodology of psychiatry entitled, *Allgemeine Psychopathologie* (*General Psychopathology*), which was published during his research activities as a young psychiatrist in 1913. The book focuses on the relevance of phenomenological and hermeneutical methods in psychopathology. Although this work is grounded in the clinical thought and practices of the late nineteenth and early twentieth centuries, Jaspers's delineation of psychiatric methods in this work is still evaluated as "unmatched to this day," a work that is "indispensable" to contemporary psychiatry.[2] Jaspers also contributed important articles and book reviews to psychiatric periodicals during the first two decades of the twentieth century.[3]

His second major book, *Psychologie der Weltanschauungen* (*Psychology of Worldviews*), sets forth a psychology of worldviews from the perspective of hermeneutic psychology, and was written while lecturing in psychology in 1919. This book marks Jaspers's cognitive transition from psychology to philosophy. The book contains numerous nascent ideas that would be explicated in detail later in his three-volume *Philosophy* (Vol. I: Philosophical World-Orientation, Vol. II: Existential Elucidation, Vol. III: Metaphysics).

Second, Jaspers suffered from an incurable lung disease that significantly influenced his daily physical activities and philosophical reflections. Diagnosed with this disease at the age of eighteen, he explains in his *Philosophical Memoir* the existential impact of the diagnosis in this way: "One basic fact of my existence qualified all the decisions of my life: I was organically ill from childhood on (bronchiecstasis and cardiac decompensation). I was eighteen . . . when the correct diagnosis was made. Until then, false treatment of my condition had brought on frequent fever spells; now I learned to adjust my life to this disease. I read a treatise by Rudolf Virchow which described my ailment in every detail and gave the prognosis: in their thirties at the latest, these patients die of pyemia. I realized what mattered in treatment. I slowly learned the procedures, partly inventing them myself. They could not be carried out properly if I led the normal life of the healthy. If I wished to work, I had to risk what was harmful; if I wished to go on living, I had to observe a strict regimen and to avoid what was harmful. My existence passed between these poles. Frequent failures, by allowing fatigue to poison the body, were inevitable, and every time recovery was essential. The point was not to let concern about my illness turn the illness into the sum and substance of life. My task was to treat it properly almost without noticing it, and to keep working as if it did not exist. I had to adapt everything to it, without giving up to it. Time and again I made mistakes. The exigencies arising from my illness touched every hour and affected all my plans."[4] The permanent confrontation with the imminence of death not only determined Jaspers's decision to study medicine, but also influenced one of the most important ideas of his existential philosophy, namely, that the experience of the "boundary situations"[5] of death, suffering, struggling, and guilt are basic to human existence and shape our fundamental orientation to the world, self, and transcendence.

A third feature of Jaspers's life that is vital for understanding his philosophizing was his marriage to Gertrud Mayer. The deep personal relation with his wife provided an important stimulus for his "existentialism," especially the concept of interpersonal communication. In his *Philosophical Memoir*, Jaspers recalls enthusiastically his first encounter with Gertrud: "Loneliness, gloom, self-consciousness—everything changed in 1907, at twenty-four years of age, when I met Gertrud Mayer. I have never forgotten the first time I entered her room, with her brother. She was seated at a large desk. She got up, still with her back to the arrivals, slowly closed a book, and turned to us. I watched her every move; in their clearness and calm, without gestures, without conventionality, they seemed to me like unconscious expressions of her purest nature, of the nobility of her soul. It seemed a matter of course for the conversation to turn quickly to great, fundamental questions of life, as if we had known each other for a long time. An inconceivable accord, never anticipated even as possible, reigned between us from the very first hour."[6]

During the Nazi period in Germany, when people of Jewish origin were insulted, prosecuted, and murdered, and their Germanic husbands were pressed to agree to divorce, it was never a question for Jaspers to stand in unconditional solidarity with his wife without compromising her identity. "If I cannot protect against brute force, I, too, have to die—this is simple human dignity. . . . To become one in death is the fulfilment of love—it is like a kindly fate that permits us to die together, while mere nature, when it causes death, forces the survivor to go on living. My philosophy would be nothing if it were to fail at this decisive point. Somewhere, fidelity is absolute or it is not at all."[7] We know that he and his wife retained a poison capsule in their pockets in order to commit suicide if they had been imprisoned by the Gestapo and transported to an extermination camp.

Fourth, Jaspers's confrontation with the Nazi regime brought about radical changes in his life and philosophical thinking. After the Nazis came to power in 1933, Jaspers was excluded from all administrative duties at the University of Heidelberg. In 1937 he was denied the right to teach, and a year later he was forbidden to publish. Until the very end of the Second World War, he and Gertrude, were in constant danger of deportation to an extermination camp. Offers to leave Germany and to emigrate to the United States could not be accepted because of his unstable health. Given his physical condition, he would not have been able to overcome the radical changes, threats, troubles, and burdens that necessarily accompany life in emigration. The experience of Nazi terrorism was one reason why Jaspers and his wife left Germany after the war, and moved to Switzerland in 1948, where Jaspers continued his academic career at the University of Basel. The experience of Nazism was the dominant motivation for Jaspers to turn from *Existenzphilosophie* to a "philosophy of reason" and political philosophy.[8] Jaspers writes in 1950: "Many years ago I spoke about existentialism and at the time I added that it was not a new or special philosophy of its own but the one eternal philosophy. Since this had been momentarily lost in the merely Objective I argued that it was permissible to characterize it by Kierkegaard's basic concept.

Today I should prefer to call Philosophy the philosophy of Reason, since it appears urgently necessary to stress this age-old essence of philosophy. Once Reason is lost, philosophy itself is lost."[9]

While Jaspers's pre-war existentialism was mainly concentrated on problems of individual existence, his post-war philosophy treats public affairs and actual problems of politics: The question of German guilt for the Nazi regime was discussed in his 1946 work *Die Schuldfrage* (*The Question of German Guilt*), the problem of totalitarianism, the chance for worldwide communication among different nations in the face of the atom bomb and the cold war, the possibility of world peace, the ideal of democracy, and the moral implications of that ideal (problems discussed mainly in *The Atom Bomb and the Future of Man*). The role of human "Umkehr," a "redirection" or turn-about, in Jaspers's thinking, is present in his call to purification in his discussion of German guilt, exploration of the role of reason and of the individual in the political situation engendered by the dual threat of atomic annihilation and totalitarianism, and again in his warning against the political lethargy of the German people with respect to past transgressions and renewed threats to political freedom. As Leonard Ehrlich notes, Jaspers's conception of redirection "is that of philosophizing as continuous learning to die, which is Plato's simile for the constant task of 'rebirth to a true life.'"[10] It was during his later years in Basel, and after the Second World War, that Jaspers also published his principle works in philosophy of religion, namely *Der philosophische Glaube* (*The Perennial Scope of Philosophy*) in 1948 and *Der philosophische Glaube angesichts der Offenbarung* (*Philosophical Faith and Revelation*) in 1962.

In *Freiheit und Wiedervereinigung* (*Freedom and Reunification*) Jaspers brought together political writings originally published in the summer of 1960. The book includes the text of a television interview where Jaspers argued that any historical legitimation of Germany's reunification was both politically and philosophically unrealistic. Jaspers accepted the German Democratic Republic officially as a second sovereign German state in the hope of gaining more freedom for its citizens who were under the sway of the Soviet Bloc.

Wohin treibt die Bundesrepublik? (*The Future of Germany*) was published in 1966. No less of a thinker than Hannah Arendt described his analysis as the politically most important book to appear in Germany after the Second World War. Not surprisingly, it was the political bestseller of the year. Jaspers argues that the Federal Republic of Germany had for years been moving toward an "oligarchy" of political parties that spelled the end of parliamentary democracy. The emergency laws proposed at that time laid the political groundwork for a "dictatorship of politicians."

It is remarkable that Jaspers was able to write so prolifically and to contribute to such a wide range of philosophical fields and disciplines given his unstable state of health. In the fields of epistemology and philosophy of science, Jaspers made significant contributions to the meaning and scope of rationality (*Verstand*) and to reason (*Vernunft*) in the tradition of Immanuel Kant, as well as meta-reflections upon the task of science and the principle limits of scientific method and empirical rationality. In his psychiatric studies, Jaspers opposed dogma and methodological approaches that concentrate research solely on neurobiological explanatory methods. Contrary to biological reductionism, he tried to integrate elements of a descriptive psychology into the methods of psychopathology drawing upon the phenomenological and hermeneutical works of Edmund Husserl and Wilhelm Dilthey. Concerning the relation of cognitive scientific knowledge to values, Jaspers holds the same position as Max Weber by insisting on the dualism of cognition and decision. Max Weber's influence on Jaspers is evident in his numerous methodological reflections that distinguish between science and philosophy, as well as the high esteem Jaspers had for Weber's liberal attitude toward politics. "Philosophy which does not become political is not genuine philosophy. In political thought and in one's attitude toward concrete situations, human beings have been tested by their philosophy. This has always been the case."[11]

Jaspers wrote about the deep impression of Weber's personality and scientific work upon himself in his *Philosophical Memoir*: "Among my contemporaries I found the reality of greatness, the measure of historically distant men, uniquely and wonderfully embodied in Max Weber. . . . By his thinking and his personality, Max Weber came to be as important to my philosophy as no other thinker to this day—as I publicly acknowledged in my memorial address of 1920, and in a treatise of 1931. It was only after his death that I became increasingly aware of his importance. He is often present in my philosophical writings, and the understanding of his reality has remained a lifelong challenge to me."[12]

In the fields of philosophy of history and philosophy of culture Jaspers holds the "Axial Age" thesis concerning the development and evolution of world history and cultures. In *The Origin and Goal of History* (*Vom Ursprung und Ziel der Geschichte*) he argues that during the axial age (800–200 BCE) basic categories of human thought, culture, and religion were developed in China, India, and the West. These categories have continued the self-understanding of humankind up to the modern period. The historical consciousness of the Axial Period reminds us not only of certain cultural highlights of humankind (in China the thoughts of Confucius and Lao-tsu, in India the Upanishads and Buddha, in Palestine the prophets, in Greece the great philosophers and tragedians), but also of the threefold origin of the culture of humankind. The axial age shows the importance of pluralism in world history, and historical consciousness of this empirical origin of human culture should provide impulses for a worldwide communication beyond all differences of creed and political opinion. Jaspers's Axial Age thesis makes clear that he does not defend a Eurocentric position in cultural and historical affairs.

Jaspers's contributions to metaphysics and philosophy of religion reject every type of metaphysical system that intends to bridge the gap between immanence and transcendence. Such approaches are always illegitimate objectifications and anthropomorphizations of transcendent Being, which is ultimately unknowable and cannot be objectified in rational categories. For Jaspers, any historical revelation of God necessarily entails human mediation, and implies a claim to an absolute certainty and knowledge of God. Such claims, however, may breed intolerance, fanaticism, restrictions of individual freedom, and an incapacity for genuine mutual communication with persons of other religious traditions and beliefs. For Jaspers, God is "hidden" forever and cannot speak to us in an objectifying language through mediators.

In contrast to any religious faith grounded on an objectification of God in revelation, Jaspers holds out the conception of philosophical faith. Philosophical faith has no objectively guaranteed proof of the existence of Transcendence or God, as he argues in *The Perennial Scope of Philosophy* and *Philosophical Faith and Revelation*. Philosophical faith is not bound to rituals, churches, priests, and theologians who pretend to be the interpreters of God's revelation. It is, rather, an optimistic credo and confidence in the possibility of individual freedom and humanity, and in the existence of a meta-empirical dimension of Being that he calls Transcendence, absolute being, being-as-such, God, and the Encompassing. Traditional symbols of God, the Transcendent, and the Absolute must be understood as ciphers of transcendence and not as direct embodiments of transcendence. For Jaspers everything in the world can become a cipher, although he mentions explicitly nature, history, creations of the arts, metaphysical systems, myths and religions, and most important, the human being as such. Jaspers's metaphysics and philosophy of religion cannot be subsumed under theism, pantheism, or atheism. His concept of philosophical faith stands close to the otherness of the Transcendent as embodied in the life and writings of the Jewish prophets and may be stated in propositions such as "God is," "There is an absolute imperative," and "The world is an ephemeral stage between God and existence."[13] Philosophical faith affirms the indeterminate character of all modes of known reality, the hermeneutical character of all understanding, and believes that all being is apprehended within the subject-object dichotomy of human existence manifest in the Encompassing. Philosophical faith is ultimately an act of Existenz "by which Transcendence becomes conscious in its actuality."[14]

Key tenets of Jaspers's existentialism are also highly relevant for the fields of ethics and philosophical anthropology, such as the thesis that the realization of Existenz, authentic humanity, and individual, existential freedom is necessarily bound to the experience of boundary situations and to interpersonal communication. Another important idea is his conception of the human being, especially the distinction between an empirical and a nonempirical dimension of human existence. This distinction stresses the absolute singularity of every person, and the open and nondefinable potentialities of human self-realization.

Jaspers's contribution to the philosophy of education is most obvious in his conception of the idea of the university, *Die Idee der Universität* (*The Idea of the University*). Throughout his life, Jaspers was animated by the idea of the university as witnessed by the publication of three different monographs with the title *Die Idee der Universität*, the first one in 1923, the second in 1946, with a third version appearing in 1961.[15] In addition, he wrote a series of "Theses" on university rejuvenation at the end of July and beginning August 1933 entitled *Thesen zur Frage der Hochschulerneuerung* or *How Can the Universities Be Rejuvenated?: Some Theses*.[16] The "Theses" represent a fourth essay on the idea of the university whose immediate historical context was Jaspers's response to Martin Heidegger's rectoral address given at the University of Freiburg on May 27, 1933, and to the developing Nazi university constitutions throughout Germany. Jaspers's understanding of science and the fundamental ideas of university education expressed in the "Theses" stand in sharp contrast to Heidegger's address.[17] In his version of the university idea, Jaspers warns against the perpetual tendency to transform the university to a mere institution of professional training. His basic intention is not to offer a body of doctrines about the institutional shape of the university, but rather to draw attention to the cultural and moral background of scientific enterprises and educational activities. He favours a Socratic method of education, maintaining that students should be given the opportunity to participate in an open dialogue in the adventure of scientific research at the university. Such an adventure has to be guided by an unrelenting search for truth, intellectual integrity, objectivity, open-mindedness for unusually creative ideas, tolerance for counterarguments and falsifying facts, etc. In this context, as elsewhere, Jaspers's basic liberal ethos of humanity is evident.

The Atom Bomb and Future of Man is Jaspers's most developed political philosophy.[18] He calls for a "new politics" governed by reason because humankind as a whole is in a boundary situation. Human beings have the possibility of annihilating all life on earth with atomic weapons, as well as the technical possibility of establishing a world-wide totalitarian regime. Jaspers was one of the first philosophers of the twentieth century to address the radically new situation of humankind in the nuclear age, but his political ideas were not without controversy. His call for a "new politics" governed by reason, was criticized by some politicians and political scientists as a moralistic approach to politics, far removed from political reality. The critique concerns the problem of the role of morality in politics. Some critics held the opinion that politics should be free from moral demands and appeals because such demands tend to intensify political conflicts and prevent conflict resolution. Other critics of Jaspers held the view that politics is inevitably governed by ethical ideals, and it is necessary to point out these ideals explicitly. From the latter perspective, Jaspers's conception of a new, reasonable politics is quite contemporary. One thing is certain. Jaspers's political philosophy presents a counter conception to exclusively technocratic and pragmatic conceptions of politics. From his liberal (and communitarian) perspective, his political philosophy also provides a valuable analysis of totalitarian thought patterns.

The prolific scope of Jaspers's research and writing throughout his life is revealed in numerous unfinished manuscripts, expositions, notes, and references found in his literary remains. His last personal research assistant at the University of Basel, Hans Saner, has edited many of Jaspers's posthumous writings during the last four decades. Those writings include: *Provokationen Gespräche und Interviews*, 1969 (a collection of interviews Jaspers gave during the sixties), *Notizen zu Martin Heidegger*, 1978 (critical comments about Heidegger's style of philosophizing and his personality), *Die Großen Philosophen. Nachlaß* Bd.1 und 2, 1981, (*The Great Philosophers*, Vols. 3 and 4, 1993/94), and the letter correspondence with Hannah Arendt (*Hannah Arendt/Karl Jaspers: Briefwechsel 1926–1969 / Hannah Arendt/Karl Jaspers: Correspondence 1926–1969*) published in 1985, and with Martin Heidegger (*Martin Heidegger/Karl Jaspers: Briefwechsel 1920–1963/The Heidegger-Jaspers Correspondence [1920–1963]*) published in 1990.[19]

The influence of Jaspers on twentieth-century philosophical thinking is difficult to estimate. One reason is the fact that Jaspers explicitly rejected the idea of becoming the founder of a philosophical school to which disciples might be recruited. For him, true philosophizing is always original and dependent upon subjective impulses and personal efforts that cannot be taught like a set of doctrines in the natural and social sciences. Nevertheless, his works have been translated into over twenty-five foreign languages, and his German paperback editions have sold numerous copies. His philosophy has provided fruitful impulses to prominent thinkers such as political scientists Eric Voegelin and Dolf Sternberger, and the historian Golo Mann. Prominent theologians like Fritz Buri have critically appropriated Jaspers's ideas for philosophical theology. Rudolf Bultmann was involved in a public discussion with Jaspers concerning the problem of demythologization of religion, which was published in their jointly edited book *Die Frage der Entmythologisierung* (*Myth and Christianity*) in 1954. Jaspers's treatment of the relation between philosophical faith and the faith in revelation has the Protestant theologian Karl Barth as a key interlocutor. Jaspers has had a significant influence on hermeneutical and phenomenological thinkers such as Gabriel Marcel, Paul Ricoeur, Hans Georg Gadamer, and Jürgen Habermas, and in the philosophy of education, on the work of Otto Friedrich Bollnow. Finally, he has greatly influenced two modern female philosophers Jeanne Hersch and Hannah Arendt. When Hannah Arendt wrote her doctoral thesis in the late twenties in Germany, Jaspers was her adviser. After her emigration to the United States, the two continued an ongoing correspondence noted above. Jaspers also wrote the preface for the German edition of Arendt's book, *The Origin of Totalitarianism.* Arendt visited Jaspers and his wife in Basel as often as she could during her trips to Europe, and their visits entailed intensive discussions of philosophical problems as well as German and international political affairs. Arendt's appreciation of Jaspers was so high that she maintained Jaspers "is the only successor Kant ever had," and the only thinker that can help us, as no other, "to overcome our distrust"[20] of the public and political realm.

The distinguished international contributors to this work treat the foregoing essential aspects of Jaspers's philosophical thinking in expositional form and with analytical depth. S. Nassir Ghaemi teaches us how to read the *General Psychopathology*, which is arguably Jaspers's most significant scientific work, and he discusses its main themes in connection with the relation between philosophy and psychiatry, especially when both disciplines are confronted by the limits of what we can know about the human person. Ghaemi reconstructs the methodological and structural elements that characterize Jaspers's work. He argues convincingly that Jaspers's legacy for contemporary psychiatry lay in his clarification of scientific method in psychiatry, including the distinction between the method of "understanding" (*Verstehen*) and the method of "causal explanation" (*Erklären*). But Jaspers's impact goes far beyond the biological and psychoanalytic approaches in psychiatry today. Jaspers's "methodological pluralism" is still felt in the "pluralists" (Havens) and the "life story perspective" propounded by the Johns Hopkins University Department of Psychiatry (McHugh, Slavney).

The question concerning the distinction and relation between philosophy and science has been raised anew in our present historical situation by relativity theory, quantum mechanics, Big Bang cosmology, chaos and complexity theory, views of nature/nurture in the evolution of human beings, transfinite mathematics, and artificial intelligence, as well as the global economic, social, and political developments that science and technology spawn in the world. Gerhard Knauss explains why Jaspers regarded the relationship between philosophy and science as a basic philosophical question, and analyses why and how Jaspers treats the historical and the systematic aspects of the distinction and relation between philosophy and science. For Jaspers, Marxism, racism, and psychoanalysis conflate science and philosophy. The tasks of contemporary philosophy require overcoming the conflations between philosophy and science so that true science can emerge. Jaspers goes so far as to maintain that whoever is not a scientist, or has not practiced science, cannot really engage in philosophical reflection. Without science, philosophical work is meaningless, and yet, only when we understand the *limits* of empirical scientific methods can we begin to understand the tasks of philosophy in relation to science. Jaspers repeatedly stresses the distinction between philosophy and science as related to the distinction, defined by Wilhelm Windelband, between the natural sciences (*Naturwissenschaften*) and human studies (*Geisteswissenschaften*). Knauss meticulously elucidates Jaspers's understanding, which turns on key questions concerning the object of scientific inquiry, the "object" of philosophy, the methods used in scientific research and in philosophy, and the meaning connected with philosophy and scientific research. Crucial in this context is Jaspers's "transcending" method as a systematic-methodical transgressing of the limits of objectivity, but without ever falling into the void or crystallizing into a new holistic objectivity.

Hans Saner, Jaspers's personal assistant from 1961 to 1969, provides a nuanced treatment of Jaspers's preliminary and definitive plans to write a "world history of philosophy" and his idea of a coming "world philosophy." Jaspers's experience under National Socialism led him to reflect on the radical rupture of communication between persons and the political implications of philosophical thought. Does thinking itself pave the way to political terror? Or can philosophy be creative and protective of the forces that work against it. Both unfinished projects are grounded on the possibility of universal communication; hence, his work on "philosophic logic" (*Von der Wahrheit*) as an instrument of universal communicability and a world history of philosophy that could provide the framework for universal communication across cultures.

Jaspers's political thinking has been one of the most discussed aspects of his work, and many scholars have been anxious to assess the political implications of his philosophical method. Gregory J. Walters presents Jaspers's idea of democracy and the role of the "supra-political" element (ethos, sacrifice, reason) in Jaspers's call for a moral-political *Umkehr* (conversion or redirection) and a "new politics" for Germany and the world. Walters provides an analytic overview of Jaspers's main political works and themes, his idea of democracy, and teases out the numerous "supra-political" values that must guide the new politics if it is to succeed in finding a global political mean between the possibility of human self-destruction and new forms of political totalitarianism.

Jaspers's early three-volume philosophy articulates the close connection between freedom and the will. Joseph W. Koterski argues that freedom and truth are dialectically related in Jaspers's philosophical thinking. Freedom is a condition of possibility for attaining truth, but, at the same time, truth, and the will to truth are the *sine qua non* for authentic human freedom. Jaspers's understanding of human freedom is highly nuanced and includes the formal sense of freedom informed by knowledge and the absence of coercion and cooperation with moral and legal norms. As a guiding "idea" for one's life projects, freedom appears in the choices and acts of one's unique historicity. Freedom exists as volition, but attempts to grasp the will as an empirical object are inadequate. Human beings remain self-determining with each act of volition willing some intended object or end. In the very act of willing, itself, human freedom is instantiated and habituated over time and in the temporal development of the self toward greater freedom and truth.

Questions concerning the proper relations between science, philosophy, and religion have been on the rise in our present historical situation. Andreas Cesana shows us why Jaspers's concepts of philosophical faith, transcendence, and ciphers "dare us to live out of uncertainty" in our relations to the world, our self, and to transcendence. Modernity has left us with a crisis of orientation, a "modern tripartition" left in the wake of the splintering of modern science (knowledge or cognition effected by the understanding), philosophy (philosophic faith or Kant's "faith of reason"), and religion (the faith in revelation). Cesana systematically explains, out of the richness of Jaspers's corpus, the relations between philosophic faith and science, philosophic faith and religion/theology, and the faith in revelation. He does this by situating philosophic faith within the context of Jaspers's image of the human being as espoused in his Existenz-Philosophy, his unique and original understanding of "ciphers" of Transcendence, transcending methodology, and the nature, meaning, and scope of the language of ciphers. Religionists or theologians will find Cesana's treatment of Jaspers's approach to biblical hermeneutics and rejection of Rudolph Bultmann's "demythologization" program of particular interest.

Alan Olson frames Jaspers's university "idea" against the deconstructive analysis of Jean-François Lyotard's *The Postmodern Condition* and in light of the classical Greek notion of *paideia* as a cipher of transcendence. As a "supra-political" institution, the university is the last best hope for the future of humankind, but only if the university remains true to its own "idea" by remaining open to the call of transcendence. Jaspers's conceptualization of the university is one of the most cogent and comprehensive twentieth-century restatements of the Humboldtean university whose "legitimacy" Lyotard critiques by shifting the referent of the university idea from the question of *meaning* to the question of *legitimacy*. Olson compellingly argues for the contemporary relevance of Jaspers's idea of the university amidst the plethora of works that treat the crisis of higher education. Essential to Jaspers's view of education is that it ought to prepare individuals for responsible citizenship and personal self-transcendence, beyond reductionist aims tied to vocationalism and commodification.

Ram Adhar Mall's contribution reveals the creativity and richness of Jaspers's axial age theory and its relevance to contemporary cross-cultural philosophy. Mall links Jaspers's axial age theory, idea of philosophic faith, and perennial philosophy to the tasks of contemporary "cross-cultural" philosophy or "intercultural philosophy." In accordance with Jaspers's hope for a "new world vision," interculturality stands for the conviction that no culture is the one culture for the whole of humankind without deconstructing terms such as philosophy, truth, culture, and religion; but inteculturality *does* deconstruct the monolithic, absolutistic, and exclusivistic use that is far too often made of these terms.

Central to Jaspers's philosophy are the concepts of Existenz, boundary situations, and communication. Kurt Salamun argues that these concepts are only comprehensible when illuminated in the context of Jaspers's basic philosophical anthropology. The human being is both empirical and nonempirical and attains self-realization in modes of being as vital existence, consciousness as such, spirit, and the nonempirical dimension of the self (Existenz). The realization of Existenz is possible only in the experience of "boundary situations" and in authentic communication with others. Because communication is the basic aim of Jaspers's philosophical thinking, he distinguishes types of communication that are correlative to the modes of being human, deficiencies and ruptures in communication, and communicative situations. He links Jaspers's concepts of "boundary situation" and existential communication to what he calls Jaspers's "liberal ethos of humanity."

George B. Pepper discusses the crucial, but often neglected or inadequately discussed, concepts of the Encompassing, foundering, and the tragic individual in Jaspers's philosophy. He approaches the tragic individual by identifying the historically important religious persons, scientists, eastern inspirational leaders, and artists who are found in Jaspers's corpus, and how Jaspers's key interpretive criterion, Existenz, helps us understand the philosophical dialogue he entertains with great figures in history. While Jaspers provides no generic criteria for conducting the philosophical dialogue, Pepper points to what he calls "existential markers" for detecting authorial creativity in relation to others. These markers are illuminated out of the context of Jaspers's treatment of periechontology, boundary situations, and the concept and reality of foundering. Pepper identifies these markers and defends their hermeneutical cogency for understanding the supreme importance that the tragic individual holds for Jaspers and why the tragic individual must be compared with other historically important persons. Pepper explains why communication across theoretical and cultural boundaries is compelling, and analyzes Jaspers's influence on contemporary literary theorists who often miss the mark in understanding the differentiation and specification that Jaspers connects with tragedy.

Complementing Mall's exposition and interpretation of Jaspers's world philosophy and world history of philosophy is Indu Sarin's exposition of Jaspers's humane renderings of the philosophies of Buddha and Nagarjuna and a critical analysis of Jaspers's comparison between Eastern and Western thought. Jaspers's scholarly rendering of their ideas is not with the goal of presenting an encyclopedic knowledge, but rather with fostering a personal encounter with their thinking and its relevance to our present historical situation. The quest for freedom, the radical break with the faith in revelation, and emphasis on the spiritual dimension of the human being, without believing in an essentialist view of the soul, are common to Jaspers and Buddhist philosophy. Jaspers interprets the Buddhist doctrine of "momentariness" and the "law of dependent origination" in light of levels of truth and Buddha's idea of being. Jaspers had a profound understanding of Nagarjuna's "middle path" to redemption, penetrating critique of the world, self, ultimate reality, and any final formulation of knowledge. He contrasts Nagarjuna's anti-metaphysical philosophy with the metaphysical philosophy of *Vedanta* and provides nuanced differences between Indian and Western forms of detachment and the role of action in the world.

Jaspers interprets Buddha and Confucius as "paradigmatic individuals" (along with Socrates and Jesus). Sawako Hanyu stresses the importance of Asian philosophy to Jaspers after the Second World War and in light of the development of his postwar work on a "world philosophy." Jaspers communicates with Asian thinkers by highlighting Confucius's basic idea concerning the renewal of antiquity, his moral-political ethos and idea of government, "basic wisdom" tied to the *li* ("imperatives of conduct") and idea of *jên* (humanity and morality as one). Jaspers appreciates Confucius's profound awareness of the limits of education, communicability, and knowledge. She illuminates striking similarities and differences between Jaspers's philosophy of the encompassing, communication, and reason in comparison with the open-ended nature of Confucian thought. She closes her contribution with a discussion of the reception of Jaspers in postwar

Japanese culture and offers reasons why he is able to "communicate" with Asian philosophers.

Jaspers includes Lao-tzu in his project on "world philosophy." Unlike Confucius, however, Jaspers places Lao-tzu in a secondary subgroup of seminal thinkers called "intellectual visionaries," and then with further nuance places him within the group, "original metaphysicians," who he argues arrived at a closed system and handed it down to posterity. In his analysis of Jaspers's interpretation of Lao-tzu, Young do Chung argues for a range of remarkable similarities between Jaspers's conceptions of transcendence and the encompassing and Lao-tzu's understanding of the Tao. These similarities extend to both positive and negative affirmations of being and the Tao, as well as the essential unity of reality and the transcendent source of self-being. Chung also illuminates both Jaspers's critical evaluation of Lao-tzu's philosophy and key differences between Western and Chinese worldviews.

When available, the contributors to this volume have used existing English translations of Jaspers's major works and articles. Where necessary for clarification or emphasis, the editors have checked them against the original German.[21] Jaspers takes his basic philosophical vocabulary from Kant, especially Kant's distinction between *Verstand* and *Vernunft*. Hannah Arendt notes that the distinction between the faculty of thinking and the faculty of cognition for Kant, as for Jaspers, lies in the fact that concepts of reason serve us *to conceive*, whereas concepts of the intellect serve us *to apprehend perceptions*. Stated differently, the intellect (*Verstand*) desires to grasp what is given to the senses, but reason (*Vernunft*) wants to understand its meaning.[22] As Leonard Ehrlich explains,

> all thought is determinative by virtue of the forms of thought which are explored in formal sciences such as logic and the theory of knowledge. Jaspers, like Kant, calls this 'consciousness as such.' Some human thinking fulfills the requirements of the universal forms of thought, for other human thought the forms of thought are as inadequate as they are unavoidable. Instances of the former are scientific knowledge and everyday experience. It is this that Kant and Jaspers call "Verstand" and Locke and Hume, for example, the "understanding." However, understanding has too many uses, particularly when speaking of Jaspers in the English language.[23]

Linguistically distinct from *Verstand* or intellect is Jaspers's use of *Bewusstsein überhaupt*, which has been variously translated into English as "consciousness in general," "consciousness at large," and, as we will use herein, "consciousness as such." Jaspers distinguishes the Kantian concept of *Bewusstsein überhaupt* not only from a singular individual consciousness, but also from post-Kantian psychological phenomena such as the subconsciousness and the unconscious.[24] We have taken editorial license to use the English consciousness as such, but remind the reader that Jaspers uses the terms "intellect" and "consciousness as such" as virtual synonyms.

Existenz is a technical term in Jaspers's philosophy,[25] and stands very close to Kierkegaard's use of it in his philosophy. The term "existential" (*existentiell*) is generally used as the adjective of Existenz unless the context clearly suggests the adjectival form of physical existence (*Dasein*). In the German language and ethos, "existentialism" has a broader meaning than even in the English language and ethos where "existentialism" normally refers to philosophers like Sartre and Camus. In German the term used to describe the French existentialism is *Existentialismus*.[26]

In his search for being, Jaspers distinguishes three general, formal concepts: objective being, subjective being, and Being-in-itself.[27] Because the appearances of objective and subjective being are always mediated through consciousness as such and encompassed by the horizons of the modes of being that we are as humans and the external world, we use the term "being" (lower case) throughout in order to capture the boundedness of what is in relation to the self and the self's relation to the external world. Where Jaspers's idea of "Being-in-itself" or "Being as such" is invoked by contributors in reference to the radical otherness of the Encompassing of all encompassings or "absolute Being," we have tried to consistently use the term "Being as such." The use of the term Transcendence (upper case) should be understood as synonymous with "God" or the Encompassing of all encompassings.

Notes

1. On the term "existentialism" see below, note 26.

2. Paul R. Mc Hugh, M.D., "Foreword to the 1997 Edition," *Karl Jaspers: General Psychopathology*. Vols. I, II. Translated by J. Hoenig and Marian W. Hamilton (Baltimore and London: The Johns Hopkins University Press, 1997), p. v.

3. While nearly all of these articles and others related to Jaspers's psychopathological writings have been translated into Spanish and Japanese, there exists only one major article that has been translated into English. See Karl Jaspers, "The Phenomenological Approach in Psychopathology," in *British Journal of Psychiatry, Journal of Mental Science*, vol. 114, Nr. 516 (1968), pp. 1313–23. Some of these early articles have been col-

lected and published as Karl Jaspers, *Gesammelte Schriften zur Psychopathologie* (Berlin/Heidelberg/New York: Springer-Verlag, 1963).

4. Karl Jaspers, "Philosophical Memoir," in *Karl Jaspers, Philosophy and the World. Selected Essays and Lectures*. Translated by E. B. Ashton. (Chicago: Henry Regener Company, 1963), pp. 198–99. Hereafter cited as PW [eds.].

5. Other English translations of Jaspers's German term *Grenzsituation* are "limit situation," "borderline situation," and "ultimate situation." "Boundary situations" is the term used by E. B. Ashton in the English translation of Jaspers's three-volume *Philosophie*.

6. Jaspers, *Philosophy and the World*, p. 201.

7. Karl Jaspers, "Journal Entries: 1939-42," in *Karl Jaspers: Basic Philosophical Writings-Selections*, edited, translated, with introductions by Edith Ehrlich, Leonard H. Ehrlich, George B. Pepper (Athens/Ohio/London: Ohio University Press, 1986), p. 524.

8. This change becomes evident in the books *Von der Wahrheit*, 1947, *Vom Ursprung und Ziel der Geschichte*, 1950 (*The Origin and Goal of History*), *Vernunft und Widervernunft in unserer Zeit*, 1952 (*Reason and Anti-Reason in our Time*), and *Die Atombombe und die Zukunft des Menschen*, 1958 (*The Future of Mankind*, or, *The Atombomb and the Future of Man*).

9. Karl Jaspers, *Reason and Anti-Reason in our Time*, translated by Stanley Godman (London: The Camelot Press, 1952), p. 63.

10. Leonard H. Ehrlich, *Karl Jaspers: Philosophy as Faith*, p. 122.

11. Karl Jaspers, *The Great Philosophers*, Vol. IV. Edited by Michael Ermarth and Leonard Ehrlich. Translated by Edith Ehrlich and Leonard H. Ehrlich (New York/San Diego/ London: Harcourt Brace & Company, 1994), p. 326.

12. Jaspers, *Philosophy and the World*, pp. 221–22.

13. Jaspers, *The Perennial Scope of Philosophy*. Translated by Ralph Manheim (London: Routledge & Kegan Paul Ltd., 1950), pp. 34–45.

14. Jaspers, *The Perennial Scope of Philosophy*, p. 22.

15. Karl Jaspers, *Die Idee der Universität* (Berlin: J. Springer, 1923). Second version: *Die Idee der Universität* (Berlin/Heidelberg/New York: J. Springer, 1946). English translation, *The Idea of the University*, edited by Karl W. Deutsch, translated by H. A. T. Reiche and H. F. Vanderschmidt, Preface by Robert Ulich (Boston: Beacon Press, 1959). The English translation by Reiche and Vanderschmidt was also published in England with a preface by Oliver L. Zangwill (London: Peter Owen Ltd., 1960). Third version: *Die Idee der Universität. Für die gegenwärtige Situation entworfen von Karl Jaspers und Kurt Rossmann* (Berlin/Göttingen/Heidelberg: Springer, 1961).

16. Karl Jaspers, *Thesen zur Frage der Hochschulerneuerung* (1933), were first published by Hans Saner in the *Jahrbuch der Österreichischen Karl-Jaspers-Gesellschaft* (*Yearbook of the Austrian Karl Jaspers Society*), Vol. 2 (1989), pp. 2–28, and republished in the original German and translated into English by Edith Ehrlich as "How Can the Universities Be Rejuvenated? Some Theses (1933)," in Richard Wisser and Leonard H. Ehrlich, eds., *Karl Jaspers: Philosopher Among Philosophers/Philosoph Unter*

Philosophen (Würzburg: Königshausen & Neumann, 1993), pp. 293–311 (German) and (Amsterdam: Ed. Rodopi, 1993), pp. 312–31 (English).

17. See Hans Saner, "Jaspers's 'Theses' on the Question of University Rejuvenation (1933): A Critical Comparison with Heidegger's 'Rectorial Address,'" in Richard Wisser and Leonard H. Ehrlich, eds., *Karl Jaspers: Philosopher Among Philosophers/Philosoph Unter Philosophen*, pp. 139–52. See also the defense of Jaspers—against his imputed support of the *Führerprinzip*—by Leonard H. Ehrlich "Heidegger's Philosophy of Being from the Perspective of His Rectorate," in *Heidegger & Jaspers*, edited by Alan M. Olson (Philadelphia: Temple University Press, 1994), pp. 29–48, esp. p. 32.

18. See the article by Gregory J. Walters herein.

19. *The Heidegger-Jaspers Correspondence (1920-1963),* edited by Walter Biemel and Hans Saner, translated by Gary E. Aylesworth (Amherst, NY: Humanity Books, 2003).

20. Hannah Arendt, "Karl Jaspers: Laudatio," in *Men in Dark Times* (London: J. Cape, 1970), pp. 71–80, at p. 74.

21. On the problem of English translations of Jaspers's philosophy, see Charles Wallraff, "Jaspers in English: A Failure of Communication," *Philosophy and Phenomenological Research* 37 (1977), pp. 537–48, and the response by Adolph Lichtigfeld, "Jaspers in English: A Failure Not of Communication but Rather of Interpretation," *Philosophy and Phenomenological Research* 41 (1980/81), pp. 216–22.

22. Hannah Arendt, *The Life of the Mind* (New York and London: Harcourt Brace Jovanovich, 1978), pp. 13–14 and 57, citing Kant: "Vernunftbegriffe dienen zum Begreifen, wie Verstandesbegriffe zum Verstehen der Wahrnehmungen."

23. Leonard H. Ehrlich, *Karl Jaspers: Philosophy as Faith* (Amherst: University of Amherst Press, 1975), p. 240, n.19.

24. See further, E. Ehrlich, L. H. Ehrlich, G. B. Pepper, eds., *Karl Jaspers*, 146–49.

25. See the contribution by Kurt Salamun in this volume.

26. The term "existentialism" is used in German and in English in different ways. In German the term refers to the French "existentialists" such as Sartre, Camus, and Marcel, while the term existentialism in English is used in a much broader sense to emphasize the values of human freedom and responsible action. See Kurt Salamun, "Existentialism," in *Dictionary of Existentialism*, edited by Gordon Haim (Westport: Greenwood Press, 1999).

27. Karl Jaspers, *Philosophy*, vol. 1, translated by E. B. Ashton (Chicago and London: University of Chicago Press, 1969).

Part I
Philosophy and the Sciences

ON READING THE *GENERAL PSYCHOPATHOLOGY*

The Importance of Karl Jaspers's Methodological Pluralism for Contemporary Psychiatry

S. Nassir Ghaemi

> *I would like my book to give the reader a wide education in psychopathology. It is indeed much simpler to learn up formulae and technical terms and appear to have the answer to everything. An educated attitude has to grow slowly from a grasp of limits within a framework of well-differentiated knowledge. It lies in the ability to think objectively in any direction. An educated attitude in psychiatry depends on our own experiences and on the constant use of our powers of observation—no book can give us that—but it also depends on the clarity of the concepts we use and the width and subtlety of our comprehension, and it is these which I hope my book will enhance.*[1]

It is commonly assumed that the most important or influential figure in modern psychiatry is one of two persons. For most of the lay public and the majority of psychologically oriented clinicians, the overwhelming choice would be Sigmund Freud. For the majority of biologically oriented clinicians, it would be the German psychiatrist Emil Kraepelin, who laid out the classic distinction between the major psychoses of schizophrenia and manic-depressive illness. The history of psychiatry over the past century has been a yin and yang between the two. First Kraepelin's views were popular (from the late 1890s until the 1930s), then Freud's views were supreme (from the 1930s until the 1970s), and then Kraepelin made a rebound in the 1970s, with many considering current psychiatry to be "neo-Kraepelinian."[2]

It is my view that the person who deserves to be the most important figure in psychiatry, however, is Karl Jaspers. Today what psychiatry needs to learn from Jaspers is that there is something available after Freud and Kraepelin, i.e., there is something beyond the conflict between natural science-like biological psychiatry and the pseudo-"understanding" psychology of classical psychoanalysis. Within biological psychiatry and psychoanalysis, there certainly are currents that seek to breach this chasm as well, but they can only go so far. What is needed is a total new conception of what psychiatry is all about, and this "new" conception was actually laid out for the field by Jaspers almost a century ago.

Thus, Jaspers is very important for contemporary psychiatry.

But psychiatry is also important for an understanding of Karl Jaspers. Many know that Jaspers was a psychiatrist, but a common interpretation of his biography is that he evolved from psychiatry to psychology and from psychology to philosophy rather early in his career, and he never looked back. Psychiatry is seen as an early stepping stone, while his move to philosophy is made through his experience with the philosophical approach of phenomenology, derived from Edmund Husserl and worked out in parallel lines to the work of his sometime friend Martin Heidegger.

The reality is, I believe, that one cannot appreciate Jaspers the philosopher completely until one comprehends Jaspers the psychiatrist. The two are intertwined, and, indeed, Jaspers never completely stopped being a psychiatrist, in the sense of his interest in and attention to the subject matter, even though he never practiced clinically.

There is no evidence, especially in a careful reading of his letters and other papers assessed in a recent first full-length English biography,[3] that Jaspers simply lost interest in psychiatry or had philosophical reasons for giving it up. Rather, he seems to have simply been physically unable to do the clinical work, due to his own severe lifelong lung ailment, diagnosed at the time as chronic "bronchiectasis with cardiac decompensation,"[4] though he had been worried it might be tuberculosis. Jaspers loved the clinical work he experienced during his psychiatric training, but he could not exert himself physically to do that work for his entire career. He clearly went into medicine and science and psychiatry to a great extent because he was thirsty for knowledge, and in that sense philosophy made sense as a next step. But his interest in philosophy also grew out of his family background (his father also had such interests), his environment (he experienced the impact of Max Weber in Heidelberg and attended philosophy courses during his psychiatric training), and most importantly from his psychiatric training itself. What Jaspers realized as he neared the end of his training was that psychiatry was conceptually adrift. This field, dedicated to understanding human beings *qua* human beings in a scientific manner, was adrift in competing schools of thought without any coherence to them. *General Psychopathology* (GPsy) was Jaspers's attempt to provide such coherence, and when he was finished with it, Jaspers had already created a road map for his own future contributions to philosophy.

Jaspers's originality lay not in the introduction of the method of phenomenology to psychiatry, through extensive use of case material, as is most commonly assumed. Rather, I believe, his most original contribution, and what provides the conceptual structure for psychiatry in GPsy, is his methodological pluralism, which I will discuss in detail below. Unlike his phenomenological contribution, which has connections to Husserl, Jaspers's methodological contribution is most closely derived from the mentorship of Max Weber, which I discuss in more detail elsewhere.[5]

Jaspers had an impact in psychiatry. But his impact was mostly among those who appreciated the benefits of the phenomenological method. This approach led to a great deal of clinical work on the signs and symptoms of various conditions such as depression and schizophrenia, and indeed even today Jaspers's ideas regarding the nature of psychosis are frequently discussed.[6] But his major philosophical contribution to psychiatry, the conceptual structure of pluralism, has not been as well appreciated. In the last few decades, two groups, one at Harvard University, led by Leston Havens, and one at Johns Hopkins University, led by Paul McHugh and Philip Slavney, provide an exception to this rule, and I will examine their contributions as well.[7]

On Reading the *General Psychopathology*

Medicine existed in ancient times, although psychiatry was not an organized discipline, and it is noteworthy that John Locke was a trained physician. One might also call Aristotle a proto-physician, since that was his father's profession and he closely observed and followed its practitioners. But the closest philosophical personality to Jaspers, in the sense of his background in medicine and psychiatry, might be William James, who also trained in medicine and then studied and taught experimental psychology before turning to philosophy. Indeed, it was James who made the comment that the first philosophy course he ever attended was the first one he taught! There are, interestingly, many similarities between James and Jaspers such as a pluralistic theory, a strong interest in science, a respect for religious faith, a mistrust of philosophical systems, a devoted coterie of students, and political liberalism, which leads up to the point of this introduction: Jaspers believed strongly that the way into philosophy passed through the fields of science. And in his case, the particular science he experienced was the medical science of psychiatry. As a result, his first major work, the psychiatric tome entitled the *General Psychopathology*, was not simply a psychiatric book, but a compendium of thinking that marked his transition to philosophy. For the field of psychiatry, Jaspers's work was more than an introduction to his philosophical career, however; it was an uncommon achievement in itself that has continued to influence this branch of medicine for almost a century. "Here . . . was a rare bonus for psychiatry," commented the psychiatrist Michael Shepherd. "One of the foremost thinkers of the day, a trained physician, had spent a long enough period in the practice of the subject to write a major volume on its foundations."[8]

Due to his chronic lung condition, Jaspers spent his final year of residency in the library, working on a dissertation on the theoretical basis of psychiatry. This is how Jaspers describes the setting:

> Stagnation of scientific research and treatment was widely felt in German psychiatric hospitals. . . . In view of their own infinitesimal knowledge and skill, intelligent but intellectually sterile psychiatrists took refuge in skepticism and in the elegantly phrased hauteur of men of the world. In Nissl's hospital, too, therapy was unambitious. At bottom, we were therapeutically hopeless but kind. . . . All this I found when I came. Fascinated by each fact and method, I tried to absorb everything. . . . Often the same thing was said in other words, usually vague ones. Several schools had terminologies of their own. They seemed to be speaking different languages, and the divergencies extended to the jargon of each individual hospital. . . . At our regular staff meetings and demonstrations I sometimes felt we were constantly starting all over. One cause of this intellectual jumble seemed to me to lie in the nature of the case. For the subject matter of psychiatry was man, not just his body. . . . Our subject was also that of the *Geisteswissenschaften* (the human sciences). They had developed the same concepts, only far more subtly and distinctly. One day we were taking down utterances made in states of confusion or paranoid talk, and I told Nissl, 'We must learn from the philologists.' I started looking for what philosophy and psychology might have to offer us.[9]

Paul McHugh has pointed out that the publication of the GPsy in 1913 came at a unique time.

> The year *General Psychopathology* was published—1913—was pivotal in the history of psychiatry. It was the culmination of the most productive decade of this century. It was also the last year before the great German tradition of university-based empirical psychiatry was drowned in the chaos of war. . . . The initial collision between empirical and interpretive psychiatry occurred in this

> decade and originated in two linear Teutonic thinkers (Kraepelin and Freud). Their contention demanded resolution, but—with the exception of this great book—no such effort was made. . . . Enervating as it is to teaching and practice, this psychiatric conflict festers to the present day. . . .[10]

Jaspers was writing to both audiences: Initially, he wanted to convince his more "tough-minded" (James's phrase) empirically oriented colleagues that it was worthwhile reading both long volumes so as to conceptualize more clearly what psychiatry was all about. Soon, as his psychoanalytic star rose, the task became to convince the "tender-minded" (again James) analysts that there were other worthwhile methods in psychiatry, including empiricism.

The history of the book is tied to its revisions and its translations. It ran to nine editions. The second came out in 1920, and the third was an expanded version. Jaspers rewrote the book with detailed changes for the fourth edition in 1941/42, when he was in an enforced period of inactivity due to his opposition to the Nazi regime in Germany. Later editions exist in Germany, but the English translation is based on the fourth edition. This translation was made by Hoenig and Hamilton in 1963.[11] The translators have generally received both praise and criticism for their efforts.

While Jaspers has always had an influence on psychiatry and philosophy in his native Germany, the extension of his impact to other nations required adequate translation into English. This has proven difficult, and observers in psychiatry have adduced this problem chief among reasons for Jaspers's relative obscurity among rank-and-file practitioners. "It is not an easy work to read," noted the British psychiatrist Michael Shepherd in a generally laudatory article in 1982, "concentrated in argument and diffuse in form, difficult enough in the original German and often understandably opaque in another language despite the heroic efforts of the translators."[12] Even after enough of the translation could be understood for readers to realize that something of importance was being said, the actual content of the book eluded easy summary. "There is an apocryphal saying," noted the British psychiatrist Paul Harrison, "that in order to pass the membership examination of the Royal College of Psychiatrists, Jaspers's name should be invoked at some stage, preferably being followed by a comment as to the great significance of his *General Psychopathology* and of how much is lost in translation."[13]

Professor Leonard Ehrlich and his colleagues have done much in the last decades to provide new and more accurate translations of Jaspers's philosophical work.[14] But the daunting task of retranslating the GPsy remains undone. Another task has succeeded, however. Since the English edition of 1963 had been long out of print until recently, readers had to search used book stores or rely on luck to find a copy of the book. In 1997, though, the Johns Hopkins University Press published a new version of the English translation,[15] with a wonderful Foreword by Paul McHugh, chairman of the Hopkins department of psychiatry. As will be noted below, McHugh's work is probably the chief living example of Jaspersian psychiatry today. His department, as a result, has long explicitly seen Jaspers's work as an important part of psychiatric training, and the field owes a great debt to the Johns Hopkins group for providing easier access to the new edition of Jaspers's GPsy.

Thus, today, the GPsy again is easily found, although the translation remains a difficult read. There is another factor, however, which has complicated the reception of this book, one which Michael Shepherd first noted: "Perhaps the principal difficulty posed by the book for the reader is that of fitting it into a recognizable and familiar mould. *General Psychopathology* cannot be classified as a textbook. Rather it should be regarded as an intellectual map, a guide to a series of separate but related areas of knowledge. . . ."[16] As a result, the GPsy is not the kind of book that one should begin on page one, with hopes of smoothly passing from chapter to chapter to a satisfying conclusion. The GPsy is not a novel. Nor is it a psychiatric textbook. Unlike a text, one cannot easily skim the table of contents and move to interesting sections, or look up specific matters in the index and read a few pages of neatly summarized material. Not a medical text, it fails also as a book of philosophy; the bulk of it consists of descriptions of psychopathological states, rather than conceptual arguments or exercises in logic. The GPsy is none of these things, but a bit of them all. Shepherd's phrase, "an intellectual map," probably best captures its nature. One might call this purpose to understand the conceptual basis of what we do in psychiatry. Shepherd again best captures the spirit in which the GPsy should be approached for the first time, after noting the above quote by Jaspers:

> The attainment of this objective depends primarily on the clarification of a host of concepts which are traditionally either ignored or over-simplified in the psychiatric literature. To do justice to such themes as the mind-body relationship, the role of scientific inquiry, the principles of classification, personality, the subjective-objective dichotomy, or the notions of health and disease calls for a familiarity with the history of ideas in other disciplines. It is here that Jaspers comes into his own, bringing a massive tradition of philosophy and social theory to bear on these perennial problems in relation to psychopathology.[17]

Paul McHugh presents his view in the Foreword to the 1997 edition:

> Jaspers sensed that psychiatry inhabited a middle ground between science, where laws of nature are discerned, and history, where fateful events are conceived as

emerging from human choices and actions. . . . He believed and emphasized in his phenomenological studies that the individual human being—even afflicted by mental disorder—was always more than we can know. In essence, Jaspers's object was to show psychiatrists exactly what they know, how they know it, and what they do not know and cannot claim. He wrote this book with these aims in mind. . . . I call this book indispensable even though it was written eighty-four years ago—before the discovery of the EEG, DNA, or norepinephrine. . . . We have more information than Jaspers found crowding the shelves of Heidelberg, but we still disagree about how best to order this information so as to encourage its steady progress and to read its fundamental messages.[18]

Jaspers would argue that all this can be summed up by saying that the GPsy was not a psychiatric text or a philosophical book, but a book on psychopathology, a field that stands in a middle relation to both psychiatry and philosophy. This is what makes the GPsy of interest to professionals in both fields. In fact, since Jaspers explicitly discusses the nature and goals of GPsy in its introduction. It is perhaps best to let him speak for himself:

> General psychopathology is not called upon to collect individual discoveries but to create a context for them. Its achievement should be to clarify, systematise, and shape. It should *clarify* our knowledge of the fundamental facts and the numerous methods used; it should *systematise* this knowledge into comprehensible form and finally shape it so that it *enriches the self-understanding of mankind.* It thus specifically assumes the function of furthering knowledge, a function which far exceeds the simple process of fact-finding. . . .[19]
>
> *Conscious critique of methods in place of dogmatism.* . . . Instead of forcing the subject-matter into a strait-jacket of systematic theory, I try to discriminate between the different research methods, points of view and various approaches, so as to bring them into clearer focus and show the diversity of psychopathological studies. No theory or viewpoint is ignored. I try to grasp each different view of the whole and give it place according to its significance and limitations. . . .[20]
>
> *Classification according to methods*: . . . We obtain our facts only by using a particular method. Between fact and method no sharp line can be drawn. The one exists through the other. Therefore a classification *according to the method used* is also a *factual classification* of that which is, as it is for us. . . .[21]
>
> *Overlapping of chapters*: . . . In each chapter there is only one method that is paramount, and the reader's gaze is directed to all that it reveals . . . but [each method has] some relation to other subject-matter which is duly comprehended by other methods. . . .[22]

Then Jaspers provides the most succinct summary of his aim, quoted at the beginning of this chapter:

> I would like my book to give the reader a wide education in psychopathology. It is indeed much simpler to learn up formulae and technical terms and appear to have the answer to everything. An educated attitude has to grow slowly from a grasp of limits within a framework of well-differentiated knowledge. It lies in the ability to think objectively in any direction. An educated attitude in psychiatry depends on our own experiences and on the constant use of our powers of observation—no book can give us that—but it also depends on the clarity of the concepts we use and the width and subtlety of our comprehension, and it is these which I hope my book will enhance.[23]

The GPsy consists of two volumes and six parts. The first part is a section on phenomenology, where Jaspers carefully describes various psychopathological states. The second part consists of a discussion of those phenomena using the method of understanding (*Verstehen*), and the third part does the same using the method of causal explanation (*Erklären*). These being the two ways of knowing that Jaspers introduces into psychiatry, the fourth part ("Conception of the Psyche as a Whole") seeks to connect the two, and does so most interestingly in discussions of nosology and personality. The fifth part touches on social and historical factors affecting psychiatry, factors often ignored among the biologically oriented. And the sixth and final part ("The Human Being as a Whole") seeks to discuss the connection between philosophy and psychiatry in more detail and to introduce Jaspers's philosophical ideas. This last step makes sequential sense of Jaspers since he sees his entry to philosophy as occasioned by recognizing the limits of what he could know through science (specifically psychopathology). The Introduction and Appendix both function as largely general reviews of the major topics discussed in the text, particularly the understanding/causal explanation distinction, and the importance of conscious methodological awareness.

I will comment on some highlights in the text, which must of necessity fail to do justice to the entire work. I want to give a flavor of some of the language that is relevant in particular to my emphasis on Jaspers's methodological pluralism.

In the introduction, Jaspers provides the conceptual background for the book and outlines the general theory that he seeks to detail in the book. This general concept, as will be discussed further, is that any science utilizes specific methods, and that these methods both allow the science to discover certain things and limit the ability of that science to know about other things. One needs to know one's methods, consciously and clearly, to adequately apply one's science and comprehend the object of that science. In the case of psychopathology, the GPsy intends to apply just this "methodological consciousness." The introduction should lead to recognition that this is the method and the ultimate outcome of the whole endeavor of the GPsy. Jaspers lays out this central core of his thinking in sections

3 and 4 ("Prejudice and Presupposition" and "Methods")[24] of the Introduction. In my opinion, if a reader had to choose just one section of the GPsy to read, these twenty-three pages would be it. Hence I will quote extenstively from what Jaspers writes there:

> [There] were periods in which philosophy tried to create from "above" what only experience could bring from "below." Nowadays we seem to have abandoned this orientation but it reappears here and there in the form of abstruse theories. Behind our accepted systems of general psychopathology the old spirit hovers and can be identified. Our rejection of purely deductive and barren philosophical theorising is justified but it is often linked regrettably with the opposite misconception, that the only useful approach is to go on with the collection of particular experiences. It is thought better to amass data blindy than sit down and think. From this follows a contempt for the activity of thinking, which alone gives a place to facts, a plan to work to, a standpoint for observation and the passionate drive for rewarding scientific goals.[25]
>
> Reality is constantly seen through the spectacles of one theory or another. We have, therefore, to make a continual effort to *discount* the theoretical prejudices ever present in our minds and train ourselves to *pure appreciation of the facts*. We can only appreciate these latter in terms of category and method, and we have therefore to be fully aware of the presuppositions lying in every discovery according to the nature of its subject-matter—"theory lurks in every fact."[26]
>
> The investigator, however, is more than a vessel into which knowledge can be poured. He is a living being and as such an indispensable instrument of his own research. The *presuppositions* without which his enquiry will remain sterile are contained within his own person. Clarification may free us from prejudice, but presuppositions are a necessary part of understanding. They appear as tentative ideas which we then take as experimental hypotheses. . . . Presuppositions provide guiding ideas, and form the mental life of those engaged in research; they need to be strengthened and cultivated and they should be acknowledged. They do not prove the correctness of an insight but are the source of any truth or relevance it attains.[27]
>
> *Prejudices (that are false)* are rigid, circumscribed presuppositions which are wrongly taken as absolutes. . . . *Presuppositions (that are true)* are rooted in the investigator himself and are the ground of his ability to see and understand. Once elucidated, they will be well and truly grasped.[28]
>
> In psychiatric literature, there is much discussion of mere possibilities and a great deal of subjective and speculative comment that lacks the substance of authentic experience. . . . It is a pity to waste time on tortuous, meaningless argument or on imaginary models, however much they clamor for attention. If we are to apperceive essentials with certainty, our guide should be a clearly grasped methodology.[29]

> Every advance in factual knowledge means an advance in method.[30]
>
> A clear definition of *the original data* is of decisive importance. If it is not unequivocally defined and identifiable by any other research worker at any time, calculation becomes meaningless. Exact method based on inexact data can lead to the most remarkable mistakes.[31]
>
> The main problem is to find those methods that will extract some definite realities from the endless and confusing flood of life. . . . Discovery of a way to make certain facts comprehensible, so that they can be re-identified by others, is the beginning of all research.[32]
>
> Some scientists tend to deny the validity of any psychological source of scientific knowledge. They only accept what can be perceived objectively by the senses, not what can be meaningfully understood through the senses. Their viewpoint cannot be refuted since there is no proof of the validity of any ultimate source of knowledge. But at least we might look for consistency. Such scientists should abstain from talking of the psyche or even thinking in terms of psychic events. They should give up psychopathology and confine themselves to the study of cerebral processes and general physiology. . . . This seems a sterile nihilism shown by people who would persuade themselves that their incompetence is due to their subject-matter, not to themselves.[33]

Jaspers warns against certain particular methodological errors in psychiatry, such as "*unlimited 'ad hoc' hypotheses*:"

> We need working hypotheses for the interpretation of our facts. . . . [But frequently] we keep on making more and more far-reaching concepts, develop our theoretical constructions and employ one concept after another simply for the sake of concept-building. . . . We must, therefore, ask of every method whether it increases our knowledge and gives it depth and shape, and whether it makes it more possible to identify phenomena as they arise. Does it widen our experience and increase skill? Or does it lead to a void of abstractions and so entangle us with ideas and paper-schemes that we suddenly find ourselves in a world remote from what we see or do, and ourselves moving from one vacuum into another?[34]
>
> According to Kant expert opinion in the courts on mental states should fall within the competence of the philosophical faculty . . . in practice of course it will not do. . . . Kant's dictum stands, however, in that the psychiatrist's competence is really commensurate with how far his education and knowledge would qualify him to belong to the philosophic faculty. This goal is not served where (as has occurred in the history of psychiatry) he learns a certain philosophical system by heart and applies it automatically. This is worse than if he had learnt nothing at all. But he should acquire some of the viewpoints and methods that belong to the world of the Humanities and Social Studies.[35]

In Part I ("Individual Psychic Phenomena"), Jaspers engages in his classic detailed descriptions of psychopathological states. In this section he is engaging in "phenomenology," the school of thought in existential philosophy with which he would be most associated. This approach, derived from the philosopher Edmund Husserl, sought to know the phenomena of the world without presuppositions of any kind. Thus, Jaspers seeks to describe varied psychopathological states without reference to any theory or any concepts regarding their etiologies. He seeks to be as unbiased as possible, merely observing and describing.

> The simple *separation of observation and value-judgment* is something that must be required from every psychopathologist in his work, not so that all human values must be relinquished but that, on the contrary, we shall possess truer, clearer, and profounder values the more we observe before we judge. What is needed is a quiet absorption into the facts of psychic life without the adoption of any specific attitude to them. Human beings have to be approached in an unbiased fashion with lively interest and without any kind of appraisal.[36]

This part in itself has exerted an immense influence on psychiatry, where it forced the field to notice certain phenomena that were often ignored due to biological or psychoanalytic biases.

In Parts II and III, Jaspers seeks to comprehend the psychopathological material just detailed by the two methods of *Verstehen* (understanding, meaningful connections) and *Erklären* (causal explanation), respectively. This distinction is another crucial aspect of Jaspers's work, which he lays out most explicitly in the introduction to Part II. It derives from previous thinking in Germany in the disciplines of history and nascent sociology, as is discussed further below.

> In the natural sciences we find causal connections *only* but in psychology our bent for knowledge is satisfied with the comprehension of quite a different sort of connection. Psychic events "emerge" out of each other in a way which we understand. Attacked people become angry and spring to the defence, cheated persons grow suspicious.[37]
>
> The evidence for genetic understanding is something ultimate. When Nietzsche shows how an awareness of one's weakness, wretchedness and suffering gives rise to moral demands and religions of redemption, because in this roundabout way the psyche can gratify its will to power in spite of its weakness, we experience the force of his argument and are convinced. . . . Such conviction is gained *on the occasion* of confronting human personality; it is not acquired inductively *through repetition of experience*.[38]
>
> In any given case the judgment of whether a meaningful connection is real does not rest on its self-evident character alone. It depends primarily *on the tan-*

> *gible facts* (that is, on the verbal contents, cultural factors, people's acts, ways of life, and expressive gestures) in terms of which the connection is understood, and which provide the objective data. All such objective data, however, are always incomplete and our understanding of *any particular, real event* has to remain more or less an *interpretation* which only in a few cases reaches any relatively high degree of complete and convincing objectivity.[39]
>
> Psychological understanding only serves psychopathology in so far as it makes something visible to our experience and fosters our observation. As I understand, I find myself asking what are these facts I am looking at and what am I indicating? When do I reach the limit of my understanding?[40]

In sum, Jaspers used this distinction to explore two different ways of comprehending psychopathological states. In Part II ("Meaningful Psychic Connections"), the meaning of such states, in terms of subjective understanding, is pursued. In Part III, the causal explanation of such states, based on biological and empirical research, is intended.

Part II is the more interesting, for time has not faded its impact, as Jaspers seeks to empathize with the experiences of psychiatric patients. In this section Jaspers also borrows the method of "ideal types" from his mentor and friend, the sociologist Max Weber,[41] and applies it to the classification scheme of personality disorders. In particular, it is noteworthy that Jaspers perceives the nosology of personality disorder as utilizing the ideal type method, and thus being useful, but limited, by not exactly applying in all its details to specific individuals in the real world. I would suggest that this analysis of ideal types as the underlying method of psychiatric nosology might be extended to the entire current *Diagnostic and Statistical Manual of Mental Disorders* (DSM) system for all psychiatric disorders:

> If we think of a property as something lasting, understandable in its manifestations, in modes of reaction and expression and the general behavior of the individual, we are in process of developing a type. We form the property and all its consequences into a construct and viewing it as a whole recognise it as something obviously connected. If we then make one or several such properties the basis of a comprehensive totality and proceed to apply it to the person as a whole, noticing the meaningful connection between this and what the individual experiences and does, we are in the process of designing a personality-type.
>
> Such types remain *ideal types* even if we have conceived them from our scrutiny of real people. . . . They only occur in reality as approximate forms, as classical borderline cases.

> Thus the whole meaning of types makes it impossible for any one individual to be sufficiently characterised by any single type.[42]

In Part III, he provides a useful theoretical review of the strength and limitations of the causal explanatory method in psychiatry.[43] For instance, he discusses the view that psychiatric conditions are at base brain disorders in a manner that could have been written in a contemporary philosophical article on the mind/body problem:

> [The view has been held that] "*mental illness is cerebral illness*" (Griesinger, Meynert, Wernicke). This declaration is as dogmatic as its negation would be. Let us clarify the situation once more. In some cases we find connections between physical and psychic changes taking place in such a way that the psychic events can be regarded with certainty as consequences. Further, we know that in general no psychic event exists without the precondition of some physical basis. There are no "ghosts." But we do not know of a single physical event in the brain which could be considered the identical counterpart of any morbid psychic event. We only know conditioning factors for the psychic life; we never know *the* cause of the psychic event, only *a* cause. So this famous statement, if measured against the actual possibilities of research and the actual findings, may perhaps be a possible, though infinitely remote, goal for research, but it can never provide a real object for investigation. To discuss statements of this sort and try to solve the problem in principle indicates a lack of critical methodology. Such statements will vanish from psychiatry all the more quickly in proportion as philosophic speculations vanish from psychopathology and give place to a philosophical maturity in the psychopathologist.[44]
>
> All categories and methods have their specific meaning. It is nonsense to play off one against the other. Each can realise itself fruitfully if it preserves its independence, accords with its facts and observes its limitations. But if we turn it into an absolute, this will end every time in empty claims, ineffective discussion and attitudes which destroy any free approach to the facts. In relation to causal events in particular, it is a basic impulse of knowledge to advance constantly in the direction of more profound compelling causality. Hope may lend wings but the goal is difficult and calls for patience. But however far our causal knowledge goes, we shall never be able to know the event simply in itself and as a whole, and so be able to manipulate it. Causal knowledge is always faced by something which no matter how we operate it implies that in the end all the well-being of man is still dependent on something decisive in himself, which is only approachable if we understand.[45]

He also provides a critique of Freud in this context:

> Freud's new attempt at psychological understanding was epoch-making for psychiatry: A critique of Freud's teaching might resolve itself into the following theses. . . .
>
> 1. Freud is actually concerned with the *psychology of meaningful connections* and not with causal explanation as he himself believed.
>
> 2. Freud teaches us in a most convincing way to recognise many particular meaningful connections. We understand how complexes repressed into unconsciousness reappear in symbolic form. . . . To some extent here Freud fills out in detail the teachings of Nietzsche. . . .
>
> 3. The falseness of the Freudian claim lies in the mistaking of meaningful connections for causal connections. The claim is that *everything* in the psychic life, every psychic event, is *meaningful*. . . .
>
> 4. In a great number of cases Freud is concerned neither with understanding the meaning of unnoticed connections nor with the bringing of them into consciousness but with a "*hypothetical understanding*" *of extra-conscious* connections . . . [such as] Jung thought he had discovered in the case of dementia praecox [schizophrenia].
>
> 5. One lapse in Freud's teaching consists in the increasing *naïveté of understanding* which goes with the transformation of meaningful connections into theory. Theories call for a certain simplicity whereas the understanding of meaning uncovers an infinite manifold. As it is Freud believed that practically everything psychic could be traced back to sexuality in a broad sense as if it were the sole and primary power. In particular the writings of many of his followers are intolerably boring by reason of this very naïveté. One knows beforehand that the same thing will be found in each one of them. The psychology of meaningful connections cannot make any progress here.[46]

Jaspers goes on to link the errors of the two extremes, Wernicke's totalistic biological psychiatry and Freud's totalistic meaningful psychology, which as discussed below, foretold that seesaw of psychiatry in the next nine decades between the two approaches:

> Wernicke started with his theory from the "outside," with the brain. Freud on the other hand started his theory from the "inside," with what is psychically understandable. Both review a whole field of facts and both generalise what has only a circumscribed validity and apply it over the whole realm of psychopathology and psychology; both end in abstract constructions. They are complete opposites as regards the content of their study and interests . . . yet their two modes of thought are structurally related. They are indeed opposites but on the same plane and with the same limitations and restrictions on their thinking.[47]

In Part IV, "The Conception of Psychic Life as a Whole," Jaspers takes on the problem of diagnostic classification ("The Synthesis of Disease Entities, Nosology–Nosologie."[48] Here again Jaspers inaugurated a discussion, touched on earlier in the chapter on personality, that has continued to this day, and his ideas continue to be in the center of the discussion. Jaspers directly addresses the perspective of the empirical/biological school, led in his age by Emil Kraepelin. This discussion remains relevant today, especially as mainstream psychiatry has returned to the basic nosology established by Kraepelin, but which is now termed "neo-Kraepelinian."[49] This nosology is purely empirical, and has been criticized, in the spirit of Jaspers, for not allowing for meaning-oriented approaches in psychiatry.[50] Further, the Kraepelinian nosology held that psychiatric diagnoses could be delineated by careful clinical observation, and that eventually the underlying brain pathology for these diagnoses would be discovered. This is still the mainstream view in psychiatry today. Kraepelin's opponents in 1913 held the "unitary psychosis" model, holding that psychiatric diagnoses could not be accurately separated from a single general psychotic condition. A few prominent psychiatrists continue to hold this view,[51] and some even argue that there are no psychiatric diagnoses or diseases at all, but that mental conditions are defined by social and legal deviations from the norm of human behavior.[52] Jaspers came out against the concept that psychiatric illnesses would be reduced to diseases of the brain, but he also recognized the utility of the clinical empirical approach:

> There has been *no fulfilment* of the hope that clinical observation of psychic phenomena, of the life-history and of the outcome might yield *characteristic groupings* which would *subsequently be confirmed in the cerebral findings*, and thus pave the way for the brain-anatomists. . . .
>
> The original question: are there only *stages and variants* of one unitary psychosis or is there *a series of disease-entities* which we can delineate, now finds its answer: *there are neither*. The latter view is right in so far that the idea of disease-entities has become a fruitful orientation for the investigations of special psychiatry. The former view is right in so far that no actual disease-entities exist in scientific psychiatry.[53]

Earlier, in the introduction, Jaspers also had added:

> In the psychiatric assessment of a case . . . except in the case of well-known cerebral changes, diagnosis is the least relevant factor. If it is made the main issue, it will prejudge what ideally should emerge from the investigation. What matters is the process of analysis. The chaos of phenomena should not be blotted out with some diagnostic label but bring illumination through the way it is systematically ordered and related. Psychiatric diagnosis is too often a sterile

> running round in circles so that only a few phenomena are brought into the orbit of conscious knowledge.[54]
>
> But here in Part IV, Jaspers explains why a classification scheme is important in psychiatry and provides one that is remarkably similar to the current nosology in psychiatry, arrived at in 1980 with the major changes enacted in DSM-III in the United States.
>
> We have detailed knowledge of particular phenomena, of causal connections and meaningful connections, etc., but complex disease entities remain an endless, inextricable web. The individual configurations of disease are not like plants which we can classify in a herbarium. Rather it is just what is a "plant"—an illness—that is most uncertain.
>
> *What* do we diagnose? . . . Diagnosis is expected to characterise in a comprehensive manner the whole morbid occurrence which has assailed the person and which stands as a well-defined entity among others. . . . But however we devise [a diagnostic schema] we realise that it cannot work; that we can only make temporary and arbitrary classifications; that there are a number of different possibilities which account for the fact that different workers construct entirely different schemata; and that classification is always contradictory in theory and never quire squares with the facts.
>
> Why then do we keep on making this vain attempt? In the first place we want to see properly what this idea of disease-entity has *achieved* in respect of the *over-all picture* of existing psychic disorders, and particularly where we have failed because it is the basic and radical failures which make us aware of the actual state of our knowledge. In the second place every *presentation of special psychiatry* requires some classification of psychosis at its base. Without some such schema it cannot order its material. In the third place we need a classification in order *to make statistical investigations* of a large case material.[55]

Jaspers goes on to provide his proposed diagnostic schema:

> An ideal schema would have to satisfy the following requirements: It must be such that any given case would have only one place within it and every case should have a place. The whole plan must have a compelling objectivity so that different observers can classify cases in the same way. . . .
>
> We abandon the idea of disease-entity and once more have to bear in mind continually the various points of view (as to causes, psychological structure, anatomical findings, course of illness and outcome) and in face of the facts we have to draw the line where none exists. Such a classification therefore has only a provisional value. It is a fiction which will discharge its function if it proves to be the most apt for the time. There is no "natural" schema which would accommodate every case.[56]

With those caveats, Jaspers proposes a nosology quite similar to the big shift in 1980 with DSM-III in modern US psychiatry. He proposes dividing psychiatric conditions into three main groups: Group I, "Known somatic illnesses with psychic disturbances" (such as cerebral tumours, meningitis), coincides with DSM's "Axis III," which describes psychiatric conditions secondary to known medical illnesses. Group II, "The three major psychoses" (genuine epilepsy, schizophrenia, and manic-depressive illness), would correspond with the major mood and psychotic disorders on DSM's "Axis I" of primary psychiatric conditions (with epilepsy now moved to Axis III since a cerebral basis has been established for it). Group III is the "Personality disorders," which corresponds to DSM's "Axis II" also defined as personality disorders. Heuristically, with the caveats given previously, Jaspers goes on to accept Kraepelin's definition of the distinction between schizophrenia and manic-depressive illness based on the outcome criterion as the main factor, i.e., invariably poor outcome with schizophrenia and frequent recovery with manic-depressive illness. This too is a distinction that mainstream psychiatry dropped in most of this century in favor of psychoanalytic theories, but to which the field returned in 1980 with the "neo-Kraepelinian" nosology of DSM-III.

Jaspers's acceptance of affective disorder/schizophrenia distinction in the nosology debate was based on the distinction between conditions with which one could empathize, those in whom meaningful connections could be made, and those which were not understandable. He felt that this distinction would provide one of the few organizing principles for nosology:

> The most profound distinction in psychic life seems to be that between what is meaningful and *allows empathy* and what in its particular way is *ununderstandable*, "mad" in the literal sense, schizophrenic psychic life (even though there may be no delusions). Pathological psychic life of the first kind we can comprehend vividly enough as an exaggeration or diminution of known phenomena and as an appearance of such phenomena without the usual causes or motives. Pathological psychic life of the second kind we cannot adequately comprehend in this way. Instead we find changes of the most general kind for which we have no empathy but which in some way we try to make comprehensible from an external point of view.
>
> The affective illnesses appear to us to be open to empathy and natural but the various types of "madness" do not seem open to empathy and appear unnatural.[57]
>
> Part V assesses social and historical aspects of psychiatry, and in Part VI ("The Human Being as a Whole"), he engages in his most clearly philosophical writing. He reviews the role of "Psychopathology in Retrospect:"[58]
>
> We do not accept any group of facts as genuine reality. We have opposed

> the tendency of all dogmatic theories of Being to build a structural whole and have pursued a systematic scrutiny of methods. The meaningful question for us is whether the differentiations are sufficiently clear and in what way they could be improved. . . . [59]

He discusses "the Problem of the Nature of Man:"[60]

> The retrospective survey of our psychopathology has been bringing us to the problem of human nature itself. . . .
>
> As with all the sciences we have to find the limits of psychopathology as well, and see the concrete problem with which we are presented so that while we note the *wide expanse free for scientific enquiry* and its specific methods, we keep *within the limits of science* when we evaluate the findings and make use of them. It is just through science encountering its limits in this way that we can trace out [the ultimate nature of Man]. . . .
>
> What is of decisive importance for theory and practice in relation to Man is that there should be a basic philosophic attitude and no philosophical dogma.[61]
>
> The human being is not merely a kind of animal nor is he any kind of purely spiritual creature of which we have no knowledge and which earlier times conceived to be angelic. Man is rather something *unique*; he partakes in the series of living things and in the series of *angel*, belonging to both and differing from both. . . . The human being is *open possibility*, incomplete and incompletable. Hence he is always *more and other than what he has brought to realisation in himself*.[62]

He explores the relationship between "Psychiatry and Philosophy"[63] with important comments on scientific method in psychiatry:

> Science is knowledge that is generally valid and compelling. It is based on methods that are designed deliberately and which can be tested by anyone and it is always related to individual objects. . . .
>
> In the name of science we have been wrongly satisfied with mere *conceptualisation*, with mere logical method, mere clarity of thinking. . . . When simple thinking is confused with an objective knowledge science becomes lost in empty speculation and the resultant endless possibilities.
>
> Science is wrongly identified with *Natural Science*. . . . Natural science is indeed the groundwork of psychopathology and an essential element in it but the humanities are equally so and, with this, psychopathology does not become in any way less scientific but scientific in another way. . . . The scientific attitude is ready to adopt any methods and asks only for those universal scientific criteria; general validity, convincing insights (which can be proved), clarity of method and the possibility for a meaningful discussion.[64]

In my opinion, this short section of GPsy is among the most important, as it lays out more clearly Jaspers's important contribution to identifying scientific method for psychiatry, i.e., the understanding/explanation methodological distinction, and the emphasis on methodological consciousness and pluralism. Jaspers later expanded his discussion of philosophy of science in future works, which has been expertly interpreted by Professor George Pepper.[65]

Jaspers goes on to make the most cogent argument for the relevance of philosophy for psychiatry:

> Where is the place for the many non-scientific discussions of traditional and contemporary psychopathology? Should we simply drop them as not belonging? Not so. They are the expressions of something inevitable, namely, that philosophy is operative in every living science and that without philosophical science is sterile and untrue and at best can only be correct.
>
> Many a psychiatrist has said that he did not want to burden himself with a philosophy and that this science has nothing to do with philosophy. Nothing can be said against that, inasmuch as the correctness of scientific insights in general and in psychiatry is not proved by philosophy. But the exclusion of philosophy would nevertheless be disastrous for psychiatry . . . since in psychopathology in particular scientific knowledge is not all of one kind, we have to distinguish the different modes of knowing and clarify our methods, the meaning and validity of our statements and the criteria of tests—and all this calls for philosophic logic.
>
> The psychopathologist . . . must set his face against every attempt to create an absolute and to claim that particular methods of research are the only valid, single objectivities. . . . He must also take sides on behalf of meaningful understanding in the face of biologism, mechanism, and technics without denying them their validity within their own appropriate area. He has then to set his face against any attempt to turn scientific knowledge as a whole into an absolute so that consciousness may be kept free and with it the effectiveness of life at its source, which gives all practice its meaning. In this he stands on the side of differentiation as against a general confusion and of synthesis as against isolation. He is against the confusion of science with philosophy and of the physician's role with that of a saviour. But he is also against an isolation that plays off one thing against another instead of keeping them properly apart.
>
> To sum up: If anyone thinks he can exclude philosophy and leave it aside as useless he will be eventually be defeated by it in some obscure form or other.[66]

In an appendix, Jaspers reviews "The History of Psychopathology as a Science,"[67] again touching on by now familiar figures like Wernicke, Kraepelin, and Freud, and concluding with further expression of his conception of scientific method in psychiatry and the relevance of philosophy:

> [Kraepelin] was responsible for one of the most fruitful lines of research, the investigation of the whole life-history of the patient. . . . [He] laid the foundations for psycho-pharmacology. . . . But Kraepelin's basic conceptual world remained a somatic one which in the company of the majority of doctors he held as the only important one for medicine, not only as a matter of preference but in an absolute sense. The psychological discussions in his Textbook are brilliant in parts and he succeeded with them as it were unwittingly. He himself regarded them as temporary stopgaps until experiment, microscope and test-tube permitted objective investigation.[68]
>
> The tenable observations [of Freud's psychoanalysis] . . . found a defender in [Eugen] Bleuler and also a promoter. His critical penetration and its purging effect salvaged the tenable substance of Freud's teaching for the whole body of scientific psychiatry.[69]
>
> The new element in the situation is the general uncommittedness and the breadth of approach possible today. We can ignore all theories, every established viewpoint and may investigate from any angle. . . . What our situation lacks is the absence of any over-all view, but this is only the negative side of something quite positive. The basic question is whether any fresh dogmatic idea will arise or what will take its place. Since 1913 my own effort has been to make a contribution here through an attempt to systematise methods.[70]
>
> Everything creative usually tends to be converted into an absolute. The creator, however, experiences enthusiasm and a sense of fruitfulness—not the ruin. It is his successor who pays for the enthusiasm, becomes one-ideaed and sterile and acquires a vested interest in the legacy, in being right because of it and in that power that lightly-won knowledge confers.[71]
>
> Scientific knowledge is precisely that which is independent of philosophy, opinion, and world-outlooks in general. It is valid for everyone, universal, and compelling. The vital thing therefore is whether our basic philosophical attitude contains the unconditioned will to get to know and therefore impels us to take the paths of science, or whether our philosophy makes conditions for our knowledge and so unfailingly inhibits or destroys any scientific advance.[72]

THE IMPORTANCE OF JASPERS'S METHODOLOGICAL PLURALISM FOR CONTEMPORARY PSYCHIATRY

As previously mentioned, Jaspers's main influence on psychiatry is conventionally assumed to rest on his emphasis on the importance of phenomenology in psychiatry, or perhaps in his application of the understanding/explanation dichotomy. While these are both important contributions, I will emphasize his most underappreciated contribution, methodological pluralism, as expressed in sections of GPsy reviewed above.

It is perhaps not an exaggeration to state that Jaspers was the first psychiatrist to clearly identify the need to be clear about one's methods. Jaspers took it as a given that each human being, including each patient, is unique. There is an aspect of each person that transcends any attempt to understand or capture that person by a certain way of knowing, whether it be science or anything else. This transcendence is the ultimate source of human freedom, Jaspers believed. Simply recognizing that we are each unique could also be understood biologically as, for instance, due to genetic differences, however small, between individuals. No matter how one views human freedom, Jaspers begins with this first intuition: A human being can never be completely understood by a single method of knowledge. If one begins with this assumption, one is led inexorably to its corollary, every method of knowledge has its limitations. If no single method is sufficient, then multiple methods should be used. Complementary information should be obtained with multiple methods, leading to a better and better understanding of an individual's mental life or condition. Yet multiple methods never exhaust the uniqueness of individuals; hence clarity about one's methods is essential. Each method has an advantage and strength, certain aspects which it captures more effectively and accurately than other methods; and each method has disadvantages and weaknesses, certain aspects which it fails to see. Each method begins with certain assumptions, which both hones its ability to capture certain aspects of reality and limits it ability to capture other aspects of reality. Methodological pluralism, then, consists of recognizing the strengths and limits of each method, and applying the ones that are best suited for specific circumstances, e.g., diseases, diagnoses, and conditions. This was perhaps Jaspers's most important contribution to a theory of scientific method for psychiatry.

The specific methods Jaspers introduced into psychiatry were *Erklären* (causal explanation) and *Verstehen* (meaningful understanding) as discussed above in parts II and III of GPsy. But his main contribution, in my view, is not these specific methods, which as described below, can be reformulated in different ways, but rather the pluralistic concept itself.

Approaches in Contemporary Psychiatry

In contemporary psychiatry, in my opinion, there are two major attempts at a theoretical understanding of the field, beyond the psychoanalytic and biological approaches, and both of these attempts are highly influenced by Jaspers's ideas. The first is the work of the Harvard psychiatrist Leston Havens, who in the years after Jaspers's death in 1969, was among the first in academic psychiatry to seek a pluralistic renewal of psychiatric thinking. The second is the work on the "perspectives" of psychiatry propounded by Paul McHugh, Philip Slavney, and the Johns Hopkins department of psychiatry over the last two decades.

Havens's 1973 book, *Approaches to the Mind*,[73] reprinted in 2004 as *Psychiatric Movements*,[74] takes up the Jaspersian theme of cutting through the clutter of dogmas by emphasizing the methods underlying theories rather than comparing innumerable theories.

Havens's own approach, which remains one of the most helpful, is what he calls "pluralism." Havens organizes differing approaches in psychiatry into four schools of thought. The key advantage of his work is that he divides the schools based on their methods, not on their content, which clears away many differences in theory that obscure larger underlying agreements in methods. The four schools defined by Havens are the objective-descriptive school, the psychoanalytic school, the existential school, and the interpersonal school.

First, *the objective-descriptive school* is based on the traditional scientific method of empirical observation and statistical analysis. Its leader was Emil Kraepelin, the most prominent psychiatrist, perhaps other than Freud, who first clearly established the diagnoses of schizophrenia and manic-depressive illness. This school of thought emphasizes the classical medical approach of obtaining a list of symptoms and signs in the course of psychiatric history and mental status examination, relating these symptoms and signs to collections of syndromes, and relating those syndromes ultimately to underlying diseases. These diseases would then be treated, as any medical diseases, "somatically," that is, with medications or other physical treatments such as surgery or electroconvulsive therapy. The causes of these diseases are mostly biological, such as viruses or brain abnormalities. Thus, Kraepelin's student, Alois Alzheimer, discovered the brain abnormalities underlying the dementia that now bears his name; also, many of the psychotic patients Kraepelin studied were discovered to suffer from syphilitic infection of the brain, a discovery that much influenced Kraepelin and others to pursue possible theories of underlying viral infections as the etiology of schizophrenia. While the content of objective-descriptive theories can vary, Havens makes the point that all the theories share one thing: the methodology of empirical observation and description as in the traditional medical model.

The second school is *the psychoanalytic school*, founded by Freud. Its basic method is free association, which is the use of "free-floating attention" so that the doctor or therapist is not pursuing the description of signs and symptoms, as above, but simply listening in a completely neutral way and not forming any judgments initially. By allowing the statements discussed to wander in whatever direction they take, Freud found that a certain logic imposed itself to the therapy that was not accessible to the objective-descriptive approach. That is, if the therapist tried to make sense of things, nothing made sense. Once the therapist stopped and simply let things go wherever they went, a sense of order grew up out of the apparently meandering associations produced. A major benefit of Havens's achievement in stripping the psychoanalytic school down to this bare essential is the ability to prevent confusion in trying to understand the differences among the myriad sub-schools produced by his followers. Whether Adlerian, Jungian, Reichian, Kleinian, or Kohutian—whatever the sect—all subscribed, at base, to free association as their basic method. This approach is similar to the many biological theories in psychiatry, e.g., infectious disease models, hormone theories, neurotransmitter models, epilepsy analogies, and so on, whose theory content differs, while their objective-descriptive methodologies remain the same. Freud's method helped its founder with a group of conditions poorly assessed and treated with the predominant objective-descriptive models of nineteenth century Vienna: hysteria.

The third school is *the existential school*, whose leader in psychiatry was Ludwig Binswanger[75] and among whom later leaders included R. D. Laing.[76] The main method of this school is empathy, placing oneself in the position of the other person. Like the psychoanalytic school, from whom some of the existentialists derived, the therapist began with a neutral listening to the patient, but unlike psychoanalysis, the existential therapist would not later try to organize what was thus learned into a theory. The therapist's role was simply to understand the patient, not theorize about her. In fact, the patient/treater difference was annulled, with the goal of treatment being a coming together where the patient, to use an objective-descriptive term, moved toward the therapist and the therapist moved toward the patient. The whole subject-object divide upon which the objective descriptive school is based is thus erased in the existential school. Some of the most interesting work that has arisen from this school is research on the subjective experience of psychosis and the psychology of depression.

The fourth school is *the interpersonal school*, or what Havens sometimes calls the social psychiatry school. One of its undisputed leaders is Harry Stack Sullivan,[77] the only American among founding leaders of these schools. Later proponents include Erich Fromm, Erik Erikson, Carol Gilligan, and others. The methodology of this school, as derived from Sullivan, involves "clearing the interpersonal field." This refers to Sullivan's view that any interaction between two persons, such as a psychiatric interview between doctor and patient, involves interpersonal reactions which influence the psychological phenomena observed. These reactions frequently tend to distort the interpersonal interaction; this occurs not only in psychosis due to the effect of paranoia, as described by Sullivan, but also in nonclinical interactions, such as communication between men and women. Before the recent popularity of the Sullivanian notion of clearing the interpersonal field of distortion, the psychoanalytic view held more prominence, whereby such interpersonal phenomena are viewed as "transference," as necessary stages toward gaining a deeper understanding of the patient's inner psychic life. Sullivan was unsatisfied with this approach, among other reasons, because by focusing on the transference, psychoanalysis often seemed to only worsen the distortions produced. Sullivan's work largely consists of proposed methods of actively combating these transferential distortions.

Havens is very clear that his approach to this conceptual structure for psychiatry is methodological. Each school is identified by the methods it uses, not the specific contents of its theories:

> "In growing sciences," Newton wrote, "examples teach more than precepts." The foundation of this book is case material from the principal investigators. It is necessary to grasp the empirical basis of psychiatry first, then the methods by which the various observations were made, and only cautiously the grand ideas through which psychopathology is too often approached. The central questions concern what has been discovered and what methods were used to make the discoveries. Psychiatry has evolved a powerful group of methods—we can say technologies—that govern the relationships of therapists and investigators with their patients and subjects in each of the major schools.[78]

Thus, while there are many variants of psychoanalysis, in theory, they are all similar in their methods and to that extent can be lumped together. The same holds for differing biological theories as well as with the other schools. Havens emphasizes that no school is groundless, but each school has its limitations. Further, he is quite explicit about his reliance on a pluralistic structure, which is essentially the same as the viewpoint described by Jaspers in GPsy:

> The schools comprise a rich psychiatry, perhaps already ordered into a rough succession of tasks. . . . We can spot patients seemingly designed for each method, although it is more likely that the methods developed from the patients. Affective disorders often need the battering encounter of existential work to surrender their denial. Paranoid patients, almost by definition, need the counterprojective techniques of interpersonal work. How readily some hysterical patients develop their transference neuroses and almost work them through by themselves, on couch or chair. . . . Finally many patients need, despite our most sophisticated intentions, the observations, manipulation, and medical control of the oldest school. . . .

> Of course every period produces manuals of practice in which the clinical lore of the time is collected. These books offer solutions rather than dilemmas and slide over the systematic difficulties of mixing methods. . . . Each offers superb advice: specific prescriptions for specific problems. Reading them, we feel that nothing is beyond us.
>
> Eclecticism is the name for these efforts at synthesis. Usually it has meant grasping the ideas of all the schools and taking from them those most appealing to us. It has usually not involved the much more taxing matter of mastering all the methods of the schools and discerning when to use them. Eclecticism has tended to underplay differences, to homogenize complexities, so that the powerful school methods lose their edge.
>
> I believe that the future lies with refining methods, not mixing them, just as physical treatments have moved toward more and more precise methods and medicines. Such a refinement would mean pluralism in psychiatry. . . . Having achieved that pluralism, we could look back on psychiatry's school days with both nostalgia and relief.[79]

Havens was very complimentary of Jaspers and the GPsy: "Jaspers's book . . . is a work of extraordinary interest, standing as the still unsurpassed high-water mark of psychiatric erudition and sophistication."[80] While he was not explicit about the influence of Jaspers, Havens has since personally communicated to me the central role Jaspers's work has had to his thinking. In fact, Havens wrote, to his knowledge, the first full-length article about Jaspers in an American psychiatric journal in 1967.[81] In a recent reprinting of his book, Havens and I have written a new introduction which makes the connection to Jaspers explicit: "The basic concept of pluralism has been around for almost a century, having been introduced by Karl Jaspers in *General Psychopathology* in 1913."[82] Further, in the section of his book that examines the existential school he discusses Jaspers at length:

> Karl Jaspers knew Kraepelin's work at first hand in Heidelberg, and psychiatric phenomenology, which was to a considerable extent Jaspers's creation, sprang from the limitations of Kraepelin's work. . . . What Jaspers did was to make clear a fresh difference between psychosis and normal or neurotic life. He did so by studying carefully patients' reports of their experience, as Kraepelin had studied their physical movements, stream of speech, and handwriting, and Freud their mental content. And just as the objective schools of descriptive psychiatry and psychoanalysis fathered detailed methods, so the study of inner experience fathered its own technique.[83]

McHugh and Slavney's *Perspectives of Psychiatry*,[84] like Havens's work, focuses on identifying different methods underlying basic conceptual approaches in psychiatry. Unlike Havens, they did not focus on different schools of thought in psychotherapy to a large degree, and they did not emphasize a historical approach in denoting founders and followers among the different schools of thought. Yet they are very explicit about deriving their basic ideas from Jaspers. In this debt, they are carrying on the tradition of the British school of psychiatry (and, in fact, McHugh obtained some of his training with Aubrey Lewis). McHugh and Slavney propose a theoretical framework for psychiatry that would rest on four different perspectives:

1. **Disease:** What the patient *has*. The goal of treatment in this perspective is cure. This view agrees with Havens's objective/descriptive approach and consists of categorical knowledge: one either has or does not have the disease.

2. **Dimension:** What the patient *is*. The goal of treatment in this perspective is counseling, and this perspective is similar in parts to Havens's existential approach, where the focus is on the human being who may be suffering the illness, not the disease that underlies the illness. This involves continuous rather than categorical knowledge, since all human beings have certain characteristics, and what is relevant is how much of each characteristic someone has. Unlike diseases, which one either possesses or does not possess, the dimensional model applies better to aspects of psychological functioning such as personality traits, which everyone possesses, but which may differ among individuals due to having more or less of particular traits.

3. **Behavior:** What the patient *does*. McHugh relates treatment to a type of re-education in which the patient learns new methods of controlling or changing one's actions. This is the underlying method behind popular behavioral approaches to treatment of depression or obsessive-compulsive disorder, for instance. Havens classified this type of treatment under the objective-descriptive approach, since behavioral treatments subscribe to traditional methods of describing objective signs and symptoms and attempting to alter them directly through a form of relearning behavioral habits.

4. **Life story:** What the patient *wants*. The goal of treatment is a kind of rescripting of one's life goals. This perspective is future-oriented and takes an overtly hermeneutic perspective in the sense that objective truth is not the purpose one sets; this is similar to the major difference between the existential approach, as described by Havens, and the other approaches that seek to obtain objective accurate knowledge. Just as the existential approach simply seeks to understand things rather than explain them, the life story perspective is focused on understanding one's goals or one's ideals, what might be rather than what definitely will be or what has been.

Like Havens, McHugh and Slavney also emphasize that their basic approach to psychiatry is formulated around methods. Each perspective is a method, and it provides a way to organize the field of psychiatry. Each perspective is valid in its own field to a greater or lesser degree, and one perspective is better than the rest for a specific condition. The task of the clinician is to match the best perspective for the condition being faced; to justify the choice of one perspective rather than another, and then to apply it effectively. Again, this is a modernization of the pluralistic approach offered by Jaspers in GPsy.

The perspectives approach has been quite influential at Johns Hopkins University Department of Psychiatry and has formed the conceptual core of training of decades of psychiatrists from that institution. The connection to Jaspers's ideas is quite explicit, alluded to in the *Perspectives of Psychiatry*, itself, as well as quite clearly in McHugh's introduction to the reprinting of GPsy, as discussed above. McHugh's connection to Jaspers appears to have been mediated by his own breif experience as a trainee under the British psychiatrist Sir Aubrey Lewis. Lewis headed the Maudsley Hospital in London for decades in the mid twentieth century, and was informed about Jaspers's ideas by German immigrant colleagues. It is also notable that McHugh briefly worked as a medical student with Havens, who at the time was a psychiatric resident, and thus those thinkers may have cross-pollinated ideas over the years. In practice, McHugh's interests have tended in the biological direction, and those of Havens, after some initial biological work, in a psychological direction. I think it is a fair assessment, however, to maintain that scientifically they are both "grandsons" of Karl Jaspers.

Critical Evaluation

It should be clear that there is a good deal of overlap between the theoretical structures advanced by Havens and by McHugh and Slavney. However, certain differences in emphasis and in content also stand out. Havens more clearly establishes a historical background to his theory, and he links the different methods to different historical schools of psychotherapy. McHugh and Slavney provide a more precise distinction of the cognitive-behavioral perspective in psychiatry, but Havens provides better descriptions of the unique methods of the psychoanalytic and the interpersonal schools of thought. The positions described by these authors can be put to empirical testing.

The theoretical approaches of Havens, McHugh, and Slavney also fall into the divisions of explanation and understanding that Jaspers proposed, although the contemporary authors do not enter into a discussion of this distinction to any major degree. The psychotherapy schools in Havens's paradigm, and the life story perspective in the Johns Hopkins approach, would appear to be variations on the understanding method, while the explanation approach would apply to Havens's objective-descriptive school and to the three other perspectives described by McHugh and Slavney. In all this, Havens, McHugh, and Slavney are proposing an explicit methodological pluralism. Each school or perspective has advantages and disadvantages, strengths and weaknesses, and is more or less applicable to particular illnesses or patients, much along the lines first argued by Jaspers.

"ECLECTICISM" OR METHODOLOGICAL PLURALISM?

Thus, these contemporary theoretical models of psychiatry are consistent with, and indeed indebted to, Jaspers's earlier formulations. They provide a way above and beyond the historical seesaw between biological reductionism and psychoanalytic orthodoxy. In this manner, Jaspers's ideas have been clearly rediscovered and resonate again in psychiatry almost a century after he first propounded them.

Yet, while academic thinkers in psychiatry like those described above may have come close to Jaspers's ideas, the mainstream of psychiatric academicians have not carefully followed these theoretical developments and have shown little interest in them. Havens made the important distinction between eclecticism and pluralism. For this mainstream group, "eclecticism" has become their catchword. They claim to be "ideologically neutral," by which in reality they simply ignore conceptual attempts to understand what they are doing when they study and practice psychiatry. They hide this lack of interest under the rubric of the "biopsychosocial" approach to medicine, initially introduced by George Engel as a means of attempting to include psychological and social factors in the largely medical disease model practiced in medicine.[85] Today, the biopsychosocial approach, combined with eclecticism, has too frequently come to mean simply avoiding a discussion of methods and assumptions in one's psychiatric work.

Thus, a Jaspersian "pluralism" conflicts with "eclecticism," the mainstream philosophy of modern psychiatry. This is so because by eclecticism modern psychiatrists mean abjuring all talk of theories and methods, thus denying them all. Unable to place the rise and decline of biological psychiatry and of psychoanalysis in context, some have given up altogether on the attempt to comprehensively understand human nature. Since unified dogmas fail, no doctrines are allowed. This is an explanatory nihilism as sterile as the earlier therapeutic nihilism that Jaspers found irksome. Hidden under the rubric of a "biopsychosocial" approach to understanding human nature, this eclecticism takes no stands.[86]

It does not pay attention to the methods of biological, psychological, or social knowledge; it simply labels different theories under those concepts, appends them to each other, and does not attempt to weight their advantages or disadvantages critically. Therapeutically, it ends in the opposite of nihilism, a shooting from the hip of all types of treatments. Everyone gets medication and psychotherapy because everything is biological and psychosocial. But little work is done on specifying when and why medications work or do not work, when and why psychotherapy is effective or not, and when they might—or might not—work best together. Empirical research in psychiatry is beginning to ask these questions, but at the theoretical level, biopsychosocial eclecticism remains accepted doctrine, rather than the methodological pluralism proposed by Jaspers, Havens, McHugh, and Slavney.

The rediscovery of Karl Jaspers, I conclude, may help modern psychiatry drop its presumed ideological neutrality, which actually hides a biopsychosocial eclecticism, and turn to principled methodological pluralism.

Notes

1. Karl Jaspers, *General Psychopathology*, Vols. 1 and 2 (Baltimore, MD: Johns Hopkins University Press, 1997 [1959]), p. 50. [Hereafter, cited as GPsy.] [Karl Jaspers, *General Psychopathology*. Translated from the fourth German edition by Julius Hoenig and Marian W. Hamilton, eds. (Manchester, England: Manchester University Press, 1963)].

2. Peter D. Kramer, *Listening to Prozac* (New York, Viking, 1993).

3. Suzanne Kirkbright, *Karl Jaspers, A Biography: Navigations in Truth* (New Haven, CT: Yale University Press, 2004).

4. Karl Jaspers, "Philosophical Autobiography," in *The Philosophy of Karl Jaspers*, Second Augmented Edition, edited by Paul Arthur Schilpp, 5–94 (La Salle, IL: Open Court Publishing Company, 1981 [1957]), p. 9.

5. S. Nassir Ghaemi, *The Concepts of Psychiatry: A Pluralistic Approach to the Mind and Mental Illness* (Baltimore, MD: Johns Hopkins University Press, 2003), pp. 81, 83–85, 90–92.

6. Gerhard Huber, "The Psychopathology of K. Jaspers and K. Schneider as a Fundamental Method for Psychiatry," *World Journal of Biological Psychiatry*, vol. 3, no. 1 (2002), pp. 50–57; Michael Shepherd, "Review of *General Psychopathology*," *British Journal of Psychiatry*, vol.141(1982), pp. 310–12.

7. Ghaemi, *The Concepts of Psychiatry*, pp. 14–16, 57–69, 142.

8. Michael Shepherd, "Review of *General Psychopathology*," *British Journal of Psychiatry*, vol. 141 (1982), pp. 310–12.

9. GPsy, p. 7.

10. Paul R. McHugh, "Foreword: Genius in a Time, Place, and Person," in *General Psychopathology*, vol. 1 (Baltimore, MD: Johns Hopkins University Press, 1997), pp. v–vi.

11. Karl Jaspers, *General Psychopathology*, Vols. 1 and 2.

12. Shepherd, "Review of *General Psychopathology*," pp. 310–12.

13. Paul Harrison, "*General Psychopathology*: Karl Jaspers: A Trainee's View," *British Journal of Psychiatry*, vol. 159 (1991), pp. 300–302.

14. Leonard E. Ehrlich, Edith Ehrlich, and George B. Pepper, eds., *Karl Jaspers: Basic Philosophical Writings* (Atlantic Highlands, NJ: Humanities Press, 1994).

15. Jaspers, *General Psychopathology*: Volumes 1 and 2.

16. Shepherd, "Review of *General Psychopathology*," pp. 310–12.

17. Ibid.

18. McHugh, "Foreword: Genius in a Time, Place, and Person," in Jaspers, *General Psychopathology,* pp. v–xii.

19. GPsy, pp. 38–39.

20. GPsy, p. 41.

21. GPsy, p. 43.

22. GPsy, p. 47.

23. GPsy, p. 50.

24. GPsy, pp. 16–37.

25. GPsy, p. 16.

26. GPsy, p. 17.

27. GPsy, p. 21.

28. Ibid.

29. GPsy, p. 22.

30. GPsy, p. 23.

31. GPsy, p. 24.

32. GPsy, p. 25.

33. GPsy, p. 28.

34. GPsy, p. 33.

35. GPsy, p. 36.

36. GPsy, p. 17.

37. GPsy, p. 302.

38. GPsy, p. 303.

39. Ibid.

40. GPsy, p. 312.

41. George B. Pepper, "A Re-examination of the Ideal Type Concept," *American Catholic Sociological Review*, vol. 24 (1963), pp. 185–201.

42. GPsy, p. 434.

43. GPsy, pp. 451–62.

44. GPsy, p. 459.

45. GPsy, p. 462.

46. GPsy, pp. 539–40.

47. GPsy, p. 546.

48. GPsy, pp. 564–616.

49. See Donald W. Goodwin and Samuel B. Guze, *Psychiatric Diagnosis* (New York: Oxford Unitversity Press, 1989 [1974]).

50. John Z. Sadler, Osborne P. Wiggins, and Michael A. Schwartz, eds., *Philosophical Perspectives on Psychiatric Diagnostic Classification* (Baltimore, MA: Johns Hopkins University Press, 1994).

51. Timothy J. Crow, "From Kraepelin to Kretschmer Leavened by Schneider: The Transition from Categories of Psychosis to Dimensions of Variation Intrinsic to Homo Sapiens," *Archives of General Psychiatry*, vol. 55 (1998), 502–505.

52. Thomas S. Szasz, *Ideology and Insanity: Essays on the Psychiatric Dehumanization of Man* (New York, Doubleday, 1970).

53. GPsy, pp. 568–70.

54. GPsy, p. 20.

55. GPsy, p. 604.

56. GPsy, pp. 604–605.

57. GPsy, pp. 577–78.

58. GPsy, pp. 747–56.

59. GPsy, p. 747.

60. GPsy, pp. 756–67.

61. GPsy, pp. 756–57.

62. GPsy, pp. 765–66.

63. GPsy, pp. 768–78.

64. GPsy, p. 768.

65. George B. Pepper, "Karl Jaspers on the Sciences," in *Karl Jaspers Today*, edited by Leonard H. Ehrlich and Richard Wisser (Washington, DC: Center for Advanced Research in Phenomenology and University Press of America, 1988), pp. 185–201.

66. GPsy, pp. 769–70.

67. GPsy, pp. 844–59.

68. GPsy, pp. 852–53.

69. GPsy, p. 855.

70. GPsy, pp. 855–56.

71. GPsy, p. 857.

72. GPsy, p. 859.

73. Leston Havens, *Approaches to the Mind: Movement of the Psychiatric Schools from Sects toward Science* (Cambridge, MA: Harvard University Press, 1987).

74. Leston Havens, *Psychiatric Movements: From Sects to Science* (New Brunswick, NJ: Transaction Publishers, 2004).

75. Ludwig Binswanger, *Being-in-the-World* (New York: Basic Books, 1963).

76. R. D. Laing, *The Divided Self: An Existential Study in Sanity and Madness* (Baltimore, MA: Pelican, 1969).

77. Harry Stack Sullivan, *The Psychiatric Interview* (New York: Norton, 1954).

78. Havens, *Psychiatric Movements*, pp. 4–5.

79. Ibid., pp. 328–30.

80. Ibid., p. 342.

81. Leston Havens, "Karl Jaspers and American Psychiatry," *American Journal of Psychiatry,* vol.124, no.1 (1967), pp. 66–70.

82. Havens, *Psychiatric Movements*, p. xiv.

83. Ibid., pp. 124–31.

84. Paul R. McHugh and Phillip R. Slavney, *The Perspectives of Psychiatry* (Baltimore, MA: Johns Hopkins University Press, 1986).

85. George L. Engel, "The Clinical Application of the Biopsychosocial Model," *American Journal of Psychiatry*, vol. 137 (1980), pp. 535–44.

86. N. McLaren, "A Critical Review of the Biopsychosocial Model," *Austrailian and New Zealand Journal of Psychiatry*, vol. 32 (1998), pp. 86–92.

KARL JASPERS ON PHILOSOPHY AND SCIENCE
DISTINCTION AND RELATION

Gerhard Knauss

Endnotes enlarged with cross-references to the English editions by the editors. In this article "science" is a translation of the German word "Wissenschaft." *While the English word ordinarily connotes the natural sciences such as physics, chemistry, and biology,* Wissenschaft *comprises any methodically disciplined inquiry, including history, psychology, and sociology. In Professor Knauss's contribution "science" is used in this broader sense. Appropriate distinctions among disciplines are mentioned in the article.* **Eds.**

In his inaugural lecture at University of Basel in 1948 Jaspers regarded the relationship between philosophy and science as a problem of the first order and presented his fundamental position on this question in an exemplary manner.[1] The lecture deals with the systematic as well as the historical aspects of the topic; it can, therefore, serve as the basis for an account of Jaspers's analysis of the problem, which is the topic of the first three sections. The remaining three sections will discuss Jaspers's treatment of systematic aspects of the problem.

THE RELATIONSHIP OF PHILOSOPHY AND SCIENCE: HISTORICAL ASPECTS

According to Jaspers the relationship between philosophy and science has undergone various changes over the course of time. In its Greek beginnings philosophy

Translated by Edith Ehrlich. The cross-referenced citations to *Way to Wisdom* (WW) are only tentative because the translator has translated Jaspers's German text directly. She does not appropriate the English translation versions from the book *Way to Wisdom* (see also note 1).

presented itself as a science, indeed as *the* science, that is, the highest and most certain of all possible cognition. The fact that over the years this became subject to doubt was the consequence of the self-understanding of philosophy as well as the development of the sciences. In the nineteenth century the modern sciences achieved their development in most instances without reference to philosophy, in opposition to it, or in indifference toward it. Jaspers, writing in 1948, summarized the most common views then current as follows: "The age of philosophy is over. According to the new criteria philosophy cannot be counted among the sciences. All sciences originated in philosophy as the universal science and have now supplanted it."

In opposition to this perception of the demise of philosophy, Jaspers identifies three ways of reacting:

First, withdrawing to the position of preserving the tradition. Philosophy is reduced to history of philosophy. The underlying interest is esthetic, focusing on the greatness of the cultural legacy.

Second, all previous philosophy is in fact discarded and a new philosophy is constituted as a strict science that consists, in the main, of logic, epistemology and phenomenology. In this way philosophy, imitative and servile, turns itself into the handmaiden of science. Formal logic arrogates philosophy unto itself. Thus philosophy becomes one science among many, practiced by specialists.

Finally, the attack on philosophy is countered by rejecting the claim that it is a science. Philosophy, it is said, is not a science and never has been. It is something entirely different, based on feeling and intuition, fantasy and genius. Being conceptual conjuring rather than cognition, it is wrong to ascribe scientific character to it; the sciences are themselves an aberration leading to ruinous consequences for the soul and all of existence.

For Jaspers, all of these reactions—which he describes and by doing so, characterizes certain trends current at the time—signify the end of philosophy. Renouncing philosophy in favour of science and despairing of it, these positions make philosophy impossible. In this situation, which mirrors the state of affairs in the 1920s and 1930s, Jaspers envisions the emergence of new tasks for a new philosophizing. These tasks can be fulfilled only when one recognizes the historical reasons for the decline of contemporary philosophy. These are contained in the confluence of three distinct motives: (a) the significance and concept of modern science; (b) the erroneous but ever re-emerging attempt of science to become "totalism"; and (c) the philosophic concept of truth.

(a) In modern science there occurred a shift in the traditional conception of science. This new concept of science was known neither in Greek antiquity nor in the European Middle Ages nor in Asia. Not only did the modern sciences develop further as regards method, the claim of certainty and of validity, but they conceived anew the meaning of research, the parameters of their subject matter, and the demand for unity. The ground they cover is, for all intents and purposes, universal. Everything can become their object, nothing may be excluded, no secret may remain hidden. Whereas ancient and Asiatic desire to know was directed toward a conclusion, i.e., was searching for a finite canon of knowledge regarding a finite cosmos, modern science remains in principle open-ended.

It is clear to modern science that closed worldviews are impossible. It recognizes a plurality of principles as well as the multidimensional inexhaustibility of subject matter. At the same time it is sustained by the consciousness of a general connection within this plurality, in the idea of the unity of knowledge. Developments such as those in physics exhibit this impetus toward unification coupled with the realization of incompletability.

The ancient relationship between theory and empiricism has been fundamentally altered. The old attitude toward theory as a thought possibility has given way to a practice of using theory as a tool of research, leading to proof or refutation. Very early on Jaspers recognized the principle of "trial and error" to be decisive for modern science, perhaps even earlier than Karl Popper and independently of him. Modern science is radical in posing problems and proceeds to the very limits by venturing to think by way of abstraction and counter to appearances, and ultimately dispenses with intuitability altogether. Modern science is sustained by an ethos of unbiased critical knowledge, a clear differentiation of knowing and not-knowing, as well as of the modes of knowing, supposing, believing, and doubting.

(b) In spite of the development toward a modern ethos of knowledge, the attempt and claim of a total and definitive pseudo-knowledge has survived and gained acceptance time and again, due to the fact that falsely understood science and falsely understood philosophy are intermingled. For Jaspers, René Descartes, a renowned scientist who misunderstood philosophy, considering it to be the fundamental and total science, is paradigmatic for this confusion. On the other hand, his contemporary Galileo took his cue from Platonic thought. But such amalgamation of scientific systems of philosophy had a disastrous effect on science as well as on philosophy. In the autonomous philosophic systems the sciences became sterile, their questions dull, their answers predetermined. On the other hand, philosophic self-consciousness fell prey to the self-deception of scientific certainty and was criticized mercilessly from outside. The fact that in spite of these monstrosities, grandiose philosophic speculations were achieved and scientific insights arrived at is to be credited to a "nonetheless" rather than to a "therefore."

(c) Inherent in the amalgams of scientific philosophies is a misunderstanding of what had been originally and authentically thought by Plato in his conception of knowledge as expressed in the allegory of the cave and the play of dialectics. In a similar vein, Jaspers considers the philosophic truth of Being and of that which transcends all being to be fundamentally different from scientific truth, which concerns the appearances of what there is (*Seiendes*). At another place Jaspers differentiates between philosophic truth and scientific correctness. He characterizes them not only with respect to the different kinds of subject matter, i.e., "Being" (*Sein*) on the one hand and "that which is" (*Seiendes*) on the other. Basing himself on the seventh Platonic letter, he also opines that philosophic truth cannot be written down but can only be understood at a propitious moment among those who think alike, whereas scientific "correctness," which can be arrived at by all rational creatures, is recognized as cogently correct. For this reason philosophic truth is also called "philosophic faith."

Contemporary examples of the conflation of science and philosophy are, for Jaspers, Marxism, racism, and psychoanalysis. By taking over Hegelian perspectives of the whole, Marx universalizes the approach to economic problems, and thereby the nature of capital, and surplus value turns into a dialectical-materialistic pseudo-philosophy that considers itself competent to deal with just about any problem. Jaspers was one of the first, if not the very first, thinker to express the thesis of totalitarianism grounded on the situation of man in modern terms as described by him, a thesis that later on was disseminated by his pupil Hannah Arendt in her research into totalitarianism. Marxism pretends to be all-inclusive as to subject matter, monolithic as to method, and, based on its claim of validity, to be universally valid as the definitive philosophy and definitive science.

Psychoanalysis, starting out from medical-psychopathological questions, arrives at comprehensive notions about the nature of man, his culture, and the way he perceives and regards the world. Particular insights, meaningful in their relativity, are distorted by absolutizing them and turning them into pseudo-philosophic views of the world.

However, true science, according to Jaspers, leads us "to know how, for what reasons, within what boundaries, and in what way one knows." Its certainty is tied to an awareness of its relativity by relating it in each case to the respective presuppositions and research methods. All this is lost in all-inclusive views. There is no room for criticism in psychoanalysis and Marxism. The way science appears publicly today is ambiguous. It is an "open secret," in principle accessible to all, but de facto misunderstood everywhere and in danger of falling prey to totalitarian ways of seeing. In spite of this ambiguity the history of science seems to demonstrate that, in the long run, only what is authentically cognized will maintain itself, criticism will prevail, and pseudo-knowledge will be abandoned. "Science is the deepest caesura of world history."[2]

The Relationship of Philosophy and Science: Systematic Aspects

Based on this general diagnosis of the relationship between philosophy and science, Jaspers sees three tasks for contemporary philosophy:

(a) Pseudo-philosophic all-embracing knowledge is to be "dissolved" through criticism coming from the sciences. The philosophic monstrosities pretending to be science will be destroyed by the true sciences, a result hoped for by authentic philosophy.

(b) The purity of the sciences is to be regained. This will take place in the concrete research projects of specific sciences. The necessary fundamental clarity about knowledge and ignorance will return as soon and as long as there is freedom of criticism within science. But whosoever wants to examine, from the standpoint of philosophy, the veracity of scientific cognition, must do so by engaging in the process of concrete scientific research.

(c) The purity of the sciences can be achieved only together with the authenticity of philosophy, for philosophy is always a vital element of the sciences. The great researchers were guided by philosophy; yet philosophy was not itself part of the scientific endeavor but was present as its goad and gave it its aim. One cannot prove through science that there should be science; neither can one give a scientifically grounded answer to the question as to the meaning of scientific activity.[3] The guiding ideas of science are not themselves objects of scientific inquiry. The decisions regarding the importance of the objects of research, i.e., the choice of which among the random endless array of objects are worthy of scientific research follows from philosophic consideration, not from scientific insight. The purity of science demands the authenticity of philosophy.

But the place of philosophy is not outside of the sciences. Conscious of its difference from them, it is tied to the sciences. Whoever is ignorant of the ways of science will also stumble around in philosophy. History is full of examples of uncontrolled projects being presented as science. Control by the sciences is the only safe way to authentic philosophic ignorance. "Whoever philosophizes urges on toward scientific knowledge because it is the only path to authentic not-knowing."[4] Philosophic knowledge is knowing that one does not know. What is philosophical is found at the limits and horizons of the sciences. In this sense one could call philosophy a science even if it is not, because the sciences, in a non-axiomatic sense, are the "presuppositions" of philosophy.

In this connection Jaspers holds the following noteworthy view: Whoever is not a scientist nor has, at one time, practiced a concrete science, cannot philosophize; for only the experience of the limitation of scientific research leads—in shipwreck and transcending of boundaries—to philosophizing. Jaspers goes even further and states that today philosophy is no longer practiced from the academic chairs of philosophy but within the sciences themselves, where these encounter their limits and the scientists are aware of these boundaries.

In the debates over the dangers of science, which were carried out with great intensity after 1945, Jaspers clearly came down on the side of science and against the arrogance of a number of philosophers. Keeping in mind his view of the relationship of philosophy and science one can understand that, in the dispute about the atom bomb, he did not join the ranks of the opponents of science. As early as the 1920s, in the early debates about the role of technology, he already saw the dangers arising out of the modern development of technology, and so also for medicine. However, in weighing the entirety of chances and risks growing out of the new scientific-technical developments, he came to consider their positive influence on the development of humankind to be decisive. In no way could he agree with those critics of science and technology "who even want to make modern science responsible for the calamities and inhumanity of our age."[5]

Thus philosophy is unconditionally on the side of modern science over against the superstitious belief in science and the contempt for science. It is the marvelous, incomparably reliable phenomenon, the deepest caesura in world history; to be sure, it is the source of great dangers but of even greater chances, and from now on the condition of all human dignity. Without this science, as every philosophizing person knows, his own activity is meaningless.

THE TASK: THE DISTINCTION BETWEEN PHILOSOPHY AND SCIENCE

The differentiation between philosophy and science is one of several differences whose necessity Jaspers stresses time and again in his writings. The differentiation between philosophy and religion as well as between philosophy and art appear to him at various times to be worthy of consideration. These differences furnish us with important insights regarding philosophy. While the differentiation between philosophy and religion will continue to be an eternal struggle, the difference between philosophy and science is such that it can lead to unity.

Jaspers's conception of philosophy is truly distinctive. One cannot say with certainty who most shaped his notion of science. In the section on "Psychiatry and Philosophy" of his *General Psychopathology*, he presented his briefest and most concise statement regarding the nature of science.[6] Jaspers took over the customary division into natural sciences (*Naturwissenschaften*) and human studies

(*Geisteswissenschaften*) and their characterization as nomothetical and idiographical (even though he does not use this terminology) from Wilhelm Windelband. The *Geisteswissenschaften* are, in their root, historical studies. Their true subject is simply the historicity of the spirit in its multifariousness.[7] For the *Geisteswissenschaften* the universal has its value only in its historical application, and the historically unique cannot be derived from it in any way whatsoever. The universal as subject of research, i.e., the attempt to find something in common in its various objects, has meaning only for the auxiliary disciplines of the human studies and seduces us falsely to assume a relationship with the natural sciences. The attempt to grasp the spirit as a whole in its historicity in the concept of a universal history eludes our research and leads to the philosophy of history. The method of the *Geisteswissenschaften* is always the philology of texts.

The natural sciences are pure world orientation. Here the proximity of Existenz and research—unlike in the human studies—does not lead to unclarity. Freedom from value considerations, possible for the human studies only conditionally and in a limited way, is possible for the natural sciences in principle and in their entirety because they are able to limit themselves to the cogent knowledge of factualities and the methodical knowledge defined by their presuppositions. They direct themselves toward that which is timeless and bound by laws; the historical is merely secondary, relevant only for natural history. It is mathematics that is the *organon* of the natural sciences. Their subject, nature, is studied in view of the universal but only in its particularity. If natural history means to deal with nature in its totality, it misunderstands itself, but, recognizing its limits, becomes philosophy.

What the sciences of natural actuality have in common is, then, ". . . the cogency of empirical cognition through methods for the purpose of objective determinations."[8]

There are a number of sciences that Jaspers considers to be "borderline sciences," whose subject matter lies between freedom and transcendence, such as sociology and psychology. Their subject is the boundary of all encompassing being that we ourselves are, and hence they make the claim to be universal sciences: The soul, for example, which according to Aristotle, is *tamquam omnia*, and the society of men, which, according to Auguste Comte, touches upon all Being.

For Jaspers, the relations between philosophy and science, by means of which the difference between the two can be elucidated, are manifold: Seen historically, the sciences have developed out of philosophy, and ever new disciplines arise in this manner. Philosophical speculation can be concretized and become scientific research. There is a historical alternation among those sciences that stand in close relation to philosophy. Once upon a time it was theology, then mathematics and the natural sciences and history, and finally, in the present it is sociology and psychology. Philosophy and science sometimes live side by side in the same person. It is not a coincidence that almost all great philosophers have also mastered a science. On the one hand, philosophy gives meaning and purpose to science and propels it forward. On the other, philosophy needs the content of scientific knowledge of the world in order to transcend with respect to it.

Jaspers's understanding of the mutual relationship between philosophy and science did not change from the *General Psychopathology* of 1913 until his very last utterances on his deathbed in 1969: "Everything is subject to doubt except philosophy."[9] He furnished further arguments for his basic conception, moved the one or the other aspect into the foreground, but he always maintained: Philosophy is more as well as less than science, it differs from science, but it cannot be without, but only with, science.

The fact that he began his career as a psychiatrist and changed over to philosophy by way of psychology did not alter his opinion regarding the mutual relationship between philosophy and science. He never looked down on science from a later superior philosophical position. He continued to work over his extremely successful *General Psychopathology* up to its seventh edition in 1959 and enriched it with philosophy; but he did not revise his statements regarding the relationship between philosophy and science. Even the fact that in the half century between around 1910 and 1960 a lot, including fundamentals, had changed in philosophy and the sciences, and that new philosophical schools and new scientific disciplines have come into being, did not alter his point of view. Jaspers himself was active and published in both fields and his contributions to both have won him recognition. He saw the relationship between philosophy and science in 1910, as a scientist, no differently than he saw it in 1969 as a philosopher. His changeover from scientist to philosopher did not influence his point of view; rather, his point of view had brought about his career change.

The only break in the continuity of his point of view concerns the so-called *verstehende* or hermeneutic psychology, founded by Wilhelm Dilthey to differentiate it from Wilhelm Wundt's experimental approach to psychology. In his psychiatric studies at the university clinic in Heidelberg, Jaspers declared the former, besides Husserl's phenomenology, to be a new invaluable method for dealing with psychiatric patients. There is no doubt that he considered psychiatry, as he studied it under Franz Nissl in Heidelberg, to be a science; at the same time he held that Freudian psychoanalysis in all its variations was not one.[10] On the one hand, he considered *verstehende* psychology essential for the work of the psychiatrist who does not merely want to consider neurological findings. On the other, he had doubts about it as a science because, even though it is not a natural science but is given recognition as such because of its methodological structure, it does not lead to scientific progress but merely discloses meaning contents.[11] It is not the pathology of mental illness that constitutes the *verstehbaren* phenomena; rather it is the causality that comes into play from the outside, as it were. *Verstehende* psychology, in Jaspers's sense, means understanding the patient's utterances and behavior, to the extent that they can be understood as meaningful out of healthy connections. The psychiatrist applying the method of *verstehen* advances only as far as the borders of the pathological. Of course the causal interpolations are also "understandable," in the way in which we can ordinarily understand causal connections. But these causalities do not become meaningful in terms of the clinical picture but disturb the image of the appearing phenomenon.

Jaspers evaded the problem as to the status of *verstehende* psychology; while he did not explicitly pose this question, he did, finally "solve" it by letting it be absorbed into illumination of Existenz. The latter, however, belongs to the realm of philosophy. "Existenz itself cannot be understood."[12] Jaspers introduced *verstehende* psychology in the first edition of *General Psychopathology* (1913), discussed it in *Psychologie der Weltanschauungen* (1919), but no longer mentioned it in his *Philosophy* (1931) as a separate method. In *Von der Wahrheit* (1947) Jaspers points to the special status of psychology, which he claims is not a science, and characterizes it neither as a natural science nor as *verstehende* psychology.[13] In his lecture, "The Physician in the Technical Age" of 1958 he says: "Progress is achieved by means of scientific research; by means of *Verstehen* a world of meaning contents is opened up, but it lacks the progress of a science." And further: "Here at its boundaries *Verstehen* leads back to scientific comprehension."[14] It is not the hermeneutically comprehensible meaning, but rather the mechanism that is medically essential.

The Object of Scientific Inquiry and the "Object" of Philosophy

From a systematic standpoint Jaspers's conception of the relationship between philosophy and scientific inquiry can be divided into three problem areas. These concern the following questions: (a) What can be considered to be the "object" of philosophy and in scientific inquiry? (b) What methods are used in philosophy and scientific inquiry? (c) What meaning is connected with philosophy and with scientific inquiry?

Determination of scientific objects are usually given by tradition, being based on varying circumstances, purposes and conventions, and are thus predetermined for the sciences in part by history and in part by the subject matter. Philosophy, on the other hand, determines its object itself because there is no position outside of itself. It determines in what way it wants to be philosophy, and thereby also what its object is to be. There is no more universal determination of philosophy than the one it gives to itself. Starting with his *Vernunft und Existenz* (*Reason and Existenz*) of 1935, Jaspers called the "object" of his philosophy the Encompassing. He means by this the all-embracing Being, i.e., that beyond which nothing else can be thought and what, strictly speaking, is no longer object. The origin of the concept of the Encompassing coined by Jaspers is the Kantian dichotomy of subject and object, which, according to Jaspers, is embraced by the Encompassing. The underlying opposition is not finite—infinite, but rather, particular object—encompassing All. This fundamental opposition points to the difference between science and philosophy. Infinity can still be particular and mastered in mathematics. This particularity, and not finiteness, is the fundamental determination of all scientific endeavors. There is no universal science. The claim to a universal science leads to pseudo-science and superstition. The underlying critical idea is: what is valid for a part is not valid for the whole. The object of the sciences is that which confronts a cognizing subject. Jaspers calls the cognizing subject, by a term borrowed from Kant, "consciousness as such." The object of cognition facing it is, as object, always merely a part of the whole, a whole that includes the subject as well.

Science studies actual being (*Dasein*) that is independent from the being of the scientist. Philosophy, too, poses the question of Being, which is experienced in that I am myself; in this sense, philosophy is also self-assurance.[15] This self-assurance is not a science, neither is it psychology. The object of science, located in the subject-object dichotomy, is for us not as it is in itself but as it appears to us. Therefore all scientifically objective knowledge is a knowing of appearances and not of Being as such. But even the cognizing subject, as it becomes its own object in an act of self-reflection, does not experience itself as a being as-such but rather in modes of its appearance. The character of being-appearance applies not only to the objects of science but also the subjects of philosophy. Reason and Existenz are located within the subject-object dichotomy; we can confront them in cognition only in their being appearance. Philosophy however, understanding that it is not a science, tries to think in terms of the Encompassing, i.e., not of objects. Such thinking is expressed indirectly in ciphers, and the reading of ciphers is called metaphysics. The experience of itself as possible Existenz is called illumination of Existenz. Propositions of science are direct, and are said to be "correct"; the thinking of philosophy searches for an encompassing meaning of truth that embraces all partial aspects of being-correct.[16]

Philosophical truth is not incorporated into scientific correctness but does not disregard it. What is scientifically false cannot be philosophically true; however what is scientifically correct need not be philosophically true. Properly understood, science and philosophy need not oppose each other as do religion and philosophy; neither do they need to correct each other. Instead, they are critically to validate and, cautiously, to affirm each other. Philosophy sees through the excesses of science in its generalizations; science calls the attention of philosophy to its false claims. The Encompassing appears in the seven modes; these are always the "object" of philosophy and not of science. These modes of the Encompassing do not correspond to the steps of Being, i.e., matter-life-soul-spirit, which Jaspers may have taken over from Nicolai Hartmann, including their determination from lower to upper as well as their intermediate steps, though he does not refer to Hartmann.[17] In his *Philosophie* he discusses in detail this "fourfold actuality"; in *Von der Wahrheit* he refers to it as the "levels of openness to investigation" of the world and differentiates it from the modes of the Encompassing.

The subject of science is consciousness as such, i.e., the ideally identical consciousness of all subjects of cognition. The subject of philosophy is reason, or rather the absolute consciousness of Existenz that is grounded in unconditional freedom. Therefore the aim of the sciences is the cognition, valid for all, of objects within world orientation; the aim of philosophy, however, is the understanding of itself as possible Existenz in the appearance of its being-in-the-world.

The Question of Method in Scientific Research and in Philosophy

From Jaspers's perspective, philosophy does not have a specific, prescribed method; otherwise it would be determined from without. The sciences are determined, through and through, by methods that have been prescribed for them or which have developed within them. Certain scientific research can be done only with certain methods. In principle, philosophy must be familiar with all methods; it must see through their nature and import. In its self-representation philosophy must of course proceed methodically, but the method of representation is not constitutive of its contents. In philosophy, results cannot be forced through the use of certain methods.

In the sciences, on the other hand, the methods are constitutive and are meant to lead to results. In the sciences there is research. In philosophy there is nothing that can be achieved through research. It does not stand within the "continuity of research."[18] The results of scientific inquiry aim to be universally valid, i.e., everyone who is in a position to reconstruct the steps of the research must be able to accept them as valid. This universal validity comes about because the individual steps of the research, whether in the intuitability of the experiment or in the theoretical argumentation, constitute cogent insights. Jaspers does not speak of evidence but time and again of cogent insight, cogent cognition, and cogent certainty. And this comes about because the steps must be repeatable and the results verifiable. Being universally valid, the scientific results are also communicable. They can be expressed unequivocally through language, can be understood by all rational beings, can be translated into all languages, and can be preserved for all time.

In the sciences one can discern clear and incontestable progress. This does not apply to philosophy. "The simple fact that scientific knowledge is spread identically throughout the world, but that philosophy, in spite of all its claims of validity, cannot become universally valid in any form, cannot be overlooked."[19] The insights of philosophers are, even if true, not cogent; if true for a few, still not true for all; if they arrive at certain convictions these are not communicable through reason. Philosophy sounds esoteric where it expresses what is most obvious to the one who philosophizes. Its messages are indirect, by way of ciphers, because it knows that what it discusses is appearance but does not know what it is that appears. Hence it does not speak in an assertive manner but in a summoning one. Philosophy challenges us to show our agreement out of similar experiences of Being; for it does not address the categories of the intellect but the ideas of reason.

The old differentiation of intellect (*Verstand*) and reason (*Vernunft*) serves Jaspers also to differentiate between science and philosophy. For him, reason is one mode of the Encompassing, the one that constitutes the medium for connecting the other modes. It is "the bond of all modes of the Encompassing."[20] Here, too, in connecting reason and ideas, Jaspers follows Kant's usage. Reason embraces intellect but does not deny it. Certainty is only categorical-partial, but the superordinate connections become clear through the guiding ideas of reason. And just as there are no universally recognized results in philosophy, there is also no incontestable progress in its knowledge.

Saying that science is determined by method means the same as saying that scientific knowledge is determined by methodical research activity. Its findings are subject to presuppositions in the determination of its objects and its methods. Talk of "science without presuppositions" does not make any sense because science does not want to be without presuppositions. It is bound to methods, either theoretical or empirical. The presuppositions of science are both limiting and assuring. By restricting validity to precisely these presuppositions, they make possible their strict validity. This restriction means, on the one hand, the limitation of applicability to certain spheres of being (matter, life, soul, and spirit) but in this way assures, on the other, the cogent validity within the particular sphere.

In principle, philosophy has no presuppositions apart from the actual conditions of existence, i.e., that the thinking individual can exist. It knows no presupposition that it does not give to itself or which it proposes freely for itself as conditions of its own cognition. The Encompassing and the world as a whole have no presuppositions, and for this very reason evade any sort of cognition that is certain as well as contingent on method. The insights of philosophy are never cogent, even though, in the last analysis, it is philosophy that explains the meaning of "cogency." Cogent knowledge concerns something specifically finite in the world and is subject to conditional presuppositions; it is particular and relative. For this reason cogent knowledge leaves us ultimately dissatisfied, satisfaction is possible only in philosophy.

In Jaspers's view, philosophy, not being determined by any specific method, sees through all methods. Philosophy is characterized, if at all, by only one method: transcending. To be sure, Jaspers explains that transcending is not a new method. In *Von der Wahrheit* he calls it "the fundamental philosophic operation,"[21] but he merely wants to differentiate it in this way from scientific methods. In *Philosophy* he does speak about "methods of transcending, by way of categories, above oneself."[22]

What Jaspers means by "transcending" is something unique and original that cannot be found in any other philosopher. He means the systematic-methodical transgressing of the limits of objectivity, neither falling into the void nor resorting to a new objectivity. He does not mean the crossing over the borders of a realm of Being into another one which is possible only through a "leap," but a transcending of objectivity altogether. Jaspers likes to refer to Kant, and does so here, specifically to his doctrine of antinomies: For example, thinking of the world as a thing in itself, i.e., as if it were an object of science, leads to the contradictory result that it is finite as well as infinite. From this Kant concludes that we must not think the world as a thing in itself. That contradiction forbids something, and because of the contradictions the sciences abide by this negative consequence. Jaspers tries to find a positive meaning in the contradictions (in the meaningful contradictions, not in every trivial one). The *coincidentia oppositorum* attests precisely to the transcendence of the object that is falsely conceived of as immanent: the world as a whole is not an object of scientific inquiry but all objects of scientific inquiry are in the world. All philosophical systems that are attempts to think the whole of Being as if it were an object are based on logical contradictions, circular reasoning, or tautologies. This attempt may be cast in a trivial form, as in Schopenhauer: the brain creates the world, the world creates the brain; or, in a more profound way, as in Kant: the category of unity is not the unity of the categories. The basic form of the contradictory or tautological thought is always: Being is Being—Being is not Being—Being is the cause of Being. Since determinate, consistent thinking is always a thinking of objects, determinate thought of the nonobjective Encompassing is contradictory or circular or tautological. Hence thought of the Encompassing must be nonobjective thinking. "Only because there is such [thinking] is there philosophy." Such thinking is called transcending and "philosophizing is transcending."[23] For Jaspers, formal transcending means having the formal means of thinking and the philosophical contents at the ready in order to gain insights at the limits of scientific objectivity. These insights are understood not as universally valid cognition but as an assurance of Being, as a new consciousness of Being, as a transformation of consciousness. Such transcending takes place everywhere where philosophy discovers limits: in cosmology, when it asks after spatial and temporal beginning and end; in the question regarding the nature of matter and spirit, as well as the meaning of life, the where from and where to of Existenz, and the origin and goal of history.

The fundamental operation of transcending is a thinking that goes beyond "each determinate being, beyond every still visible horizon . . . to the Encompassing in which we are and which we ourselves are."[24] In doing so, we remain within our world and do not surrender our objective thinking. For Jaspers, transcending is a logical foundering experienced in thinking,[25] without it being a *sacrificium intellectum*, which would mean the abandonment of thinking altogether. Rather, it means staying with the intellectual means up to their very limits with full awareness of the limits. The dialectics of transcending thought is a "not-thinking that illuminates by not thinking Something and not thinking Nothing."[26] Transcending has the effect of liberating from objectivity; it awakens us to hear what authentically is; it enables us to perceive the origins, and it is a becoming aware of the Encompassing."[27]

PHILOSOPHY AND THE QUESTION OF THE MEANINGFULNESS OF SCIENCE

The question of meaning is the question of significance and of value. Regarding existence to be meaningless would be paramount to regarding calling it devoid of significance or value. The question of meaning is decisive for the differentiation of philosophy and science insofar as it constitutes the question of the "why?" and of the "for what purpose?" of this difference.

Strictly speaking, the sciences themselves do not pose the question as to the why of their activity, nor do they ask after its purpose. These questions do not belong within the scope of their task and are not the object of scientific investigation. Of course the individual motivation of certain scientists, or the orientation toward a purpose or hidden dependence on a goal on the part of scientific groups or disciplines can be made into the subject of historical, sociological, and psychological investigation. But this exceeds the primary object sphere to which these groups direct themselves. The mathematician as such does not examine why he practices mathematics and what it is good for. And if he does, he is no longer acting as mathematician, is no longer applying the methods of mathematics, and no longer expects the application of mathematical criteria of judgment. He either becomes a sociologist or historian or psychologist, who then has to transcend anew his sociological-historical-psychological methods if he wants to render an account once more of his sociological-historical-psychological efforts. He will have to go beyond his realms of objectivity until he realizes that he is doing philosophy.

This situation regarding the exclusion of the question of meaning from genuinely scientific problems is connected with the problem of wholeness and is the consequence of the particularity of objects of science. The question of meaning forces the scientist necessarily to reflect about his own person. The question of meaning includes the subjective side of the fundamental subject-object relationship. "Meaning" always means "meaning for someone." Something has significance for someone. Something has value in relation to something. The self-reflection of the person asking about meaning cannot come to rest anyplace because the objectivized subject demands a new subject. The question: "Why do I pursue mathematics?" demands the further question: "Why do I pursue psychology or sociology of mathematics?" Reflection drives in the direction of an infinite regress, and the question about meaning can be approached only from a whole that also encompasses the subject. Each particular finding or imparting of meaning is dependent on an encompassing finding or imparting of meaning. The question of the meaning of scientific activity can be answered only out of the meaning of the totality of human activity; the particular meaning of the life of a human being can be sought only out of existence as a whole, and the latter out of Being as such. If existence as a whole has no meaning, then personal Existenz does not either. Modern science, considered since Descartes as an aid to life, only seems to determine its meaning itself. If it is said that the meaning of science is the domination of the conditions of life, the further question immediately arises as to the meaning of this domination.

To ask and to think in terms of such totalities is, from Jaspers's perspective, philosophical questioning and thinking. For this reason, science as an activity, and not merely as a collection of facts and theories, urges beyond itself to philosophy. The scientist can also be a philosopher, but that does not turn science in its narrow sense into philosophy. Neither are meaning determinations that transcend science scientific just because they were made by a scientist.

It has always been the task of philosophy, from the time it began to make statements about the whole, to occupy itself with the question of meaning; for the whole is at the same time the meaning of the whole. Wherever it has rejected such questioning it has abdicated and has assumed a scientific posture as in positivism and the analytic philosophy of our time. In attempting to remain scientific by giving up the question of meaning it has become a pseudo-science. And by claiming to be able to solve all problems through forcing silence on the others, it has become pseudo-philosophy.

The meaning of any particular can only be thought out of an Encompassing: the meaning of each individual existence out of human existence as a whole, the meaning of any one item of knowledge out of the whole of science, the unity of the sciences. Concrete pragmatic purposes which, being obvious, do not need any justification, apparent necessities of life, and theoretical constructs, are steps in the hierarchy of meaning connections. These connections grow together, for example in the idea of the unity of the sciences in which each individual science gains meaning. Therefore the question about the unity of the sciences is "a basic question of philosophizing about the meaningfulness of science,"[28] but it is not the subject matter of any one science.

Hence: "The meaningfulness of science . . . itself cannot be proved through science."[29]

If when the meaning derives from the whole in which the individual is located, then the individual item is transcended in the question of meaning. This transcending is infinite. Even the most certain scientific knowledge points beyond itself in the question of its meaning, and ultimately to the Encompassing. But from where does the meaning of the Encompassing come if there is nothing else beside itself? The meaning of the Encompassing can be thought only as the Being whose meaning is Being, that is, it cannot be thought rationally. We are within a circular self-reference: Being is the meaning of Being. Thought rationally, meaning is always relative and has an end, for example in death. The insight we derive from this transcending in the question of meaning is: "It is impossible to question the universe . . . about meaning."[30] There are merely "answers that, as rationalistic, are erroneous." The "erroneousness" consists in the particular meaning being posited as absolute, and in that being applied to the whole that is valid only for the part.

Ultimate meaning could only result from the whole, but the whole cannot be thought except in the shipwreck of "absurd thought."[31] Thinking meaning is not possible, but one cannot live without meaning. "To live truly without meaning—this I cannot do even for a moment."

The question of meaning is a philosophical question that transcends every science. Yet only meaningful life and significant existence motivates scientists to do research, guides them through ideas of unity on their search for connections, presents them with goals and purposes; but within their task of research the question of meaning has no place. Because, properly understood, science remains particular it not only cannot give an answer to the question of its meaning, but the question cannot even arise without the context of their research task. One could summarize Jaspers's position in the paradoxical formulation: meaningful science is through philosophy—authentic science is without philosophy.[32]

Notes

1. I am quoting this lecture from: Karl Jaspers, *Rechenschaft und Ausblick. Reden und Aufsätze* (München: Piper & Co., 1958). [Hereafter, cited as RA] (In English this lecture appears as "Appendix I: Philosophy and Science" in Karl Jaspers, *Way to Wisdom* (New Haven: Yale University Press, 1954), pp. 147–67. [Hereafter, WW]

2. RA, p. 253; cf. WW, p. 160.

3. RA, p. 251; cf. WW, p. 158.

4. RA, p. 252; cf. WW, p. 159.

5. RA, p. 253; cf. WW, p. 160.

6. Cf. Karl Jaspers, *Allgemeine Psychopathologie*, p. 9. unveränderte Auflage (Berlin/Heidelberg/New York: Springer-Verlag, 1973), p. 642. [Hereafter cited as AP, eds.]

7. Cf. Karl Jaspers, *Philosophie* I, 4. unveränderte Auflage (Berlin/Heidelberg/New York: Springer-Verlag, 1973), pp. 188ff. [Hereafter cited as P 1, eds.]; cf. Karl Jaspers, *Philosophy*, vol. 1., translated by E. B. Ashton (Chicago/London: The University of Chicago Press, 1969), p. 206f. [Hereafter cited as PH 1, eds.]

8. P 1, p. 185; cf. Ph 1, p. 204.

9. Cf. Hans Saner, "Sterben können" in *Karl Jaspers in der Diskussion,* Klaus Piper & Hans Saner, eds. (München: Piper & Co., 1974), p. 325. About his "writings as a whole" and his "basic disposition" Jaspers said: ". . . there have been no changes of conviction, no breaks, no instances of crisis or renascence." (Karl Jaspers, "Philosophical Memoir" in *Philosophy and the World* (New York: Henry Regnery, 1963), p. 298.

10. Jaspers, AP, pp. 641, 646ff.; also "Zur Kritik der Psychoanalyse" in Jaspers, RA, pp. 260–71.

11. Cf. Jaspers, *Der Arzt im technischen Zeitalter* (München: Piper & Co., 1986), pp. 48 ff.

12. Jaspers, P 2, p. 12; cf. Karl Jaspers, *Philosophy*, vol. 2, translated by E. B. Ashton (Chicago and London: The University of Chicago Press, 1970), p. 12. [Hereafter cited as PH 2, eds.]

13. Cf. Karl Jaspers, *Von der Wahrheit,* Neuausgabe (München: Piper & Co., 1958), p. 1041. [Hereafter cited as VdW, eds.]

14. Jaspers, *Der Arzt im technischen Zeitalter*, p. 48.

15. P 1, p. 262; cf. PH 1, p. 268.

16. Cf. Jaspers, *Von der Wahrheit,* pp. 457ff.

17. VdW, p. 200; also P 1, pp. 165ff.; cf. PH 1, pp. 187ff.

18. VdW, p. 338.

19. RA, p. 254, cf. WW, p. 162.

20. VdW, p. 50.

21. VdW, p. 39.

22. Karl Jaspers, *Philosophie* III, p. 4. unveränderte Auflage (Berlin/Heidelberg/New York, 1973), p. 40 [Hereafter cited as P 3, eds.]; cf. Karl Jaspers, *Philosophy*, vol. 3, translated by E. B. Ashton (Chicago and London: The University of Chicago Press, 1971), p. 36. [Hereafter cited as PH 3, eds.]

23. P 3, p. 40; cf. also PH 3, p. 36; also RA, p. 253; cf. WW, p. 160.

24. VdW, p. 39.

25. See the article by George B. Pepper herein.

26. Jaspers, P 3, p. 39; cf. PH 3, p. 36.

27. Cf. VdW, p. 40.

28. Jaspers, P 1, p. 130; cf. PH 1, p. 158.

29. P 1, p. 129; cf. PH 1, p. 156.

30. P 3, p. 54; PH 3, p. 48.

31. Ibid.

32. P 1, p. 135; PH 1, p. 160.

Part II
World History of Philosophy, World Philosophy, and Politics

UNFINISHED PROJECTS

KARL JASPERS ON WORLD HISTORY OF PHILOSOPHY AND WORLD PHILOSOPHY

Hans Saner

On March 2, 1938, Jaspers wrote to Heinrich Zimmer, the Indologist at University of Heidelberg, that he was engaged in studying Confucius and was experiencing an enthusiasm "akin to the discovery of something tremendous."[1] "I am now much more interested in approaching philosophy from a universal-historical viewpoint. It is as if we are standing here before the gates of an extraordinary insight—but have yet to succeed in flinging the gate open."[2] This passage from the letter is the earliest indication that in the late 1930s a change had occurred in Jaspers's philosophic-historical endeavors. His publications up to this point,[3] as well as his lectures and seminars[4] dealing with the history of philosophy, dealt exclusively with European, and among these, predominantly German, philosophers. Starting in 1937, according to Jaspers in his "Philosophical Autobiography," he began to include first Chinese and then also Indian philosophy, whose original thinking, from that time on, was no longer considered of lesser importance than Western philosophy. His opening of himself up to the realms of East Asian culture, followed by the Near East, was connected to his idea of a "Universal History of Philosophy," which later on he more often called "World History of Philosophy." "In 1937 I conceived of the plan of a world history of philosophy. . . . "[5] In the winter semester 1951/2 Jaspers lectured about this topic at the University of Basel for the first time.[6] Almost all of his work that deals with the history of philosophy written since the war is included in this master plan, about which our knowledge is only fragmentary, in part from the writings that Jaspers himself had published,[7] in part from the *Nachlass* (unpublished papers), which appeared in the early 1980s.[8]

Translated by *Edith Ehrlich.*

THE IDEA OF A WORLD HISTORY OF PHILOSOPHY

In his "Philosophical Autobiography" Jaspers mentions the occasion that suggested to him the "Idea of a World History of Philosophy."[9] At the end of the spring semester 1937 he was pensioned off "by order of the Ministry in order to simplify the administration"[10] because his wife was Jewish. As a citizen there was practically nothing at all that he could do against his exclusion in his own country and against the terror of National Socialism. As philosopher he saw in both the "most radical rupture of communication from person to person."[11] Now the question arose in his mind whether thinking itself could either pave the way for the condition of terror, or be "creative" and "protective" of that which is able to resist it. Based on these considerations he found his task one of working "on the presuppositions of the possibility of universal communication."[12] This could—and would have to—be done primarily in two specific areas: In philosophic logic, which was to become an instrument of universal communicability, and in the world history of philosophy, which was to be the "framework" of universal communication. Jaspers needed to gain an overview of the "totality of the philosophy of mankind"[13] and on this basis to venture the envisagement of the spatial and temporal universality of thought. From the very beginning it was clear to him that a single individual must at first run aground on this task. Yet he considered it necessary because the consciousness of the times themselves assigned it to him, and he believed that it could be performed in principle because the moment of history facilitated a solution through the technology of travel and news reporting. Jaspers was convinced that this solution was not to be expected from a team in the manner of an encyclopedia, by simply juxtaposing epochs and cultures. An encyclopedia of the world history of thought would always be merely an accumulation of knowledge and material, lacking a framework. Only a single main framework can be capable of projecting and elaborating an overview of the entirety out of the idea. It will always remain controversial because there simply is no single correct conception.

In what sense can an overview of the entirety become a task at all? There has never been a universal history consisting of a constant mutual exchange of information, or of a continuous interaction, neither in the realm of political action nor of philosophic thought. Instead, to Jaspers it is a fundamental fact that philosophy can be proven to have had several independent origins—in India, in China, in the Near East, in the West—as did cultural history altogether. Notwithstanding all influences and parallels that might have been present through the millennia, there was always an "independent separate development" of the different cultural realms. For this reason the task consists of finding that certain "questions, answers and motives objectively belong together," which cut across all these differences. Hence the "unity of the world history of philosophy"[14] is not a matter of seeing a mirror image of a whole but an overview of an idea that is understood and whose meaning is envisaged.

However, the truth that understands the meaning is not the same truth everywhere but an extensive realm of possibilities in which people encounter each other in their thinking. In the breadth of this realm Jaspers finds, on the one hand, the permanent "struggle among forces" in which all are engaged who think truthfully, and, on the other hand, something like a living center of human thought to which the different thinking of all men are anchored. The seemingly endless material of history is organized toward this center, albeit by way of the struggle of understanding. This process is itself a matter of philosophizing and not merely an arrangement of philosophies. Hence the world history of philosophy calls for philosophers, to whom the differentiated thinking of history becomes transparent, thereby directing toward the wholeness of a *philosophia perennis*.

Jaspers's Preliminary Plan of the World History of Philosophy

Most likely the first plan of a world history of philosophy was conceived at the beginning of the 1950s. There Jaspers proceeds from the idea that the history of philosophy takes place within "the whole of universal history" and therefore is "connected to the entire real and spiritual world of its time."[15] It is "the consciousness of existence as a whole and of being-human in particular at a given time."[16] Whoever wants to reconstruct it must be present within the space of the time in which it had been thought; he must not carry out mere abstract thought operations as if these were ahistorical. In particular, according to Jaspers, "one must get acquainted with the conditions under which philosophizing was being carried out in each situation,"[17] in accordance with the following five approaches:

1. One has to study "*the social conditions in the particular worlds*,"[18] such as, the histories of the country, the economy, the culture; indeed everything that has brought structure and order into the common existence of these worlds.

2. One must understand the "*ways of thinking and the world views*" that are constitutive of the pre-philosophic thinking in the particular cultures, and also mold philosophy and are molded by it. In them are displayed the "spiritual forces . . . that are predominant"[19] and determine the epoch and the people down to their basic disposition.

3. One must get to know "*the sciences*" of the particular time, and that means, in principle, all of them. They are "indispensable for the understanding of the history of philosophy" for they are everywhere "an essential presupposition of philosophizing"[20] no matter whether reference is made to them or not.

4. One must acquaint oneself with the "*religions*" practiced during the times in question. "Religion is the prehistory . . . and . . . the parallel history of philosophy, is itself or becomes philosophy and . . . [is] shaped by philosophy in turn."[21] This does not mean that philosophy itself is religion. It speaks different languages of transcendence. For this reason it is always engaged in a struggle with religion, at least in modern times. This struggle is a road to its self-understanding. In this way philosophy is awakened by religion and forced into a history of its own. "No history of philosophy without a history of religion."[22]

5. One must also come to grips with the far-flung realm of "*poetry and art*." For the arts, too, "are a way of understanding Being, as are religion and philosophy"; in comparison to the heydays of the arts, philosophy may "appear even as a narrowing and impoverishment." Art not only is able to tell what man is but also to show or, in music, to let us feel. Wherever philosophy achieves a certain depth, it is always related to the arts; and in the phases of greatness on the part of different cultures the philosophies and the arts form "the indivisible whole of a spiritual world."[23]

What is decisive for Jaspers is that one would have to recognize or sense the "interwovenness of all in the One," right through the divisions of the understanding into science, philosophy, *Weltanschauung*, religion, art, and history. One has to acquire the fundamental attitude of sensing the One that runs through everything in the manifold of spiritual and real configurations of being-human, the infinite relationships that tie everything together in enmity and amity. For "the realm of the spirit is the universal comprehensibility (*Verstehbarkeit*)"[24] that knows not only the one area of philosophy but all modes of *Verstehen* that speak to us at times in ways that complement, or run parallel, or in a contrary direction. The necessary breadth of thinking along with others in the history of philosophy is therefore not merely an acknowledgment of the spiritual framework; rather, this breadth fans out to give us alternative interpretations of Being that reveal to us the differing ciphers of the One.

This does not mean that all of this should be presented explicitly in a world history of philosophy, merely that one would have to know all this in order to be able to write a world history of philosophy. For one must "not ever forget even what one does not present oneself."[25] Jaspers defends himself against all precipitous delimitations of this knowledge, perhaps based on the argument that such a breadth of consciousness would be impossible, in the following manner: "All great spiritual achievements come about by attempting the impossible."[26] In the presentation itself, however, boundaries will have to be set between the history of philosophy and the other histories; but for these delimitations there are "no external and mechanically applicable criteria,"[27] merely a leading idea, albeit a powerful one:

> For one thing will forever remain as the subject matter of the history of philosophy: The encompassing One, albeit objectified for thought, actual as existence and spirit, visible and experienceable as being-human grounded as Existenz, permeated by reason, focused on the One of transcendence, assuring itself in the world.[28]

Within this inclusive whole, the history of philosophy is divided into "specific topics."[29] These allow us to recognize the actual delimitations.

Jaspers arranges the topics into three groups: The history of philosophy is (1) history of the forms of thought, (2) history of the philosophic contents, and (3) history of the philosophic personages. The horizons of these groups are the particular forms of the Encompassing: The horizon of the forms of thought is consciousness as such; the horizon of the philosophic personages is Existenz; the horizons of content are existence, spirit, world, and transcendence. Thus the horizons of all the groups together are all the modes of the Encompassing of Jaspers's philosophical logic. Reason, as always, is given the function of combining everything with everything and thus bringing about unity across all of the groupings.

Jaspers presents us with certain considerations regarding the three groups:

1. The *history of the forms of thought* is, at the same time, a) the history of concepts, b) the history of the formulation of questions, and c) the history of the systems.

a. The *history of concepts* is, as history of the *categories*, also the history of the forms of thought and of objects. Together with the development of the categories there is a simultaneous historical development of the *methods*, that is, "the modes of their movement, application, and fulfillment." The history of the forms of thought is thus the elucidation of logic, i.e., of "knowledge according to form," and therein especially an elucidation of the forms of philosophic thought. This history brings to mind how, through the ages, one has proceeded in philosophizing, and makes us aware of how one may and, at times, should proceed. In this function it carries out the "cleansing of the act of philosophic thinking."[30]

b. The *history of the questions* that are posed is the *history of problems*; it exhibits the progressing and forgetting exhibits in the consciousness of problems. It comprises perennial questions as well as those that disappear. Insofar as it points out areas of progress, developments, and solutions, it is related to the history of science. As a rule, what is philosophically essential for Jaspers are "the deviations" because they introduce new contents into a problem. However, whatever remains identical becomes the "universal tool of philosophizing"[31] that claims objective correctness.

c. Finally, the *history of systems* was meant to differentiate between "systems as structures" that are rationally closed arrangements, and systems "as the unitariness of the ways of thinking and intuition,"[32] systems which cannot be closed off through logic. Not all philosophies by far are systems in the strict sense; but all philosophy is carried out systematically or systemically because it always aims toward a whole and not merely at particulars as do the sciences. Therefore the history of systems must show "where and for what reason the conscious, methodical concept of system appears and how it proceeds by means of logical deduction, be it syllogistic, dialectical, classificatory or in some other way."[33] It must also show how "the internal coherence of language and ways of thinking that cannot be logically completed," or "the unity of a vivid infinite vision" proceeds. Systems are not exclusively creations of individual thinkers but are at times unities of thought created by schools, movements, cultures or epochs, such as the stoic or the positivistic or the medieval system. Systems are not overcome by immanent arguments or improvements but only through "a different system"[34] that sees itself as a radical renewal.

In each of the three disciplines—of the history of concepts, problems, and systems—the history of the forms of thought concentrates on differing moments of form. But in all of its moments, form always molds content, and becomes itself, as structure, a part of this content.

2. The *history of philosophic contents* brings to mind not only the material or the contents of philosophy, but also "the fulfilment of Being" of these contents "through spiritual ideas, existential relevance, vital substance and transcendent significance."[35] It explores how the Encompassing of the world, of existence and of transcendence have been imagined or thought. It therefore becomes history, in three respects:

a. As the *history of the images of the world* it is a gallery, as it were, in which the succession of "world landscapes"[36] reveals the Encompassing, which has been thought as world.

b. In the *history of self-reflection* the various ways in which man relates to himself, cognizes and deals with himself, reveal the contents of being-human, which also have become perceivable in images of human beings.

c. In the *history of symbolism* there is revealed how finite complex unities and infinite transcendence have been visualized in symbols and ciphers. Those contents become visible in which man ultimately "was certain of Being."[37]

Philosophic contents are thought by *philosophic individuals*. What they are as human beings becomes evident indirectly in the way in which they grasp the world, themselves, and Being. Thus the history of contents merges into a history of philosophic personages.

3. In the *history of philosophic personages* Jaspers directs "the attention to the person by way of their thoughts,"[38] and not the other way around. Wherever he finds reports about a person's thinking, he counts reports about a person's thinking as a thinking person, as philosopher. Nonetheless Jaspers differentiates between those thinkers who are philosophers in the more narrow sense, and those thinking individuals whose philosophical relevance is based on their original humanness.

a. He ranks among the *figures of original humanness* those people who have either become "*exemplary for many,*" or have realized "*the utmost of radical possibilities*," or are "*valid exceptions*." Among these we find, for example, Homer and the tragedians, Shakespeare, the representatives of epochs and peoples such as Napoleon, but also figures from literature, for example, from medieval epics or from tragedies. Such literary figures have often presented in a pure form, "what in the actuality of history we find merely in an opaque reflection even though in empirical and documentary form." Jaspers merely hints at other possible types. These might, for example, be "*the well-bred and final ones*," or "*the initiators and trailblazers,*" or just "*the great exceptions without closure or successors*,"[39] who show us the limits of being-human. Only later did Jaspers work out a satisfactory grouping that does not overlap with that of professional philosophers.

b. *Philosophers in the narrower sense* are those "who have made their life in thought their calling and communicate their thought in their writings."[40] Jaspers made two attempts at grouping them. In the one he differentiates between the "*irreplaceable unique ones*" who are "indispensable," the "*classical representatives*," who are rarely, though not in principle, "irreplaceable," and the "*replaceable examples of those who represent a certain type*,"[41] of whom there are many and who are or can become important in some partial respect. In this particular attempt at a typology he does not name any names.

The other attempt draws distinctions among the *philosophers of the highest caliber*, who are at the same time "completion and beginning" and for all time awaken others to their own creativity. He only mentions "the two unique ones: Plato and Kant." These Jaspers distinguishes from "*the universal system builders*: Aristotle, Thomas Aquinas, Hegel;" then "*the great metaphysicians*: Plotinus, Nicholas of Cusa, Spinoza, Schelling," as well as "*the disturbers and probers*," "*those who experiment and those who break through*," and the "*doubting and the despairing ones*," hence a group consisting of groups, among which he explicitly places the Stoics, Descartes, Kierkegaard, and Nietzsche. And from these he separates the philosophers "*who live at all times in the continuity of the great ones*:" monks, saints; teachers, scientists, scholars; priests and statesmen. These are the philosophers who play "their role in the world" and also take it consciously upon themselves.[42]

Within the first plan of a world history of philosophy Jaspers differentiates and typifies the philosophers in an altogether inadequate way. He mentions only a few names, among them, moreover, not a single non-European philosopher. Also, there he hardly included the alternative interpretations of Being in the arts, sciences, and religion in his world history of philosophy. It is as if the novel aspect of Jaspers's attempt had not really broken through the barriers but had become their victim instead—perhaps with the one exception of the idea of a multi-aspective historiography.

We do not know whether Jaspers made use of this plan to collect his material for a world history of philosophy. Perhaps his next step already consisted of a reformulation of his plan in order to find a better orientation for his future research.

THE DEFINITIVE PLAN OF THE WORLD HISTORY OF PHILOSOPHY

In his preface to *The Great Philosophers*[43] Jaspers expands the idea of a multi-aspective world history of philosophy to five aspects, with the personal one assuming central importance. It is only from the voluminous philosophical-historical *Nachlass* holdings—and there are over 20,000 sheets with many detailed tables of content—that we gain sufficient clarity in what order and with what material he meant to present the whole of the world history of philosophy in its six aspects.[44]

The following idea lies at the base of the total concept: Whoever wants to present the universal history of philosophy in its totality faces the difficulty that this totality does not become a unitary image or object for him. He cannot grasp it from the outside since he is himself on its inside. He can, however, penetrate it more deeply. But this cannot be done satisfactorily under a single aspect. If he wants to achieve clarity as he penetrates it he must do this always under certain methodical presuppositions that, being tied to differing aspects, break apart this whole into several wholenesses. The number of aspects remains an open question, yet is limited in practice by the factor of relevance and by the ways philosophy factually exists in the world.

How, then, does philosophy exist in the world? Jaspers answers this question in six parts:

1. Philosophy occurs always in a certain epoch, within the framework of natural givens and under the changeable conditions of a society. Seen under this *historical aspect* the typical modes of thought of an age appear as "the historical garb of eternal questions"[45] and the philosophers as children of their age. A *chronological world history of philosophic epochs* came into being, which became *Book I: The World History of Philosophy.*

In the *Nachlass* there are about 3,000 sheets dealing with this topic. It is prefaced with the "Introduction into the World History of Philosophy," which was discussed above. The emphasis of the following chapters rests on the individual characterization of the epochs and cultures. A first part then tells of the prehistory and beginnings of philosophy among the primitive peoples and the early civilizations, a second breaks down the body of the main epochs of the history of philosophy and finds the triple origin of this history in India, China, and Greece, followed by the epoch of Christian philosophy and that of the more recent Western philosophy up to the end of the eighteenth century. A third part deals with the provisional end of philosophy, i.e., the nineteenth century, then with contemporary philosophy, and concludes with a preview of the philosophy of the future. An appendix was to have traced the structure of the course of history, the parallels in the development of the different epochs, their mutual relationship and their importance for a history of thought. The whole volume has been outlined down to the details. There are voluminous notes about all epochs and some parts are written out. The "Introduction" and the presentation of the early civilizations are completed.

2. Philosophy poses questions and supplies answers. Under this *substantive aspect* Jaspers worked out, "without considering chronology,"[46] a systematic covering all that had at any time been the subject matter of philosophy. This becomes *Book II: World History of Philosophic Contents*. A first part was to present, on the one hand, the philosophical speculations about world, God and Being, on the other hand, philosophical thought about man, history, and society in their essential changes. This arrangement is structured so as to include a history of all relevant contents. A second part was to trace the relationship of philosophy and science throughout history. The third part was to show how, based on its contents, philosophy has been understood in all of history as "*Umkehr*" (turning-around, conversion, reversion).

About 3,500 sheets belong to this book. The whole first part—the history of the contents—has been written out. Everything else has been outlined in full detail, in part written out and in part sketched out.

3. Philosophy is present in persons and in their works which, according to

their rank and their orientation, are aligned with each other irrespective of their times, as if they existed in an imaginary realm of contemporaneity. Under this *personal aspect* a *world history of philosophic persons* comes to be.

This *Book III* of the *World History of Philosophy*, which was to extend over three volumes, was published under the title *Die grossen Philosophen* (*The Great Philosophers*), in part by Jaspers himself, in part taken from the *Nachlass*. We shall speak of it separately after we have discussed the conception of the whole.

4. Philosophy derives from many different sources, "in the beginning and at all times," those of language, myth, religion, and art. "The independent origin of philosophy is sheltered, as it were, in an other, out of which it is nourished or from which it distinguishes itself."[47] Under this *genetic aspect* Jaspers conceives a *world history of the groundedness and reverberations of philosophy in language, myth, religion, and art*, in which he concerns himself with the relationship of philosophy to alternative interpretations of Being. The first part of this *Book IV* of the *World History of Philosophy* was to consider the mutual relations of philosophy with the sphere of the universal spirit (language, myth, and religion), the second part considers the mutual relations of the sphere of special spiritual forces (literature and art). In both of these parts it is a matter of seeing how, in the course of history, philosophy delimits itself over against these other spiritual spheres and thereby defines itself, but also how it influences these areas and takes part in their interpretation of Being.

The *Nachlass* contains about 800 sheets on this topic, all in the form of notes. The big topics are sketched out but not worked out in detail.

5. Philosophy has consequences in the world. It is actualized in the conduct of one's life and is itself subject to the influences and conditions of the conduct of life. Under this *practical aspect*[48] Jaspers conceives of a *world history of the effect and actualization of philosophy*. A first part considers the forms of its actualization in writings such as the creation of system or the different literary genres, as well as in education. A second part analyzes the form of its conscious actualization in one's life, in the formulation of maxims, in psychological-pedagogical techniques, life ideals, etc. A third part was to show how and by what means philosophy had influence on public life: through popularization, political programs, through blueprints of utopias, and so on.

There are about 650 sheets dealing with this topic. All the topics are sketched out, but not worked out.

6. Philosophy is actualized in the mutuality and opposition of the philosophers. It lives as a struggle of minds grounded in the internalized "forces" (values). Under this *dynamic aspect*[49] Jaspers conceives of a *world history of philosophical polemics and irenics*. It examines the forms of the philosophical

struggle (discussion and polemics) and their connection to real [brute] force, then turns back to look at the origin of these battles, exposes their "powers," and examines the possibilities actualized in history to free the spiritual struggle from its connection with real brute force through tolerance and communication.

About 750 sheets of the *Nachlass* treat this sixth book of the *World History of Philosophy*, which was to be called *"Der Kampf der Mächte"* (*The Struggle among the Forces*). The structure of the whole book has been worked out, and there are notes relating to all of its sections.

Thus, from about the middle of the 1950s on, Jaspers had planned to write the world history of philosophy six times and under six aspects. Each of these aspects by itself is "restricted."[50] In their separation from each other they complement each other. They cannot, however, be united in one "complete picture."[51] This multi-aspective quality places *The Great Philosophers* into a much more comprehensive program and gives us an inkling of the complexity of Jaspers's philosophic-historical thought.

The Great Philosophers

When Jaspers worked out the *World History of Philosophy* he gave precedence to its personal aspect. In 1957 he brought out the first volume of *The Great Philosophers*, which was to comprise three volumes. None of the volumes was going to be arranged chronologically. Instead, the arrangement was based on the *idea* that there is "*an eternal realm*"[52] of the great thinkers, arranged according to the different kinds of their greatness and according to type irrespective of chronological considerations. What they have in common is not contemporaneousness, but an inner relationship as regards their way of thinking, the impulses and aims of their thoughts. The greatness of some of them lies in their function as awakeners to philosophy, others in being summarizing systematizers, and still others are metaphysicians who are world-pious or who have turned away from the world; it is precisely these functions that bind them together.

Jaspers's typology arranges the realm of the great philosophers in three main groupings, two of which are again subdivided.

I. "The *first main group* comprises people who, by their existence and nature have historically determined, as have no others, what it means to be human."[53] Jaspers calls them "the *Measures of Mankind*." There are four of them: Socrates, Buddha, Confucius, and Jesus. They stand at the forefront as well as beyond all other philosophers, and one could hesitate calling them philosophers at all. Among them it was only Confucius who left a written record, the effect of the others was based on the spoken word and their actions. Jaspers, who created an opening in this grouping from the Western world toward India and China, did not count Mohammed among these measures of humankind, and he tells us why: "The only one who, historically, had a comparable effect, Mohammed, cannot be compared [with the others] as regards the profundity of his being."[54]

II. "The *second main grouping* comprises the great thinkers who, by universal consensus, are considered philosophers."[55] Jaspers divides them into *four subgroups*:

1. Three thinkers comprise the first subgroup of "*The Seminal Founders of Philosophic Thought*:" Plato, St. Augustine and Kant. These are for Jaspers the most creative philosophers whose "influence [is] incalculable"[56]—up to the present time and most likely way into the future. They are two European and one African thinkers. Among them, Kant was for Jaspers the most important; he was the one whose influence on his thinking was the most enduring. Jaspers dedicated to him an especially detailed essay[57] that belongs to the best treatises ever written about Kant.

2. The second subgroup, "*Metaphysical Thinkers at the Source*," brings together Anaximander, Heraclitus, Parmenides, Plotinus, Anselm, Nicholas of Cusa, Spinoza, Laotse, and Nagarjuna. This group, too, transcends European territory. The essay about Nicholas of Cusa[58] is especially long and, next to the one about Spinoza, surely the most important. The great Master Eckehardt is missing from this array. The first volume of *The Great Philosophers* concludes with Nagarjuna.

Among all the following portrayals there are, to be sure, a few that are finished; but each group as a whole remains fragmentary. There is another set of thinkers that belongs into the same second subgroup: the "*Projective Metaphysicians*." These are (a) *Metaphysicians of Piety toward the World* (Xenophanes, Empedocles, Anaxagoras, Democritus, Poseidonius, Giordano Bruno); (b) *Gnostic Dreamers of Truth* (Origen, Böhme, Schelling); and (c) *Constructive Minds* (Hobbes, Leibniz, Fichte). The finished texts among the metaphysicians of "Piety toward the World" are those about Xenophanes, Empedocles, Anaxagoras, and Democritus, while those about Poseidonius and Giordano Bruno are merely sketched out.[59] To these Jaspers added a text about Epicurus and Lucretius, which was originally destined for the third volume.[60] A text about Origen from the "Gnostic Dreamers of Truth" has been published (in German,[61] which the American edition did not include), as well as a text about Jakob Böhme.[62] The German edition of the *Nachlass* does not include any text about Schelling because Jaspers devoted a separate book to Schelling in 1955.[63] This book has not been translated into English as yet. Instead, the American edition has included a lecture[64] that Jaspers held on the occasion of the 100th anniversary of Schelling's death. From the grouping "Constructive Minds" two fragmentary texts, one about Hobbes, the other about Leibniz are included in the German edition, but only Leibniz was included in the American *Nachlass* edition.[65]

3. The *third subgroup* is devoted to the *Disturbers*, who again brought movement into all rigidified thought. Jaspers counts among them *The Probing Negators* (Abelard, Descartes, and Hume) and *The Great Awakeners* (Pascal, Lessing, Kierkegaard, and Nietzsche). From among *The Probing Negators* only a *Nachlass*-text about Descartes was printed.[66] It may serve as a supplement to the Descartes-book of 1937, which appeared in English in 1964.[67] More than 200 pages of text have been printed about *The Great Awakeners* and also translated into English.[68] This section belongs to the most important parts of *The Great Philosophers. The Great Awakeners* were almost as important for Jaspers as *The Seminal Founders of Philosophical Thought*. However, he considers them exceptions that ultimately repel; they cannot become examples for us. There is no question that Kierkegaard and Nietzsche exerted a powerful influence on the youthful Jaspers at the time when he was working out his Existenz-philosophy, just as Lessing influenced the Jaspers of the Philosophy of Reason.

4. The *fourth subgroup* is called *The Edifices of the Creative Orderers*. Among them we find Aristotle, Thomas Aquinas, and Hegel from the European sphere, as well as Shankara and Chu-si representing Far Eastern philosophy. These edifices are the "high points of long developments in [the form of] great systems."[69] Their creators devise "a total system of Being," grasp "all knowledge" and put it together into a panoramic whole. The creative aspect of their work does not lie in an encyclopedic approach but "precisely in the idea of order"[70] that is brought into being by each of the systematists. No texts have been found dealing with Shankara and Chu-si; there is, however, a fairly long text about Hegel, in particular a study about his dialectics, and shorter texts about Aristotle and Thomas.

In the area of the great thinkers who are "unanimously called philosophers," [*The Creative Orderers*] are the great counterexamples to the *The Seminal Founders of Philosophical Thought*; they are those who bring an epoch to an end. To Jaspers they present the danger of transforming the processive nature of thought into a systematic, ordered body of knowledge. *The Edifices of the Creative Orderers* were to conclude the second volume. In the 1950s Jaspers estimated that the completion would require about one more year.

III. The *third main grouping* comprises, according to Jaspers's plan,[71] the philosophical thinking in *literature*, in *research*, in *political thought*, in *Bildungswille*, and in *literary criticism*, in *worldly wisdom*, in *realms of practice*, in *theology*, and in the *teaching of philosophy*. In part these are persons who philosophize in the *medium of other professions*, as, for example, the natural scientist Galileo, the physician Paracelsus, the statesman Frederic the Great, or the historian Jacob Burckhardt; in part they are also philosophers in the narrower sense such as Epicurus and Lucretius, Seneca, Cicero, Epictetus, Boëthius, Bacon, Vico, Rousseau, Voltaire, and Schopenhauer, whose importance as philosophers lies, for Jaspers, rather at the frontier of philosophy as, for example in worldly wisdom or literary criticism. Jaspers enumerates altogether about sixty people whom he wanted to characterize within the framework of the third volume. He did, however, forget to mention Solon among the statesmen, as well as Leonardo da Vinci, about whom he had written a philosophical study[72] as early as 1953, neither did he mention any artists other than in literature. The third volume had not progressed far enough in preparation, and, as Jaspers himself says, in its final form there would have been "digressions, eliminations and additions."[73] There are completed texts about Solon,[74] Epicurus,[75] and Lucretius,[76] about Leonardo and Max Weber,[77] also essays about Goethe[78] and Schopenhauer[79]; however, these are not comprehensive in the same way as the presentations in *The Great Philosophers*.[80] Some textual fragments dealing with Dante, Shakespeare, Cicero, Voltaire, Marx, Einstein, among others, have been included in the *Nachlass* edition.

Jaspers considered it entirely possible that at certain times a great philosophy appears in a different guise, as it were, for example as literature at the time of Greek tragedy, or as theology in the Middle Ages, or as research in the scientific-technical age. Thus he thought that in the twentieth century the thinkers who are philosophically most relevant perhaps are no longer philosophers but rather natural and social scientists like Albert Einstein or Max Weber. When, in the winter semester 1960/61 he held a lecture course entitled "Philosophy of the Present Age," he spoke primarily about these two.

We see that *The Great Philosophers* as a whole has remained a large fragment that encourages us to look for philosophy also among those individuals who cannot be found under the philosophers in a "cultural history" (*Bildungsgeschichte*). This broadening of the field of philosophical thought has the function of preventing philosophy from deteriorating into becoming the "province of rationality"[81] and to atrophy there. However, the fragment of *The Great Philosophers* is, in turn, overarched by the much greater fragment of the "World History of Philosophy," which opens up new aspects for the writing of history, and innovates it as a multi-aspective procedure.[82] But the "World History of Philosophy" too is, in turn, overarched by a far bigger fragment that, in his later years, Jaspers called "World Philosophy."[83]

The Idea of a World Philosophy to Come

In his lecture "Mein Weg zur Philosophie" ("My Road to Philosophy"), which Jaspers held in 1951, we find the sentence: "We are on the way from the dusk of European philosophy through the twilight of our times to the dawn of world philosophy."[84] Jaspers never defined outright what he meant here by "world philosophy." Most likely he did not think that it could be, since our age does not do world philosophy, as yet, but is merely on the way toward it. But this much is clear: The term "world philosophy" stands over against "European" philosophy, whose era is drawing to a close. World philosophy is the philosophizing that follows upon national philosophies and European philosophy, namely global philosophy.[85] Here "world" means the horizon of mutual understanding. World philosophy is the future philosophy of universal communication.

In order to clarify this idea, three questions need to be asked: Is the idea of world philosophy new or does it have precursors? Are we able to sketch out the idea based on the few hints supplied by Jaspers? How are we to interpret Jaspers's late works in light of "world philosophy"?

(a) The term "world philosophy" reminds us of *German classicism*. At the end of the eighteenth century Kant spoke of a "philosophy as world concept" (*Philosophie als Weltbegriff*), which, in distinction from "academic philosophy" (*Philosophie als Schulbegriff*), not only supplies the technical wherewithal of the professional philosophers and considers their esoteric problems, but also asks about the "ultimate goals of human reason" and thereby about problems that are necessarily of interest to all. In this way, according to Kant, does philosophy go, "in accordance with the world concept," beyond all that is local and assumes an "importance for the citizens of the world."[86]Are we to assume therefore that world philosophy is a new edition of Kantian thought, which circles around the problems of men and humankind that of necessity interest us? Is the novelty of Jaspers's conception perhaps merely an original, but belated, neo-Kantianism? However, for as long as he lived, Jaspers considered all philosophy worthy of the name to be not an academic but a world concept. The term "world philosophy" of his later years therefore must have had a meaning for him that pointed beyond Kant's differentiation.

(b) Could this meaning have been indicated analogously in Goethe's concept of "world literature," whose time as an epoch,[87] according to Goethe, was inexorably approaching "due to the constantly increasing speed of contact (or traffic [*Verkehr*])."[88] Jaspers also points out that the coming world philosophy is unavoidable.[89] Its time was approaching, and he himself assigns an important role to the development of traffic engineering. Hence it seems that he was influenced by Goethe in several instances down to the terminology.

However, for Goethe world literature meant primarily the European conversation of the national literatures, by means of which the different nations "only become aware of each other, comprehend each other and . . . at the least learn to tolerate each other."[90] For Jaspers, on the other hand, world philosophy means taking leave of merely national and European thinking and is never only a means of tolerance for him.

The eighteenth-century conceptions of world citizenship may thus have anticipated some of Jaspers's ideas of a world philosophy; but what was decisive for him lay beyond their range of vision.

(c) We do find the word "world philosophy" in the nineteenth century. In a letter of confession, written by Karl Marx, aged nineteen, to his father, he also reported about his turning away from literature, his debates with philosophical friends and his gradual turn toward Hegel's philosophy: "Here, in the argument, many a conflicting view made itself heard, and I tied myself all the more tightly to today's world philosophy that I had wanted to escape. . . ."[91] Obviously "world philosophy" is a construct based on the older word "world wisdom," which meant secularized philosophy. But perhaps there was already then, among the *Circle of Hegelians*, a certain assertion hidden in this term. In any case, three decades later, Karl Ludwig Michelet, an adherent of Hegel, issued on the occasion of Hegel's one hundredth birthday (1870) a book in his honour, entitled *Hegel, the Irrefutable World Philosopher*. The claim that is connected here with the term "world philosopher" is already evident in the preface: Michelet writes: ". . . thus we now have found not *one* philosophy, to which a new one may be added in turn, but *the* philosophy."[92] Evidently Hegel was now called the "World Philosopher" because he had brought the one and only philosophy that was to assume world domination in thinking altogether.

Can we find such a claim to importance and power also in Jaspers's term "world philosophy"? Absolutely not. For him, world philosophy was not a kind of thinking that laid claim to world-wide validity, but one that was to make possible the world-wide understanding of all that was and could be thought. A philosophy that claimed exclusive dominance was precisely the enemy to be fought, namely a thinking that thwarts universal understanding by force. Jaspers's idea was not borrowed from the Hegelian tradition.

Some other figures of the nineteenth century however seem to have influenced the direction of his thinking: Schelling, Schopenhauer, Paul Deussen, and perhaps also Eduard von Hartmann. All of them introduced Indian thinking into the German philosophical discussion and in this way broke through the horizon of European philosophizing. Schopenhauer even spoke of metaphysics as "an exalted conversation of the geniuses of all times and peoples across time and place."[93]

Schopenhauer anticipated Jaspers's idea of a timeless community in time of all great philosophers, even though he did not develop it further in written form.

There remains one possible precursor in the twentieth century: Max Scheler. In 1924 he outlined, in his essay "Problems of a Sociology of Knowledge," a "doctrine of phases of the history of philosophical theories." Here he differentiates between the "supranational" scholastic philosophy of the Church, that was upheld by the estate of priests and monks, "the national-mythically tinged philosophy of the young European nations," the "downright nationally intended philosophy of the 19th century," and [on the other hand] a "truly cosmo-political world philosophy that comprises lively discussion among the philosophical leaders and representatives of the great civilizations as a method of their scholarship." Figures such as Schopenhauer and Deussen had, according to Scheler, broken ground "like a seed" for this world philosophy; but it became a task only "in the wake of . . . the first overall experience of all of humanity,"[94] in the wake of the First World War.

We may assume that Jaspers knew this doctrine of phases[95] but did not share its understanding of a world philosophy as the "discussion of philosophical leaders." Hence one must take hold of his idea out of the meager remarks that he made about it.

(a) In the Introduction to Jaspers's *World History of Philosophy* there is a short passage, entitled "The Idea of a World Philosophy to Come."[96] Here he states first of all, somewhat defensively, that this idea is "not true if it amounts to the dilution of something that has become universal."[97] As examples of such dilution he names ancient Stoicism and the "Anglo-Saxon-pragmatic language that is heard at the present time all around the globe."[98] Neither the acceptance of appealing contents nor the universal comprehensibility of language are thus the decisive qualities of a world philosophy. Rather, philosophy becomes world philosophy in that the specific historicity of each specific philosophizing becomes transparent to [philosophy] as it points toward the universal historicity of being-human altogether. One would have to understand all thinking in its peculiarity in order to be able to understand the thinking of humanity in its entirety; one would have to understand this entirety in order to allow each peculiarity to become transparent in relation to it. "A global philosophy to come will have to be the space in which the specific historicity of each particular philosophizing becomes clear to itself in regard to the historicity of mankind as a whole."[99]

Therefore world philosophy must become the *organon of reason*, a systematics of all possibilities of thought, from its origins and in its actualizations in history. Two disciplines in particular will aid in this endeavor: the *world history of philosophy* and the *philosophical logic*. The world history of philosophy is the *universal realm of what has already been thought*, hence of the historical *actualizations* of philosophizing, and philosophical logic is the *universal realm of what can be thought*, hence of the *possibilities* of philosophizing. Both realms mutually bring each other forth in their elucidation. But a third element is indispensable here: The courage of one's own historicity that does not get lost in the fanaticism of exclusivity but becomes transparent to itself in regard to the historicity of humanity as a whole.[100]

Compared to this organon of reason all national philosophies, and so also Western thought, exhibit a touch of "folk art."[101] They do not have to be overcome in their contents as much as they have to be surpassed in their historic narrowness. At the same time, each cutting off of possibilities of thought, which is the seed of new "isms," of new ideologies and of magic, must be stopped. Each structured thought edifice harms the idea of world philosophy through its aspect of considered or unconscious exclusivity.

This maximal opening of the realm of thought and history is so broadly conceived that anyone who today would attempt to work it out, will be "left behind."[102] For Jaspers it is still so much a utopia that we approach it "anticipating rather than knowing, attempting rather than attaining,"[103] in part still like blind men who would like to take part, by philosophizing, "in the transition to the new, still unknown . . . world."[104] All that can be seen clearly is the inevitability of the task.

(b) The task is not something merely thought up. Rather it is a given because of the spreading era of science and technology, hence through the historical conditions under which increasingly all people live. For Jaspers, this new era was the "entirely new development in the spiritual and material spheres"[105] as measured against history up to this point. Jaspers experienced a "new consciousness of the world."[106] The development of the technology dealing with traffic and the dissemination of news for the first time turned the globe into a single entity: "The unity of the earth has arrived."[107] For the present this means no more than that we have a comprehensive territorial overview; but as a common spiritual space and as a political unity it must yet be discovered and created. This project, however, presents itself with great urgency due to the development of the techniques of waging war. For the atomic bomb had created an "altogether novel situation."[108] Until now the individual person could take his own life; he could kill and be killed. Whole peoples could be exterminated. "Now mankind as a whole can be wiped out by men."[109] Concern about humanity and the world calls for a corresponding openness to reason that embraces the whole planet. The concrete world unity in the making thus demands a world philosophy and this can only be a kind of thinking that is commensurate with the age to come. As thinking beings in transition to this epoch we take part "in the founding of a new world,"[110] but as a generation we are condemned to suffer shipwreck because it must of necessity bring into being something that it cannot achieve.

(c) Since the new actuality to come demands the new thinking, the latter cannot be satisfied being the thinking of thinking, no matter how wide it may open the space of thought. Instead it must, in anticipation of this actuality to come, elucidate prognostically as well as diagnostically our transition to it. In this respect world philosophy is also utopia, namely the thinking of the future spiritual and political world unity and the common future world history. And it is criticism of the present world, that is, analysis of the present reality in order to lead it into a more reasonable future. But the reality of the present cannot be understood and transcended toward a new reality without bringing to mind the past, what actually has been. For this reason world philosophy is always trifold: The thinking of thought, the thinking of actuality, and the challenge to actualization; and it unfolds under three aspects: Keeping in mind the full scope of the past, clarification and criticism of the present within the wide space of possibility, anticipatory appeal to and illumination of what may be actualized under the guiding idea of universal communication. The thinking of thought protects the thinking of actuality from the precipitous synthesizing of mere pragmatism. The envisaging and thinking of actuality protects the thinking of thought from eccentricity, and appellative thought protects both against lack of commitment.

Jaspers's Later Works in Light of World Philosophy

In his own obituary Jaspers wrote the following about his time in Basel: "All the powers of these years [I devoted] to the continuation of [my] philosophical work, which by its nature cannot be brought to a conclusion, a labor by means of which . . . [I] wished to take part in the task of the times, namely to find the way out of the end of European philosophy to a world philosophy to come."[111] Hence Jaspers understood his later writings as a continuous work in transition to a future world philosophy. In this way the abstract idea assumes for us more concrete contours.

The philosophical logic and the world history of philosophy are the two basic pillars of world philosophy. The idea common to both—namely that there is, beyond the historicity of the philosophizing individual, a historicity of humanity as a whole—had to be given an empirical foundation in history. This is the reason for Jaspers's work about philosophy of history, *The Origin and Goal of History*, which demonstrates that historical basis in the axial period (approximately 800 to 200 BCE). The axial period is the "leaven that draws humanity into a single context of world history."[112] Insofar as this philosophy of history only displays the common origin, whereas the common goal is given as a task, it called for a philosophy of world politics, which Jaspers worked out in his book *The Future of Mankind*. This philosophy of world politics was, on the one hand, a criticism of current politics, and there primarily a critique of totalitarianism, and, on the other hand, a draft of a future politics of world unity and world peace, under the condition that there be truth and that freedom remain possible. However, since, for Jaspers, ultimately all philosophizing was grounded in a faith, world philosophy also called for a clarification of faith, which Jaspers presented most convincingly in his work *Philosophical Faith and Revelation*.[113] It is a strong criticism of the claim to exclusivity on the part of faith based on revelation, which it counters with the idea of "philosophic faith" for which all that is can point to the transcendence that, as such, is hidden. But Jaspers indicates that all of these works are parts of the altogether fragmentary world philosophy, and does so by anchoring them all in the "fundamental knowledge" (*Grundwissen*) of philosophic logic, which is the logic of world philosophy.

NOTES

1. Endnotes revised and enlarged by the editors.

2. Karl Jaspers to Heinrich Zimmer, March 3, 1938, in *Jahrbuch der Österreichischen Karl-Jaspers-Gesellschaft*, edited by E. Salamun-Hybasek and K. Salamun, VI (1993), p. 14.

3. Karl Jaspers, "Max Weber as Politician, Scientist, Philosopher" (originally published in 1932), Karl Jaspers, "Descartes and Philosophy" (originally published in 1936), both in Karl Jaspers, *Three Essays: Leonardo, Descartes, Max Weber* (New York: Harcourt, Brace & World, 1964). [Hereafter cited as TE, eds.] Karl Jaspers, *Nietzsche. An Introduction to the Understanding of His Philosophical Activity* (originally published in 1936), translated by Charles F. Wallraff and Fredrick J. Schmitz (Tucson: University of Arizona Press, 1965).

4. Cf. Index of Jaspers's lectures and seminars at the University of Heidelberg, in *Karl Jaspers in seiner Heidelberger Zeit,* edited by Joachim-Felix Leonhard (Heidelberg: Heidelberger Verlagsanstalt, 1983), pp. 103–106.

5. Karl Jaspers, "Philosophical Autobiography," in *The Philosophy of Karl Jaspers*, edited by P. A. Schilpp (New York: Tudor Publishing Company, 1957), p. 83.

6. Paul Meyer, "Karl Jaspers in Basel," *Basler Stadtbuch 1970. Jahrbuch für Kultur*

und Geschichte, p. 154. [pp. 153ff. contain a listing of Jaspers's lectures and seminars at Basel University, eds.]

7. Cf. Karl Jaspers, GP 1. Also: Karl Jaspers, "Gibt es eine Weltgeschichte der Philosophie?" in Karl Jaspers, *Aneignung und Polemik. Gesammelte Reden und Aufsätze zur Geschichte der Philosophie,* edited by H. Saner (Munich: Piper, 1968), pp. 9–12.

8. Cf. Karl Jaspers, GP 3, GPy 4. See also Karl Jaspers, *Weltgeschichte der Philosophie. Einleitung*, edited by Hans Saner (Munich: Piper, 1982). [Hereafter cited as WP, eds.]

9. Cf. section "XI. The Idea of a World-History of Philosophy" in Jaspers's "Philosophical Autobiography," in *The Philosophy of Karl Jaspers*, edited by P. A. Schilpp, pp. 81–84.

10. Par. 6 of the Nazi law "Law for the Reestablishment of the Professional Civil Service of 1933."

11. Jaspers, "Philosophical Autobiography," in *The Philosophy of Karl Jaspers*, edited by Schilpp, p. 82.

12. Ibid.

13. Ibid., p. 83.

14. Jaspers, "Gibt es eine Weltgeschichte der Philosophie?" in Jaspers, *Aneignung und Polemik*, p.10.

15. Cf. Jaspers, WP, p. 100.

16. WP, p. 100f.

17. WP, p. 101.

18. WP, p. 102.

19. WP, p. 104.

20. Ibid.

21. WP, p. 105.

22. Ibid.

23. WP, p. 106.

24. WP, p. 107.

25. WP, p. 101.

26. WP, p. 109.

27. WP, p. 112.

28. WP, p. 113.

29. Ibid.

30. WP, p. 114.

31. WP, p. 115.

32. WP, p. 116.

33. Ibid.

34. WP, p. 117.

35. Ibid.

36. Ibid.

37. WP, p. 118.

38. WP, p. 120.

39. WP, p. 120f.

40. WP, p. 121.

41. WP, p. 158f.

42. Cf. WP, p. 122f.

43. Cf. Jaspers, *The Great Philosophers 1: The Foundations*, edited by Hannah Arendt, translated by Ralph Manheim (New York: Harcourt, Brace & World, 1962), 1, pp. vii–x. (Hereafter GP 1).

44. Cf. Jaspers, *Die grossen Philosophen: Nachlass 2: Fragmente*. Anmerkungen, Inventar. Hrsg. von Hans Saner (Munich, Zurich: R. Piper, 1981), pp. 1023–1140. (Hereafter Grph/N2).

45. Jaspers, GP 1, p. viii.

46. Ibid.

47. Ibid.

48. Ibid.

49. Ibid.

50. Ibid.

51. GP 1, p. ix.

52. Jaspers, GrPh/N1, p. 43f.

53. GrPh/N1, 46 [translated by Edith Ehrlich; for Ralph Manheim's translation of the same. Compare Jaspers, GP 1, p. 6.

54. GrPh/N1, p. 218f.; for Manheim's translation, Jaspers, GP 1, p. 97.

55. GrPh/N1, p. 44; in English, Jaspers, GP 1, p. 7.

56. GrPh/N1, p. 231; in English: Jaspers, GP 1, p. 109.

57. Cf. GrPh/N1, pp. 397–616; in English: Jaspers, GP 1, pp. 230–382.

58. Cf. Karl Jaspers, *Nicholas Cusanus* (Munich: R. Piper, 1964). This essay was not included in the German edition of the *Die grossen Philosophen*, in part because it was too long (about 260 pages), in part because it was written at a considerably later time. It has, however, been integrated into the American edition. Cf. Jaspers, GP 2, pp. 116–272.

59. The American edition of the *Nachlass* (cf. GP 3) does not include the texts dealing with Anaxagoras and Poseidonius.

60. Epicurus and Lucretius were to form their own subgroup, to be called *Serenity without Transcendence*, to be included in the third volume, in the group *Philosophers of Worldly Wisdom*. In this way Jaspers planned to stress their singular position within the history of thought. Their later positioning in *Metaphysicians of Piety toward the World* is debatable.

61. Cf., GrPh/N1, pp. 158–88.

62. Cf., GP 3, pp. 117–42.

63. Cf., Karl Jaspers, *Schelling. Grösse und Verhängnis* (Munich: Piper & Co., 1955).

64. Cf., GP 3, pp. 143–67.

65. Cf., Jaspers, GrPh/N1, "Hobbes," pp. 214–23; "Leibniz," pp. 224–35. Jaspers, GPsy. 3: "Leibniz," pp. 171–84.

66. Cf. GP 4, pp. 7–31.

67. Cf. Jaspers, *Three Essays: Leonardo, Descartes, Max Weber.*

68. Cf. Jaspers, GP 4, pp. 35–310.

69. Jaspers, GP 1, p. 7.

70. "The Edifices of the Creative Orderers: Introduction" in Jaspers, GP 3.

71. Cf. ibid., vol. 1, p. 7.

72. Cf. Jaspers, "Leonardo as Philosopher," in Jaspers, *Three Essays. Leonardo, Descartes, Max Weber* (New York: Hartcourt, Brace & World, 1964), pp. 1–58.

73. Jaspers, GrPh, p. 49.

74. Cf. Karl Jaspers, "Solon," in Karl Jaspers, *Existentialism and Humanism. Three Essays*, edited by Hanns E. Fischer, translated by E. B. Ashton (New York: Moore, 1952), pp. 19–33.

75. Cf. Karl Jaspers, "Epikur," in Karl Jaspers, *Weltbewohner und Weimaraner. Ernst Beutler zugedacht*, edited by Benno Reifenberg and Emil Staiger (Zürich/Stuttgart: Artemis, 1960), pp. 111–33. This essay has not been translated into English; it is not identical with the entry on "Epicurus" in Jaspers, GP 3, pp. 67–111.

76. Cf. Karl Jaspers, "Lukrez," in Jaspers, GrPh/N1, pp. 115–40. "Epikur" and "Lukrez" are parts of the chapter "Transzendenzlose Ruhe: Epikur und Lukrez." The section on Lucretius is not contained in the American edition.

77. Cf. Karl Jaspers, "Bemerkungen zu Max Webers politischem Denken," in Jaspers, *Antidoron. Edgar Salin zum 70. Geburtstag*, edited by Erwin von Beckenrath et al. (Tübingen: Mohr, 1962), pp. 200–14. Not translated into English as yet.

78. Cf. Karl Jaspers, "Our Future and Goethe," in Jaspers, *Existentialism and Humanism,* pp. 35–64. "Goethes Menschlichkeit," in *Baseler Universitätsreden* 26 (Basel: Helbing & Lichtenhan, 1949), pp. 11-33. From this essay only excerpts are translated.

79. Cf. Karl Jaspers, "Arthur Schopenhauer. Zu seinem 100. Todestag (1960)" in Karl Jaspers, *Aneignung und Polemik. Gesammelte Reden und Aufsätze zur Geschichte der Philosophie* (Munich: Piper, 1968), pp. 287–95. Not translated into English.

80. The presentation of the individual persons in *The Great Philosophers* always follows the same pattern: First Jaspers orients us briefly about the life and writings, then develops the structure of thought, submits it to his critique and finally reports about the history of its influence.

81. Jaspers, GrPh/N1, p. 49.

82. Regarding a "World History of Philosophy," cf. also the papers presented at the introductory session of the Third International Jaspers Conference (Moscow 1993) in *Karl Jaspers. Philosophy on the Way to "World Philosophy"/Philosophie auf dem Weg zur "Weltphilosophie,"* edited by Leonard H. Ehrlich and Richard Wisser (Würzburg: Könighausen & Neumann, 1998), esp., Leonard H. Ehrlich, "Ausblick: Vernunft, Geist, Geschichte," pp. 39–44; Richard Wisser, "Projekt und Vision einer 'Weltgeschichte der Philosophie' und 'Welthilosophie' als Folge der 'Grundverfassung' von Karl Jaspers," pp. 61–70; Andreas Rinofner, "Periechontologie und Weltgeschichte der Philosophie. Systematische Bemerkungen zu einem aufschlussreichen Verhältnis," pp. 51–60. See also Jeanne Hersch, "Das Lesen der grossen Philosophen als Übung der Freiheit," in *Karl Jaspers. Philosopher among Philosophers/Philosoph unter Philosophen*, edited by Richard Wisser and Leonard H. Ehrlich (Würzburg: Könighausen & Neumann, 1993), pp. 5–8.

83. Concerning the idea of a world philosophy, cf. Hans Saner, "Jaspers' Idee einer kommenden Weltphilosophie," in *Philosophy at the Threshold of the Future,* edited by Leonard H. Ehrlich and Richard Wisser (Washington: University Press of America, 1988), pp. 75–92; Hans Saner, "Weltphilosophie und Globalkultur im interkulturellen Vergleich mit den Konzepten 'Weltmusik' und 'Weltkunst,'" in *Karl Jaspers: Philosophy on the Way to "World Philosophy,"* pp. 241–55; Leonard H. Ehrlich, "Tolerance and the Prospect of a World Philosophy," in *Karl Jaspers Today,* edited by Leonard H. Ehrlich and Richard Wisser (Washington: University Press of America, 1988), pp. 93–100.

84. Karl Jaspers, "Mein Weg zur Philosophie," radio lecture delivered in February 1951 on Radio Basel, in Jaspers, *Rechenschaft und Ausblick. Reden und Aufsätze*. 2. Aufl (München: Piper, 1958), pp. 323–32, at 331. [This work is not translated into English; hereafter cited as RA, eds.]

85. On Jaspers's global philosophy, see the article by Ram A. Mall herein [eds.].

86. German reference: Immanuel Kant, *Immanuel Kant's Logik. Ein Handbuch zu Vorlesungen* (*Gesammelte Schriften*, vol. 9, Akademie-Ausgabe), Preußische Akademie der Wissenschaften (Berlin/Leipzig: DeGruyter, 1923), p. 24f.

87. Cf. Johann Peter Eckermann, "Gespräche mit Goethe in den letzten Jahren seines Lebens," in *Goethe: Artemis Edition, vol. XXIV* (Zurich: Artemis, 1948), p. 229.

88. Johann Wolfgang von Goethe, "Betrachtungen zur Weltliteratur," in *Goethe: Artemis Edition, vol. XIV, Schriften zur Literatur* (Zurich: Artemis, 1950), p. 914.

89. Cf. Jaspers, WP, p. 76.

90. Goethe, concerning "Edinburgh Review" (1828), in *Goethe: Artemis Edition, vol. XIV, Schriften zur Literatur*, p. 956.

91. Karl Marx. Letter of November 10, 1837, to his father, in *Karl Marx, Frühe Schriften*, edited by Hans-Joachim Lieber and Peter Furth (Stuttgart: Cotta-Verlag, 1962), p. 15.

92. Carl Ludwig Michelet, *Hegel, der unwiderlegte Weltphilosoph. Eine Jubelschrift* (Leipzig: Duncker und Humblot, 1870), p. vi.

93. Quoted from: Max Scheler, *Probleme einer Soziologie des Wissens*, in Scheler, *Die Wissensformen und die Gesellschaft* (*Gesammelte Werke, vol. VIII*) (Berne & Munich: Francke Verlag 1960), p. 91.

94. Ibid.

95. Jaspers had in his library a copy of the 1924 edition of *Probleme einer Soziologie des Wissens*, which, however, did not exhibit any signs of having been read.

96. Jaspers, WP, p. 76f.

97. Jaspers, WP, p. 76f.

98. Ibid.

99. Ibid.

100. Ibid.

101. A jotting from the *Nachlass*.

102. Jaspers, "Philosophical Autobiography," in *The Philosophy of Karl Jaspers*, edited by P. A. Schilpp, p. 69.

103. "Obituary by Karl Jaspers Himself," in *Karl Jaspers. Philosophy on the Way to "World Philosophy,"* edited by Ehrlich and Wisser, p. 6.

104. Jaspers, "Mein Weg zur Philosophie," in Jaspers, RA, p. 331.

105. Karl Jaspers, OGH, p. 23.

106. OGH, p. 97.

107. OGH, p. 127.

108. Jaspers, FM, p. vii.

109. FM, p. 3.

110. A jotting in the *Nachlass*.

111. "Obituary by Karl Jaspers himself," in *Karl Jaspers. Philosophy of the Way to "World Philosophy,"* edited by Ehrlich and Wisser, p. 6.

112. OGH, p. 51.

113. Cf. PFR.

KARL JASPERS ON DEMOCRACY AND THE RELEVANCE OF THE SUPRA-POLITICAL ELEMENT IN POLITICS

Gregory J. Walters

> Philosophy has political consequences. . . . No great philosophy is without political thought, not even that of the great metaphysicians, not that of Plotinus, not at all that of Spinoza, who even went so far as to take an active, spiritually-effective role. From Plato to Kant, to Hegel, to Kierkegaard and Nietzsche goes the grand politics of the philosophers. What a philosophy is, it shows in its political appearance. This is nothing incidental, but of central significance. It was no accident that National Socialism, as well as Bolshevism, saw in philosophy a deadly spiritual enemy. . . . It seemed to me that only after I became deeply stirred by politics did my philosophy become fully conscious of its very basis, including its metaphysics. . . . Since then I inquire of each philosopher concerning his political thinking and action and see the magnificent, honourable and effective line of this kind of thinking in the history of the genuinely philosophical spirit.[1]

With these words Karl Jaspers concludes section "VIII. Political Ideas" in his "Philosophical Autobiography."[2] In this context it is noteworthy that his reflection on "political ideas" (not politics) is by far the longest single section of all the categorical entries that pertain to his philosophy in the autobiography. Jaspers devotes more reflection to political ideas than to "II. *Psychopathologie*," "III. *Psychologie der Weltanschauungen*," "V. *Philosophie*," "IX. *Philosophical Logic*," "X. Theology and Philosophical Faith," and even the "XI. The Idea of a World-History of Philosophy." It is perhaps equally significant that in his "Reply to My Critics," which comes at the very end of the Schilpp volume on *The Philosophy of Karl Jaspers*, he first begins with a methodological reflection on the place and the task of the reply to his eminent interlocutors, and then immediately begins by addressing the question "2. Concerning Politics."[3] The priority with which Jaspers treats political ideas and politics reinforces the importance of his statements that all philosophy has political consequences, is not without political ideas, and, indeed, that the true nature of a philosophy shows itself in its *political appearance*.

That philosophy shows its substance in its *political* appearance should give us pause from the outset, for philosophy in the Western tradition has as far back as the pre-Socratic thinkers, been essentially identified with contemplation or the *vita contemplativa*. Jaspers's emphatic admission is that it was only after he was existentially engaged by his Nazi regime experience that his philosophizing, including his metaphysics and cipher-theory,[4] became conscious of its very condition of possibility. The political realities of post-war Germany and a world in search of new political and humanist cultural orders behooved him to begin reading the great philosophers with questions concerning the political implications of their philosophical worldviews. Did they succeed in the challenge and task of integrating their thinking and action in their political ideas and action? In this context we may say that what Jaspers says about Kierkegaard is quite true of Jaspers also: "The thinker refers us to what he has thought, the thought refers us to the thinker."[5] As an activity of the human spirit, "philosophizing"[6] is intimately connected with the life of the person, and it requires the habituated and virtuous integration of thought and action in both the private and public realms. Jaspers exemplifies a remarkable integration of his life and thought, especially his political philosophical thinking and action.

Jaspers's idea of democracy and his emphasis on the "supra-political" (*Überpolitischen*) element in politics are intimately connected. In order to argue this basic thesis, my method will be expositional and interpretational at the same time. I cannot here address the import of Jaspers's political philosophy for our current historical and political situation, marked as it is by the rise of complex terrorism. Instead, I begin with (1) a broad historical portrayal of Jaspers's major political works and main ideas. One of the most discussed aspects of his philosophy as a whole, Jaspers's political thinking has drawn a wide readership across disciplines. Scientists, historians, political scientists, sociologists, theologians, philosophers, and other humanists have been interested in assessing the political implications of his philosophical method or "transcending" philosophizing (a going-beyond in thought) as set forth in his *Philosophy* is not without political implications; nor is it devoid of metaphysical questions of human meaning in the categorical domains of world orientation, existential elucidation, and cipher-reading as these three "horizons" of objectivity in the world, self, and Transcendence (God) bear on the formation and sustainability of the socio-political realm.[7]

While some commentators have debated the nature and extent of Jaspers's political commitments and involvements, there is no doubt that his experience under National Socialism had a profound impact on his political thinking and action. After the Second World War, he would embark in earnest on his projected "world history of philosophy," "world philosophy," and study of the great philosophers (East and West) with a view to their *Lebens-praxis* (life-action, that is, the realization of philosophical thinking in their action in the world).[8] The post-Nazi period forced, if not called, Jaspers into a rather new role, what we would today call a "public political philosopher," thus marking yet another developmental stage in his remarkable and productive career as a psychopathologist and philosopher. The decade of the 1950s would find him in explicit conversation—via scholarly press, magazines and journals, and radio and television media—with German political developments during the Cold War such as the issue of the reunification of West and East Germany, as well as the then heated debates concerning international relations between the European countries, the United States and the Soviet Union.

What does Jaspers mean by the idea of democracy? In order to answer this question, (2) I turn first to Jaspers's presupposition that the political world is directly affected by the "unconditionality of Existenz and by ideas;" for, in one sense, we may say that the true and sustainable foundation of politics is for Jaspers grounded in the unconditional action of political leaders and democractic citizens alike. Unconditional action is necessary, but not sufficient, with a clear view to the "idea" of democracy. Jaspers's democratic idea functions as a Kantian "regulative idea," which is embodied in the self-actualization of reason and freedom, the uniqueness and dignity of every individual, and active, democratic participation. I close this section with six broad theses that capture some key elements that inform his idea of democracy

Because political thinking and action must spring from the depths of the self and take guidance from the "supra-political" element in politics, (3) I connect Jaspers's call in *The Future of Mankind* for a "new politics" to his understanding of the supra-political element in politics (ethos, sacrifice, and reason). Jaspers draws his concept of the supra-political most directly from Nietzsche's distinction between the unhistorical (*Ungeschichtlichen*), the historical (*Geschichtlichen*), and the supra-historical (*Übergeschichtlichen*), but it holds a different meaning than Nietzsche's idea of the supra-historical.[9] For Jaspers, a dialectical relation exists between existential freedom (individual will) and political freedom (state will). Existential freedom is "pre-political" (not unhistorical as in Nietzsche) and "supra-political," whereas political freedom concerns the actual conditions of government and circumscribes existential freedom. Can these supra-political elements provide political guidance for us today?

Rational communication, its institutionalization in communities of reasonable human beings around the world, and leadership provided by reasonable "statesmen" are all essential to a new politics that can overturn the *Realpolitik* and will to power (4). Rational communication grounds the social and political tasks of what Jaspers call "the community of reasonable human beings" (*Die Gemeinschaft der Vernünftigen*)[10] in civil society and state institutions. Political authority must flow from a new "boundless" communication that counteracts the age-old principles of lying, secrecy, and terror that mark the will to political power. As for the future of humankind, Jaspers conjoins Kant's idea of perpetual peace to Max Weber's ethic of responsibility, but adds a sense of urgency that surpasses both given the entirely new general boundary situation that humanity finds itself in now that we have the power to destroy ourselves as well as new technological means that may serve totalitarian political ends.

Finally, (5) is the realization of human reasonableness and personal political transformation possible? Can we actualize a *global* idea of democracy in our present historical situation? Can we convert the violent struggle for existence into the "loving struggle" for Existenz?

POLITICAL WORKS AND THEMES

Politics was not foreign to Jaspers's family. His grandfather and father (who, also, was president of the Oldenburg City Council for decades), were state representatives in Oldenburg. As a student, he confesses, "I felt little responsibility for the course of [political] events as a whole."[11] Like any serious student he was devoted to his academics until political events forced a self-transformation. Jaspers was terrified by the flight of the dirigible Zeppelin and the nationalistic "intoxification" it provoked in 1908. He was thirty-one years old when the First World War erupted in 1914, and his physical environment, which was always precarious because of his chronic health problems, as well as his academic existence, were seriously threatened.

> The historical earth trembled. Everything which seemed long to have been secure with one stroke appeared threatened. We felt that we had gotten into an irresistible, opaque process. Only since then do our generations know them-

> selves thrown into the stream of catastrophic events. Since 1914 these have not stopped. They keep going in a frantic tempo. This our human fate I sought from then on to comprehend, not as the knowable necessity of a dark supernatural process of history, but as a situation whose results—on the basis of what is properly knowable, which is always something specific—are decisively determined by our human freedom.[12]

Jaspers's political thought took initial guidance and inspiration from Max Weber, especially his understanding of nationalism and a vision of Germany that would be different from both Russian and Anglo-Saxon hegemony. Like Weber, he understood that political realities force politicians and nations to act, that one cannot evade the spirit of political liberalism, personal freedom, and the serious stakes involved in the Western political tradition,[13] but nonetheless distanced himself from Weber's Prussianism, military spirit, and regard for Bismarck. He felt ridicule for Emperor Wilhelm's pomposity and provocative actions, as well as the political "stupidity" of Erich Ludendorff who was Germany's chief military strategist during World War I. While Jaspers was not directly involved in politics at this time, it is incorrect to say that he had no "political" involvement between the two world wars. For example, as a *Privatdozent* (lecturer), he refused to sign a petition that was circulated in 1919 throughout all the German universities by the rector of the University of Berlin. The petition opposed the conditions of the Versailles peace treaty. Jaspers objected to the petition because he felt it compromised the intellectual or academic freedom of the university. A similar incident occurred in 1924 when he defended a statistics lecturer, Emil Gumbel by name, against the wrath of nationalist professors at Heidelberg. An avowed pacifist, Gumbel opposed the re-establishment of the German military and decried the loss of soldiers during the war. Patriotism ran high at the university and he was viewed as dishonoring the German war dead. Jaspers defended Gumbel by appealing to the long-standing principle of academic freedom in the German university.

> If today because of political pacifist convictions and because of actions disclosing a political breach of treaty, an instructor can be reprimanded under the guise of an insult to national honor which carefully veils those facts, then tomorrow another one (may suffer this same fate) because of his atheism, and day after tomorrow still another because of his nonconformity to the existing regime of the state.[14]

Jaspers's first quasi-political reflection came in 1929 when he was commissioned to write a work for the Göschen-Series on the "spiritual" or intellectual movements at that time. *Die geistige Situation der Zeit* (*Man in the Modern Age*), however, was not so much an analysis of the German political situation as it was an analysis of an "epochal consciousness" that Jaspers identified as dominated by new technologies, techniques, and mechanization.[15] The book was completed in September 1930 at the very same time as the victory of the National Socialists in the Reichstag. Jaspers initially viewed the election as "impossible" and simply thought that the political crisis was certain to pass. He grew completely incredulous when the Nazi-Putsch came in 1933. Hannah Arendt asked him what he would do in light of the "election" and he responded that it was an "*Operette*" in which he would not play a hero's role. When Ernst Mayer said to Jaspers in the summer of 1933 that the Nazis would "one day bring us Jews into barracks and set the barracks on fire,"[16] he thought the idea was insane. Reflecting late in life on the political events of 1933, Jaspers confesses that "at first I deceived myself. I think of it with shame. I still did not think of the extreme consequences [of the Putsch]. . . . I wanted the fear not to have the likeness of truth."[17]

During the National Socialist (NS) era (1933-1945), political events in Germany moved from bad to worse: Jaspers was excluded in 1933 from the University of Heidelberg administration, whose Nazification had become complete by the summer of 1935. Jaspers stood alone at this time. He was independent of all groups, including the German resistance movement. As Hannah Arendt remarks of Jaspers's political standing in 1933:

> It was self-evident that he [Jaspers] would remain firm in the midst of catastrophe. But that the whole thing could never become even a temptation for him—this which is less self-evident, was his inviolability, and to those who knew of him it meant far more than resistance and heroism. It meant confidence that needed no confirmation, an assurance that in times in which everything could happen, what Jaspers represented then [1933], when he was entirely alone, was not Germany but what was left of *humanitas* in Germany. It was as if he alone in his inviolability could illuminate that space which reason creates and preserves between men, and as if the light and breadth of this space would survive even if only one man were to remain in it.[18]

By 1937 Jaspers was no longer allowed to teach at the university and in 1938 was forbidden to publish anything by the Nazi censorship board (*Reichsschrifttumskammer*). He made several attempts at emigration. Although banned from the University of Heidelberg and from publishing, his self-discipline allowed him to continue working on his philosophical logic. By 1939, Jaspers felt that Nazi political developments had come to mark the beginning of the end for Germany (*finis Germaniae*). Two political ideas were foremost in his mind during and after the NS-era. The first concerned the meaning of being German, which he defined in terms of "language," "home," and "heritage." The second idea concerned the very meaning of Germany as a political entity. The nation could no longer be morally or spiritually grounded upon "restoration" tendencies or past laurels. Two necessities arise in the crisis situation. "We must learn to talk with each other, and we mutually must understand and accept one another in our extraordinary differences. These differences are so great that in borderline cases we appear to each other like people of different nations."[19]

Germany would have to be created anew after the catastrophes of the two wars and Hitler's totalitarian fascism. Jaspers's belief in an international court of law, his support for human rights, his vision of world citizenship, and his staunch critique of the United Nation principles of "non-interference" and "absolute sovereignty" had their insemination during this time. In 1941 Jaspers worked on the philosophical logic (*Von der Wahrheit*) and a universal history of philosophy as the foundation of a world philosophy (*Weltphilosophie*).[20] He saw both as complementary in thought, and opposed to any "system" in which being and truth are reified or made absolute. The dangerous four years that followed eventually sapped his ability to work, and eventually made any philosophical work impossible. In the dark night of war, his political insights must have been keenly honed by the allied bombing raids. He and his Jewish wife, Gertrud Jaspers, were scheduled to be taken from Heidelberg to a concentration camp on April 14, 1945, but American forces liberated the city on April 1, 1945.

After the war Jaspers tried to gain a larger public voice as a political writer, and Germany's chaotic political situation under the Allied government soon demanded his energy, attention, and thinking. "As Germans," Jaspers writes, we "must try to find our way as thinking people in the unprecedented distress."[21] With economic assistance from the Allies he hoped to help build a new, democratic German state; but with all political power in the hands of the allied military government, he knew that his focus could not be on German politics per se. Instead, the philosopher's immediate task was to address the mental and moral state of Germans whose existential and moral health would be the very condition of possibility for a new democratic polity in Germany.

The importance for Jaspers of the question concerning German guilt is illustrated by the fact that he directly addressed the question at the solemn reopening of the School of Medicine at the University of Heidelberg on August 15, 1945, in a lecture on the "regeneration" (*Erneuerung*) of the German university.[22] Only if there were candid admissions of personal guilt and culpability for the atrocities committed during the NS-era would it be possible for the much-needed healing or regeneration to occur in the university (and, by implication, the new German state):

> The rebirth of our university could never mean that we merely want to continue where we left off in 1933. Too many things have happened; too vast and far-reaching has been the disaster. And we ourselves are no longer the same as we were in 1933. It was possible to seek death in the disgrace of that year when, after the breach of the constitution, dictatorship was established through sham legality, and all opposition was brushed aside by the wave of intoxification that carried away a major part of the people. We might have sought death when the crimes of the regime came to light on June 30, 1934; when our Jewish friends and fellow-citizens were robbed, deported and murdered; when to our everlasting shame the synagogues of all Germany were blazing. We might have sought death when during the war the government from the very beginning acted against the principle stated by our greatest philosopher, Kant: that as a condition of international law "nothing should be done in war that would absolutely preclude the later reconciliation of the belligerents." Thousands of Germans, most of them anonymous, have sought—or found—death in opposition to the regime.
>
> We, the survivors, did not seek it [death]. As our Jewish friends were taken away we did not demonstrate in the streets, we did not shout until in turn we, too, were destroyed. We chose to survive on the weak but correct ground that our death would amount to nothing. Our guilt is to be still alive. We know before God what has happened to us. During these twelve years we have gone through what one may call the remolding of our very being. We have been cudgeled by the devils who dragged us along into confusion and left us stupefied. We have won insights into the reality of world and man and of our own selves—insights that we shall never forget and whose consequences for our thinking cannot be measured.[23]

The Heidelberg lecture was the first time Jaspers was able to speak publicly since his ban from teaching in 1935 by the Nazis. He sets forth his early conception of metaphysical guilt, one of four types of guilt along with criminal, political, and moral guilt that would be developed at greater length in his 1946 monograph entitled simply *Die Schuldfrage* (*The Question of German Guilt*). Jaspers hoped that Germans and others would avoid superficial understandings of guilt that could result in serious conflation of both the concept and the degrees of ethical responsibility and political accountability involved by citizens. Jaspers identifies a fourfold schema of guilt types:

He first distinguishes *criminal guilt*: "Crimes are acts capable of objective proof and violate unequivocal laws."[24] These laws include natural, positive, and international laws, which reflect Jaspers's understanding of the reasonableness and legitimacy of legal traditions invoked at the Nuremberg trials. In respect to criminal guilt, jurisdiction rests with the court and the judge who sentences the guilty party for freely determined and willfully guilty acts.

Political guilt pertains to those specific actions of both politicians and citizens of the state. Citizens bear the consequences of the public policies and actions that the state legislates in so far as state power inevitably governs and orders the lives of its citizenry. Jurisdiction, in both domestic and foreign policy, for political guilt rests with the power and will of the victor as was the case with the allied military government that was set-up in Heidelberg after the war. Liability for political guilt entails reparation, as well as the loss or restriction of political power and rights.

Moral guilt entails the unique responsibility that the individual, as a moral agent, exercises. In this context, Jaspers specifically names those actions carried-out in the execution of political and military orders. Every deed that you or I perform is subject to moral judgment, according to Jaspers, all the while acknowledging that there may be mitigating circumstances, such as the degree of danger that was involved, whether or not blackmail was involved, or even if terrorism could apply in a given situation. Jurisdiction for moral guilt rests with the agent's conscience and those significant others with whom the individual is most intimate. Insight into one's culpability is not enough. Insight must involve "penance and renewal" that leads, in turn, to real self-change and a transformation in one's actions with others, in any nascent political state, and in relation to the ideals of democracy and human rights throughout the world.

Metaphysical guilt results from the solidarity among human beings and reminds us that we are co-responsible for human injustice committed against others, especially in the case of crimes committed in our presence or with our knowledge. If I do not risk my life to prevent murder or injustice, I too am guilty. Situations arise that force us to choose either to risk our lives unconditionally, or to stay alive because we see no reasonable hope of success (as, for example, in attempts to assassinate Hitler). The sacrifice of those who acted unconditionally retains utmost substance, while those who remained alive know their (metaphysical) guilt well:

> That somewhere among men the unconditioned prevails— . . . the capacity to live only together or not at all, if crimes are committed against the one or the other, or if physical living requirements have to be shared— therein consists the substance of their being. But that this does not extend to the solidarity of all men, nor to that of fellow-citizens or even of smaller groups, but remains confined to the closest human ties—therein lies this guilt of us all."[25]

Recognition of metaphysical guilt results in a transformation of the self in relation to others and God (Transcendence). Human pride or *hubris* is broken: "This self-transformation by inner activity may lead to a new source of active life, but one linked with an indelible sense of guilt in that humility which grows modest before God and submerges all its doings in an atmosphere where arrogance becomes impossible."[26] Jurisdiction in the case of metaphysical guilt rests ultimately with God.

Jaspers's lectures on German guilt do not offer us any concrete political proposals. He is more interested in reflecting on the necessary *pre-condition* for any political judgment in a post-Nazi Germany, namely, the "purification" (*Reinigung*) of the soul. "Our use of the word purification in the guilt question has a good sense. We have to purge ourselves of whatever guilt each one finds in himself, as far as this is possible by restitution, by atonement, by inner renewal and metamorphosis."[27] Jaspers gives popular voice to German purification in an analogous fashion to the way his philosophizing calls for a repeated turning in the basic philosophical position (subject-object dichotomy) and in on-going transformations of the self toward greater existential and political freedom.

Jaspers delivered another "political" lecture at the *Rencontre Internationales de Geneve* (The Geneva International Conference) entitled "Vom Europäischen Geist" or "The European Spirit"[28] on September 13, 1946. Before the European intellectual community, and amidst the ashes of war, he asks: "Is this indeed Europe's decline, or is it a crisis of rebirth?"[29] Both were possible. Europe's foundations were shaken by the war and the dominance of modern technology. Now "every people must either come to terms with technology and its results or become extinct."[30] Jaspers identifies the mental aims of a European self-consciousness along lines that anticipate some of his later political themes, including the need to broaden the de facto Eurocentric philosophy into "world philosophy" and the idea of humanity, the transformation and reappropriation of "biblical religion" in the Western churches, and the transformation of revelational faith into philosophic faith in order to facilitate communication across pluralist faiths and cultures and, thus, hopefully avoid another major world war.

Immediately after the defeat of Germany, Jaspers also helped establish the journal *Die Wandlung* with the help of Werner Krauss and Alfred Weber. The journal was a forum for moral and political renewal that ran from 1945 to 1949. With contributing authors such as Arendt, Brecht, Buber, Mann, Eliot, Auden, Sartre, and Camus, the journal maintained a high professional standard until its termination. Jaspers was one of the clearest and most respected voices for Germany after the war, even though he craved neither publicity nor fame. Eventually the tide changed, however, and he would become saddened by what he understood as Germany's "missed turn about" (*verpasste Umkehr*) toward an authentic political path. In a letter dated January 31, 1947, referring to his book on the guilt question *Die Schuldfrage* (*The Question of German Guilt*) and other political writings, he laments that what he had written was all but "virtually ignored."[31] He even underwent a form of character assassination when the German press considered his move to the University of Basel in 1948 as a betrayal and desertion. In an open rebuttal in the newspaper *Rhein-Neckar-Zeitung*, dated March 24, 1948, he spoke of his philosophical duty as being "fulfilled in the service of an absolutely supranational task."[32] Just as his previous work at the University of Heidelberg had not been a profession of ultimate loyalty to Heidelberg, so too his move to take a call from the University of Basel was not to be understood as such. Jaspers merely continued to live out his idea of the university,[33] but now in the cultural context of Switzerland.

Jaspers's ambitious task of thinking through a universal history of philosophy materialized, in part, with the publication of the book *Vom Ursprung und Ziel der Geschichte* (*The Origin and Goal of History*) in 1949. The "end of Germany" had really meant the end of a historical epoch, and raised fundamental questions of world history and Germany's place therein. There remained the philosophical task of clarifying the moral presuppositions and real conditions of politics, as well as orienting his political thinking toward the idea of world citizenship. "Philosophy which does not become political," as he remarks in reference to Weber's work, "is not genuine philosophy."[34] Personal beliefs and actions and political involvements and realities are of whole cloth. Freedom is decisive in both the private and public sphere: "There is no law of nature and no law of history which determines the way of things as a whole. The future depends upon the responsibility of the decisions and deeds of men [. . .] upon each individual. By his way of life, by his daily small deeds, by his great decisions, the individual testifies to himself as to what is possible. By this, his present actuality, he contributes unknowingly toward the future."[35] The book identified the completely different vista technology opened up in the shape of the atom bomb and political totalitarianism and the perils of both for humankind on the path to a world order, but order still under the illusion of "total planning" policies in the social, political, and economic spheres.

Jaspers first lectured on the problem of atomic warfare and totalitarianism in 1950 in "Das Gewissen vor der Bedrohung durch die Atombombe" ("The Conscience Confronted by the Threat of the Atom Bomb").[36] This text marks the beginning of what would become a substantive and unique analysis of the existential, political, and moral problems posed by the invention of the atom bomb and rise of Soviet totalitarianism during the decade of the original Cold War. In the fall of 1956 he delivered a series of radio lectures on "The Atom Bomb and the Future of Man,"[37] and in 1958 he published the monograph, *Die Atombombe und die Zukunft des Menschen* (*The Future of Mankind*). Jaspers's atom bomb book, which remains one of the few substantive books on the nuclear age by any twentieth century philosopher, is a probing reflection of the twin possibilities of annihilation and totalitarianism made possible by the unleashed power of the atom and the technological mass-ordering characteristic of the twentieth century and the age of industrialization. The book was a direct response to the many objections and questions elicited from his German radio audience, and it won the prestigious Peace Prize of the German book trade in the same year of publication. His acceptance speech, "Wahrheit, Freiheit und Friede,"[38] provided him with the opportunity to sound a theme that encapsulates much of his political philosophy: "First, no outer peace is sustainable without the inner peace of humanity. Second, peace exists only through freedom. Third, freedom exists only through truth."[39] The aim of politics is peace, but not peace at any price. Peace requires freedom and freedom requires truth in political communication.

The atom bomb book was published at the height of the Cold War and just less than a decade after the defeat of Germany and its division of Germany into eastern and western states. It is not surprising that some Germans on the political left would respond critically to Jaspers's analysis of the twin threats of atomic annihilation and political totalitarianism.[40] For Jaspers, however, the battle against totalitarianism must be waged at both the existential and political dimensions of existence.[41] He was criticized as being NATO's military philosopher, the "henchman" of class enemies, and as articulating middle-class German decadence.[42]

Jaspers's first specifically German political work was firmly established with the 1960 publication of *Freiheit und Wiedervereinigung* (*Freedom and Reunification*),[43] which brought together political writings originally published in the summer of 1960 in the prominent weekly journal *Die Zeit*. The book includes the text of a television interview where Jaspers maintained that any historical legitimation of Germany's reunification was both politically and philosophically unrealistic. Jaspers identified a threefold political strategy advocating the idea of world peace grounded in freedom and established by means of a world confederation; the political question concerning the self-determination of the West and the development of freedom against the danger of totalitarianism, which Jaspers emphasizes is both an external (geo-political) and existential (individual freedom) threat; and, the idea of the new, postwar German state, the Federal Republic of Germany, which could rightly take its place in the West, and elsewhere, only by truly embodying political democracy in its constitution and in the lives of German citizens. Jaspers accepted the German Democratic Republic (GDR) officially as a second sovereign German state in the hope of gaining more freedom for its citizens who were under the sway of the Soviet Bloc.[44]

Given the historical and political horizon out of which Jaspers was writing, it is not surprising that *Freiheit und Wiedervereinigung* would draw many threats and insulting letters. One anonymous letter decried Jaspers as a "traitor of the fatherland—the henchman of Communism—the political pig."[45] It was not so much the criticism of German politicians in power at the time that made Jaspers critical toward the nascent West German state; rather, it was their resistance and willful refusal to accept the historical reality of a Germany divided into East and West. In light of Jaspers's earlier call for a German "purification of the soul," he must have interpreted German political obstinancy as a moral and existential foundering of many German politicians. For Jaspers the political issue was clear: A divided Germany was merely the inevitable consequence of Germany's culpability for the war; failure to understand this basic political fact is a failure of reasonableness, perhaps ideologically masking a passion for the political night or the Nietzschean will to power.

Jaspers published in 1966 his controversial German political analysis, *Wohin treibt die Bundesrepublik?* (*The Future of Germany*). No less of a philosopher than Hannah Arendt describes his book as "the politically most important book to appear in Germany after the Second World War."[46] Here in what proved to be the political bestseller of the year in Germany, Jaspers argues that the Federal Republic of Germany had for years been moving toward an "oligarchy" of political parties that spelled the end of parliamentary democracy. The emergency laws proposed at that time laid the political groundwork for what Jaspers called, in striking terms, a "dictatorship of politicians."[47] Once again, Jaspers's political reflections were met by strong opposition from the political right and left. The press portrayed him as a man bitter against Germany, questioned his political and philosophical foundations, and even falsely insinuated scientific and professional lack of responsibility. Such erroneous media spin succeeded in turning some in the academic world against him, including Jürgen Habermas, who came to regard Jaspers's political writings as the "fruits of an intelligent newspaper reader."[48] Ironically, Jaspers received a favorable response, including a lengthy thirteen-page letter in June 1966 from Walter Ulbricht, who was then the president of East Germany. Jaspers acknowledge the letter, but did not respond to Ulbricht at length out of fear that his correspondence might be used for propaganda purposes in the East.

In his 1967 *Antwort: Zur Kritik meiner Schrift "Wohin treibt die Bundesrepublik"* (*Response to My Book: The Future of Germany*) he set forth a response to various critics of his analysis of Germany's failure in democracy and its implications for the future.[49] With sober candor and honesty, Jaspers challenged those who would not admit that the German state was criminal during the NS-era:

> [Nineteen thirty-three] was a breakdown—or a revelation of the character of the German majority. Considering the facts everyone could see it [1933] was possible only if one would either deny the facts or treat them as non-existent. It took criminal untruthfulness. To fail to be absolutely, unreservedly anti-Nazi in view of the criminal facts, one had to be unimpressed by lawlessness and crime wherever apparent. Without profound inhumanity it was not possible.[50]

Jaspers applied for and was granted citizenship in 1967 by the Swiss government and canton of Basel. For many reasons, we may say that the move symbolized his final falling-out with the political situation in Germany, and despite his high regard for the exemplary political principles manifested in Switzerland, he always felt himself "a pilgrim without a fatherland."[51]

THE IDEA OF DEMOCRACY

What does Jaspers mean by the idea of democracy? Before we can respond directly to the question, we must first refer to Jaspers's proposition that the political world is affected by "the unconditionality of Existenz and by ideas"[52] (which presupposes his distinction between existence and Existenz).[53] Existence (*Dasein*) is the human being taken as an object, a unique individual, but one among other individuals in the world. Existenz, in contrast, is the human being as the non-objectifiable self. Existenz is what I truly am as the encompassing of self-being. In the illumination of Existenz I can only verify Existenz by the way I am authentically with myself and with others, and through the unconditionality of my action in the world, especially in relation to the political order.

This leads to another question: What does Jaspers mean by the unconditionality of Existenz for political action? Unconditional action is "an expression of self-conscious Existenz doing in phenomenal existence, with reference to its transcendence, what it considers essential for all eternity."[54] In contrast, the meaning of a conditional action is always qualified by its *end.* Unconditional action is willed, as such, and has no final goal or *telos* in its intentionality. When unconditional action serves a merely mundane purpose, that very purpose is never a sufficient reason for the act. The drive to unconditional action is illuminated by an assurance of being, which does not lie either in the drive and its satisfaction, or in a calculated end or utilitarian outcome. To be sure, action in the political realm is most often purposive, conditional action because it is carried out in relation to the will of others. It attempts to arouse and shape the will of those with whom we work, even as it must work against willful opposition. Political action encounters limits related to the human inability to survey all of the factual conditions of the world, or even the actual will of those involved in shaping the political order. Unconditional action characterizes a true foundation of politics. Unconditional acts often occur in the boundary situations of death, suffering, struggle, and guilt, and are not visible to psychological research. Similar to Kant's categorical imperative, Jaspers's unconditional imperative demands that political action not be subordinated to the requirements of existence (Dasein). The imperative requires "a conversion from continuous self-betrayal and impurity of motives to the seriousness of the unconditional."[55] Action stops being unconditional the minute the individual acts for the good only if it is not too costly, or when the individual gets lost in mundane acts and purposes.

We have come full circle: What, then, does Jaspers mean by *the idea of democracy*? Ideas shape the political world—whether the idea of democracy or the idea of the university. Jaspers's political philosophy is deeply indebted to Kant's understanding of a "regulative idea." Jaspers researchers understand the intimate connection between Kant and Jaspers. The idea of democracy is a regulative idea, a nonperfectible ideal that lies beyond complete visualization and actualization in time. The idea of democracy always has, as its anthropological grounding, a proper awareness of human imperfectability and the need for modesty and humility in political affairs. In this context we may say that Jaspers's political thinking is closer to Plato's than to Aristotle's. For Aristotle, natural right can indeed be perfected in the *polis*. Despite the limits of instrumental rationality that dominate political agendas and goals and the antinomies of political existence, the idea of democracy is neither weak nor skeptical. Democracy may be a bad form of government because it leads to the tyranny of the majority, or a radical skepticism toward the reasonableness of human nature that requires ruling with a big stick. Jaspers and Churchill agree: Democracy is still better than all other forms of government. But for Jaspers, and as a regulative idea, the *idea* of democracy offers no practical political program. Instead, democracy is a procedural framework for rational and reasonable communication among our species, as well as a way of being-together in a human community that refuses to believe that human irrationality is the final word or that our democratic rulers must be saints or superpersons. "The democratic idea," Jaspers writes, "has its ground in human beings' task of self-actualization in reason, and in the unique, irreplaceable character of every individual, and in one's dignity based on participation in reason. . . . [T]o despair of the democratic idea is to despair of human beings."[56]

Jaspers's political humanism speaks of self-actualization in reason as a task for each and every member of society. The importance of democracy is so great that to despair in it is to despair in my self, with others, in society, in the world.

Despair writ large spells political dangers, especially the mass-ordering of human beings in technological systems or the deification of man in the political square, or the *fuga mundi* or flight from the world. Here we see clearly the importance of the supra-political element of ethos. A culture of despair manifests a cultural ethos vulnerable to the shackles of economic, political, religious, and even scientific manifestations of totalitarianism.

For Jaspers, political salvation or damnation (used ciphericaIly) follows from the actions of human beings; we act out of freedom or we act not at all. Now the philosopher and the statesman must act responsibly, and freedom makes demands on the self that will not allow the thinker or the politician to hide behind obfuscating statistical analyses or shift the blame for one's political acts to events, institutions, technological fixes, or causal relations beyond the politician's control. All freedom—whether in the political and public realm, or analogously whether in the existential and private realm, lies in the individual. Despair is the enemy of democracy.

We may now respond directly to the question posed from the outset. Six general theses characterize Jaspers's idea of democracy.

First, the reasonableness that informs democracy must guide both citizens and politicians, and requires that every one have equal opportunity to be educated to the utmost of their natural potential. Freedom of speech and association are crucial to this educational process.

Second, democracy is never final. It keeps changing shape. Like Kant, Jaspers distinguishes the various forms of government (e.g., democracy, aristocracy, monarchy) from the Republican constitution, or manner of government, whose unconstitutional opposite is despotism. Democratic or despotic rule may occur in democratic, aristocratic, or monarchical forms of government in the shape of merely a "formal freedom." The Republican form of government is set up in keeping with the principles of the freedom of the members of society, the dependence of all members on a common legislature, and grounded in the law of equality.[57] A merely formal democracy may provide a condition of possibility, as in the past, for horrific political systems such as fascism, dictatorship, or communism, or even new forms of totalitarianism unbeknownst to humankind. In Jaspers's socio-historical situation, the potential was especially great in those countries where the idea of democracy has been hastily established. Is this any different than in our time? No, and even in the best forms of democratic government the authentic realization of democracy requires constant self-education, publicity of thought, and an incessant struggle for private and public truth and self-criticism. Democracy can endure only by continual improvement and self-criticism. Like reason, itself, democracy is always *en route*. It must be won anew with every new generation of young people.

Third, the goal of democracy is to allow every individual to self-actualize freedom. Democracy aims at equality, therefore, by means of equal legal rights and opportunities. All governments founded upon the concept of right require laws that are subject to change and improvement. Stagnation and inertia are enemies of open societies that are creative and reasonable enough to change democratic structures as necessary with the increasing complexity of technological developments and global change.

Fourth, the reasonableness that informs and imbues democracy is prior to any specific state laws and institutions. As such, and against legal positivism, Jaspers maintains that human rights stand taller, ethically, than positive laws, which reveals his being rooted in the tradition of natural right, which has been excluded from legal philosophy in favor of legal positivism. Democracy defines the objects of human rights through time in the shape of moral norms, even as reason works for the promotion and protection of human dignity and potentialities. True democracy requires mutuality and an active solicitude among all members of the state. Democracy makes any injustice done to other persons a matter of grave concern to all citizens, both national and world citizens.

Fifth, the reason in democracy works by persuasion and not by force. Nonetheless, because struggle or conflict, which may involve or require police and military force, is a boundary situation of human existence, democracy must employ force against rogue, criminal, and terrorist elements in accordance with judicial order. At the same time, individuals must be protected from arbitrary and illegal violence by other citizens or by the state system. In the extreme political situation, when consensually based procedural and substantive rules are ignored or willfully violated by the state or party power, citizens have a right to revolt. This right should be understood as also having a correlative self-obligation, i.e., the self, as both subject of and respondent to the right, toward "possible Existenz" or the basic dignity and self-actualization of persons in their freedom and well-being.

Finally, the reason in democracy never forgets that fallible human beings are governing economic, social, political, legal, and health affairs. Human beings have weaknesses and make inevitable errors. Human existence and political existence both have their mental and physical limits. Democratic government requires, therefore, a healthy critical cultural ethos with respect to the power that is wielded by human beings sworn to act in behalf of both all individual citizens and the public interest or common good. In the intellectual struggle of opinions, in the distribution of public offices, and in the very procedural justice at play in the electoral process itself, Jaspers stresses that governmental checks and balances require a loving struggle for communication and rational dialogue among all stakeholders.

Jaspers's idea of democracy, as apparent from the foregoing exposition, orients itself between potential military force, on the one hand, and free association, on the other. The individual has a rightful claim to be protected by the state against force and to make his or her will felt through voluntary associations, civil society and political democracy. Power politics and parliamentary politics are opposed. The important question for Jaspers is how both potential force and the right to freedom of association may join forces in an effort to realize a "new politics" given the boundary situation created for humanity as a whole by the advent of the atom bomb and the rise of modern and technologically sophisticated forms of fundamentalism and political totalitarianism.[58] History reveals that politics is characterized by the wielding of military force, but free association exercised through public debate can act to limit this force. Indeed, our very attitude about force contains a supra-political element that motivates and shapes political thinking. Physical violence, as for example in warfare, is the extreme form of conflict. Human conflict, as a boundary situation of human existence, need not be violent however. Conflict may also take guidance from and manifest supra-political ideas such as the will to non-violence, political responsibility, soldierly discipline, and virtue.[59]

Jaspers's idea of democracy appropriates elements of Kant's essay on "perpetual peace" as a supra-political norm, but with the norms of peace, freedom and truth transformed into a triadic whole: There can be no peace without freedom, but no freedom without truth. Modernity has brought a temporal urgency related to scientific and technological developments unknown to Kant. At the end of the day, however, the political turns back on the question concerning truth: "Freedom is empty when truth, from which it springs and which it serves, is not intended. . . ."[60] We become free and truthful only when we constantly turn back to a "common room" where rational communication unites differing political factions. The basic characteristic of reason is its will to unity. As the bond between the various modes of the encompassing, reason provides the impulse toward the unity of truth that is never completely fulfilled in time. Reason affirms the historicity of truth as manifest in the modes of being that we are as existence, consciousness as such, and, ultimately, Existenz. Thus, common sense, political realism, and formal religion may grow absolute in the individual or become false substitutes for reason. When political authorities make claims about the fulfillment of truth in time, they manifest what Jaspers calls "catholicity" (*Katholizität*), a closure of thought, whether it appears in totalitarian, fascist, or imperialist forms.[61]

The Supra-political Element in Politics: Ethos, Sacrifice, and Reason

"Philosophy is not without politics," as Jaspers says, and all philosophical thinking must accomplish itself in political action. Political action, however, must take some guidance from the supra-political element. What does he mean by a supra-political element? What is the relevance of the supra-political element in Jaspers's conception of a "new politics," a fully human and democratic politics commensurate with the challenges posed to thinking and acting in late modernity by the global boundary situation in which humanity is now situated?

The supra-political element in politics defies simple definition. It is perhaps more accurate to speak of three key supra-political elements in Jaspers's moral-political philosophy as he writes at the beginning of *The Future of Mankind*:

> All politics depends on something above politics, but this supra-political element is not unequivocal. We may call it *ethics* [*ethos*],[62] *self-sacrifice*, *reason*—yet each of these three is dependent upon the others, or at one with them. Distinction is only a way to make them communicable. . . . To us, the *supra-political* element is manifested in the ethical idea and in the valor of sacrifice. They can provide the conditions for the achievement of world peace—conditions impossible to create by treaties and institutions, but growing, rather, out of man's other side which the observer of tangible reality never perceives.[63]

Jaspers refers to the supra-political element in ethics, the power of sacrifice, and reason or reasonableness (*Vernunft*). The reasonableness that infuses the political order is democratic and participatory. It is grounded in a unity of wills whose procedural conditions of discourse are not short-circuited by existing political powers, and which are embodied in a legal state constitution and human rights.

To this threefold distinction between components of the supra-political element, we must add supra-political ideas or norms as well, such as may be found in Jaspers's distinction between conflict and violence, or, his distinction between the violent struggle for existence (*Dasein*) and the loving struggle for *Existenz*. Jaspers reminds us that in the effort to move away from violence to communicative forms of discourse marked by conflict (a boundary situation of human existence), we may take guidance from supra-political ideas, e.g., the will to nonviolence, political responsibility, soldierly discipline, and virtue.[64] The supra-political, in its various elements, in turn, shapes and directs a cultural ethos. Then again, in turn, the cultural ethos permeates and shapes the private realm in an on-going feedback loop.

Jaspers draws his concept of the supra-political most directly from Nietzsche's distinction between the unhistorical (*Ungeschichtlichen*), the historical (*Geschichtlichen*), and the supra-historical (*Übergeschichtlichen*). For Nietzsche the unhistorical, historical, and supra-historical man are different. The unhistorical man designates "the art and power of *forgetting* and of enclosing oneself within a bounded *horizon*," whereas the supra-historical man refers to "the powers that lead the eye away from becoming towards that which bestows upon existence the character of the eternal and stable, towards *art* and *religion*."[65] The historical man, despite his or her preoccupation with the process of history, thinks and acts unhistorically. The preoccupation with history merely serves individual "life" and not pure knowledge. The supra-historical man, by contrast, sees no salvation in the historical process per se. For Nietzsche the world is complete; it reaches its finality at each and every moment. And when history is employed for the process of present "life," the supra-historical outlook possesses a certain wisdom.

Jaspers's concept of the supra-political holds a different meaning than Nietzsche's concept of the supra-historical.[66] For Jaspers, a dialectical relation exists between existential and political freedom, between the individual will and the state will. Existential freedom is both *prepolitical* (not "unhistorical") and *supra-political*, whereas political freedom concerns the actual conditions of government and circumscribes existential freedom. Political freedom cannot exist without the will to existential freedom, but existential freedom is menaced in its realization if political slavery engulfs a people or nation. To be sure, a despotic state can maintain external political freedom, just as a free democratic constitution can rule a nation of existentially unfree persons. Political freedom requires a combination of essential variables if it is to be authentic: "*Freedom begins as freedom of the individual, gains communal form in the Republican form of government, [and] maintains itself against oppression from alien states. In the entirety of these three elements is freedom real.*"[67]

Political freedom cannot be learned from the disciplines of political science, law, or history texts per se. There is no means-ends formula that might neatly be applied to obtain political freedom because the actualization of democracy rests in the possibilities of human freedom, ethos, sacrifice, and reason.

Jaspers distinguishes negative political freedom from positive freedom. State law may provide for the free play of a libertarian will through which individuals shut themselves off from others. This is merely a negative freedom. An ethically based freedom consists in openness to others without compulsion. Positive freedom springs from motives of love and reason. When this more excellent, positive freedom is realized on the basis of legal safeguards for negative freedom, only then does Jaspers affirm that "man is free in the measure in which he sees freedom around him, i.e., in the measure in which all men are free."[68]

Political freedom requires legitimate authority. All freedom is empty "unless it heeds authority, but authority is false if it does not stimulate freedom."[69] Jaspers grounds political authority in tradition and Transcendence. The authority of tradition and Transcendence are both threatened by preoccupation with technological authority in our present historical situation. Echoing Weber, Jaspers affirms that all forms of authority need faith for legitimation. "The crucial hallmark of free conditions is faith in freedom."[70] When faith and trust prevail in the constitutional state this is because the state is grounded in a legitimate authority. Where there is legitimacy, there is internal political freedom because legitimate authority puts violent force in fetters through the law.

Jaspers's upholds an ineradicable faith in human possibilities for existential and political freedom. Just as existential freedom requires a continual "turnabout" within the Encompassing in order not to be blinded by the darkness of reductionism in the other modes of being that we are, so, too, the condition of possibility for the new politics requires a transformation, redirection, turnabout, or "conversion" (*Umkehr*)[71] from the old politics to the "new politics." In *The Future of Mankind*, Jaspers identifies the limits of the old politics. Linking the technological and historical situation of the Cold War period to the larger "epochal consciousness" of modernity, his thinking takes the following form: Only world peace can remove the twin threats of the atom bomb and political totalitarianism. To think that future wars will be waged without the use of nuclear weapons, or to think that weapons of mass destruction will be used only as a deterrent is delusional thinking. World peace, however, cannot be actualized by technological or political means alone. Hence the idea of a human redirection arises:

> "Man seems doomed unless he experiences an inner change through his freedom. But such a conversion cannot be the object of a new politics: it can only be the prerequisite of a new politics."[72]

Freedom can never be propagated as such or handed down from generation to generation like a trade or business. Freedom must be appropriated by each individual. Without the existential struggle for freedom, political freedom is lost.[73] The old politics is grounded on the Hobbesian and Darwinian educational principle of the struggle of all against all for existence. In contrast, education for the new politics will act on the principle that there can be honest, rational communication and peace between all persons of good will.

Jaspers takes up but goes beyond political realism and ethical idealism (which is not the same as the supra-political element of individual and cultural *ethos* noted above) in his vision of a new politics.[74] For the political realist, the idea of eliminating human warfare appears unreal. To justify this view, the realist invokes history and the sordid nature of human existence for his realism. The idea that there may, indeed, be a change of human beings, a change of their reason and will, appears naïve and unrealistic. Guided as such by a pessimistic view of history and the future possibilities for humanity, the realist plans policies only for the moment, the short term. The realist does not want to upset the political status quo. He is unconcerned with the truth or rightness of human motives, only with their political consequence. He believes politics is a public affair, completely unaffected by the private sphere and ethos. An ethos, however, looses its supra-political power when it becomes moralistic and exhausts itself in prohibitions and commandments, or when it grows detached from the courage to sacrifice. Reason, therefore, must guide ethos and the courage to sacrifice; both ethos and sacrifice must stem from the unconditionality of Existenz in human beings who actively participate as good citizens in the public realm or who actively take part in political life. Jaspers's critique of political realism, then, is that it is in fact unrealistic in its proper understanding of politics; and as history has also illustrated clearly, when political realism turns absolute it can become a ruthless terror of history.

Absolutist political realism, or what Jaspers synonymously implies by his use of the term, "*Realpolitik*," wills power for its own sake. Left to its own devices, realpolitik leads to nihilism and doom. Without the supra-political element in politics—without existential freedom in dialectical relation with political freedom, without reasonableness, ethical substance, or sacrifice—Realpolitik will inevitably sweep humankind over the precipice. Even Machiavelli was far more creative than modernity's political realists. For what the political realist ignores in Machiavelli's political discourses is the *virtu* of the great statesman who goes his successful way in conflict leagued with *fortuna*. Like ethos and sacrifice, *virtu* and *fortuna* are supra-political forces that help make up the substance of political reality. With giants like Thucydides and De Tocqueville, Jaspers affirms that great statesmen demand more than political realism to ground their political actions and policies and lead to a lasting peace.[75]

Communication skills are crucial in the political realm. Jaspers contrasts the existential communication of the great statesman with the "political intercourse" of Realpolitik. Political intercourse is characterized by untruthful discourse, political lies, trickery and deception. Any authentic passage from the old politics to the new politics requires the passage from falsehood to truth. "Existenz does not touch Existenz . . . until men cease to deal with each other as enemies locked in a struggle for existence."[76] Jaspers's "ethic of responsibility," which is indebted to Max Weber, includes accountability for the consequences of one's actions, readiness for any kind of sacrifice, though not for a sacrifice that would destroy the meaning of politics itself.[77] What Jaspers writes about Weber is highly appropriate to his own political thinking. He is not so much concerned with the articulation of normative political proposals as with a "way of thinking about politics, its grandeur, dignity, truthfulness, seriousness."[78]

What then determines and grounds responsible political action? There is no guarantee. The statesman makes an authentic political decision, one that is based neither on some calculable consequences following from an ethic of responsibility, nor on the unequivocal consequences of one's deepest moral and spiritual convictions (ethic of conviction). For Jaspers, all political decision is grounded in unconditional action, which, in turn, springs from the actualization of possible Existenz. Unconditional action is capable of leaving its moral-political imprint upon the community because it issues from a responsible, accountable, and trustworthy *Lebens-praxis*. The statesman reaches a point where he understands and accepts the consequences of his action, but nonetheless says "I can do no other, here I stand."[79] The ethic of responsibility seeks to avoid moral absolutism, the will to power, and dogmatization of an unlimited reason of state.

To be sure, Jaspers has an eye for political realities and is able to sense the potential consequences of present historical and political events. Whereas Weber could justify power politics for the protection of the nation or *raison d'etat*, Jaspers views politics in light of the inevitable struggle for existential order (*Daseinornung*), the protection of freedom, and peace. Where Jaspers and Weber differ is that Weber's politics (*das Machtpragma* or power politics) become for Jaspers part of the problem of our new historical situation, wed as it is to the old politics. Weber was not confronted with the same twin threats that Jaspers was. While there is no political *telos,* per se, in Jaspers's concept of Existenz,[80] there is an inextricable link between world peace, existential and political freedom, and freedom's relation to truth. The integration of freedom, ethics, sacrifice, reason, and truth—in politicians as well as the body politic—is crucial to the actualization of political democracy in history.[81]

Along with ethos, sacrifice is another crucial supra-political norm that must be acknowledged and lived if a new politics is to succeed. Gandhi realized the power of sacrifice better than any other person living in the twentieth century. He incarnated the supra-political basis of politics by his consistent principle of non-violence (*ahimsa*) and truth (*satyagraha*). Gandhi's life stands as an inspiring reminder that sacrifice is essential to realize our true humanity,[82] even if Jaspers's philosophic faith believes that the pacifist renunciation of all force cannot show us an absolute way out of the modern political predicament.

DEMOCRACY AND THE COMMUNITY OF REASONABLE PERSONS

Rational communication is essential for the new politics, and grounds the tasks of the community of reasonable individuals (*Die Gemeinschaft der Vernünftigen*) in civil society and state institutions. Such a community consists of existentially free individuals who concretely embody supra-political solidarity, which is not abstract. Solidarity takes the form of constructive and enduring political action and depends upon reason's prevailing in states, political parties, churches, schools, unions, and bureaucracies. No strategic think tank, peace movement, or government leadership can produce rational communication and the ethos and conscience of the reasonable community. Jaspers's reasonable community differs from the idea of the sovereign will of the people.

> Democracy is every individual. Everyone . . . is responsible for the way he lives, thinks, and works, for the actions he decides to take, and for the way he does all this in common with his neighbors. To feel free of this responsibility is the basic perversion of democracy.[83]

From whence springs the authority of the community of reasonable individuals? Authority flows from "boundless communication," which counteracts the principles of the "old politics:" *lying*, *secrecy*, and *terror*. Error and the possibility for correction are not only permitted by boundless communication, they are required and encouraged by it. The existential source of boundless communication is humanity as such. The community of reasonable individuals rises and falls in accordance with those "hidden existential forces that well up and contract the loving communication itself."[84] The indispensable condition for the global expansion of such a community is freedom for the public clash of minds without censorship, and support for the promotion and protection of human rights.[85] Jaspers rejects Plato's view that the ideal state should subject the power of poetry, music, and art to censorship because of their potential negative influence. Instead, he retains the call to responsibility contained in the Platonic precept, but chooses the path of freedom's potential peril over the destruction of creative potentialities entailed in various forms of censorship. Like Kant before him Jaspers defends the freedom of the spirit as the premise of cultural creativity, and upholds political freedom against state censorship. Jaspers also goes beyond Plato's conception of philosopher-kings. An egalitarian, democratically based philosophizing, grounded in existential freedom, is the guiding rule for the new politics. Even the most astute statesman will turn to others for political insight and understanding. The true statesman will be persuaded by the community or reasonable individuals in which each citizen helps to control and correct the other in the building up a democratic and participatory common good.

The reasonable statesman in a world marked by a new politics must relinquish the old political principles: *Fac et excusa*—commit the war act and explain it later; *Si fecisti, nega*—if you did it, deny that you are at fault by blaming others or human nature; *Divide et impera*—set the leaders or the people against each other, then conquer them all. The political realist becomes ashamed of these "sophistical maxims" (cf. Kant) only if he fails to carry them out on the political faith that all honor lies in the aggrandizement of political power. Jaspers wants the new politics to shame the realists on the Kantian ground that morality holds theoretical precedence over politics. The "radical evil" in humanity typically reverses moral duty for a will to happiness. And yet, supra-political norms of right have objective reality. They can be applied in the political arena despite objections raised by an empiricist-based political worldview. To paraphrase Kant, political freedom cannot take a step for Jaspers without rendering homage to the ethos of possible Existenz. For Kant, the moral ought implies a political can. For Jaspers, the link between morality and politics lies in a philosophic faith in the human ability to be both rational and thus moral. But as long as political realists espouse the old politics, moral duty needs reason's political wisdom to guide the rational statesman through the uncertainty of force and political action. In this way Jaspers conjoins Kant's idea of perpetual peace to Weber's ethic of responsibility. And yet, Jaspers is even more the realist than Kant with respect to the "progress of history." He adds a temporal urgency to Kant's idea of eternal peace, an urgency that is no less pressing in the present situation and the war against terrorism:

> We have a breathing spell. . . . If this interval is not utilized to prevent war as such, the doom of mankind seems inevitable. . . . Nothing short of unprecedented fear could perhaps, as a natural factor, compel the assurance of peace; but as a mere institution this would have lasting success only if man were to permeate it with a new ethos, with a new spirit of sacrifice, with a new reason. Man will escape perdition only if he is changed in the Kantian concept of a "revolution of the way of thinking." Today he faces a great choice: the doom of mankind, or a transformation [*Wandlung*] of man.[86]

Politics, Philosophic Faith, and Terrorism

Is the realization of human reasonableness and personal transformation possible? Can we actualize a *global* idea of democracy in our present historical situation?

In Jaspersian terms, can humankind convert the violent struggle for existence into a loving struggle for Existenz? Jaspers's answer to these questions is a resounding yes, but only if we presuppose a faith in the possibilities of human reasonableness and solidarity. What is vital is that the community of reasonable persons, not guided by the instrumental rationality of technological means, alone, will seek untiringly to turn violent struggle into the loving struggle for Existenz and reasonable communication. Jaspers's gives us his definition of peace and the stakes involved in an age of atomic, biological and chemical weapons. His words are as insightful today as they were during the early 1960s:

> Peace is not the absence of struggle. But man can convert the struggle from a violent one into a spiritual and loving struggle. The violent struggle dies in communication. Instead of superiority in victory, the result is communal truth. By means of such struggle each individual comes to him or herself. The loving struggle places all means of power— also the means of intellectual forcefulness, which as a stronger rationality corresponds to physical strength—at the disposal of the partner in the same manner in which oneself makes use of them, and thereby cancels its fatal effects.[87]

Jaspers's political thinking has been charged as idealistic, as doing violence against the politically particular in favor of the universal, of moralizing a realm that putatively defies the logic of the ethical and the supra-political element in politics. If Jaspers privileges the concrete universal in his political ideas, however, he only does so on the basis of a tolerant and humanist *philosophical faith*, which includes faith in the one historicity of humankind and a belief that "whatever is grasped and brought forth by the human race possesses a unity of meaning by virtue of the inter-relatedness of everything."[88] Philosophical faith affirms that human beings can, indeed, realize the idea of democracy and the supra-political element in politics, but not without ethos, sacrifice, and reason; more precisely, not without philosophic faith in the possibilities of human freedom and reasonableness.

A "new politics" that puts an end to violent conflict by means of global democratic procedures and legal policies remains a task. Now in an age of "complex terrorism,"[89] this task extends to the global community of reasonable persons who are ready to act freely, responsibly, and unconditionally in both existential and political action, all the while knowing that the idea of democracy is never perfectible. Reason, itself, tells us that there is no absolutely right and perfect political ordering of the world, and our awareness of human limitation and imperfectibility is a corollary of Jaspers's democratic idea. Jaspers's "new politics" is badly needed today in an age where technological advances have brought greater destructive capacities to terrorist groups and individuals, especially, the dramatic developments in information technologies and communications, more powerful weapons, and more abundant opportunities to divert non-weapon technologies to destructive ends. Terrorist threats against the idea of democracy are real, but the struggle against terrorism cannot be achieved through information and communication technologies.[90] And yet, to paraphrase Max Weber, you cannot "argue against warriors of the faith," but must be prepared to face the reality of struggle even where deadly force is involved. What if we fail as a human species to actualize democracy, reasonableness, and a new global political order commensurate with the general "boundary situation" that humanity as a whole faces in our present historical and technological situation? Jaspers asks a similar question in light of the potential destruction of our species by the use of thermonuclear weapons:

> Would the doom of reason be the revelation of nothingness? No, for where there is reason it is certain of not being nothing. To have striven for it is worthy of man—and possible for man, because his own self was given to him in the gift of reason, he knows not whence. Because it is certain of itself only if it is conscious of being a demand from elsewhere, reason has an unknown, unknowable actuality in the eternal.[91]

NOTES

1. Karl Jaspers, "Philosophical Autobiography," in Paul Arthur Schilpp, edited by *The Philosophy of Karl Jaspers*, augmented edition (La Salle, IL: Open Court Publishing Co., 1981 [1957]), p. 70. [Hereafter cited as PAE].

2. PAE, pp. 5–94.

3. Karl Jaspers, "Reply to My Critics," in PAE, pp. 747–869 at pp. 751–56.

4. See the article by Andreas Cesana herein.

5. Karl Jaspers, *The Great Philosophers*, Vol. IV, edited by Michael Ermarth and Leonard Ehrlich. Translated by Edith Ehrlich and Leonard H. Ehrlich. (New York/San Diego/ London: Harcourt Brace & Company, 1994), p. 231. [Hereafter cited as GP 4, eds.]

6. Jaspers uses the verbal form "philosophizing" rather than "philosophy" in order to capture the open-ended, periechontological nature of his thinking out of the Encompassing. On "philosophizing" as a rejection of "philosophy," especially when the later becomes satisfied with the reductionist knowledge of tangible objects in the world, and thereby turning philosophizing into the practice of science, see Karl Jaspers, "Reply to My Critics," in PAE, pp. 749–869, at pp. 793ff.

7. See Gregory J. Walters, *Karl Jaspers and the Role of "Conversion" in the Nuclear Age* (Lanham, MD and London: University Press of America, 1988); Godfrey

Robert Carr, *Karl Jaspers as an Intellectual Critic: The Political Dimension of His Thought* (Peter Lang: Frankfurt am Main, 1983); Fritz Böversen, Hrsg., *Philosophie der Politik: Ein Symposium zum 100. Geburtstag von Karl Jaspers* (Wuppertal: Bericht des Faches Pädagogik, Nr. 12, 1984); Kurt Salamun, *Karl Jaspers* (München: C.H. Beck, 1985), 102ff; Werner Schneiders, *Karl Jaspers in der Kritik* (Bonn: H. Bouvier, 1965); *Karl Jaspers—Philosophie und Politik,* Hrsg. Reiner Wiehl and Dominic Kaegi (Heidelberg: Universitätsverlag C. Winter, 1998).

8. As Alan Olson notes in his comparison of Jaspers and Nicholas of Cusa or Cusanus, "it is Cusanus 'the man of action,' moving from *praxis* to *theoria* as distinct from being a purely academic philosopher or retiring contemplative, that seems to impress Jaspers. . . . Jaspers believed . . . the ultimate validation of philosophical existence is *Lebens-praxis*." Alan Olson, "Cusanus as Postmedievalist," in *Karl Jaspers: On Philosophy of History and History of Philosophy*, edited by Joseph W. Koterski, S. J. and Raymond J. Langley (Amherst, NY: Humanity Books, 2003), pp. 155–65, at 156.

9. Reiner Wiehl, "Jaspers' Bestimmung des Überpolitischen," in *Karl Jaspers—Philosophie und Politik,* Hrsg. Reiner Wiehl and Dominic Kaegi, pp. 81–96.

10. E. B. Ashton translates the German expression, *die Gemeinschaft der Vernünftigen* as "the community of men of reason."

11. Karl Jaspers, *Nachlass*, quoted in Hans Saner, *Karl Jaspers in Selbstzeugnissen und Bilddokumenten* (Rowohlt, 1970), p. 43.

12. PAE, p. 55.

13. PAE, pp. 55–56.

14. PAE, p. 50.

15. Dolf Sternberger, "Jaspers und der Staat," in Klaus Piper, edited by *Karl Jaspers. Werk und Wirkung* (Munich: R. Piper, 1963), p. 134.

16. Ernst Mayer (1883-1952) was Jaspers's friend from their early days together at medical school until the time of Mayer's death. He was also Jaspers's brother-in-law, the man who had "the greatest possible significance" for his three-volume *Philosophy. Cf.* PAE, "VI. Ernst Mayer," pp. 40–45, at 43.

17. Karl Jaspers, quoted in Saner, *Karl Jaspers*, p. 44. Cf., Karl Jaspers, *Schicksal und Wille. Autobiographische Schriften*. Hrsg. Hans Saner (München: Piper, 1967), p. 35.

18. Karl Jaspers, quoted in Saner, *Karl Jaspers*, p. 44.

19. Hannah Arendt, *Men in Dark Times* (London: Jonathan Cape, 1970), p. 76.

20. Karl Jaspers, *The Question of German Guilt*, translated by E. B. Ashton, new introduction by Joseph W. Koterski, S. J. (New York: Fordham University Press, 2001), p. 11. [Hereafter cited as QGG].

21. See the essay by Hans Saner herein, eds.

22. Karl Jaspers, quoted in Saner, *Karl Jaspers*, p. 51; Cf., HS, p. 30.

23. Karl Jaspers, "Erneuerung der Universität," in HS, pp. 31–40. The German original first appeared in *Die Wandlung* 1, Nr. 1, Heidelberg (L. Schneider), pp. 66–74. In English, "The Rededication of German Scholarship," translated by Marianne Zuckerkandl, *The American Scholar,* vol. 15 (Spring 1946), pp. 181–88.

24. Jaspers, "The Rededication of German Scholarship," pp. 181–82.

25. QGG, p. 25.

26. QGG, p. 26.

27. QGG, p. 30.

28. QGG, pp. 97–98.

29. Karl Jaspers, "*L'Esprit Européen,*" *in L'Esprit Européen, Rencontres internationales de Genève*, translated by Jeanne Hersch (Paris: La presse française et étrangere, O. Zeluck, 1947), pp. 291–323. German, Karl Jaspers, *Vom Europäischen Geist.* Munich: R. Piper, 1947; also in Jaspers, *Rechenschaft und Ausblick: Reden und Aufsatze*, second edition (Munich: R. Piper & Co., 1958 [1951]), pp. 275–312. [Hereafter cited as RA.] English, *The European Spirit*, translated by R. G. Smith (London: SCM Press, 1948) and (New York: Macmillan, 1949).

30. Karl Jaspers, "Is Europe's Culture Finished?" translated by E. B. Ashton, *Commentary* IV (1947), pp. 518–26, at 519.

31. Jaspers, "Is Europe's Culture Finished?" p. 520.

32. Karl Jaspers, *Briefe*, quoted in Saner, *Karl Jaspers*, p. 55.

33. Karl Jaspers, "Öffentliche Erklärung," *Rhein-Neckar-Zeitung* (am 24. März, 1948), quoted in Saner, *Karl Jaspers*, p. 56.

34. See the article by Alan Olson herein, eds.

35. GP 4, p. 326.

36. PAE, pp. 69–70.

37. In RA, pp. pp. 370–77 (my translation).

38. Karl Jaspers, "The Atom Bomb and the Future of Man." Translated by Norbert Guterman in the *Evergreen Review* 2 (1958), pp. 37–57. German, HS, pp. 153–72.

39. Karl Jaspers, "Wahrheit, Freiheit und Friede (1958)," in Karl Jaspers, *Hoffnung and Sorge: Schriften zur deutschen Politik, 1945–1965* (Munich: R. Piper & Co., 1965), pp. 173–85. [Hereafter cited as HS, eds.]

40. HS, 174: "Erstens: Kein äusserer Friede ist ohne den inneren Frieden der Menschen zu halten. Zweitens: Friede ist allein durch Freiheit. Drittens: Freiheit ist allein durch Wahrheit." [my translation].

41. For the political debate and discussions by Robert Spaemann, Golo Mann, Julius Ebbinghaus, Richard Schaeffler, and Georg Mende, see Werner Schneiders, *Karl Jaspers in der Kritik* (Bonn: Bouvier, 1965), pp. 91–134. See also, Gregory J. Walters, *Karl Jaspers and the Role of "Conversion" in the Nuclear Age* (Lanham, MD: University Press of America, 1988), pp. xviii-xxviii; Godfrey Robert Carr, *Karl Jaspers as an Intellectual Critic: The Political Dimension of His Thought* (Frankfurt am Main, Germany: Peter Lang Verlag, 1983), pp. 116–36.

42. See, e.g., Karl Jaspers, "The Fight Against Totalitarianism," in *Philosophy and the World: Selected Essays and Lectures*, translated by E. B. Ashton (Chicago: Regnery, 1963), pp. 68-87. [Hereafter cited as PW eds.]

43. Cf., Saner, *Karl Jaspers*, p. 60.

44. Karl Jaspers, *Freiheit und Wiedervereinigung* (München: R. Piper, 1960). [This book has not been translated into English—eds.]

45. Ibid., p. 13.

46. Cited in Saner, *Karl Jaspers*, p. 61.

47. Hannah Arendt, "Foreword," Karl Jaspers, *The Future of Germany*, translated by E. B. Ashton (Chicago: University of Chicago Press, 1967), p. v (italics added). [Hereafter cited as FG, eds.]

48. FG, p. 36.

49. Jürgen Habermas, "Deutschland—wohin?" *Die Zeit*, May 13, 1966, quoted in Saner, *Karl Jaspers*, p. 63.

50. Karl Jaspers, *Antwort: Zur Kritik meiner Schrift "Wohin treibt die Bundesrepublik?"* (München: R. Piper, 1967). English, FG, pp. 116–22, 140–50, 163–73. The English translation of FG brings together material from *"Wohin treibt die Bundesrepublik?"* and Jaspers's book *Antwort: Zur Kritik meiner Schrift "Wohin treibt die Bundesrepublik?"* but the English translation does not include all the German original source material, and frequently paraphrases at times, as is also the case in the Ashton translation of *Die Atombombe und die Zukunft des Menschen.*

51. FG, p. 167.

52. Karl Jaspers, quoted in Saner, *Karl Jaspers*, p. 64.

53. PHT I, p. 149.

54. On the concept of Existenz, see the contribution by Kurt Salamun herein [eds.]

55. PHT II, p. 256.

56. WW, p. 60. (emphasis added).

57. BPW, p. 429; FM, p. 209.

58. PW, p. 91.

59. KST, p. 49.

60. FM, p. 31; cf. Karl Jaspers, *Die Atombombe und die Zukunft des Menschen: Politisches Bewusstsein unserer Zeit.* 4th edition (Munich: R. Piper, 1960 [1958]), p. 57. [Hereafter cited as AB, eds.]

61. FM, p. 334; AB, p. 484. Cf., PW, pp. 97–98.

62. VdW, p. 857.

63. In the English translation of *The Atom Bomb and the Future of Mankind*, E. B. Ashton translates the German term *Ethos* as "ethics." Ethics is an inadequate translation, however, because Jaspers was critical of all conceptions of ethics as a definitive rational system. He prefers to speak of a cultural ethos. This reading is further justified by Jaspers's treatment of ethos and its crucial relation to the wide variety of worldviews as discussed in the *Psychologie der Weltanschauungen.*

64. FM, p. 13.

65. FM, p. 31; cf. AB, p. 57.

66. Friedrich Nietzsche, "On the Uses and Advantages of History for Life," *Untimely Meditations*, edited by Daniel Breazeale, translated by R. J. Hollingdale (Cambridge and New York: Cambridge University Press, 1997), pp. 59-123, at 120.

67. Reiner Wiehl, "Jaspers' Bestimmung des Überpolitischen," in *Karl Jaspers—Philosophie und Politik,* Hrsg. Reiner Wiehl and Dominic Kaegi, pp. 81–96.

68. HS, p. 175 (italics in the original).

69. OGH, p. 160.

70. PW, p. 37.

71. OGH, p. 170. Cf., Karl Jaspers, "Liberty and Authority," in PW, p. 35.

72. The role of "redirection" or "transformation" (*Verwandlung*), "turn about" (*Umkehr*), "turn around" (*Umwendung*), or "change" (*Veränderung*) in our way of thinking is central to Jaspers's philosophical thinking as a whole, and not simply his political ideas. Neither should the above terms be conflated with the idea of a religious conversion, e.g., from one faith denomination to another, or from one faith tradition to another one. In the latter case, the proper German word would be *Bekehrung*. There are, however, precedents in existing English translations for the use of "conversion" to capture Jaspers's concept of the moral-political *Umkehr* required by the contemporary technological and political situation. See further, Walters, *Karl Jaspers and the Role of "Conversion" in the Nuclear Age*, p. x; *idem*, "The Role of 'Conversion' (*Umkehr*) in the Nuclear Age: Moral-Political Dimensions in the Thought of Karl Jaspers," *Jahrbuch der Östereichischen Karl Jaspers Gesellschaft*, vol. 2 (1989), pp. 88–106.

73. ABR, p. 50 (emphasis added). Cf., HS, p. 165.

74. PHT III, p. 26.

75. HS, p. 166; Cf., ABR, p. 52.

76. FM, pp. 249–51; AB, pp. 343–46; Cf., ABR, pp. 50–51.

77. PHT II, pp. 90–91.

78. Karl Jaspers, *Three Essays: Leonardo, Descartes, Max Weber*, translated by Ralph Manheim (New York: Harcourt, Brace and World, 1964), p. 223.

79. GP 4, p. 330.

80. AB, p. 77.

81. Gerhard Knauss, "Karl Jaspers: Philosophie wider die Politik," in Fritz Böversen, Hrsg., *Philosophie der Politik*, pp. 10–29, at 18.

82. Alexander Schwan, "Die Zusammengehörigkeit von existentieller und politischer Freiheit bei Karl Jaspers," in *Philosophie der Politik*, Hrsg., Fritz Böversen, pp. 30–48.

83. Karl Jaspers, "One of Karl Jaspers' Last Commentaries: Gandhiji," *The Courier* Vol. 22 (October 1969), pp. 26–27.

84. FM, p. 308; AB, p. 439.

85. FM, p. 222; AB, p. 305.

86. I have developed the idea of a global community of human rights at great length in Gregory J. Walters, *Human Rights in an Information Age: A Philosophical Analysis* (Toronto, Buffalo, London: University of Toronto Press, 2002), pp. 238–53; See also, *idem.*, "Human Rights, World Philosophy, and the Quest for Global Solidarity: Jaspers's Abiding Contribution," *Yearbook of the Austrian Karl Jaspers Society*, 10 (1997), pp. 127–50.

87. Karl Jaspers, "Kant's 'Perpetual Peace,'" in PW, p. 123; PW, p. 134.

88. Karl Jaspers, "Wahrheit, Freiheit und Friede," in HS, p. 174.

89. Karl Jaspers, *World History of Philosophy, Second Volume: History of the Substantive Contents of Philosophic Thought*, in *Philosophy on the Way to "World Philosophy"/Philosophie auf dem Weg zur "Weltphilosophie,"* edited by Leonard H. Ehrlich and Richard Wisser (Würzburg: Königshausen and Neumann; Amsterdam: Rodopi, 1998), p. 19.

90. Thomas Homer-Dixon, "The Rise of Complex Terrorism," *Foreign Policy*, No.128 (January-February, 2002), pp. 1–8. Also, Frank P. Harvey, *Smoke and Mirrors: Globalized Terrorism and the Illusion of Multilateral Security* (Toronto, Buffalo, London: University of Toronto Press, 2004), pp. 11–32.

91. BPW, p. 439.

Part III

Freedom and Will, Philosophic Faith, and Metaphysics

KARL JASPERS ON THE RELATION OF FREEDOM AND THE WILL TO TRUTH

Joseph W. Koterski, S.J.

For Karl Jaspers, freedom and truth are dialectically related. Freedom is a condition for the very possibility of reaching truth in any sphere, and truth is crucial for the authenticity of human freedom. To appreciate his sense of the relation between truth and freedom, we need to be remindful of the general context of his philosophizing: rather than asking the traditional metaphysical questions about what is being, Jaspers always asks what is being for us, in our temporal existence. The result is that reflection on the temporal character of all human experience of truth and freedom becomes for him the ground for thinking all things about being. Jaspers's polysemous understanding of truth includes the compelling cogency of truth-claims in science as well as the trans-temporal truths of being contemplated by metaphysics (periechontology) and the truths of commitment realized in the realm of value. His understanding of the nature, the purpose, and the possibilities of human freedom is framed by his treatment of the will and of boundary situations.

One finds discussion of these themes recurrently throughout Jaspers's corpus, in the creative *Psychologie der Weltanschauungen* (*Psychology of World-views*), in the massive *Von der Wahrheit* (*On Truth*), and in specialized articles such as "Philosophie und Wissenschaft" ("Philosophy and Science"), but of special importance by reason of the explicit connections of this theme to other parts of Jaspers's thought is the second volume of *Philosophy: Existential Elucidation* (*Philosophie: Existenzerhellung*).[1] A number of specialized monographs, including works by Elizabeth Young-Bruehl and Sebastian Samay,[2] have explored various aspects of this theme within Jaspers's own works, and the insights found in Jaspers's original philosophizing have proven fruitful for thinkers trying to do their own creative work within a Jaspersian framework.[3]

From Jaspers's earliest works in psychology and psychopathology we find him convinced of the pluralistic methodology required for sound anthropological thinking.[4] The study of human existence will necessarily involve using various perspectives that are irreducible to one another, including the physical and biological, the psychological, the social, and the properly philosophical. In the case of freedom we have a perfect example of precisely this need for a pluralism of perspectives. The reality of economic, civil, and political freedom, for example, can be known through categories of commerce, law, history, and the sociology of knowledge,[5] but none of these considerations settles questions about the inner personal basis of human freedom that psychology explores. Neither the fulsome determinism presumed by biological science in the investigation of embodied human existence nor the epistemologist's logical exclusion of freedom or choice from any of the knowledge that is scientific cognition in the strict sense may abrogate assertions of the reality of human freedom, even though these considerations remain entirely valid within the proper sphere of their disciplines. In short, Jaspers's methodological commitment to as much pluralism as a subject demands reinforces the need for a certain complexity on the present topic. It requires us to make certain distinctions, including the formal sense of freedom that is marked by the presence of knowledge and the absence of coercion, the freedom involved in determining oneself to comply with law, the sense of freedom as a guiding Idea[6] for one's life, and the existential sense of freedom in which one's choices are historically decisive for one's life-course.

The dominant perspective of the second volume of *Philosophie* is the elucidation of human existence, that is, the indirect illumination of what cannot be "objectively conceived" without being destroyed or at least irretrievably altered by the patterns of objective cognition. For the notion of freedom, this means situating one's reflection in the context of the will and boundary situations. Like most thinkers who have ventured to probe freedom, Jaspers acknowledges[7] that pursuit of the quarry by the means of objective research tends, if anything, to lead to denial of freedom on the presupposition that there is always a previous cause to be found. Only in the conscious volitions of the subject who is not being treated as a determinate object of a science that proceeds under the standards of universally valid demonstration and compelling cogency (articulated, for instance, in the discussions of the first volume of *Philosophie)* can one encounter with certainty the reality of freedom.[8] Helpful as it may often be to think of the play of differently directed forces within consciousness, the mechanism intrinsic to this model will ultimately prove unable to discern genuine volition from the involuntary processes in the company of which it dwells within a person: "The will which we call free cannot be directly observed at all; it can only be elucidated by appealing to it, in direct contrast to such objective observation."[9] For this reason the philosophical method most appropriate will be elucidation rather than, say, the experiment and demonstration more typical of the empirical sciences; but there will be need in the second part of this essay to return to consideration of the various senses of "truth" in general and as known by the specialized sciences, for Jaspers clearly regards knowledge as a necessary but not sufficient condition for freedom.[10]

Freedom and the Will

If freedom always exists as a volition, as some form of willing, the attempt to grasp the will empirically may tend to appear as the top rung on a scale of reactions that range from (1) *reflex* movements that happen involuntarily and unconsciously in a mechanically determined fashion as responses to particular stimuli, through (2) the *instinctive and impulsive* actions that manifest a certain striving that is oriented toward various goals and yet remains blind and ignorant of those goals, to (3) what is properly *volition* because it is marked by a genuine consciousness of the end being pursued and the means being selected. Although any choice by the will presupposes the organism's reflex movements and impulsive strivings, volition itself involves deliberation and eventually some choice. It may not be reduced to those reflexes and impulses any more than it may be described wholly in terms of the *motives* at play within one's conscious thought, as if freedom were merely the name for the victory produced by natural necessity in a struggle among motives. "A choice is not the preponderance of a force—for I can decide for the psychologically weakest motive, for the one least affective and impelling."[11] This point is the proper corollary to the claim that knowledge is a necessary condition of freedom: a person cannot choose an option that remains unknown, and yet knowledge of the alternatives (including knowledge of the relative strength of one's motives) does force the will: "*Willkür* does not amount to freedom; but without *Willkür* there is no freedom."[12]

Despite Jaspers's own abiding confidence for certain purposes in the naturalistic explanations offered by the empirical psychology of his medical training, he resists any promissory reductions of the sort which proffer that "more data" will someday explain psychological processes without remainder:

> The direct translation of the will into physical motion [such as a deliberate arm movement] . . . is a fact whose instantaneity is as familiar to us as it is miraculous upon reflection. . . . No matter how many mechanistic and psychological

> causal connections we might discover, this translation would remain a primal fact with which nothing can compare.[13]

Given the immediacy of most instances of our efforts to direct the actions of our bodies, it may only be when we are learning some new skill or perhaps when age, illness, or psychopathology makes us fail to move our limbs as we will that we even consider the instantaneousness with which the will acts upon our bodily being.[14] However long or short the deliberation process may take, choice occurs at some moment, as a kind of timeless instant within the flow of time. Yet, Jaspers insists, our volitional power has a relatively settled structure, noticeable especially in the dispositions acquired by habit slowly over the course of time, such that it operates in certain ways and not in others. So thoroughly integrated do many of our volitional patterns become within the social mechanisms of our communal life and the bodily resonances of our physical being that many actions of a voluntary nature come to seem spontaneous rather than strictly deliberative, and thus they often become more places within us where actual freedom of choice may become manifest but need not.

Although intransigently resistant to philosophies that in any way mechanize the concept of will, Jaspers joins many another philosophical tradition (both the Aristotelian and the Kantian, for instance, would do so) in distinguishing intellect and will: "When my will, my clear sense of purpose, wills a thing, both the thing and the means to it must have been set before me by my intellect."[15] Yet, curiously, even this inner determination of the options presented by what an agent comes to know cannot in principle explain the will as the source of agency: "The will is psychologically incomprehensible, but in uniting purposive and existential clarity it can move me originally because I myself am it. Indirectly it can be elucidated."[16] A crucial aspect of the mystery that resists full comprehension here is that by one's will the human being is self-determining, and with each act of volition the will not only wills some object but "wills itself."[17] This is to say that by whatever one wills, one makes oneself, for better or worse, a little more of the sort of person who wills that sort of object. Likewise, one's freedom is not some "invariable" quantity but "grows along with one's true self-being."[18]

Alert to the difficulties in accounting for the will that had been encountered in the then emerging discipline of psychology, Jaspers directs his own effort at least to describe something that so persistently evades strict definition toward the distinction between "formal will" and "grand will." The formal will names the lower domain of human volition, which is above the level of involuntary processes, but thoroughly informed by what has been presented by the intellect. One's sense of purpose (both the goal and the means thereto) might be quite clear to a person, but always within the immediate limits of cognition as "an orderly channeling of one's psychological forces."[19] But for Jaspers these forces are not yet the real person and the will which we call "free" cannot be directly observed in the way that a psychological observer can at least in principle identify the "finite psychological impulses" that provide the motive power of the formal will (the will as formed by intellectual cognition). For this purpose Jaspers also articulates the notion of a "grand will"—the will as encompassing rather than encompassed. The grand will, he says, is "volition by ideas on the ground of *Existenz*."[20]

Existential Freedom: Real but Indemonstrable

Although questions about our ultimate ends are, strictly speaking, unanswerable for the intellect, human beings still need to deal with the larger questions of purpose and meaning; in doing so, they show themselves to transcend the boundaries in which the objects of formal will are finite and formalized:

> Though we may seek the utmost clarity about our motivations and our ends, this clarity remains encompassed by the font from which the will draws its substantial forces. . . . Not intelligible is the way volition rests on the idea and on *Existenz*. What the actor clearly knows as consciousness at large is complemented—in place of mere darkness at the bounds of self-observation—by the possibility of being clearly sure of himself as *Existenz*: this is what I must do, to be true to myself. This will is psychologically incomprehensible, but in uniting purposive and existential clarity it can move me originally because I myself am it. Indirectly it can be elucidated.[21]

Much of one's ordinary life does little to disclose the depths of the self of which Jaspers speaks here. But "boundary situations" (like the inevitability of death, or the impossibility of living without struggle or suffering), which we can neither comprehend nor avoid,[22] force us to precisely the sort of choices that manifest what Jaspers has called grand will:

> We can avoid the boundary situations only by closing our eyes to them. In the world we seek to preserve our existence by expanding it . . . but in the end we can do nothing but surrender. The meaningful way for us to react to boundary situations is therefore not by planning and calculating to overcome them but by the very different activity of *becoming the Existenz we potentially are*; we become ourselves by entering with open eyes into the boundary situations.[23]

The responses one makes at this level thus constitute the level of authentic existential freedom. For cognition these choices may seem dark and arbitrary, and they do have the character of a "leap" that originates from myself rather than from anything that could ever be cognized as compelling and cogent objective in the terms intelligible to *Bewusstsein überhaupt* (consciousness as such).

Rather, it is these decisions about where to take the course of one's life that are decisive. Because they take place in historically definite situations, each such leap runs the risk of going astray and the person of "suffering shipwreck," but without undertaking such risks the person would never manifest the freedom that is most authentically human, that is, the self-determination of possible *Existenz* that is at the heart of freedom as Jaspers tries to elucidate it. Further, although the corpus of Jaspers's writings always remains noncommittal on questions about the truth of religious claims, he does allow for at least the possibility of a genuine relation to a deity by virtue of another sort of life-determining "leap"—that is, the self-determination that consists on belief or some comparable act of an unconditional nature that brings one into relation with Transcendence.[24]

Now, the assertion of the freedom of the will needs to be distinguished both from the delusion of complete independence championed in some notions of libertarian freedom and from the poor science involved in denials of free will in the name of determinism, whether in its statistical or strictly causal variety.[25] For Jaspers, determinism is simply bad science, inasmuch as it pretends to have the totality of human existence in a scientific grasp, as if it were the case that where scientific comprehension exists, there is no freedom. In fact, genuine science cannot destroy freedom because it does not presume to apprehend the totality of human existence. Only false science, one that mingles the choice of a deterministic stance in philosophy with data derived from the objective cognition of science, would even dream of absolutizing a particular theory of human existence and thus try to destroy freedom. For Jaspers, this is the error of the followers of Marx and Freud, whose genuine scientific comprehension of some things is made into a falsifying absolute.

In the previous case, the tendency is to treat freedom as if it were purely uncaused. If there ever were a demonstration of such a completely arbitrary selection as the spontaneity suggested in the famous story of Buridan's ass,* the argument would for Jaspers prove nothing but "coincidence and license, not

*John Buridan (ca. 1300–after 1358) was a Parisian nominalist and naturalist philosopher. He refers to an ass or donkey that is trapped by the attraction of two bales of hay. The ass cannot decide which bale of hay to eat, and is determined thereby to starvation. Buridan locates the will's freedom in our ability to choose as humans, between alternatives, especially when they are doubtful or uncertain. Jaspers's reference to Buridan entails the idea that freedom is more than mere choice. Freedom is a regulative Idea in Kant's sense.

freedom proper."[26] Rather, genuine freedom needs to be situated somewhere between the spontaneity of voluntarily acting out of one's own essence and the compulsion of acting under coercion, duress, or even fear of threatened force. The experience of deliberate review of one's individual motives and personal reasons for desiring and choosing something do help in the process of elucidation, and yet they still do not show us the will itself as if it were an object. Freedom in the genuine sense is "neither demonstrable nor refutable"[27] theoretically but must be approached indirectly as "an idea" (in the characteristically Jaspersian way of noticing the idea as the "whole" that we "project" to encompass our experience but which we can never strictly "know" as an object).[28]

As in the case of other key "ideas"—such as God, the world, and the idea of freedom that anyone can derive from the variety of motives and experiences that constitutes that person's experience—ideas create an order and a structure for thinking about freedom without having freedom becoming an object in the normal sense of the word "object." By way of example, the awareness that one might have of deciding to bow to a civil or moral law that does not force one's compliance by natural necessity in the same way that, say, the law of gravity invariably does force a physical body to move, can be a stimulus for becoming aware of one's freedom and calling it explicitly by that name. The freedom in which we find ourselves by obeying valid norms is not an object of cognition in the strict sense but rather an idea by which we guide our thinking in the realm of action, where alone freedom can be proven.[29]

Crucial to Jaspers's reasoning in this matter is his sense that the person, the "I," is never a finished totality but always an ego in process, on the way, situated within particular circumstances and at particular times.[30] Hence, he regards the notion of absolute freedom devoid of all restriction as a pure fantasy, as unhelpful to the process of personal maturation since it is unrealistic for the guidance of life. Freedom proves to be something one can lose by inauthenticity as well as something that one can acquire and increase by action and choice. The need to live and to make all sorts of decisions at definite times might at first generate more of a sense of "unfreedom" than of freedom, and yet further reflection permits even the confrontation with mundane limits, not to mention the anxious moments of confrontation with such profound boundary situations as suffering, death, or guilt, to be the occasions of becoming aware of one's "fundamental" (*ursprüngliche*) freedom "because only there do I know myself as my true self."[31] Important as correct calculation is within a deliberative process of rational willing, freedom for Jaspers is not merely the result of the deliberation. It is not mere seeming to decide in a situation in which I can do nothing else but admit the evidence tabulated by calculative reason. Rather, even if what I decide to do is to acquiesce in what reason determines to be the correct result of the weighing of the evidence, "the crux of the choice is that I choose."[32]

While the process of deliberation is thoroughly time-bound, the resolution of the process in the decision that is a choice is different. It has the character of a "leap" that permits us to speak of the "point" or "moment" of decision that determines our course of action thereafter. Fearful as one may prudently be about the demands of any genuine commitment, the inclination to flee from freedom is a sign of inauthenticity, of being untrue to oneself. "It is the essence of phenomenal Existenz in temporal existence that there must be a decision."[33] For Jaspers, freedom as elucidated in this manner is the core from which springs the entire range of phenomena that manifest freedom, from the spontaneity of bodily movement possible in a healthy human organism to the most sophisticated expressions of political liberty and the most subtle forms of friendship and commitment.

THE DIALECTICAL RELATION OF TRUTH AND FREEDOM

Just as freedom has a number of distinct meanings for Jaspers, so does truth. There are some truths that are universally valid, that is, compellingly cogent for any mind whatsoever. Jaspers calls this the sphere of *Bewusstsein überhaupt* or consciousness as such, the domain of objective cognition that is possible for any one who is attentive and sufficiently trained to appreciate the evidence and argument presented. But there are also truths that arise by personal commitment, the truths by which one lives, and this is the sphere of moral life. And there are transcendent truths, the ciphers to which one can at best point but never grasp, truths that encompass us but which our minds in principle can never encompass as objects— the sphere of religion and metaphysics.

The place of freedom in the latter two groups is more readily apparent, for the truths to which we commit ourselves in moral life and in the quest for the transcendent entail by definition a constitutive role for free choice. The freedom of the subject searching for wisdom about how one should conduct oneself and about what is beyond all possible worldly experience is axiomatic. But with respect to compelling and cogent cognition there arises a revealing paradox that actually offers some illumination about the other groups as well. It would seem *prima facie* that the realm of compelling cogency excludes freedom. As Golo Mann puts it: "Perfect comprehensibility logically excludes freedom, that is, choice, or creative decision. If the concept of freedom is nevertheless to be saved, then it is defined as comprehended necessity as Marx has done."[34] Yet, as we have seen above, Jaspers considers and rejects the notion that we can save freedom by reducing it to the acceptance of unavoidable necessity. Even when resignation to the inescapable is the content of a particular free act, he insists that freedom must be elucidated in terms of self-determination and choice. Paradoxically, even in the most objective sphere of truth, there remains a role for freedom, for even there the knower must choose to conform the mind to the objects being known. Upon analysis this choice too is philosophically disclosed to be a kind of willing oneself, that is, a choice that determines oneself to be the sort of person who will be a tough-minded researcher; and yet, one who always remains open to discovering reality as it is rather than, say, the sort of inquirer who insists, for whatever reason (stubbornness, for instance, habit, or reputation) on seeing things in a way that arbitrarily denies or distorts the evidence.

The interdependence of truth and freedom here thus implies a dialectical relationship: each is a necessary condition for the other, but there is a difference in regard to what each gives to the other. Freedom is a necessary condition for the possibility of acquiring the truth of objective knowledge, even as there can be no freedom without knowledge in relation to "otherness" (*Gegenständlichkeit*), for without a basic openness to recognize extra-mental reality as it is without creating, controlling, or altering it, one will never be able to achieve any truths in the sphere of universally valid cognition. But truth is also a necessary condition for freedom in the sense that without knowledge there can be no freedom; for without appreciation of the objective realities within which one is situated, one would not be able to choose and act realistically in the world. This applies not only to the researcher as researcher, but more generally to anyone at all, in the domain of morals, metaphysics, or just in general. For Jaspers this dialectic pervades the very structure of consciousness, since it is precisely the temporality intrinsic to the subjective pole of human being that makes freedom so crucial for even the most rigorous and sound scientific cognition.

For Jaspers, the basic concept of epistemology is the polar relation between subject and object constitutive of all human consciousness. However many forms human thinking can take, all of them exhibit a certain "otherness" with regard to the conscious subject, a certain "unity" (*Einheit*) that the subject gives them, and a certain "generality" (*Allgemeinheit*) developed by the subject in order to deal with the concreteness and particularity received in sensory intuition.[35] Now, Jaspers is ever mindful of the need to respect the abiding differences between the sphere of objective cognition, where the person is primarily receptive to being informed by objects, which the thinker in no way creates, controls, or alters, and the spheres of ethics and metaphysics, where the thinker has to employ, in the one case, practical reason to generate norms of action and value and, in the other, a critical speculative reason to produce symbols for transcendence. Nonetheless, despite the difference in the type of objects with which the subject has a polar relationship, both the moral and the periechontological uses of reason continue to exhibit the fundamental subject-object polarity of all human consciousness. In this way the relation of freedom to truth appears less problematic for ethics and metaphysics, but paradoxical for the realm of objective cognition.

FREEDOM AND THE TRUTH OF OBJECTIVE KNOWLEDGE

In order to appreciate the insight about freedom as a condition for even the truth of objective knowledge, it may prove helpful to explore the ground for the paradox that objective certainty logically excludes choice and yet that freedom is the condition for the possibility of knowledge. Jaspers takes objective knowledge to refer to cognition's most rigorous and advanced form as found in modern science. Hence, if freedom is still present here, it will necessarily be present as well in any lesser case of objective cognition.

One of the relevant factors for Jaspers is the endlessness of science. Although the sciences always remain incomplete owing to the inexhaustibility of the world that they investigate, they are often able to reach sufficient objective knowledge to permit one to claim a distinctive degree of cogency upon the demonstration of some universally valid truth-claim.[36] Thus, the comprehension of the truth possible in science is not a claim to have reached absolute totality, for the process of research is without end. But scientific work is not just a site for freely chosen activity because it is unfinished in principle; it is also a site for freedom because it is necessarily relative to all sorts of free human decisions about the appropriate framework of discussion and inquiry. Even so, truth-claims may be made, for the relativity intrinsic to an open-minded inquirer here does not imply arbitrariness, and careful rigorous work permits the researcher to attain universal validity and compelling cogency.

For Jaspers, the type of cognition typical of rigorous science will embody three characteristic features: (1) deliberate adherence to method, (2) exigent certainty, and (3) validity anyone sufficiently trained in the science can recognize. Needless to say, these traits cannot be expected at every moment of scientific work; the process of discovery, for instance, is much more a matter of art, constructive intuition, and even good luck rather than just method. But even during the process of discovery anyone who wants to think scientifically will display signs of the freedom of self-determination in the consciousness of needing to choose to undertake the discipline of the science out of the desire for knowledge. This will mean undertaking some sort of order and method, including (1) an awareness of the appropriate method needed to gain the knowledge as well as mindfulness of the limits of that method, (2) an appreciation for certainty when that judgment is warranted as well as a sensitivity to uncertainty and to degrees of probability, and (3) an alertness to the standards of general verifiability that give anyone else who cares to investigate the same subject access to one's reasoning.[37] The "exact knowledge" (*Wissen*) that can be attained by the sciences is "binding to the intellect" (*zwingend dem Verstande*) as universally valid. This is to assert that it will prevail on anyone's mind if proper attention is given to the evidence and argument. Now, to arrive at such exigent certainty and thus be warranted in judging a claim as objective knowledge in the strict sense, the intellect must obtain its conclusions with a degree of cogency such that no one is any longer free to reject it for private reasons. To reject it would require a scientific demonstration just as forceful as the proof that has been provided, judged by the same standards. Acceptance of the claim would imply that a given proposition has to be admitted because of the evidence and argument mustered.

Now the emphasis here is on the objective and impersonal standards of scientific rationality that generate the paradox. How can the subject-knower (whose freedom can only begin to be elucidated by reference to the spontaneity and indeterminateness that are at the grounds of choice and self-determination) ever be the source of claims to universal validity and compelling cogency? While there are various nonrational components involved in the process of scientific discovery (including feeling, intuition, and good luck in one's experiments), these factors are not, as such, what permits the claim of having achieved objective truth. A strong truth-claim presupposes a mind able to recognize and represent in intellectual terms how the world outside the mind necessarily acts. Granted, there is a choice on the part of the subject to have pursued the truth about some part of the world and this choice has brought the scientist to do the work that has resulted in cognition that is independent of one's personal preferences, feelings, and beliefs. The truth-claims made for objective knowledge imply the conviction that one has attained a sufficiently compelling rigor of argument that no one adequately prepared to follow the argument could honestly dissent.

At various places in his work Jaspers insists that the subjective contribution to such knowledge is not limited to the pre-demonstrative moment of science, that is, not confined to such factors as one's motivation for beginning the research or carrying on despite obstacles and weariness so as to bring it to its conclusion. Rather, Jaspers testifies to the ongoing role of volition in all cognition, for instance, in this passage from *Von der Wahrheit*:

> One might suppose that thinking cognition is exhausted in the recognition of valid propositions, that one observes a timeless constant in a temporal process. Such attentiveness is supposed to be knowledge. But cognition is always more. It is a doing, and this doing is led by a will. Cognition is related to actuality through the content of the activity which is its vehicle. Attentiveness and having knowledge are, admittedly, one moment of cognition, but the whole of cognition which takes hold of truth is encompassing activity.[38]

This is to take notice of both the active and the receptive aspects of intellect. In cognition the mind grasps what is constant amid the flow of change and preserves what it has managed to grasp. But the retention of concepts and propositions is merely one aspect of the will-infused activity of cognition.[39] For Jaspers, temporality is a crucial aspect of knowing, for scientific knowing is thoroughly temporal, as objective knowledge, as method, and as discipline. It is not merely that science is psychologically temporal because scientists are persons in time, but that even science as objective knowledge is marked by an intrinsic temporality. While the freedom of the subject does not guarantee the truth of any truth-claim, it is the free exercise of the power of choice to be the sort of subject who is open to being conformed to reality as it is that makes the truth of objective cognition, even in science, its most rigorous form, possible. The free will of the knower is intrinsically temporal and thereby is a condition for the truth of the objective claims made in any science.

In his various writings on the objective cognition characteristic of science, Jaspers is intent on displaying the temporality intrinsic to the object as well as the subject. The search for trans-temporal laws that govern the changes studied in any particular area of science aims at the patterns of invariance behind all the temporal fluctuations of the particular objects studied and of the person making these studies. In order to validate a scientific claim, one must thus take into account all the intrinsic temporality within the objects studied in order to find a nontautological basis for the claims of science. If the only invariance were to derive from the mind of the subject, scientific claims would ultimately be tautological. But the truth-claims made by science avoid such tautology if there is a basis in the objects investigated. Jaspers's recognition of the receptive capacity of the mind to discover the structure of objects is evident in his account of the objects of *Bewusstsein überhaupt* (consciousness as such), namely, that which can become evident to any intelligence whatsoever, provided only that the inquirer has the same evidence, a sufficient background, and the ready attentiveness to consider the problem.

The ways in which temporality can figure into a scientific problem are theoretically endless and range from the variations in the data studied through the process of growth typical of the investigator to the communal understanding of what constitutes a scientific theory or an adequate demonstration. In this way time can be an integral aspect of what the scientist chooses as a suitable problem[40] and what the individual researcher observes; and yet, scientific theories and laws dealing with the prediction and measurement of time-dependent phenomena are no less objective for that, since the theoretical structures and concepts that the scientist uses transforms the time-dependent features of the world[41] into laws and theories that are structurally trans-temporal. But there is also the factor of change that occurs within the scientist, whether in what a given individual comes to accept as true or false, or in what that individual comes to regard as acceptable scientific procedure.[42] This is to note that the concepts and judgments which a scientist uses have a stability, a fixedness, when considered in themselves, and this invariant structure is what makes them potentially falsifiable; but what readily changes is the use that scientists make of these concepts and judgments, and sometimes even the methods that constitute a given discipline, for example, when new formalisms are introduced. For Jaspers, this implies a dialectic between facts and theories that reflects the intrinsic temporality of science and thus the pervasive influence of freedom in coming to the truths of objective cognition:

> Once we possess a fact of natural science, or a document, or monument of the intellectual sciences, it may acquire a vast new import; but we can no longer get around it. . . . Yet facts need to be determined. What makes them accessible is not pure sense perception but *reflective apperception*. Consciousness of the method in which we bring them to mind is the critical test of whether, and in what sense, they are factual. . . . The blind compulsion of facts as random contents of perception leads *ad infinitum*. To be of interest, the fact must have significance. The relevance, and largely even the discovery, of facts, depends on *theories*, on mental structures of connections and entireties. A theory is cogent if the facts bear it out. The more heterogeneity it unifies without being contradicted by a fact, the more compelling its truth. But it can never be definitive. . . . In regard to facts, therefore, cogency in empirical science is tied to theory, and in regard to theory, to facts.[43]

Jaspers's central assertion is the need for scientific awareness of the limitations on cogency in a given discipline; but in passing his comments on the temporality of the processes involved, he discloses the freedom of the scientist to appraise new data, new and old theories, and the reliability of methods in the efforts to determine reliability and objectivity. The changes that come about in science over the course of time in this way bear witness to the place of freedom in the scientist as crucial to the very possibility of advancing cogent nonsubjective truth-claims.

The interaction of the scientist with the community of research may well produce an increasingly profound sense that what had previously been assumed to have been known without presuppositions in a given discipline needs to be examined. Jaspers points to this phenomenon when speaking of the limits of cogency:

> When cogent empirical knowledge anticipates an individual reality, the endlessness of possible factors will always make it uncertain. Coincidence may interfere with predictions and technological productions, and even the most irrefutable astronomical calculations apply only with a probability great enough to be counted a practical certainty. From there we can move gradually down to predictions in which antithetical possibilities strike a balance. There is no field in which we can control reality with absolute certainty, as a perfect mechanism.[44]

Further, for Jaspers, one of the fundamental dispositions required in the scientist is the conscious relativizing of perspective, a condition that he identifies at the very start of his account of world-orientation in the first volume of *Philosophie*:

> By way of research, of knowledge, I try to free myself from *my* world so as to find *the* world. . . . Having taken the step from the particular and accidental world of my individual existence, having set out to overcome and discover the one world, I am still always occupying a particular "standpoint." Only the change in standpoints will relativize every previous one, and finally, every one. It is only relatively, by *a universal mobility of standpoints*, that I can free myself from the standpoint of a specific mundane being; it can never be done absolutely, as by reaching a *standpoint outside* as the only true one.[45]

The relativism Jaspers espouses here is not some universal arbitrariness, for it is precisely the objective structures of beings that make science possible. Rather, the method of relativizing one's perspective that is asserted aims to escape the absolutizing of any particular, limited point of view as if it were an encompassing and comprehensive view of the totality. For our present purpose, the significance of this stance lies in the decisive role played by the will in deliberately choosing to vary one's outlook. An intentional flexibility of this sort is for Jaspers only possible by the thoroughgoing penetration of the will to know in every instance of objective cognition.

In summary, Jaspers's reflections on the pervasiveness of temporality in objective cognition, such as is found in even the most rigorous science, testifies to the freedom that is a condition for the possibility of truth, which is in turn the goal of the freedom with which a scientist pursues work in any given discipline. Although the aspect of science most highly prized is properly an objective knowledge that bears the marks of necessity and universal cogency, temporality is indispensable to its acquisition but does not mar this objectivity.[46] While the truth of a proposition that expresses some objective knowledge depends on the conformity with reality in such a way as to be objectively verifiable for any intellect with enough training to appreciate the evidence and argument, the proposition ultimately has no existence apart from living minds, whose very structure requires a polar relationship between subject and object for consciousness. The temporality that the subjective pole introduces into scientific knowledge means in turn that there is an inescapable but methodologically controlled presence of human free choice at the heart of even the most rigorous scientific endeavor:

> In taking up the pure object we would always *abstract from something else*, from something we had to eliminate so as to come to generally valid truth. . . . Timeless are the structures of consciousness as such, the form of identity and of contradiction, the categories. . . . There is need for the actuality of motive, of interest, of will, for this cognition to occur in time; a choice is thereby stipulated as well as an emphasis for the temporal matrix, but the meaning is timeless.[47]

In this way there is no escape from the compelling rigor of the conclusion and one has objective knowledge, for the universally valid demonstrations of science cannot be denied. But in another sense even the recognition of generally valid truths requires the free assent of the mind, not in an uncontrolled sense of freedom by which one person could arbitrarily decide to allow or to ignore the conclusions reached by another, but a tempered sense of freedom in which the knower is abiding by a prior and ongoing choice to accept certain standards of cogency, rigor, and meaning.

Conclusions

The dialectical relation of truth and freedom that Jaspers describes has sweeping implications for all branches of human thinking. Appreciating the comprehensive range of its applicability is consonant with Jaspers's basic project of shifting questions about the meaning of being to questions about the meaning of being for us.

When philosophy attempts to understand the reality of human freedom, it must factor in knowledge and truth or else one will not yet have risen to the properly human sphere of volition and deliberate choice. When we attempt to grasp the significance of claiming to know the truth about some object, let alone when committing ourselves to a truth by which we want to live or contemplating truths beyond the scope of our understanding, we need to take into account such factors as will and free choice. Invariably Jaspers's attempts to take stock of this dialectic bring him to connect both the subjectivity of *Existenz* and the commitment to remaining open to being changed by reality with the possibility of objectivity in our cognition, as in this passage from *Von der Wahrheit*:

> Knowledge is related to reality and is itself real only through the fact that I will something in it. In knowledge, a will fulfills itself; but this will is a manifold one, for example. . . . *I will to become I myself.* The reality of thinking is an inner action, in which I come to myself and determine myself. I am as thinker, not separated from that which I become, but identical with it. The object is not the known thing, as thinking, but in thinking the objects, I am brought to myself, I cognize myself not as object but in the embodiment of myself. . . . *I will to become aware of the being which really exists.* The reality of thinking is that which in thinking assures itself of being itself.[48]

In the first case Jaspers analyzes the motive of the knower in terms of the intention to become more completely actual as knower, and does this by producing an adequate mental representation of those aspects of the world under consideration. Yet, in the course of achieving this, the knower incorporates the object into the intellect and produces a significant change in the mind itself. But here Jaspers detects a willed restraint, for if the knower were to allow already operative categories or personal predilections to dominate, the other that is being investigated would be altered or destroyed and the knower would defeat the project of becoming truthfully altered by the object; all the knower would end up knowing is some aspect of the mind that started the process.

On the other hand, the recognition that even the most rigorous of knowers are constantly involved in choosing is not a superficial observation about the practicalities of, say, a scientific process, but a genuine measure of respect for creativity in science. Whether one adverts to the hypothetical assumption of various ideas or theories, the tentative rejection of others, the selection of certain data as relevant, or even whether a given difficulty is worth one's trouble investigating, the endless decision-making turns out to be substantially significant for the methodological control over endlessness required by objective cognition. The precise significance of this recognition for science is that the concepts and judgments of science are not merely acts of intellect alone, as if one could blindly follow the ruts and grooves of the trail of compelling cogency, but are also genuine and appropriate contributions of the will and its power to accept and reject.[49]

The freedom that Jaspers found to be involved in science is not pure randomness or arbitrary choice, or the haphazard quality that might be suggested by unmotivated or purposeless behavior. The extremely purposeful work of any objective cognition, but of science in particular, bespeaks a sense of freedom as personal goal-directedness that is operative even when the answers (and sometimes even the precise problems) may not yet be clear. In this way the crucial contribution of freedom can be recognized not only at the start of inquiry and during the process but even in the accomplished result, for then the errors and the correct choices will be clearer by virtue of hindsight about what was selected in accord with truth and what with prejudice or ignorance.

The dialectic also cuts in the opposite direction. Truth is also a condition for freedom, and the effort to gain a philosophically adequate conception of truth requires that one have genuine knowledge about human existence as well as a self-critical appreciation of the limits of knowledge. The human being is always more than anyone knows about one's own mind, motives, or condition, and this "more" is an indication of human freedom. It is impossible to make the totality of a human being the object of empirical research; only partial aspects of any human existence can be successfully objectified. Yet, even partial comprehension can cause significant change in the one who achieves such knowledge, for freedom depends on such knowledge even though it cannot be reduced to such knowledge. For Jaspers, freedom then is not an object of empirical research so much as a matter of philosophical faith. Science neither confirms nor refutes its reality. But freedom can come to appear for us through reflection on science, that is, through reflection on the process of confronting endlessness of the scientific process in the steady steps toward objective cognition.

Notes

1. Karl Jaspers, *Psychologie der Weltanschauungen* [1919], 6th edited by Berlin: Springer Verlag 1971). [Hereafter cited as PSW.] *Von der Wahrheit* (München: R. Piper & Co., 1947). [Hereafter cited as VdW.] "Philosophie und Wissenschaft" (1948) appears in *Rechenschaft und Ausblick, Reden und Aufsätze*, 2nd ed. (München: R. Piper Verlag, 1958), pp. 204-20; *Philosophie* (1932), 3 vols., 3rd ed. (Berlin: Springer Verlag, 1956). [Hereafter cited as P 1, 2, 3.] German edition translation by E. B. Ashton as *Philosophy*, 3 vols. Chicago: University of Chicago Press, 1969-71). [Hereafter cited as Ph 1, 2, 3.]

2. Elisabeth Young-Bruehl, *Freedom and Karl Jaspers's Philosophy* (New Haven: Yale University Press, 1981); Sebastian Samay, *Reason Revisited: The Philosophy of Karl Jaspers* (Notre Dame: University of Notre Dame Press, 1971).

3. See Gregory J. Walters, "Human Rights, World Philosophy, and the Quest for

Global Solidarity: Karl Jaspers's Abiding Contribution," *Jahrbuch der Österreichischen Karl Jaspers Gesellschaft/Yearbook of the Austrian Karl Jaspers Society*, Studien Verlag Innsbruck-Wien, Herausgegeben von Elisabeth Salamun-Hybašek und Kurt Salamun Jahrgang/Annual, Vol. 10 (1997), pp. 127–50 and, *idem.*, "Is a Global Human Rights Community Possible?" Feature Review Essay: *Confucianism and Human Rights*, edited by Wm. Theodore de Bary and Tu Weiming (New York: Columbia University Press, 1998), *International Philosophical Quarterly*, Vol. XXXIX, No. 2, Issue No.154 (1999), pp. 209–15.

4. See the selection on methodology from his *General Psychopathology* in *Karl Jaspers: Basic Philosophical Writings, Selections*, edited, translated, and with introduction by Edith Ehrlich, Leonard H. Ehrlich, and George B. Pepper (Athens, OH: Ohio University Press, 1986), pp. 8-20.

5. See P 2, p. 166; Ph 2, p. 147. One of Jaspers's more telling analyses of political freedom can be found in *Vom Ursprung und Ziel der Geschichte*, 4th ed. (München: R. Piper Verlag, 1966 [1949]), p. 89; English translation of Michael Bullock, *The Origin and Goal of History* (New Haven: Yale University Press, 1953), p. 62. On pages 205–17ff. in the German edition and pages 160-170 in the English translation, Jaspers lists sixteen chief characteristics of political freedom.

6. Professor Koterski uses the upper case letter "I" in reference to Jaspers's (Kantian) conception of "Idea," e.g., as in Jaspers's reference to the idea of freedom, the idea of a university, the idea of democracy, etc. We have retained the author's use throughout [eds.].

7. P 2, p. 163; Ph 2, p. 153.

8. The burden of much of the first volume of *Philosophie* is to present the structure of thinking in the realm of world-orientation. The assumption of a world causally regulated to the last detail is required for the very possibility of factual cognition—there can be no generally valid, objective truth-claims unless one can know mundane being under laws. For Jaspers's assessment of the inadequacy of approaching freedom by consideration of the unresolved "remainder" that appears at the bounds of universally valid cognition. See P 2, pp. 188–91; Ph 2, pp. 164–67.

9. See Ph 2, p. 156; P 2, p. 177: "Knowledge does not make me free as yet, but without knowledge there is no freedom."

10. Ph 2, p. 140; P 2, p. 157.

11. Ph 2, p. 134; P 2, p. 151. See also, PSW, pp. 330 ff.

12. Ph 2, p. 136; P 2, p. 153.

13. P 2, p. 155; Ph 2, p. 138.

14. Paralysis and even arthritis can be among the "boundary situations" that contribute to self-understanding, like the more profound and decisive boundary situations of death and guilt discussed in chapter 7 of P 2, pp. 201–54; Ph 2, pp. 177–222. See also the lengthy discussion of the topic in PSW, pp. 221–80.

15. Ph 2, p. 140; P 2, p. 158.

16. Ph 2, p. 141; P 2, p. 158.

17. Ph 2, p. 133; P 2, p. 149.

18. Ph 2, p. 154; P 2, p. 175 and Ph 2, pp. 160–61; P 2, pp. 182–83: "To realize myself, I leave possibilities behind. From the emptiness of the rich world that might be, I step into the abundance of a world that is poor compared with the other, but that becomes real and is sustained by self-being."

19. Ph 2, p. 139; P 2, p. 157.

20. Ph 2, p. 141; P 2, p. 159.

21. Ph 2, pp. 140–41; P 2, p. 158.

22. Within his *Philosophy* Jaspers treats the topic in chapter 7 Ph 2, pp. 177–222; P 2: pp. 201–54. [A thematic approach to "boundary situations" may be found in the essay by Kurt Salamun herein, eds.]

23. Ph 2, p. 179; P 2, p. 204.

24. See the brief discussion of this point at Ph 2, pp. 273–79; P 2, pp. 314–20. This is also the topic of the entire third volume of *Philosophy*, as well as of volumes such as *The Perennial Scope of Philosophy* and *Philosophical Faith and Revelation.*

25. See Ph 2, p. 149; P 2, p. 169: "Cogent insight has long shown, however, that statistical laws do not disprove individual freedom. The individual does not take his own life because of a statistical law, no more than he dies of cancer because of the statistical law."

26. Ph 2, p. 145; P 2, p. 164.

27. Ph 2, 1p. 50; P 2, p. 169.

28. Jaspers provides an account of his own version of the Kantian doctrine of ideas in the Appendix to *Psychologie der Weltanschauungen*, pp. 465–86. See also my article, "Jaspers on Realism and Idealism," *Jahrbuch der Österreichischen Karl Jaspers Gesellschaft* (*Yearbook of the Austrian Karl Jaspers Society*) vol. 11 (1998), pp. 58–69.

29. See P 2, p. 176; Ph 2, p. 155: "Freedom is proved by my actions, not by my insight. My concern with its being includes the activity I realize it in." See also P 2, p. 191; Ph 2, p. 167.

30. P 2, pp. 193–94; Ph 2, pp. 169–70.

31. See P 2, p. 180; Ph 2, p. 158. For the discussion of particular boundary situations, see chapter 7 of *Philosophie*.

32. P 2, p. 180; Ph 2, p. 158.

33. Ph 2, p. 161; P 2, p. 184.

34. Golo Mann, "Freedom and the Social Sciences in Jaspers's Thought," in *The Philosophy of Karl Jaspers,* The Library of Living Philosophers, edited by Paul Arthur Schilpp (LaSalle, IL: Open Court, 1957), p. 551.

35. See P 1, pp. 6–13; Ph 1, pp. 49–54, and VdW, pp. 231–33.

36. See Jaspers, "Philosophie und Wissenschaft," p. 216. See also Jaspers's essay "Wahrheit und Wissenschaft" (1960) in *Philosophische Aufsätze* (Frankfurt: Fischer Bücherei, 1967), pp. 62-67; this essay appears translated by Don Travis Jr. as "Truth and Science" in *The Graduate Journal*, vol. 5, no.1 (1962), pp. 24–42.

37. See Jaspers, "Wahrheit und Wissenschaft," pp. 62–63; VdW, pp. 67ff., and P 1, pp. 89–94; Ph 1, pp. 123–27.

38. Jaspers, VdW, p. 308.

39. See Karl Jaspers, *Vernunft und Existenz*, 3rd ed. (München: R. Piper Verlag, 1973 [1935]), pp. 47–58.

40. Jaspers discusses the choices a scientist makes as regards a suitably isolated problem in VdW, p. 26. See also, Karl Jaspers, *Die Idee der Universität* (*The Idea of the University*) (Berlin: Springer Verlag, 1946), p. 23.

41. For Jaspers, even the "world" is an idea we construct, and he has a healthy sense of the changes that take place by virtue of the cognitive restructuring that from time to time takes place in the scientific understanding of the "world," which the sciences are trying to explain. See especially, P 1, pp. 61–84.

42. See Jaspers's *Die Geistige Situation der Zeit* (*Man in the Modern Age*) 9th ed. (Berlin: Walter de Gruyter, 1955 [1931]), pp. 160–61.

43. Ph 1, pp. 124–25; P 1, pp. 90–91.

44. P 1, p. 125; Ph 1, p. 91.

45. Ph 1, pp. 104–105; P 1, pp. 67–68.

46. See P 1, pp. 85–86; Ph 1, pp. 120–21.

47. Ph 1, p. 121; P 1, p. 87.

48. VdW, pp. 308–309.

49. One can see this theme very clearly in the biographical studies Jaspers did of Leonardo da Vinci, René Descartes, and Max Weber, printed in *Descartes und die Philosophie*, 2nd ed. (Berlin: Walter de Gruyter, 1948 [1947]).

DARING TO LIVE OUT OF UNCERTAINTY

KARL JASPERS ON PHILOSOPHIC FAITH, TRANSCENDENCE, AND CIPHERS

Andreas Cesana*

Karl Jaspers's last great work, *Philosophical Faith and Revelation*, appeared in late fall of 1962 just a few months before his eightieth birthday. We may be justified in calling it his most perfect work, the sum and legacy of his thinking. At the height of international recognition and in his certainty that—according to a phrase by Heidegger—his "thinking has endowed a resting place for contemplation."[1] Jaspers summarizes his fundamental philosophical position and succinctly delineates his position in a much more pronounced manner than in his previous publications. The book constitutes an intellectual provocation: It informs the "man of the present" that he will become "truly human [only] in philosophizing."[2] It deals with the sciences, which he accuses of overrating their cognitive abilities in a manner akin to superstition, of being blind to the existential dimension of being-human, and of engaging in an "obfuscation" of what is essential in existence. The book treats the Christian faith in revelation, which is rebuked for distancing itself more and more from the substance of biblical faith and for absolutizing its position. Ultimately, the book establishes philosophic faith as the third modern cultural and educational force next to science and religion. Jaspers is convinced that in the present situation only philosophic faith—and not faith in revelation—is in a position to create the one basis for mutual understanding on which people from all directions of faith can meet, world-wide, in meaningful encounters.

Even though this book presents itself as surprisingly up-to-date and provocative, it essentially does not contain a single basic idea that Jaspers had not already developed in his earlier publications. This last book also confirms the astonishing

*Translated by Edith Ehrlich.

unity and consistency of Jaspers's philosophy. It centers around a great basic idea that is developed in all directions as his work progresses. This basic idea can be summarized as follows: The process of modernity has brought about a crisis of orientation and thereby essentially altered the existential situation. Jaspers stresses three reasons that are primarily responsible for the present crisis of orientation: The first concerns the sciences, whose knowledge has failed in regard to all questions of philosophical-existential relevance. The second concerns the religions, which have, to a large extent, lost their former function of bringing order in an increasingly secularized world. The third concerns philosophy itself, which has failed up to now to assert its own destiny by consciously separating itself from science and religion. In light of the existential failure of religion and science, philosophy, according to Jaspers, must again take upon itself the task of bringing to mind those dimensions that support life, and illuminate and guide action in personal existence as well as in the socio-political arena.

The character of Jaspers's early work *Psychologie der Weltanschauungen* was already determined by his consciousness of that task. According to his own statement, it constituted "the earliest writing of the—later so designated—modern Existenz-philosophy."[3] In this book, published in 1919, Jaspers is concerned about bringing to light possible beliefs, attitudes, and images of the world. Such a psychology no longer means to be merely an empirical determination of facts; rather, it means to serve, by way of clarification of the possibilities of being-human, as a means of orientation for contemplation about oneself. Mood and message of this work anticipate the leitmotifs of his three-volume *Philosophie* (1932) in which Jaspers develops and states precisely and systematically his philosophical position, all the while demarcating it from the scientific claim to knowledge and the religious claim to truth: There exists a genuine philosophical form of rationality, that is, a thinking that neither is intersubjectively valid in the sense of scientific rationality, nor arrives at objective knowledge, but claims to be true in an existential sense. This thinking does not produce any knowledge because it serves the purpose of self-assurance and aims at personal certainty; but this thinking is capable of more than knowledge because it affects the thinker himself.

The process of self-assurance, in the sense of a movement of thought that—faced with conflicting possible insights, leads to a certainty that is personal—presupposes the experience of the foundering of all attempts at finding, in the realm of genuinely philosophical questions, an objective starting point. It is precisely this experience of shipwreck that brings about the consciousness of existential freedom and independence. In the course of thinking I become aware that in the end it is my free decision how I judge and how I respond. It is a matter of the insight that at the end—but only at the end—something depends on me and solely on me. It is precisely this consciousness of existential freedom that allows for the realization of that possibility, which Jaspers presents to us as the ideal of being-human. He is speaking about the person who determines himself and who, in the process of his "self-realization"[4] and "finding himself" arrives, out of objective uncertainty, at his personal certainty.

An instance of open, critical, and independent thinking leads inevitably to the loss of ultimate foundations and to the dissolution of absolute certainties. In this sense shipwreck is immanent to all philosophical thinking. But such foundering is, at the same time, an act of self-liberation and of overcoming illusionary wishful thinking. Illusions are simulations of false realities, they are deceptions that mislead our perception of factualities. Our thinking must make an effort in order not to be deceived any longer. Not to let oneself be lied to any more, requires a decision on our part. Existenz-philosophy, in Karl Jaspers's sense, is grounded in such a decision.

Philosophic Faith

On April 19, 1947, Karl Jaspers wrote to Hannah Arendt that he had accepted an invitation of the University of Basel, Switzerland, for six guest lectures and, of course, would have to try to present something new. He was considering the topic of "philosophic faith,"—and then added, doubtfully and reluctantly: ". . . or does this sound inherently impossible?"[5] He was right in asking this question for tying together "philosophy" and "faith" seems, at first glance, to be contradictory in itself, an oxymoron: How is it possible for philosophy, the embodiment of rational cognition, to be combined with faith?

The six lectures, which Jaspers presented in July of 1947 at the University of Basel, have been published under the title *Der philosophische Glaube* (*The Perennial Scope of Philosophy*). The title establishes a new philosophical term. However, as one reads the book one soon becomes aware of the fact that Jaspers does not designate something new with this novel concept. His concern is not to found a new form of thinking but to return to a way of philosophizing that, according to his understanding, has always been present but had passed into oblivion in the process of modernity, or rather had been pushed aside by a scientific philosophy.

Jaspers makes use of the provocative concept of philosophic faith in order, on the one side, sharply to delimit philosophy from all science, and on the other, to call attention to the originary and authentic nature of philosophical thought:

From the very beginning philosophy has had its fundament in faith and not in knowledge. Faith does not possess the status of a knowledge that I can possess, have control over, or pass on. Rather, faith is the certainty that leads me personally.[6] Faith cannot be forced by knowledge or insight, it cannot be determined with finality, nor can it be imparted directly. Truth in the philosophic sense, that is, truth out of which I live, also cannot be forced through knowledge. In distinction from scientific knowledge of finite things, philosophic thought achieves the certainty of truth without ever being able to prove it. The character of the truth of faith and that of science are substantially different. Science is directed toward objects in the world, philosophy aims at the "origin out of which I live."[7]

Philosophic certainty of truth is a characteristic of faith. Philosophizing, if it is to lead to personal certainty at all, ends in faith, in philosophic faith, and this is true from the very beginnings of philosophic thinking, throughout the centuries and the diversity of cultures. As Jaspers sees it, there is a wide-ranging correspondence between his understanding of philosophy and philosophical tradition, indeed with the *philosophia perennis* altogether; and this explains why he did not hesitate accepting the title suggested by the publisher for the English translation of *Der philosophische Glaube* (*The Perennial Scope of Philosophy*). While this title is not unsuited to the actual content of the little volume, it blunts the point of the actual intention and renders harmless the audacity of the original title.

Jaspers explained the singular nature of philosophic faith and its difference from scientific knowledge by comparing Giordano Bruno and Galileo. Bruno believed, Galileo knew. True, their objective situation was the same, for both were haled before the Inquisition and, threatened with the death penalty, urged to recant their teachings. Bruno, however, did not recant and was condemned to death. Galileo recanted. Both acted rationally, for Bruno defended a truth that was grounded in his faith, whereas Galileo sacrificed a truth having the status of scientific knowledge. Obviously there is truth that suffers by being recanted and thus becomes untrue, and there is truth that does not lose anything of its verity by retraction. The first is the truth out of which I live and which has absolute validity for me; the second is truth whose universal validity is independent of me. To die for such a truth that, in the last analysis, is merely an objective correctness, would be inappropriate. Jaspers's admiration for Bruno and his sacrificial death,[8] for his naturalist philosophical convictions, express at the same time his admiration for a certain possibility of being-human: the possibility to be oneself and to actualize one's Existenz. It is the risk to live—and to die—out of oneself, that is, out of factual uncertainty, and yet out of one's own philosophic certainty of faith. Here philosophy becomes religion, as it were, here philosophic insight becomes faith. And, with great consistency, Jaspers celebrates Giordano Bruno as "the great martyr of modern philosophy, a greater hero than any Christian martyr, since he had to hold out solely on the strength of philosophical faith, without either the assurance of revelation or the community of a church, but standing alone before God."[9]

Philosophy, as Karl Jaspers understood it, is meant to be something totally different from science. At the same time philosophy is substantially different from all theology. The man of modernity thus finds himself in a field of tension determined by philosophy, science and theology. Bruno, Galilei, and the Church that brought them before the tribunal of the Inquisition represent these three powers. The same pattern of three components is repeated in the triad of philosophic faith (i.e., faith of reason), knowledge (i.e., cognition effected by the understanding) and religion (i.e., faith of revelation).[10]

Philosophic Faith versus Science

One expects from the empirical sciences—and rightly so—that they produce, within the framework of their limitations, cogent and universally valid knowledge. Precisely for this reason they remain confined to the area of particular, partial knowledge. They have no answers to questions of value and meaning because such questions lead beyond what is objectively knowable. Therefore science can not offer life goals to society or to the individual. It does not hand down any knowledge out of which one could live. It can not carry out determinations of meaning. Convictions out of which one lives, and scientifically grounded knowledge belong to different spheres. Confusing the two realms that are so different in their nature is bound to lead to error. Precisely this confusion, however, is characteristic of the concept of rationality as it was established during the era of Enlightenment, and has remained effective down to our present time. It is characterized by the confidence of being able to render actuality by means of a system of unequivocal and exact concepts. Precisely in this self-certainty this conception of reason shows itself as unenlightened.

However, the idea of Enlightenment, as Kant emphasizes, is inseparably tied to the idea of "critique."[11] Consequently it was unavoidable that the critical program of the Enlightenment would turn against its own presuppositions and question the uncritically applied concept of reason. In Kant's project of a self-critique of reason we discern—in the words of Georg Picht—the "enlightenment about the Enlightenment," which can be called, as it were, "Enlightenment to the second degree."[12] In it, reason became aware of its boundaries. This reason, aware of itself, established novel ways of thinking. The critical way of thinking projected by Kant constitutes a third, quasi-middle possibility between the alternatives of skepticism and metaphysical dogmatism. If we apply Kant's attempt, which in the history of thought was based on the situation of his own time, to the situation today, we quickly realize that any claim of a form of rational thought specific to philosophy is now a matter of opening up a sphere of competence of its own, and in this way overcoming the unsatisfactory alternatives of scientific cognition and a religious-dogmatic faith.

Who among the classical philosophers of the twentieth century has transposed Kant's attempt more decisively and with greater consistency into the present situation of thought than Karl Jaspers?

Jaspers is a Kantian. A cursory look at Kant lets Jaspers's basic position emerge all the more clearly. Philosophy goes beyond the limits of what we can know. It presents arguments in favor of positions and convictions using rationalistic means without being able to reduce them to a basis of empirical-objective cogencies. Since philosophy goes beyond the realm of what can be grasped scientifically, its ultimate basis is found not in knowledge but in faith. In his essay "Was heisst: sich im Denken orientieren?" ("What Does It Mean to Orient Oneself in Thought?") Kant coins the concept "*Vernunftglaube*" (faith of reason) for this genuinely philosophical form of cognition.[13]

The term "faith of reason" makes it possible for Kant to draw attention to some essential characteristics of philosophical cognition based on pure reason:[14] (1.) Faith of reason is characterized by the fact that it refers to no data other than those contained in pure reason. Hence it is a question of a faith that is legitimized by means of rational arguments, but not by empirical, i.e., objective reasons. (2.) Like any other faith, faith of reason is a considering-to-be-true that is subjectively adequate, but objectively inadequate. (3.) Faith of reason, hence, is the opposite of knowledge. (4.) Since the reasons for considering something to be true are not objectively valid, no exertion of thinking can ever turn the faith of reason into knowledge. (5.) Kant calls the faith of reason a "postulate of reason." This does not mean that it is a matter of insights that are capable of satisfying all criteria of certainty; rather, it means to tell us that considering something to be "true" is in no way inferior in degree to any "knowledge," even though it is totally different from it in its very nature.

Jaspers's immediate connection to Kant is evident. The conception of philosophic faith has its direct antecedent in Kant's conception of the faith of reason. Both conceptions of faith proceed from the insight that the reach of the capacity of objective knowledge, which can never go beyond the world of appearances, is fundamentally limited. If the power of scientific cognition were also to cover the realm of the normative, of meaning, and of what is fundamentally significant, then faith would be overcome. But this dimension is closed to the reach of scientific knowledge; and this insight lends a new dignity to faith, as expressed in the well-known dictum in the preamble to the second edition of the *Critique of Pure Reason*: "Hence I had to suspend (or 'restrict': *aufheben*) *knowledge* in order to make room for *faith*. . . ."[15]

Philosophic Faith versus Religion and the Faith in Revelation

Philosophy does not possess any absolute foundations and is, therefore, dependent time and again on premises that can no longer be substantiated by knowledge, but can only be appropriated by faith. In this way philosophic faith separates itself decisively and critically from religious faith, for in distinction from the latter, it does not know any revelation and contains neither creeds nor dogmas nor definite contents. Religions teach as objective actualities what, from the standpoint of philosophy, possess merely the function of existentially effective images and parables. Philosophic faith disassociates itself from the error made by religion, namely to confuse what is merely imagery and parable with objective reality. This confusion, as well as the obedience to faith demanded by religion, result in their endangering precisely that which is important to philosophical reflection: self-determination on the basis of discussion carried on by rationalistic means. Philosophy and religion share the consciousness of having to believe, but do not share the contents of faith.

Faith is the authority that guides us through life, that gives us support in the personal sphere, by which each of us, as an individual, orients himself. This is true for philosophic as well as religious faith. The essential difference between philosophic faith and religious faith lies in the faith of religion having precisely determinable contents. It possesses a canon of tenets that can be taught and learned. Philosophic faith, on the other hand, cannot turn into a confession of faith. The movement of thought cannot be rigidified into a dogma. It does not proceed to a firm footing on an objective certainty because it only makes use of its concepts, propositions, and methods without subjugating itself to them. According to its substance it is purely and simply historic and cannot be fixated in the universal propositions in which it expresses itself.

Faith belongs to being human. "Every human being needs a grounding in faith for everything that he is serious about."[16] This faith is either a philosophic or a religious faith. It is either based on reflection and carried through to personal certainty, or it is grounded in religious tradition, that is, either in conscious, explicit adherence or as a thoughtless habit. Hence there is no standpoint outside the two faith alternatives of philosophy and religion. Every person, Jaspers emphasizes, stands within this polarity on one side, and speaks about the other regarding a decisive point but without personal experience.[17] It is not revelation that is the reality but faith in revelation. At best, revelation is a "reality" for those who experience it. Jaspers did not have access to it: "I do not believe in revelation and, to the best of my knowledge, never did, not even as a possibility."[18] Thus there remains one last boundary of the ability to understand the faith of revelation, to which Jaspers admits. An entirely different thing is the lack of understanding with which the faith of revelation encounters philosophic faith: Possession of the truth of revelation makes one incapable of engaging in dialogue because the other position has no relevance. Faith of revelation, rigidified in dogma and possessing tenets of faith as if they were knowledge, lacks any understanding for the open and uncompletable character of philosophic faith. Faith in revelation tends toward the claim of exclusivity; philosophic faith, on the other hand, remains open and uncompletable; it is never tempted to advocate its tenets based on such a claim to the outside world. One cannot delimit the contents of philosophic faith. The man of philosophic faith cannot preach since he brings no tidings.

Though Jaspers delimits philosophic faith sharply from faith of revelation, it does not mean that he devalues the religious sphere on which we remain existentially dependent. Even on a personal level Jaspers always stressed his allegiance to the Christian tradition of faith: "We Westerners are all Christians because we were molded in this realm, moved in our souls by this heritage, determined in our decisions and objectives, and filled with images and imaginings that go back to the Bible."[19] At one time Jaspers said about himself that he was a Christian, but a Christian who was no longer able to believe in the incarnation of God. His Christianity was grounded in his belonging to a three thousand year-old Christian tradition.[20]

In this situation, when the certainty of faith is lost and religious orientation is lacking, it is incumbent on philosophic faith to bring to mind dimensions that are capable of bringing about a new, different orientation of meaning, and to guide action. Here philosophy, as Karl Jaspers understands it, turns to the individual person for only the individual can bring certainty to possible answers to fundamental existential questions. The movement of thought that, in dealing with arguments, insights and positions, images and symbols, leads to personal certainty, is called philosophic self-assurance. Such thinking does not produce universally valid knowledge, but it is able to do more than knowledge in that it concerns the thinking person himself. Such thinking does not result in a certainty of the kind produced by the reliability and constancy of the certainty of revelation, but it can achieve more than all certainty of revelation because it guarantees a personal certainty whose value consists in its existential commitment and meaningfulness.

First I must learn that the knowledge produced by the sciences lets me down as far as all essential questions are concerned; and it must become clear to me that the religious truth of revelation, insofar as I do not experience such revelation, cannot offer me any orientation. Then I am able to understand that I live neither out of an objective knowledge of the world nor out of a truth of revelation, but out of a quite different authority by which I orient myself: out of myself, out of my own authority and my own decision, by assuring myself philosophically of my own position.

What is involved is a fundamental situation: Questions of existential relevance, posed merely by being-human, i.e., questions about the meaning and goal of life, about values to which I know myself to be committed, about guilt and death—these are questions that each person has to answer for himself. They are, at the same time, questions that have already been decided because the course of life and the shaping of one's life had already demanded a decision, especially insofar as a decision based on reflection and made deliberately is practically impossible. And whoever avoids challenges posed by one's concrete existence, intentionally and on purpose, allows them precisely through this avoidance to influence—unnoticed—one's life. Avoidance, rejection, and suppression are all merely modes of the presence of fundamental questions in one's life.

Philosophic self-assurance, however, does not only mean arriving at a personal decision and at one's own standpoint. It also requires that one remains open to different possibilities, that one does not take a position with finality but sees it in perspective. There is no mediation between these two opposing requirements: to commit oneself and yet to remain open. Attempts to overcome this intrinsically contradictory situation would contradict the existential actuality.

The orientation achieved in philosophy—in delimitation from science as well as religion—consists in the ability to open up that consciousness of problems and those horizons and dimensions, as well as the mediation of arguments and impulses that make it possible to arrive at one's own position. By entrusting the entire burden of decision regarding faith, and the onus of assuring oneself of truth and of finding answers to the fundamental questions of being-human to the individual, Jaspers incurs the reproach that he "philosophizes past" human actuality: How could the individual human being in his concrete historic-cultural life situation be in a position to live up to these extravagant demands of Existenz-philosophy?

At this point it is imperative that we bring to mind once more the image of the human being by which Jaspers's thought orients itself. Jaspers came to philosophy by way of psychiatry. Through his experience as psychiatrist and psychologist he realized that through scientific research we really cannot come close to what is authentic and essential in being-human. This is the experience that the human being is always more than he can know about himself through science. Hence, whoever is interested in this "more" must go beyond the realm of science and turn toward philosophy. The consciousness of participating in this great new task connected Jaspers in the 1920s with Martin Heidegger. Their shared philosophical concern consisted in grasping life, existence, as well as the psychological in a radically new way. They meant fundamentally to overcome the traditional conceptualizations. In a letter from the summer of 1922, three years after the publication of the *Psychologie der Weltanschaungen*, Heidegger wrote to Jaspers:

> The psychological is not something that man "has," whether consciously or unconsciously, but something that he is and that lives in him. That is, in principle: There are objects that one does not have but that one "is." . . . The old ontology (and the categorial structures arising from it) must be restructured from the bottom up—if one means to be serious about grasping and guiding one's own present life in its fundamental intentions.[21]

This task, as presented by Heidegger, also describes Jaspers's guiding intention.

The being that we ourselves are and in which every mode of being occurs, hence our "being-I," can be categorially differentiated into "existence" (*Dasein*: lit.: being-there), "consciousness as such," "spirit," and "Existenz." As *existence*, I am, move, and experience myself as an irreplaceable individual in the concrete actuality of the world. As existence I also partake of *consciousness as such*, which designates the one consciousness that always remains the same and is common to all human beings. No one possesses it completely; we all contribute to it and are at the same time a part of it. That which man fashions by means of his imagination, he creates as *spirit*: his meaning-projects, symbolic forms, and the significance in cultural creativity. These three modes of being oneself do not exhaust all possibilities of "being-I." By virtue of these three origins of our being we are not yet, as Jaspers says, "what we can be"; they alone arouse a sense of insufficiency: "*Existence* is ephemeral life from nothing to nothing. . . . thinks endlessly even what is indifferent. . . . *Spirit* can see in the magic of its creations the magnificence of soap bubbles."[22] Jaspers asks: Am I merely this? Am I simply there, partake of consciousness as such, lose myself to the spirit? Does not being myself mean more than this? Am I perhaps, in the end, never myself?—That which indicates itself in such questions, is called Existenz.

The three categories, existence, consciousness as such, and spirit designate three perspectives under which this same "I" can be considered. Objective statements about the "I" are possible under all three perspectives. That which Jaspers calls "Existenz," however, does not possess any such objective correspondence. Differing from life, thought, and spirit, Existenz can never become an object. Existenz cannot be fixated objectively; and yet it is not simply nothing but rather an essential—according to Jaspers, *the* essential side of being-human. Here the limit of the scientific picture of man becomes evident; that it cannot do justice to the actual human being is due to the fact that man, according to his nature, is free and open to possibility. This dimension of possibility and freedom is called Existenz.

In order for Existenz to enter my range of vision I must change over to a perspective that only I can assume. If I pose this question about myself explicitly and if I can persevere even though it cannot be answered in an objective sense, then a change will occur in one's being-human that Jaspers calls "awakening," "coming to oneself," "becoming aware of myself," "the process of becoming conscious," the "process of my finding myself," or as "origin" of philosophizing. Existenz is the possibility of being myself. The two concepts "Existenz" and "being oneself" have the same meaning in Jaspers. By no means do they designate man's universal mode of being but a way of life that is possible for all but by no means realized by all. Being oneself begins where the individual human being recognizes that what he authentically is is still up to him. "I am Existenz insofar I do not become my own object. In [Existenz] I know myself to be independent without being able to see that which I refer to as my self. I live out of its possibility; yet only in its actualization am I myself."[23]

Objective knowledge of the world collides with limits of a fundamental kind. As we know, it is the task of "philosophical world orientation," the title of the first of three volumes of Jaspers's main work, *Philosophy*, to demonstrate this. As I philosophize I am struck by a contrariety that cannot be grasped rationally but can be grasped existentially, namely, that between Being as objectivity and the being that I am myself as freedom. On the side of freedom there is neither objective and universally valid cognition, nor are there direct and unequivocal forms of communicating. But that is no reason to be silent: As "elucidation of Existenz," philosophy has the task of making the realm of possible freedom communicable, as Jaspers pointed out in the second volume of *Philosophy*. On the side of the being of existents, all knowledge, though universally cognizable and objectively communicable, remains ultimately particular, historically relative, and hence variously contingent. On the side of freedom, on the other hand, it is always a matter of unconditional validity. One cannot and may not be silent philosophically. In the unconditional nature of that which is at stake on the side of freedom, we find the validation of Existenz-elucidating thought that seeks to make the inexpressible expressible, even though ultimately it must knowingly suffer shipwreck.

Jaspers's Existenz-illuminating philosophizing shows us time and again that his thinking orients itself by a very particular possibility of being-human, by an ideal of humanity whose realization is successful whenever man is not simply man but when he is himself: "The wonderful thing, the only one that is authentically being, is the human being who is he himself."[24] It may well be that this image of a human being, self-determining, independent, who, aware of his personal dignity, striving for successful self-being, misses the reality of being-human as we observe it daily. Nonetheless we must keep in mind that this open image of man suits the existential situation of the present better than its counter-image; it provides us with an important corrective to the ordinary self-understanding of the majority of people today.

Since the possibilities of orienting oneself to the world are fundamentally limited, we need a philosophy that goes beyond worldly knowledge. Hence the task of philosophy is not exhausted by pointing out the limited nature of the ability to know. This is merely a first step on the road on which Existenz becomes conscious of itself and of transcendence.

Becoming conscious of oneself as possible Existenz presupposes a movement of thought that Jaspers calls "transcending." By transcending, which simply means "going beyond," Jaspers means going beyond, in one's thinking, what is objectively knowable. Transcending is the "going beyond the objective into the non-objective."[25] If philosophy is to reach its goal and assure itself in thought of authentic Being,[26] it cannot avoid transcending the knowledge of the world since no knowledge can reach authentic Being. Philosophic transcending has two goals toward which it transcends. If the aim of the transcending movement is concerned with the being that I myself am, it is called Existenz. And if the goal of transcending is Being as such, then it is called Transcendence. Existenz and Transcendence form the two cognitive goals of transcending.

Jaspers's understanding of philosophy is directly tied to the concept of transcending: Transcending is the philosophical movement of thought of the rational step-by-step development of ideas. For Jaspers, philosophizing without transcending seems like an intrinsic contradiction. Thus he can make this categorical judgement: "Where thinking does not transcend we find not philosophy but either immanent and particular cognition of objects through science or intellectual games."[27]

Naturally, the question now arises as to why the limits of knowledge are to be transcended at all. As Jaspers himself elaborates, there is not even the *desire* within the framework of scientific world orientation to go beyond the said limits since, from its perspective, one asks about the things in the world and not about the world as such. Also, there is no *occasion* for transcending the limits of knowledge since, in the uncompletable process of world orientation, no limits appear. Moreover, the *capacity* is lacking since, given the methods of world orientation, transcending is impossible.

The justification for philosophical transcending consists simply in that the boundaries of knowledge are being crossed in the actuality of life even without methodically conscious transcending, even without much thought given to the matter. It is an anthropological fact that man is dependent on images of the whole. Religion, myth, art, and ideology have the function of transmitting images of the whole and of allowing for an orientation of meaning. Jaspers's *Psychologie der Weltanschauungen* already made it clear that man is dependent on orientation, on images of the whole, on ultimate principles. The expression "*Weltanschauung*" (worldview) after all, expresses something that is more than knowledge. It is the way in which a person evaluates things, in which he determines what has absolute validity, in which he lets himself be guided by ultimate principles. It is his inner stance in relation to that which is no longer knowable.

It would be a misunderstanding to believe that worldviews are strongly delineated, closed, unitary pictures of the world. Rather it is in the nature of *Weltanschauungen* that they can never be transformed into something conceptually systematic. One can never get an overview of them as something complete because they are not capable of completion. Furthermore, they can never be completely understood from the outside. Being in fact lived belongs to the full actuality of a *Weltanschauung*.

The core of any *Weltanschauung* is not knowledge but faith. Hence the peculiarity of a *Weltanschauung* cannot be made into the object of cogent explanations. Each lived *Weltanschauung* is the factual limit of world orientation. In it—conscious or unnoticed—knowledge of the world is transcended, for human consciousness cannot avoid to posit something as absolute. And if one were to give up what is absolute for him, then something else would automatically take its place. A *Weltanschauung* that one actually lives by—which, in the sense of world orientation, cannot be investigated and yet constitutes a vital actuality—is also an origin of philosophizing.

In the end, however, it is impossible to prove the necessity of philosophic transcending. Philosophic transcending thought simply is not a fact of existence, but merely a possibility of being-human. As possibility it can be grasped or avoided. The possibility of grasping philosophical transcending and of realizing it—this is what existential self-actualization means in the sense of Jaspers's philosophy of Existenz. "Transcending is not a factual situation that is given together with existence but a possibility of freedom within it. Man is as the existence (*Dasein*: being-there) in which possible Existence [Existenz] appears to itself; he is not only there; he can transcend, and he can refrain from it."[28]

Philosophizing is a transcending of the knowable in the direction of the no-longer-knowable. In this process the movement of transcending does not arrive at knowledge of a "higher," different kind; rather, it leads into openness as it were. Since the goal of philosophic transcending is not cognition in the sense of scientific rationality, what counts is solely the movement of transcending. What is important is not at what insights philosophizing arrives; important is only the movement of transcending, the act of going beyond. The importance of philosophizing therefore is not measured by ostensible results but by the existential consequences for the thinker himself: "The reality of *philosophizing* does not lie in objective results; it is a posture of consciousness."[29]

As Existenz becomes aware of its freedom it cannot but assume a position vis-à-vis an ultimate ground, which is called "transcendence." Self-being can be realized only in some relation to transcendence: whether through explicit denial of transcendence, that is, through a negative relationship to it, or through conscious opposition to transcendence, or, finally, through agreement with it. Without, against, or with transcendence—Existenz always stands in relation to it: "Existenz is only in relation to transcendence or not at all."[30]

The directedness of Existenz to transcendence is evident also in that it cannot succeed in considering freedom to be the ultimate, for freedom consists precisely in being able to choose the way in which one confronts an ultimate and unconditional. Without such a confrontation there is neither freedom nor Existenz. It follows that transcendence is the point of reference for both.

But what is transcendence? From the perspective of consciousness as such transcendence appears in the multiplicity of myths, metaphysics, and religions present throughout history. Of course, from this perspective all one can see is how the individual experiences transcendence and how he speaks about it, but not what transcendence itself is. For Jaspers the actuality of transcendence consists only in its immediate, nontransferable, existential experience. He defines metaphysics as thinking that seeks to express the existentially experienced actuality of transcendence in the medium of universal thought. Hence the basic difficulty of all metaphysics consists in that it seeks to reproduce something in the medium of the universal which, as universal, becomes empty and insignificant.

Metaphysics serves to illuminate the possible paths to transcendence. Transcendence designates a limit of thought, as does Existenz. There is no answer, based on knowledge, to the question what transcendence is. But where being able to know ceases, thinking does not also cease. There remains the possibility to approach transcendence by way of ciphers. Jaspers calls "ciphers" the specifically philosophic form of setting down through language something that can no longer be objectively cognized. Ciphers are the language of transcendence but not transcendence itself. Existenz assures itself of transcendence through the medium of ciphers and thereby finds its position; it gains anchoring and orientation.

Speaking about transcendence directly and by means of objective concepts is denied to present-day man. Transcendence is more transcendent than ever before, so to speak. No conceptual-theoretical cognition reaches it. Whatever has been said about transcendence in the past and is said still today, it possesses merely the cognitive status of ciphers.

The doctrine of ciphers is Jaspers's answer to the question as to how metaphysics is still possible today given the modern situation of thought. To be sure, for consciousness as such the language of ciphers remains meaningless; for ciphers are not the vehicles of unchanging meanings, they cannot be deciphered in a universally valid manner. The language of ciphers addresses itself to existential consciousness. Only for the latter do the ciphers become the language of transcendence.

The "Language" of Ciphers

That which in the pre-philosophic mythical manner of expression is called soul and God and is called Existenz and transcendence by Jaspers does not possess an objective-worldly nature; it is nonetheless not nothing. For if I leave the position of objective knowledge of the world and assume that of philosophic self-assurance—that is, the standpoint of an experience of the world and my own interpretation of it that is actual only for me—then Existenz and transcendence become realities of primary importance. Philosophic self-assurance makes use of a language whose statements are no longer meant directly but indirectly. What is said and what is thought assume the status of ciphers.

Thus it happens that what from the perspective of objective rationality seems like babbling about illusionary actualities, achieves in the perspective of philosophic reason a meaning that sustains Existenz. However, there is no way of circumventing the limit that what is illuminated by subjective reason can become reasonably certain only for me; consequently the proof of philosophic statements in the existential situation assumes the place of the intersubjective validity of objective statements.

The fascination emanating from such thinking consists in its going beyond a limit and attempting to speak about something that cannot be spoken about in an objective sense. In this difficulty and in the way in which it is overcome we must surely see the core of all debates about the value or lack of value of the philosophy of Existenz. For it goes without saying that from the very beginning this philosophy has been fiercely criticized and rejected as being an unscientific expression of opinion, as an irrational, subjective, and therefore nonbinding form of philosophizing. One can understand such reproaches and to some extent they are even justified; but they miss the point that this thinking, which explicitly wants to be something other than science, and cannot at all be measured according to the criteria of scientific rationality.

Religions teach as objective realities what, from the standpoint of philosophy, possesses merely the function of existentially effective images and metaphors. Philosophic faith knows that transcendence cannot be expressed, and it speaks of it only in ciphers. The great mistake of religion consists, according to Jaspers, in confusing the language of ciphers with objective reality. This confusion as well as the obedience of faith demanded by the religions has the consequence that the realization of existential freedom and authentic self-being become impossible. For this reason Jaspers states categorically: For the philosophizing individual faith is possible but religion is not.

In spite of this decisive rejection of the religions based on revelation, Jaspers devoted his last great work to his dispute with them. His main concern consisted in showing what the texts of religious tradition could say to us today if they were read from the position of philosophic faith. In regard to Christian revelation Jaspers states: "Not being able to believe in revelation does not mean having to deny its possibility altogether. Neither is it necessary to lose, together with the faith in revelation, the eternally true content of the Bible as well."[31] To be sure, the philosophic appropriation of biblical tradition presupposes that its central statements possess merely the status of ciphers; their word-for-word, literal, immediate meaning is lost, its meaning is now an indirect, metaphorical one. The statements of biblical tradition, read as ciphers, are transformed into the philosophical language of transcendence.

In an age determined by science and technology, biblical tradition has lost its real, word-for-word, meaning for many. Biblical tradition is able to maintain its character as wisdom and its philosophic importance in the present only under the presupposition that its mythical tales, its images, and parables are read as ciphers. Jaspers's position vis-à-vis biblical tradition is expressed especially distinctly in the great controversy with Rudolf Bultmann regarding the question of demythologizing.

Jaspers's Rejection of Demythologizing Christianity

Bultmann's program of demythologizing kept the theological discussions of the 1950s in suspense. It was based on the task theology had set itself of opening up the Christian message, written as it was in mythical language, to a present determined by science and technology, so that it again achieves binding character and the power to convince. It meant to make the Christian message "ready for today." Bultmann found this task unavoidable because the New Testament had been written for an age determined by myth and had entered, with its world of mythological imagery, into conflict with the worldview and the self-understanding of modern man. Hence it would be futile, indeed an imposition, to demand of Christians simply to believe the mythological tales of miracles where such faith in miracles has no place in our times. Bultmann made use of unequivocal, strong language when he took his position with respect to the modern situation of faith, to wit: "Can the Christian gospel demand of man in this day and age *to acknowledge the mythical world picture as being true?* That is senseless and impossible. *Senseless*: for the mythical picture of the world is as such nothing specifically Christian but simply the world picture of a past age that has not yet been shaped by scientific thought. *Impossible*: for a picture of the world cannot be appropriated through decision, rather it is given to man together with his historical situation."[32]

Demythologizing designates the process of interpreting the message of the New Testament with the aid of existential interpretation such that it can be rendered without reference to the mythological. Bultmann's existential interpretation, which in substance as well as terminology, follows Martin Heidegger's existential-ontological analysis of existence (*Daseinsanalyse* or analysis of being there), has the aim of making the core of the biblical message, the *kerygma* or Gospel proclamation, once again comprehensible and believable for the man of today who no longer thinks in mythological terms. To be sure, the all-decisive question is whether, upon the demythologizing and the existential reinterpretation of the New Testament, there still remains a substantial content or not.

Bultmann's program of demythologizing encountered, as we know, decisive rejection among many. The criticism by conservative theologians was to be expected. Unexpectedly harsh criticism, however, came from the philosophical side, from Karl Jaspers, who was known in theological circles as an implacable opponent of theological claims to absoluteness. Jaspers reproached Bultmann by claiming that the whole project of demythologizing rested ultimately on an all too simple and superficial confrontation of myth and science. It boiled down to a devaluation of the mythical and meant in the end a loss of mythical language. Jaspers's objections can all be attributed to *one* thesis, to wit: Mythical thinking is not a form of thinking that is passé, has been overcome and is now invalid. Mythical thinking constitutes a possibility that is valid through all time and therefore even today. Demythologizing, Jaspers writes in his little tract about "Truth and Calamity of Bultmann's Demythologizing," is therefore "almost a blasphemous expression."[33]

Jaspers's criticism of Bultmann rests on an understanding of myth, which attributes to myth the ability to express something graphically and vividly that cannot be expressed at all in discursive, objective-conceptual language. Obviously there are things that can be reported better and even more precisely in the form of a myth. What the myth says and tells can only be said and told mythically. As soon as it is translated into discursive, conceptual language, it is falsified. Its symbolism and pictorial quality can be transposed only inadequately into something that is told directly. Myths and symbols are ciphers, signs for what would be inexpressible otherwise. Jaspers is only being consistent when he assumes an explicit position in the controversy about demythologizing: The myths of the New Testament tradition must be read as ciphers of what cannot be expressed; they are to be read as ciphers of transcendence. If they were to be eliminated, then precisely that which is perennially true in this tradition would be lost.

The myth that is read as cipher expresses something that, as myth, is told better, more incisively, more succinctly as it were, than in its conceptual translation. Its meaning content cannot be gleaned through language. The value of myth, which cannot be replaced by anything else, consists in its untranslatability. For this reason myth cannot be "translated" in a manner that is binding, and the radical elimination of myth would, at the same time, get rid of a fundamental capability of human reason: "Demythologizing would mean allowing a basic gift of our reason to become extinct."[34]

However, both Jaspers and Bultmann agree that today it is no longer permissible to consider the truth of the stories in the New Testament to be literal. After all, even the program of demythologizing turns against a perversion of the mythical statements into word-for-word reality. For this reason, Jaspers believes, Bultmann is completely correct when he challenges the claims of incarnation and rejects a concretizing, literal, quasi-materialistic interpretation of the New Testament mythical accounts; for a corpse cannot really come alive again and climb out of the grave, and miracles are actually impossible. The difference between the two positions, however, becomes evident in that Bultmann would like to interpret away the mythical ideas in order to advance to the authentic Christian message that is hidden behind the mythical foreground. Jaspers, on the other hand, seeks to preserve the myths as myths because these make up the substantial element of the New Testament. "Existential" appropriation of the New Testament tradition means, according to Jaspers, transcending assurance of those dimensions of meaning in which we live and die, but which can never be expressed in a universally valid manner and, therefore, remain dependent on the pictorial quality of the language of myth. Hannah Arendt surely gets to the decisive point of the controversy when, in a letter to Jaspers, she comments on his polemics, saying that basically all of the criticism boils down to the proposal directed at Bultmann "to read and interpret the Bible as if it were a philosophical text."[35] And in the same vein, we find in Jaspers's tract the exhortation to read the biblical texts as we would the Greek epics and tragedies or the sacred books of Asia. What is demanded is not obedience vis-à-vis the text but personal, individual participation in the mythic contents, no matter whether they repel or attract us.

The myth that is read as cipher becomes for philosophic faith the medium of a movement of thought serving the self-assurance of each individual's own position. The cipher language of myths is not directed toward conceptual theorizing but toward existential consciousness. The myth that is understood in this way is not the vehicle of objective unchanging meanings since it cannot be "deciphered" in a universally valid manner. According to Jaspers, it is simply a fact that, existentially, we remain dependent on myth since it is impossible to live out of knowledge alone. Jaspers reduces this to the following short formula: "We all live among pictures even if in philosophical speculation we go beyond them. One may call them the unavoidable myth, whether meager or profound."[36]

What Jaspers calls "philosophic faith" does not represent any one philosophical discipline among others but constitutes, according to his conviction, the characteristic of genuine philosophizing. For authentic philosophy cannot stop at that which can be known objectively. Hence the philosophical movement of thought leads not only to the experience of the limits of knowledge and our own basic uncertainty, but also lets us know that the ultimate fundament of existential orientation can consist only in a faith. Philosophic faith, in distinction from religious faith, remains suspended. By objectifying transcendence, religious faith makes authentic transcending impossible, the process of philosophic self-assurance superfluous; it negates freedom and opposes the possibility of self-being. Thus an essential characteristic of Jaspers's philosophizing consists in keeping the progress of thought in motion, not to break it off too early, to avoid every fixation, to leave what is said in "suspension." The language of ciphers suits this form of thinking to a high degree; it is the language of philosophic faith.

Philosophically, speaking in ciphers is truthful only as long as it remains in suspension. Any fixation is a sign of untruthfulness. Such thinking finds itself confronted with the same accusation time and again: If everything is brought into suspension and kept in suspension, then this thinking no longer offers any stability or orientation, then everything drops into bottomlessness. For philosophic faith, in distinction from the faith of revelation, does not impart any concrete, substantial contents. In dealing with this criticism Jaspers regularly brings in the argument of existential freedom, which he expresses most tersely in the following counter-argument: "I myself cannot think other than with Kant: If revelation were reality then it would be a disaster for the created freedom of man."[37]

This is an opportune moment to point to a peculiarity of Karl Jaspers's philosophizing. In general, his books communicate neither factual knowledge nor specialized information nor the results of research. Jaspers neither wants to inform nor to pass on knowledge. His philosophical writings make a different claim: In them he means to demonstrate how, in the present-day situation of thinking, philosophizing can still be possible, namely as a transcending thinking that goes beyond the knowledge of the sciences without solidifying into traditional metaphysics. Since these books do not pass on any objective knowledge they force us to think along with him, to follow his lead; only in this way is what the author said to be understood at all. Because the subject of this philosophizing is not available as something that can be known, it can be communicated only indirectly: As the reader thinks along with him it is to become actual once again. Jaspers himself remarked that those who come to him to find a teaching and a doctrine in the sense of scientific philosophy would be disappointed by his books: "These readers would have to say that I really don't say anything."[38]

To the accusation that his philosophy ultimately has nothing to say, that it has no teachings, does not supply any directives, that it leaves us in the lurch just like the sciences and the religions, Jaspers replies that his philosophy deals with that which is beyond being grasped objectively. However, one can speak about the nonobjective, about what is not an object only in objective terms. It is impossible to think something without envisaging an object, indeed, one cannot speak even *one* reasonable word without immediately connecting something objective with it. The consequence of this is that the language of Jaspers's philosophy is basically indirect communication. It cannot express what is meant directly or immediately.

Therefore, the essential aspect of his books does not consist in doctrines or directives; rather what is essential has to be brought about by the reader, precisely at the time when he follows in his thinking what Jaspers has said: "All essential content of philosophizing . . . lies in that which, by way of objectivities, grows in us, recognizes itself again and feels validated in its impulses, inner state, way of seeing and judging, in readiness to choose one's response, in delving into the historic present."[39]

The Actuality of Philosophic Faith

Formerly the actuality of Jaspers's philosophizing consisted in having posed anew the question of the contents, presuppositions, and possibilities of thinking in an era that believed in science but otherwise was increasingly lacking in orientation. He understood his philosophy of Existenz to be the answer to the philosophical situation of his time. In Kierkegaard and Nietzsche he recognized the protagonists of his own philosophizing. In spite of all the differences between the two precursors in thought, Jaspers saw in them what forges a bond between them, what was essential and decisive: "The return to the Existenz of man in this present Western situation."[40]

Today we find ourselves again in the midst of epochal change. The process of modernization has entered a new stage. The event of globalization transforms the socio-cultural situation from the ground up. The push to pluralism connected with it is more radical, more uncompromising, and comes about more rapidly than all comparable processes in our history up to the present. The pluralizing and relativizing, especially in the religious and normative realms, once more alter the existential situation of the individual: He begins to doubt his understanding of himself, his socio-cultural identity is threatened, the certainty of his religious and normative convictions, lived without reflection until now, has become shaky. The dissolution of closed pictures of the world, the refashioning of the forms of life and the dynamics of the change in values speed up the loss of orientation and bring about an increasing existential insecurity. We live in an age of existential uncertainty. What is the meaning of the philosophical demand for a "return to Existenz" in the context of the pluralism of our present world situation?

The concept of pluralism designates the cultural fact that there is a multiplicity of ultimate forms of faith, thought, and life. We must learn to deal with a plurality of religious, normative, ideological, and political fundamental convictions. The main difficulty consists in that the differences between the multiplicity of convictions cannot simply be overcome by rationalistic-argumentative means, nor with political instruments since we are dealing with lived differences, that is, those that are culturally established and legitimized. It is a matter of cultural identity.

To be sure, the process of globalization is aimed at universality. However, the resulting processes have paradoxical consequences: They cause a pluralism in the normative and religious areas, bring about a multicultural imprint on modern society, and produce a growing sensitizing for cultural differences. A new consciousness arises to the effect that what men consider true and right varies in accordance with their cultural allegiance and way of life. Many, however, deeply deplore the cultural and historical contingency of that which, as norm, as sense and as meaning, offers existential stability. Only a few experience the progression of pluralism as enrichment; most, however feel threatened by it. This is understandable since it also affects the inner actuality of one's life, the personal-existential dimension of being-human. In order to avoid the threatening loss of identity, people cling all the more firmly to their own position.

Thus, in this time of existential uncertainty, a categorical rejection of pluralism is combined with a deep longing for solid and absolute orientation. How is it possible, in light of such preconditions, for a so badly needed communication between religions and cultures to succeed?

Successful communication presupposes openness for other positions and renunciation of the absolute validity of one's own position. But the central problem of interreligious and intercultural communication consists in that the demand to give up the absolute validity of one's own convictions or one's own ground of faith is neither possible nor permitted. A solution to this fundamental problem can succeed only through the consistent separation of the subjective-personal from the intersubjective-collective perspective. This is, at the same time, the starting point of philosophic faith.

Existenz-philosophy has always stressed that philosophic truth is tied to the individual. This means that truth cannot be achieved without personal effort, without acts of actual freedom, and without realizations of Existenz.[41] Whenever the individual arrives, in the process of philosophic-existential self-assurance, at his personal conviction and certainty of faith, then—for that particular individual—these constitute in fact an absoluteness that, however, must not be tied to a claim of its exclusivity. This corresponds to the insight, presented time and again, that the truly normative authority does not consist in an abstract catalogue of norms but that the person making responsible decisions is himself that authority. An analogous situation exists in regard to decisions about one's faith since the true authority of faith is not to be found in a catalogue of dogmas but in the decision of faith by the individual. It is evident that this individual cannot and may not give up the absolute validity—for himself—of his convictions and certainties of faith; if he were to do so, it would not be a matter of personal conviction and certainty of faith.

Such a personal attitude, which is appropriate for Existenz, is usually and as a matter of course transferred to the collective level of the community, the nation, the confession or the culture. This transfer is inadmissible for absolute certainty of faith always remains tied to the individual. On the intersubjective-collective plane, however, faith never achieves the status of absolute certainty. For this reason the statement that the absolute validity of joint convictions and certainties of faith can and must never be surrendered is no longer valid. All the arguments that Jaspers uses to prove the unconditional character of philosophic faith over against religion, revelational faith, and science could be cited here once more in order to clarify this central point of the difference between the subjective-personal and the intersubjective-collective perspective.

To be sure, it is a fact that the individual tends to comply with those convictions, norms and tenets of faith that make their appearance on the ground of intersubjectivity and claim universal validity. Most likely it is a specifically Western prejudice grounded in our tradition of thought that notions of value seem to us somehow "devalued" and in some way also less binding as soon as they lack such a claim to universal validity. On the other hand, a main concern of Jaspers's philosophy and a main premise of his philosophic faith consist in the insight that, subjectively, the binding character of my conviction or of a tenet that I am certain of is in no way impaired if this conviction or this tenet does not possess universal objective validity. The validity that, existentially, is unconditionally and absolutely valid, has no presupposition of unconditionality or absoluteness on the level of intersubjective-collective validity. It is this fundamental insight of philosophic faith which, based as it is on the fact that it emanates from the individual person, has the potential to open a new entranceway to the dialogue of cultures and religions, and to prepare the ground "on which people from all directions of faith could come together throughout the world in a meaningful way, ready to adopt anew their very own historic tradition, to purify it, to transform it, but not to give it up."[42]

The process of globalization and the push to pluralism triggered by it have led us into an "era of existential uncertainty." This is the right moment to remind ourselves of a philosophy that has declared the "risk of living out of uncertainty" to be the ideal of being-human.

NOTES

1. In his congratulatory letter on the occasion of Jaspers's eightieth birthday on February 23, 1963, Martin Heidegger wrote: "Today your thoughtful thanks (*denkender Dank*) are due [to the fact] that you could go so far and may abide there, where your thinking has endowed a resting place for contemplation." [Translated by Edith Ehrlich, eds.] Cf. *Martin Heidegger und Karl Jaspers: Briefwechsel 1920-1963*, hrsg. von Walter

Biemel and Hans Saner (Frankfurt a.M.: Klostermann; /Munich/Zurich: Piper & Co., & Co., 1990), 216. [Translated by Edith Ehrlich, eds.]

2. Karl Jaspers, *Der philosophische Glaube angesichts der Offenbarung* (München: Piper & Co., 1962), p. 8 [Hereafter cited as PGO]; Karl Jaspers, *Philosophical Faith and Revelation*, translated by E. B. Ashton (New York: Harper & Row, 1967), p. vii. [Hereafter cited as PFR.]

3. Karl Jaspers, *Philosophische Autobiographie*. Erweiterte Neuausgabe (München: Piper & Co., 1977), p. 33. [Hereafter cited as PA.] Cf. Jaspers, "Philosophical Autobiography," in *The Philosophy of Karl Jaspers*, edited by Paul Arthur Schilpp, Augmented Edition (La Salle, IL: Open Court Publishing Co., 1981), p. 25.

4. See the article by Kurt Salamun herein [eds.].

5. Hannah Arendt und Karl Jaspers, *Briefwechsel 1926-1969*, hrsg. von Lotte Köhler und Hans Saner (München/Zürich: Piper & Co., 1985), p. 117.

6. See PFR, p. 18.

7. Cf. Karl Jaspers, *Provokationen: Gespräche und Interviews*, hrsg. von Hans Saner (München: Piper & Co., 1969), p. 70.

8. Karl Jaspers, *The Great Philosophers*, vol. III, edited by Michael Ermarth and Leonard H. Ehrlich, translated by Edith Ehrlich and Leonard H. Ehrlich (New York/San Diego/London: Harcourt Brace & Co, 1993), p. 60: "For Bruno, philosophy had become his religion; it was sufficient onto itself. Not only did he dispense with the Church, but also he affirmed the truth of philosophy in sacrificial death, and in rejection of Christ's divinity . . . in the face of death, and in prophetic awareness."

9. Jaspers, PFR, p. 46.

10. Cf., PFR, p. 61.

11. Cf. Immanuel Kant, *Kritik der reinen Vernunft*, Immanuel Kant, *Gesammelte Schriften,* Akademie-Ausgabe, vol. 4, Preußische Akademie der Wissenschaften (Berlin: Georg Reimer, 1903), p. 9 (XII).

12. Georg Picht, *Wahrheit-Vernunft-Verantwortung: Philosophische Studien* (Stuttgart: Klett-Cotta, 1969), p. 191.

13. Cf. Immanuel Kant, "Was heißt: Sich im Denken orientieren?," in Immanuel Kant, *Gesammelte Schriften,* Akademie-Ausgabe, vol. 8, Preußische Akademie der Wissenschaften (Berlin/Leipzig: De Gruyter, 1912), p. 141.

14. Ibid., p. 141.

15. Kant, *Kritik der reinen Vernunft*, BXXX.

16. Jaspers, *Provokationen*, p. 72.

17. Jaspers, *The Perennial Scope of Philosophy*, translated by Ralph Manheim (New York: Philosophical Library, 1949), p. 60.

18. Jaspers, PGO, p. 35; cf. Jaspers, PFR, p. 8.

19. Jaspers, PGO, p. 52; cf. Jaspers, PFR, p. 20.

20. Cf. letter to Oskar Hammelsbeck of December 14, 1958; in *Briefwechsel Karl Jaspers—Oskar Hammelsbeck, 1919-1969*, hrsg. von Hermann Horn (Frankfurt a.M./Bern/New York: Peter Lang, 1986), p. 108.

21. "Letter of June 27, 1922," in *Martin Heidegger und Karl Jaspers: Briefwechsel 1920-1963*, p. 26.

22. Jaspers, PGO, p. 116; cf. Jaspers, PFR, p. 65.

23. Karl Jaspers, *Philosophie* II, vierte, unveränderte Auflage. (Berlin/Heidelberg/New York: Springer-Verlag, 1973), 1. [Hereafter cited as P2, eds.] Cf. Karl Jaspers, *Philosophy*, vol. 2, translated E. B. Ashton (Chicago and London: The University of Chicago Press, 1970), p. 3. [Hereafter cited as PH 2, eds.]

24. P 2, p. 44; cf., PH 2, p. 41.

25. Karl Jaspers, *Philosophie* I, vierte, unveränderte Auflage (Berlin/Heidelberg/New York: Springer-Verlag, 1973): p. 38. (Hereafter cited as P1, eds.) cf. Karl Jaspers, *Philosophy*, vol. 1, translated by E. B. Ashton (Chicago and London: The University of Chicago Press, 1969), p. 77.

26. Professor Cesana emphasizes thinking in relation to the whole of Being, that is, thinking in relation to the modes of the being that we ourselves are and in which every "mode of being appears to us" (*qua* existence, consciousness as such, spirit, Existenz), as well as "the encompassing that is being itself" (world and transcendence), to use Jaspers's terminology. We use the capital letter "B" to emphasize the entirety of Being, what Jaspers calls "the Encompassing of all encompassings," that stands as an *aporia* beyond the encompassing of subjectivity and the encompassing of objectivity [eds.].

27. P 1, p. 39; cf. PH 1, p. 78.

28. P 1, p. 38; cf. PH 1, p. 77.

29. P1, p. 264; PH 1, p. 270.

30. Karl Jaspers, *Philosophie* III, vierte, unveränderte Auflage. (Berlin/Heidelberg/New York: Springer-Verlag, 1973), p. 6. [Hereafter cited as P 3, eds.] Cf. Karl Jaspers, *Philosophy,* vol. 3, translated by E. B. Ashton (Chicago and London: University of Chicago Press, 1971), p. 7. [Hereafter cited as PH 3, eds.]

31. Karl Jaspers, "Der philosophische Glaube angesichts der Offenbarung," in *Philosophie und christliche Existenz, Festschrift für Heinrich Barth,* hrsg. von Gerhard Huber (Basel/Stuttgart: Helbing & Lichtenhahn, 1960), pp. 1–92.

32. Rudolf Bultmann, *Neues Testament und Mythologie. Das Problem der Entmythologisierung der neutestamentlichen Verkündigung*, 2nd ed. (München: Kaiser, 1985), p. 14.

33. Karl Jaspers und Rudolf Bultmann, *Die Frage der Entmythologisierung* (Munich: Piper & Co., 1954), p. 42. [Hereafter cited as FE eds.] Karl Jaspers and Rudolf Bultmann, *Myth and Christianity: An Inquiry into the Possibility of Religion without Myth*, translated by Norbert Gutermann (New York: Noonday Press, 1964), pp. 15–16. [Hereafter cited as MC eds.]

34. Karl Jaspers, *The Future of Mankind*, translated by E. B. Ashton (Chicago: University of Chicago Press, 1961), p. 43.

35. Arendt und Jaspers, *Briefwechsel, 1926-1969*, p. 250f.; *Hannah Arendt and Karl Jaspers: Correspondence, 1926–1969*, 1st US edition. Edited by Lotte Köhler and Hans Saner, translated by Robert and Rita Kimber (San Diego/New York/London: Harcourt, Brace, Jovanovich, 1993), p. 81.

36. Ibid.

37. Jaspers, PGO, pp. 37ff.; cf. Jaspers, PFR, p. 10.

38. P 1, p. XXIX; cf. PH 1, p. 16.

39. P 1, p. XXXI; cf. PH 1, p. 18.

40. Karl Jaspers, *Vernunft und Existenz. Fünf Vorlesungen* (München: Piper & Co., 1973), p. 121, anm., 1.

41. Cf. Karl Jaspers, *Nachlass zur Philosophischen Logik*, hrsg. von Hans Saner und Marc Hanggi (Munich/Zurich: Piper & Co., 1991), p. 387.

42. Jaspers, PGO, p. 7; cf. Jaspers, PFR, p. xxv.

Part IV
Education and Culture

THE IDEA OF A UNIVERSITY IN THE PHILOSOPHY OF KARL JASPERS

Alan M. Olson

Karl Jaspers's "idea of a university"[1] might be viewed as an admirable reaffirmation of the classical Humboldtean conception of the nineteenth-century university. When the Jaspersian *Idee* is framed against Jean-François Lyotard's deconstructive analysis of the university,[2] however, Jaspers's views can easily strike the contemporary reader as being anachronistic. Lyotard's influential essay, written only twenty years after the appearance of Jaspers's *Die Idee der Universität* (*The Idea of the University*) in its final form, seems in many ways a century removed from what Jaspers has to say.

Why is this the case? The reason for this apparent gulf is that Jaspers, unlike many if not most commentators on education in recent years, views the university as a cipher of transcendence—perhaps the *ultimate* cipher of transcendence for twentieth-century humankind. Ciphers of transcendence[3] have the power of instantiating, at least in consciousness, experiences of the temporal and the eternal, the particular and the universal, that provide a basis for understanding the nature of value and Being accessible by no other means. Ciphers have the power of providing an experience of "the fragmentary but unambiguous vision of the unity of Being," as Paul Tillich once put it regarding the power of symbol. But rather than being the basis of a system through reduction to a formula, ciphers for Jaspers are limited to occasions of personal self-transcendence or what he calls "possible self-being" (*mögliche Existenz*). Because the university idea has this cipher-status—at least, potentially, and because Jaspers works out of a highly constructive view of Western tradition, he concludes, in the face of the manifold horrors of the early and mid-twentieth century, that the university is the last best hope for the "future of mankind,"[4] but only if the university remains "true to its concept," as in Hegel, by remaining open to the call of transcendence.

Not many philosophers nowadays speak like Jaspers any more. Apart from Lyotard's influential deconstructive essay, it is interesting to note the conspicuous absence of sustained philosophical reflections on the nature and meaning of the university during the past forty years or so. As Charles MacClelland observes, ". . . no other public institution has been the victim of such a large volume of uncritical writings."[5] Given the scope and economic prominence of institutions of higher education in the contemporary world, the paucity of critical comment is indeed astonishing.

THE CIPHER-STATUS OF THE UNIVERSITY-IDEA

The two most famous and doubtless most influential statements regarding the university "idea" continue to be the early nineteenth-century works of Wilhelm von Humboldt and John Henry Cardinal Newman. Humboldt's *Über innere und äussere Organization der höheren wissenschaftlichen Anstalten in Berlin* (1810)[6] not only provided the basis for the establishment of the University of Berlin, but the basic structure for the organization of the research university worldwide. Newman's lectures on *The Idea of a University*,[7] delivered at Trinity College in Dublin in 1852, also continue to be a major point of reference (especially in Catholic circles, but not exclusively so) with respect to the "character building" function of the academic community. Jaroslav Pelikan's fairly recent book *The Idea of a University: A Reexamination*,[8] provides a positive reassessment of the validity of the *classical* (nineteenth-century) views of von Humboldt and is somewhat compatible with what Jaspers asserts, but with more attention to Newman, as one might expect from a theologically trained historian. Robert Paul Wolff's perceptive book *The Ideal of the University*,[9] written hot on the heels of the university unrest in the late-1960s, upholds the "sanctuary of scholarship" much in the same spirit that Jaspers affirms the sanctity of the "cosmos of knowledge" entrusted to the university. But Wolff also acknowledges the need for institutional change in a rapidly changing society lest universities simply become "service stations" in the humanities for students otherwise interested merely in the acquisition of technical degrees. More recent works, by contrast, have been highly critical of the directions in which the university has actually changed or developed during the past few decades, most notably works responding to or playing a major role in the culture wars of the 1980s: for example, the well-known works of Allan Bloom, Roger Kimball, Dinesh D'Souza, Bruce Wilshire, and Alasdair MacIntyre, with MacIntyre's *Three Rival Versions of Moral Enquiry* being by far the most philosophically substantive.[10] The discussion in the 1980s and early-1990s was framed to a large extent by the libertarian-communitarian debate in social and political philosophy and fueled by the perception that the "sanctuary of scholarship" and the "cosmos of knowledge," in Jaspers's terms, are precisely what have been abandoned in institutional responses to the social, political, and economic exigencies of the moment.

Through it all, Jaspers's "idea" of the university certainly continues to stand out as being one of the most cogent and comprehensive twentieth-century restatements of the "ideal" Humboldtean university, even though it is precisely the legitimacy of this view with which Jean-François Lyotard takes issue in *The Postmodern Condition* (1979). While Lyotard's essay is framed, in many ways, by the many reexaminations of Heidegger's rectoral address at Freiburg in May 1933 titled "Die Selbstbehauptung der Universität," his observations are by no means limited to the Heidegger controversy, and have primarily to do with the implications of shifting the discussion from the question of *meaning* to the question of *legitimacy*.

The absence of sustained philosophical reflection on the university idea is a bit odd, but the *oddness* is mitigated by the fact that university life during the last quarter of the twentieth century has increasingly been transformed by a transition to the so-called *corporate model* of higher education. Our growing acceptance of this state of affairs as being inevitable in an age of mass culture (or *globalization*, as we would call it today) is precisely the point of Lyotard's critique. Thus it might be said that university professors, in general, and philosophers, in particular, have in some sense become the ultimate Platonic cave-dwellers with respect to the nature and meaning of their own workplace—being "unexposed to the light," as it were, however much we like to number ourselves amongst the enlightened. Perhaps it is the case that professional philosophers (as life-long, tenured, spelunkers, being sufficiently familiar only with the ways in which the furniture of the academic cave has been moved about over the course of their respective careers) no longer have the capacity to catch the Platonic resonance of Jaspers's *Universitäts-Idee* or to be illuminated by it.

The reason that discourse on the *Universitäts-Idee* sounds so strange obviously has to do with the widening gulf between the classical notion that the university stands for, represents, or is the instantiation of some kind of special coherent ideality that can be found in no other institution, on the one hand, and the rather more mundane observation, on the other, that the university is just another business, increasingly akin to the multinational corporation with branches and affiliations in all the tourist centers of the world. Thus the cynical interlocutor might easily conclude that whether as idea or ideal, the university today is a chimera or even a fraud—a chimera in the sense that the university has no special claim upon reality nor is it the custodian of what Jaspers calls "the cosmos of knowledge," and a fraud in representing itself otherwise, especially when it comes time to raising money from alumni. Far from being the "concrete universal," as in Hegel, or a "sanctuary of scholarship," as Paul Robert Wolff puts it, we are, in fact, really dealing today with what Clark Kerr, back in 1963, first called the "multiversity," that is, with a loose and frequently incoherent academic confederation of scholarly enterprises responding to a variety of "national needs" but within whose walls, we might add, faculty rarely if ever communicate with each other on substantive matters. Kerr's observations on the multiversity were, in fact, an "unwitting indictment" of the American university since one cannot, as Wolff notes, "be both an instrument of the national purpose and a critic of national purpose," for "an instrument is a means, not an evaluator of ends."[11]

It is reasonable to ask whether Jaspers's views, written over a space of nearly forty years during the first half of the twentieth century, can shed any light on the contemporary situation. When Jaspers wrote his essays, as Raymond Langley points out, there were only about 50,000 students in fifteen German universities.[12] By the mid-1990s, and following reunification, the number of students in over one hundred universities had grown to about 2 million. The American situation runs parallel to the German situation, even apart from the devastation of war. Prior to World War II, less than 5% of graduating seniors went on to obtain a college or university education. Today approximately 60% of graduating high school students continue some form of postsecondary, higher education. Given this disparity, it might be surmised that Jaspers's idea of a university, informed as it is by an education and a career at *Ruprecht-Karls-Universität* at Heidelberg, the oldest university within the territorial boundaries of Germany, founded by charter with Pope Urban VI in 1385, has little relevance when attempting to understand the *megaversity* of today. On other hand, it might be argued that only a position informed by the historical depth of one of the oldest European universities, grounded and founded in what Jaspers calls the *Occidental Idea*, can provide us with a sense of what remains essential about the "idea" of a university and help to amplify what is otherwise missing in most universities today. In short, the step backward may be the way to a step forward since a careful consideration of the university idea of Jaspers seems otherwise unavailable in the literature of today.

Jaspers published his essay on *The Idea of the University* three times over the course of his career.[13] In each instance, the structure of his argument is basically the same with respect to fundamentals, but expanded (especially in the

1946 edition) in order to address the current problems and challenges facing the German university. This is especially true in the case of the second version of 1946, where he addresses the rise of technology and its implications for the university. Jaspers proposes that technology (or what we might call "science and engineering") might reasonably be developed as a fourth division in the "higher faculty" (*trivium*) of theology, law, and medicine, with philosophy expanding its role in the "lower faculty" (*quadrivium*) as kind of moral overseer of the operations of the university as a whole.

It is also important to note that the *Die Idee der Universität* initially appeared in 1923, four years after the publication of his *Psychologie der Weltanschauungen* in 1919, and just one year following his appointment as a full professor of philosophy at Heidelberg. Jaspers's appointment came in spite of the objections of Heinrich Rickert who, in 1916, had succeeded Wilhelm Windelband as the chair of philosophy. Rickert did not think it appropriate that a *Privatdozent* in psychiatry be appointed to the philosophy faculty. The success of Jaspers's *Allgemeine Psychopathologie* (1913), now in its tenth edition and still a standard reference in the diagnosis of mental pathology,[14] combined with his record of superior teaching skills, was sufficient for Jaspers to obtain his appointment over the objections of Rickert. The fact that the "embryonic but outspoken" (Rickert's words) young philosopher published his "university idea" within the year following his appointment probably also greatly irritated Rickert, since Jaspers had not as yet published anything that might be identified as "pure" philosophy. This irritation was heightened, as Ray Langley points out, because Jaspers, as a young *Dozent,* had also spoken out, in 1919, against the faculty for having unanimously signed a petition of protest against war reparations, arguing that because the university had an "Occidental and not a German essence and origin,"[15] it should remain aloof from political involvements.

In the expanded version of 1946 (translated into English in 1958), Jaspers developed his argument in ways responsive to the massive challenges of postwar reconstruction in Germany by calling for the "resurrection" (*Auferstehung*) of the university idea. The final and basically unaltered version of his *Idee* appears in 1961, together with a new introduction by Jaspers called "*Das Bild der Universität*," written in collaboration with Kurt Rossmann, his successor at Basel.

The publication dates of Jaspers's works on the university idea are significant in each instance since they follow immediately in the wake of major geopolitical crises. The 1923 version appeared in the midst of the disillusionment that accompanied the collapse of the German Empire following the First World War and the ill-fated transition of the Wilhelmine Reich to the Weimar Republic and the hyperinflation of the *Reichsmark.* The 1946 version came out immediately after the total moral and economic devastation of the Second World War and in the same year as Jaspers's controversial but enduring work, *Die Schuldfrage* (*The Question of German Guilt*). The cooptation of German universities by National Socialism, beginning in 1933, infamously marked by Heidegger's Freiburg rectoral address, "*Die Selbstbehauptung der Universität,*" in May of the same year, provides an important subtext in the 1946 version of Jaspers's *Universitäts-Idee*, with respect to the necessity of keeping politics out of university life.[16] The final version appeared in 1961, the year the Berlin Wall was constructed, and in the sequence of other major works by Jaspers on the human prospect in the face of thermonuclear holocaust during what arguably was the hottest period of the Cold War. Because *Krisis* defines the occasion for all of Jaspers's published essays on the university, it is fair to adduce that in each instance he believed that the future of humanity and civilization depended, in some sense, upon the university being "true to its idea" by recovering its essence as a cipher of transcendence. Far from being a mere repristination of the early-nineteenth-century German university of Wilhelm von Humboldt, Jaspers struggles, in each of these essays, to provide an account of the university and its mission that was true to what he believed to be its historic essence. Only then, he believed, could the university provide a humanely constructive path between the past and the future.[17]

In order to amplify Jaspers's position on these matters, I begin by framing his idea of a university against the foreground provided by the more recent analysis of Jean-François Lyotard in *The Postmodern Condition: A Report on Knowledge*.[18] Following this, I develop Jaspers's views by way of the classical Greek notion of *paideia.* I do so because it seems to me that *paideia* is precisely the evanescent educational notion informing Jaspers's *Universitäts-Idee* as a cipher of transcendence—especially when considered in conjunction with the Humboldtean emphasis upon *Bildung* and *Bildungsformierung*.

CHANGES IN THE UNIVERSITY-IDEA: FROM ESSENCE TO LEGITIMACY

What is distinctive about Lyotard's analysis is his shift away from hermeneutical considerations regarding the meaning of the university idea to questions regarding its legitimacy. Lyotard argues, in a quasi-Wittgensteinian way, that the legitimacy of most, if not all, propositional truth-claims is determined by the rules implicit to particular language games in which they arise. This includes discourse on the allegedly timeless idea of a university. The defining feature of the postmodern condition, of course, and as contrast with the modern and the premodern conditions, is the radical proliferation of language games. The heterogeneity or, as he calls it, the "heteromorphology" of language games today, forces one to acknowledge that traditional justifications of the university idea no longer have the compelling significance they once enjoyed. This lack of compelling significance becomes apparent when one takes the time to consider the nature of the prevailing language games informing the founding of the University of Berlin in 1810, which is precisely what Lyotard does in a major portion of his study. Because most of the great research universities of the world have been heavily influenced by the Humboldtean conception, whether directly or indirectly, Lyotard believes it important, even essential, to determine the narrative *telos* (goal) providing the "idea" of the modern university with its claim to legitimacy in the first place.

Since the Enlightenment, Lyotard argues, there have been two basic narratives within which the modern university idea finds expression: *speculative science* and *emancipation*. The largely apolitical narrative of science and scientific discovery posits the scientist or the pure researcher as the "hero" of its story, with the community or the state providing the space whereby the speculative scientific genius can work unencumbered by external constraints and unimpeded by the exigencies of the outside world. It is the story originating with Descartes, whose *Discourse on Method*, according to Lyotard, provides the basis for an unbroken narrative culminating in what MacIntyre recently describes as the European tradition of the "encyclopedia," the goal of which is the rationally encompassed (*enkyklos*) totality of knowledge.[19]

The politically charged narrative of emancipation, on the other hand, which progressively infiltrates the narrative of pure science, has its origin, Lyotard argues, in the French Revolution, Here "humanity" is posited as "the hero of liberty" with the "Rights of Man" providing legitimation for "equal access" to the education once reserved only for the elite—even when such access comes at the expense of quality, especially in higher education. While the right of education through the level of primary education or the *Grundschule* was generally accepted by the end of the nineteenth century, the extension of this right to secondary and postsecondary education during the twentieth century provides ample evidence as to why, according to Lyotard, the "general will" is frequently at odds with the devotees of higher education. For the "knowledge elite," worshipping at the high altar of the scientific narrative, normally is the privileged class with whom the collective hero of humanity is in a perpetual state of war.

While the narrative of emancipation was also manifest in early nineteenth-century Germany, it is modified in significant ways in the German instance. Reeling from the Reign of Terror, Kant, in his 1794 essay, "*Was ist Aufklärung?*" asserts that *sapere aude*, or the mandate to be emancipated from ignorance by reason, is directed to those individuals capable of critical (*wissenschaftlich*) thinking, and that enlightenment has nothing whatever to do with a collective emancipation from ignorance: "Ages are not enlightened," Kant insists, "only individuals." In the discussions leading to the Humboldtean reformation of the university, Fichte is a principal critic of privilege and the champion of merit, even if it comes at the expense of *Staatswissenschaft*. This value, which accelerated after the French Revolution and the reorganization of Germany, was thematic in the spirit of neo-humanism that constituted the prelude to the reforms in the early nineteenth-century German university, as Jaspers observes. So also Hegel, disillusioned by Napoleon's defeat of the Prussians at the Battle of Jena (1806), took a dim view of what he called the great "dis-enlighteners" who so carelessly emptied the "treasure in earthen vessels," in the Pauline phrase, without understanding that the contents might not ever be suitably replaced.[20] Hence priority is given, in the German case, to the individualistic narrative of the speculative spirit and the ideal of *Wissenschaft*. Sufficiently influenced by Fichte and Hegel, as Lyotard points out,[21] and as contrast to the rather more liberal position of Schleiermacher regarding the role of *Bildungsformierung* in higher education, Baron von Humboldt concluded that the character of students should be developed not only with regard to what Jaspers calls *mögliche Existenz* or individual growth and self-fulfillment, but also in ways that accord with the greater needs of the state, that is, *Staatswissenschaft* and the production of graduates qualified to assume leadership roles in governance. This continued to be true for Jaspers, but in ways that brought stinging response from Jürgen Habermas, who identifies Jaspers with the elitest Mandarins of the nineteenth century. Both Napoleon and Hitler despised the university for what they perceived as being its social and intellectual elitism, Hitler having been twice rejected by the *Kunstakademie* in Vienna, prior to enlisting in the Bavarian Corps of the German army during World War I.

Commenting on what he sees as the Humboldtean *Idee*, Arthur Kennedy views the Humboldtean development as an ominous portend of the future. For when Otto von Bismarck completely wrested the control of education from the Roman Catholic Church during the *Kulturkampf* (cultural struggle) that followed the founding of the German Empire in 1871, he also provided the precondition for the ideological domination of education by the state—as happened with the Third Reich, beginning in 1933.[22]And when the resources of education, in the Marxist universities of Russia after 1917, were entirely dedicated to bringing about a classless society through a "collectivized" humanity, this, according to Lyotard, is the supreme example of a deformed emancipation narrative. Nevertheless, it is a move contiguous with the Caesaropapist *paideia* of the Czars devoted to the political indoctrination of students in the dogmas of Russian Orthodox Christianity in prerevolutionary times.[23]

The narrative of emancipation, of course, continues in the influential work of Jürgen Habermas and devotees of the Frankfurt school of critical theory, where it is fused with the narrative of speculative science in "critical discourse." But critical theory has a diminishing influence today, according to Lyotard, precisely because the ambiguous interwining of these two largely incommensurable meta-narratives has contributed to the postmodern delegitimation of both.[24] It is precisely at this point in the postmodern condition, Lyotard observes, that a *pragmatics* narrative begins to supplant both the tradition-bound narratives of speculative science and emancipation. In the postmodern instance, a pragmatics narrative of *performative* legitimation is based entirely upon determinations of efficiency as contrast to the the impartial determination of truth, which was once the hallmark of the narrative of speculative science. Indeed, what is unique about the *performativity narrative,* according to Lyotard, is the absence of any need for an appeal to metaphysical predicates regarding the nature of truth, value and the good. Today one needs only to appeal to whatever *metaprescriptives* might enhance the performance and hence the stability of the system.[25] The postmodern methodological and epistemological move, therefore, is from dialectic to *paralogy* (as in *paralogism*) and the neutralization of conflicting narrative strategies for the sake of reducing complexity. This is why *Diskurs,* as deployed in the Habermasian use of dialectic in order to reach consensus regarding policy, Lyotard observes, is viewed as a destabilizing factor in attaining the postmodern fully integrated cyborgian organization of maximal efficiency. In short, the subversive intent of critical discourse (or "theory") is viewed as an attempt to relegitimate the narrative of emancipation by way of its appeal to the presumably value-free narrative of speculative science.

Tough-minded university administrators began to discover the institutional incommensurability of the speculative science and emancipation narratives during the days of student unrest of the late 1960s and early 1970s, both in America and in Western Europe. A tender-minded, quasi-romantic attachment to a metaphysical admixture of the nineteenth-century narratives of speculative science and emancipation, many university administrator's concluded, could just as easily lead to the ruination of the institution by rendering it inoperative as to any possible renewal of mission through emancipation. In any case, the conclusion to be drawn in the postmodern shift to the meta-prescriptive narrative of *performativity*, according to Lyotard (and, of course, also for Foucault), is that "ultimate validity has to do with the instrumental pursuit and maintenance of *power* as the ultimate legitimation of the system."[26]

What is distinctive in Jaspers's university-idea by contrast, and, indeed, in his philosophy of education generally, is his appreciation of the anti-instrumentalist maxim, *"You don't put fat on the hog by weighing it!"*[27] To consider the truth of this pithy saying, we turn our attention to the rather older question of *paideia*, for it is precisely this question that informs the university-idea of Jaspers.

FROM LEGITIMACY TO ESSENCE: THE UNIVERSITY IDEA AND *PAIDEIA*

The concerns of Jaspers can be elucidated by briefly calling attention to an influential essay written by one of his devoted students, Hannah Arendt. This essay, entitled "The Crisis in Education," American education, in this instance, can be found in the collection called *Between Present and Future,* published in 1961, the same year in which Jaspers's third version of his *Universitäts-Idee* appeared. In this essay, Arendt raises the seemingly self-evident but also quite impertinent and provocative question: 'What is education for?'[28] It is the same question underlying the formation of Jaspers's *Universitäts-Idee,* in which he moves from the question of self-evident legitimacy to considerations of meaning and essence.

For most people the answer to the question regarding education's legitimacy and purpose is self-evident. One needs an education, especially a "higher" education, "in order to be happy," in other words, to help one reap life's rewards in the belief that one's economic performance is more likely to be enhanced with advanced degrees than it will be without them. But even if such a conclusion is statistically accurate, it is not at all self-evident that education will lead to *eudaimonia* and self-fulfillment. Hannah Arendt raises her question regarding the essential purpose of education not in the instrumentalist sense as to how we might better improve the curriculum so as to produce better specialists and practitioners, whatever the vocational field or specialty might be, or in order to be more competitive. Rather, she raises a question of immanent teleology, as in Hegel, with respect to the kind of *paideia* that will enable students to "take responsibility for their world."[29] In so doing, Arendt not only echoes her teacher, Karl Jaspers, but also Plato. For it is from Plato that we receive the notion of *paideia* as the "true and essential education" that not only prepares individuals for productive citizenship, but also provides the means of personal self-transcendence and "eternalization"—with "eternalization" understood, in Jaspers's words, as the "philosophical analog of salvation."

In his *Laws,* Plato, through the voice of the Athenian Stranger, poses the philosophical question as to the true meaning of education to Clemias and Megillus, representatives of the contrasting cases of Crete and Sparta, as they consider the legal composition of *Megapolis* or the urban cultures of the future. Both Clemias and Megillus are familiar with divinely revealed laws and values (from Zeus and Apollo respectively) informed by a kind of hedonistic calculus designed to minimize pain and maximize pleasure. However, they admit that these traditional laws and values are in a state of stagnation and they also confess to being conflicted on the matter because they are based upon inadequate conceptions of virtue (*arête*) and the good (*agathon*).

Clemias and Megillus agree with the Athenian Stranger that if one is rationally clear regarding the differences between "virtue" and "vice," it may be fairly easy to discern what the form such an education might take. But they are fuzzy on this matter, having been too much in the sway of local traditions of Crete and Sparta and the bad moral reputations these places have. And so they are willing to be engaged in dialogue recognizing that Athenians have the reputation of being "noble by nature" and blessed with a certain "rational autonomy" on matters of ethics and education as contrast with other peoples.

They soon discover that the meaning of education (*paideia*), like the meaning of virtue and the good, is not at all that clear. Their naïve realism (or empiricism, as the case may be) has led them to believe that values and virtues have merely to do with the *performative* qualities necessary "to survive the original state of nature," which, as in Hobbes, is war and eternal conflict. They have not bothered to consider that the true meaning of *paideia* and *arête* derive from a higher set of values originating in the Idea of the Good. Once this is understood, as the Athenian Stranger points out, it becomes evident that our fundamental conflict is not with the external world, but with ourselves, that is, with the nature of our souls, and that correction and/or modification can come only by cultivating *sophrosyne* (temperance or moderation) and the "middle-way" between the extremes of pleasure and pain. For Plato in the *Laws,* as well as in the *Republic*, this is accomplished (in children at the elementary and primary levels) through musical education and the cultivation of harmony in body and soul—points reaffirmed by Goethe in "Die pädagogische Provinz" (The Educational Province) of *Wilhelm Meister*.

Upon commencing their dialogue, the Athenian Stranger enjoins his interlocutors by asserting:

> Let us not leave the true meaning of education (*paideia*) ambiguous or ill-defined. . . . We are not speaking of technical education, but of that other education in virtue (*arête*) from youth onwards, which makes a person eagerly

> pursue the ideal perfection of citizenship. . . . This is the only education which deserves the name; that other sort of training which aims at the acquisition of wealth or bodily strength, or mere cleverness apart from intelligence and justice is mean and illiberal, and not worthy to be called education at all. But let us not quibble with one another about the meaning of a word, provided that the basic proposition holds true: to wit, that those who are rightly educated generally become good men. Thus we must not slight education, which is the first and fairest thing that the best of men can ever have, and which, though individuals are liable to take a wrong direction, provides the basis for reformation. And this work of reformation is the great business of every man as long as he lives. (*Laws,* Bk I, 644ff.)

The self-same concern of Plato regarding the ultimate meaning of *paideia* directly informs Jaspers's *Universitäts-Idee*. Indeed, Jaspers develops a dialectical argument regarding the nature and meaning of a university between a Kantian understanding of the "idea" and the "ideal," that is, the *idea* understood, on the one hand, as a "regulative principle" of rigorous and critical scientific inquiry, and, on the other hand, the *ideal* understood in terms of a metaphysics of the soul as the principle of hope and aspiration. The idea and the ideal congeal, for Jaspers, in ciphers of transcendence. With respect to the *idea,* the university must conduct its scholarly activity very strictly within the boundaries of regulative principles that respect what he calls "the hierarchy of knowledge" presupposed by rational scientific inquiry. With respect to the *ideal,* the teaching activities of the university must always be conducted with a view to the challenge of *Bildung* and *Bildungsformierung*. As such, the true or actual (*wirkliche*) identity of the university is never fully realized. But to merely state that the university is in the state of becoming is not sufficient. The process of becoming must always unfold dialectically between the university idea of *Wissenschaft* and the transcendental ideal of *paideia*; otherwise, one has merely to contend with aimless changes dictated by the exigencies of the moment.

STRUCTURE AND TASKS OF THE UNIVERSITY

While the moral dimension of Jaspers's vision of the university has some similarities with the nineteenth-century model provided by John Henry Cardinal Newman and the founding of the Catholic University in Dublin,[30] it differs in important respects. To carry out its mission as the "city on the hill," Jaspers believed that the university must be entirely independent of both politics and organized religion. This distinction is consistent with the neo-humanistic views of Fichte and the general conviction of the Humboldtean reformers that higher education should be nonutilitarian, that is, limited neither to simply "making a living" (*Brotstudien*) nor reserved to those privileged by class in the first and second estates. The mission of the university is *Wissenschaft* in-and-for-itself, which, indeed, keeps it squarely within the narrative of speculative science. Here it is important to remember, however, that the ideal of "scientific" inquiry applies to all intellectual disciplines and fields, not just the natural and social sciences, for the object of science in all instances is *truth*. Accordingly, Jaspers structures his idea of the university under three carefully differentiated general headings:[31] (1) intellectual life, (2) clear programmatic objectives, and (3) the requisite institutional structures for the existence of the university.

These operational distinctions entail four functional tasks: (a) research, education, and instruction; (b) general education; (c) being as the communal locus of cultural experience and critical discourse; and (d) serving as symbolical representation of the "cosmos of knowledge" within the ideal of *Einheit* or "the encompassing." Following Humboldt, Jaspers believed it impossible to have education and instruction apart from critical inquiry and creative research. He believed this because education is not limited to students, but is an activity that should take place for all within the university, faculty and students alike. This cannot happen unless both faculty and students are engaged in the acquisition of knowledge and share in the collegial spirit of scientific discovery in the pursuit of truth.

As for instruction, Jaspers identifies three forms that follow from the corollary of research and education: (1) *scholastic* education and the mastery of basic disciplines; (2) *apprenticeship* or mentoring; and (3) "the *Socratic education* of self-fulfillment and self-realization." In order for these modalities of university life to function properly, there must be "respect" for the "hierarchy of values" that a pursuit of truth within a community of enquiry presupposes.[32] For this to happen, Jaspers believes that academic freedom is an absolute necessity—not for the sake of conveying the "half truths" of political platforms or educational programs and experiments unrelated to the university as a unity, but for the sake of open rational inquiry in the pursuit of truth. While tolerant of interdisciplinary studies, Jaspers believes that special programs generated by the exigencies of the moment, and the proliferation of special institutes and seminars, should not be taken into the permanent structure of the university unless they prove to be of genuine scientific worth,[33] and not merely capable, in the contemporary instance, of producing grants. In short, experimental programs should have trial periods during which they demonstrate intellectual value prior to being permanently integrated into a university curriculum.

In order to reach these goals, Jaspers believed it important to have selectivity criteria for student admission, but this cannot be regarded as absolutely decisive. One cannot accurately determine the success of students by advance measurements or even by testing during the process of being educated. There is no exact correlation between aptitude and intelligence, and it is "utterly impossible," Jaspers asserts, "to test creativity, curiosity, and the will to truth."[34] Hence the continuous monitoring and testing of students is an indication that students are mediocre and do not deserve to be in a university. What counts above all, Jaspers believes, are exit examinations properly designed to demonstrate that the student has, in fact, mastered a discipline or field and truly earned the degree to which he or she is entitled. In short, the university is and must remain a meritocracy and not an egalitarian institution.[35] To have it otherwise necessitates the abandonment of "unity" (*Einheit*) as having anything whatever to do with the university idea.

One of the truly notable features of Jaspers's idea of a university (and here very much in contrast to Heidegger's) is his candid acknowledgment of the revolution in technology and its implications for the future life of humanity. Thus he suggests that technology (or engineering, as we might understand this term) be added to the *higher faculty*:

> To expand the university by creating a fourth faculty next to the upper three faculties of theology, jurisprudence, and medicine, poses the real challenge today, since technology represents an entirely new and developing area of human life. Unclear as is the ultimate effect of technology upon human existence, it is involved in a development at once planned and chaotic.[36]

Philosophy, Jaspers believes, has the special role of clarifying the implications of technology precisely because of the artificial division between the natural and the humane sciences. While the objective or physical world is the primary concern of natural sciences, and while the subjective world of experience and meaning is the primary concern of the humanities, Jaspers insists that the divisions of the *Naturwissenschaften* and the *Geisteswissenschaften*, though operationally distinct and therefore necessary, must always remain in constant communication. Natural science, left to itself, Jaspers asserts, is helpless and without direction; and the humanities, apart from rigorous scientific critique, can easily drift into idle, useless speculation. Thus active communication between the "two cultures" of science and the humanities should always be concerned with the ultimate goal of unification (or "reunification") as the absolutely essential task of university life—even though "the educational ideal in which humanism and the realism of the natural sciences are completely joined to one another for their mutual enlightenment has never as yet been fully realized."[37] And while this unity will never be completely realized, Jaspers believes that it is precisely the task of the wholly "independent" lower faculty, presided over by philosophy, to keep the conversation alive by providing an authentic vision of "unity" (*Einheit*) that might serve as the encompassing guide for the higher faculties of theology, medicine, and law, which remain directly in the service of the state. If philosophy is to provide the encompassing vision as to the overall ultimate mission of the university, it must remain aloof from the day-to-day concerns of politics, and fully attuned to the calling which has its origin in Transcendence.

Insisting upon the independence of philosophy from politics frequently put Jaspers at odds with his colleagues in both philosophy and theology at Heidelberg. Not only was he the lone voice, as stated previously, objecting to the Heidelberg faculty's unanimous resolution protesting the terms of the Versailles reparations following World War I, but Jaspers was also a primary critic of the gradual erosion of academic freedom and the censorship of "worldviews (*Weltanschauungen*) unconvicted by criminal proceedings" (as the early nineteenth-century constitutions had provided) but censored for simply being hostile to the state (which was the case in the later mitigated constitutions governing the life of the university leading up to the period of National Socialism). The consistent objections of Jaspers to nationalistic "partisanship" as violations of the public and the private sphere, is based on the notion that the university, like the church, is of *Occidental* and not merely German origin, that is, both the university and the church, while distinct, have a "higher calling"[38] to which they must be true, whatever the circumstances.

In order for the university to be true to its unique calling, that is, in order to fully integrate the new world of technology in ways that will not subvert this calling, Jaspers goes on to assert:

> Only a revival of the old idea of the university can make scholars feel the magnitude of their task to the point where the creation of a new technical faculty would benefit the university as a whole. But the university as a whole would have to share in this rededication if it is to have a chance of promoting a general rebirth. The university's great task would be to create a truly comprehensive awareness of our age in terms of the sum total of knowledge and practical skills of which the integration of the technical faculty is only one aspect.[39]

By such a revival Jaspers addresses the two cultures problem that C. P. Snow famously identified far more pessimistically during the same period.[40] It is here that the *Occidental* (and Medieval) origin of his idea of a university shows its force, for he argues that the incorporation of a school of technology entails "Above all, [that] the old philosophical faculty be reunified." Hence it was imperative for Jaspers that the division of the philosophical faculty into the natural sciences and the humanities be overcome, whether such a division was *ad hoc* or formalized.

> Only reunification can impart sufficient force to the basic theoretical disciplines to counter–balance the increased impact and scope of the practical disciplines. Furthermore, such a reunification will reduce the danger that continued isolation of philosophy (both individual faculty and as a department) within the university would drive the natural sciences into the camp of technology and medicine, leaving the other [*lower*] faculties in the humanities to cherish precious memories in aesthetic isolation without vigor and without relevance.[41]

Because he views the university, in the Humboldtean manner, as being simultaneously "a professional school, a cultural center, and a research institute,"[42] only philosophy, for Jaspers, has the capacity to provide coherence to the university as a whole. But in appealing to the "old" conception of a philosophy faculty, Jaspers does not, of course, mean the departmental constitution of philosophy. What he means is that all professors in the so-called departments of arts and sciences be rigorously philosophical with respect to the task of providing substantial coherence to the university idea. Only then can the "cosmos of knowledge" and the unity of science as "meaningful aggregates" restore to the modern university its status as a truly concrete universal as contrast to incoherent aggregates simply embedded in concrete.

Such a task obviously puts tremendous pressure on philosophy, whether the philosophical resources of an arts and sciences faculty-at-large, or a department of philosophy. Some might argue that philosophy, as understood by Jaspers, and given the fragmentation of today's multiversity, simply is not up to this challenge. Moreover, while Jaspers's idea of a university is based on a distinctive philosophical concept of liberality, his concept, in Kurt Salamun's view, is not "critical enough" with respect to addressing the contemporary needs of higher education. In other words, while *liberality* in Jaspers is "anti-dogmatic," it is a concept that tends toward mysticism and the privatization of meaning; and while it is "anti-totalitarian," not only in social and political philosophy, but also in the philosophy of history, symbols of *telos*, for Jaspers, only have regulative status (in the Kantian sense), and are never really substantial. And while his concept of liberality is "anti-fundamentalistic," and hence critical of the revealed, authoritative claims of monotheistic religions which can so easily lead to intolerance, it is not at all clear that the university can of itself provide the basis for a *Kulturstätte* (Place of Cultural Interest) that can be "cultured, pluralistic, and tolerant." Finally, while Jaspers's classically liberal idea of a university is "anti-monistic," Salamun argues, with *Einheit* always being considered as an eschatological ideal and not the basis for the comprehension of reality in its totality, whether by way of an absolute system, as in Hegel, or as an entirely mundane social construction, as in the Neo-Kantians, it is difficult to say precisely *what* his concept of liberality entails with respect to the particulars of a university's actual constitution. Thus Salamun asks: "Is Jaspers's conception of liberality linked with some positive standards of value and ethical norms? Is his concept of liberality an anarchic liberalism compatible with any value standard and open to any ethical claim that is not proposed in a dogmatic, totalistic, fundamentalistic, or monistic manner?"[43]

The University Idea and Philosophic Faith

While these questions pose serious challenges to Jaspers, I suggest that Jaspers has a positive standard and that this standard does not fall prey to relativism. This does not mean the concept of liberality informing Jaspers's idea of a university can provide a recipe for its constitution as an institutional entity in all times and places. Rather, the heart of Jaspers's notion regarding the idea of a university is grounded in what he calls *philosophic faith*, precisely the kind of faith that directed Plato's queries on the nature of *paideia*.[44] In the attempt to make this notion more specific, I turn, as have so many who have commented on Jaspers's university idea, to a passage in his "Philosophical Autobiography:"

> The idea of a university lives ultimately and decisively within individual students and professors, and only secondarily in the forms of the institution. If that life would become obliterated, the institution could not possibly save it. . . . But so long as there is such a thing as the freedom of the Occidental university, the realization of that idea depends entirely upon the individual who comprehends it and is entrusted with its realization. . . . Thus the professor, in teaching, must awaken openness for everything that is knowable, for the meaning of the sciences and for the actuality of life. All of this he must encompass and penetrate by the basic operations of thinking which cause us to soar. He is called to live in the idea of the university and in doing so to acknowledge his responsibility for productive, constructive, creative activity. He must not cover up the ultimate limits but instruct in the ways of moderation.[45]

Philosophic faith is ultimately grounded in what Jaspers calls the *ethos of humanity* as distinct from the limitations always present to a particular cultural or religious ethos. Hence the idea of a university is the primary expression of the never-to-be-completely-realized ideal of philosophic faith. As in the case of the "as if" formulations of Kant's transcendental ideals, and the immanent teleology of Hegel's dialectic, the quasi-eschatological essence of Jaspers's idea of a university, far from providing the mundane basis for its falsification, is precisely the essence providing the university with its legitimacy.

NOTES

1. The task of commenting on Jaspers's "university idea" is greatly assisted owing to the presence of the collection of essays on the topic by noted Jaspers scholars; see *The Tasks of Truth: Essays on Karl Jaspers's Idea of the University*, edited Gregory J. Walters (Frankfurt-am-Main, Berlin: Peter Lang Verlag, 1996).

2. Jean-François Lyotard, *The Postmodern Condition: A Report on Knowledge*, translated by Geoff Bennington and Brian Massumi (Minneapolis: University of Minnesota Press, 1984).

3. See Jaspers's posthumous book *Chiffren der Transzendenz*, edited by Hans Saner (Munich: R. Piper Verlag, 1970). Jaspers's position on ciphers hovers between that of Cassirer and Tillich on the meaning of "symbol" (*symbolon*)—less transcendentally "generative" than Cassirer's and less "incarnationalistic" than Tillich's, but in both instances signifying the convergence of meaning and being, if only as a fleeting "event" in the experience of consciousness.

4. See *Die Atombombe und die Zukunft des Menschen. Politisches Bewusstsein unserer Zeit* (Munich: R. Piper Verlag, 1958); English translated by E. B. Ashton, *The Future of Mankind* (Chicago: University of Chicago Press, 1961). This would include Buber, Maritain, and a host of religious thinkers identified with Neo-Orthodoxy, as contrast to the rather more cynical Neo-Marxist views of Lyotard in the late-1970s, conditioned as they were by Sartre and the events surrounding the student instigated *General Strike* in France in 1968, the Vietnam war, and other destabilizing events during the 1970s.

5. See Charles E. McClelland, *State, Society, and University in Germany: 1700-1914* (Cambridge: Cambridge University Press, 1980), pp. 16–26.

6. Wilhelm von Humboldt, "Über innere und äussere Organisation der höheren wissenschaftlichen Anstalten in Berlin (1810)," reprinted in *Gelegentliche Gedanken über Universitäten*, edited by E. Müller (Leipzig: Reclam Verlag, 1990), pp. 273–84.

7. John Henry Newman, *The Idea of a University*, edited by I. T. Ker (Oxford: Clarendon Press, 1976).

8. Jaroslav Pelikan, *The Idea of the University: A Reexamination* (New Haven and London: Yale University Press, 1992).

9. Robert Paul Wolff, *The Ideal of the University* (Boston: Beacon Press, 1969).

10. Allan Bloom, *The Closing of the American Mind: How Higher Education Has*

Failed Democracy and Impoverished the Souls of Today's Students (New York: Simon and Schuster, 1987); Roger Kimball, *Tenured Radicals: How Politics Has Corrupted Our Higher Education* (New York: Harper and Row, 1990); Dinesh D'Souza, *Illiberal Education: The Politics of Race and Sex on Campus* (New York: Free Press, 1991); Bruce Wilshire, *The Moral Collapse of the University: Professionalism, Purity, and Alienation* (Albany: SUNY Press, 1990); Alasdair MacIntyre, *Three Rival Versions of Moral Enquiry: Encyclopaedia, Genealogy, and Tradition* (London: Duckworth, 1990).

11. Wolff, *The Ideal of the University*, p. 41.

12. See the articles by Raymond Langley and George Pepper in *The Tasks of Truth*, edited by G. J. Walters; see also, McClelland, *State, Society, and University in Germany,* esp., 99ff.

13. All three versions of Jaspers's *The Idea of the University* were published by the Springer Verlag, Berlin.

14. See the article by Nassir Ghaemi herein [eds.].

15. See Langley in *The Tasks of Truth*, edited by Walters, pp. 23–28. McClelland also reports, out of Franz Eulenberg, that during the Napoleonic era reforms during the first quarter of the nineteenth century, the University of Heidelberg had about 400 students—practically all of which matriculated in medicine, law, and theology, with hardly any in philosophy, indicating that the neo-humanistic reforms of northern Germany had not as yet reached Baden-Würtemberg. McClelland, *State, Society, and University in Germany,* p. 108.

16. There is an obvious symmetry between the 1961 version of Jaspers and the various issues engaged by Hannah Arendt in "The Crisis in Education." See *Between Past and Future: Six Exercises in Political Thought* (New York: Viking, 1961), pp. 173–96.

17. As Raymond Langley correctly observes, the university is for Jaspers the instantiation of a kind of "secularized" vision of the "city on the hill"—even though the terms instantiation and secularized need major qualification in the case of Jaspers. It is important here to indicate, in connection with the final version of Jaspers's *Universitäts-Idee,* that *Chiffren der Transcendenz* also appeared in its initial form in 1961 (*National-Zeitung*, Basel, Nr. 323, 16.7).

18. Jean-François Lyotard, *The Postmodern Condition: A Report on Knowledge*, translated by Geoff Bennington and Brian Massumi (Minneapolis: University of Minnesota Press, 1984).

19. See MacIntyre, *Three Rival Versions of Moral Enquiry*; also, Tom Rockmore, *Hegel's Circular Epistemology* (Bloomington: Indiana University Press, 1986).

20. See the famous section on "Absolute Freedom and Terror" as outlined in the middle-sections of Hegel's *Phenomenology of Spirit* (1807). A similar dissonance is to be found at the end of *Hegel's Lectures on the Philosophy of Religion* with respect to the post-enlightenment future of religion.

21. Lyotard, *The Postmodern Condition*, pp. 31ff.

22. Arthur Kennedy, "The University as a Constituting Agent of Culture, in *The Tasks of Truth*, edited by Walters, pp. 97–115. In the German instance, the "subversion of Transcendence" by the state during the Third Reich raises the question as to whether

Jaspers's *Universitäts-Idee*, as a cipher of transcendence, is sufficiently concrete (as contrast with the idea of Newman) to avoid this subversion, or whether it remains perpetually in a state of "hovering" so that it becomes the easy captive of totalitarian ideologies and governments.

23. This was the argument of Nicholas Berdyaev, of course, in *The Origins of Russian Communism* (1937) and also *The Beginning and the End* (1939), i.e., that Marxist-Leninism was but the secularized form of Czarist-Orthodoxism and, as such, entirely within the continuity of the Byzantine legacy of *caesaropapism*. It is of interest to note in this regard, and with respect to the role of religion in higher education, as does Edward Pace in his article on "The University" in the *Catholic Encyclopedia*, that prior to the Protestant Reformation eighty-one universities with papal charter had been founded in the Latin West. In the Russian case, as well as in the other countries in Eastern Europe dominated by the schismatic Greek Church, no universities were established during the medieval period.

24. Frankfurt University, it will be recalled, was identified by the Nazis as a "*Rote Universität*" or Red University and summarily the first to be shut down. Here Lyotard (*The Postmodern Condition*) cites the rectoral address of Heidegger in May of 1933 on "*Die Selbstbehauptung der Universität*" ("The Self-assertion of the German University") as an "unfortunate episode in the history of legitimation" precisely because the political and the scientific narratives are fused in "unbecoming ways." The incommensurability of these narratives is also manifest in Habermas's persistent critique of Jaspers as a "mandarin" and/or "elitist" defense of the Humboldtean conception. See Jürgen Habermas, "The Idea of the University: Learning Processes" in *The New Conservatism: Cultural Criticism and the Historian's Debate*, edited by Shierry Weber Nicholsen (Cambridge, MA: MIT Press, 1989), pp. 100–27. Hannah Arendt, in "The Crisis in Education," would defend her teacher, Karl Jaspers, against the critique of Habermas precisely on the latter's failure to distinguish sufficiently between "learning" and "education."

25. "Fairness" in the Rawlsian sense can be regarded as precisely such a *meta-prescriptive* (though Lyotard makes no mention of Rawls), since, for Rawls, what Lyotard calls meta-narratives are confined to the so-called veil of ignorance. See John Rawls, *Theory of Justice* (Cambridge, MA: Harvard University Press, 1973). In his discussion of paralogy, Lyotard is largely dependant upon the work of Nicholas Luhmann.

26. Lyotard, *The Postmodern Condition*, pp. 60–61. It is interesting to note that the narrative informing the 1983 report *A Nation at Risk* of the "National Commission on Excellence in Education" is almost completely informed by *performativity*. What concerns the authors, in each and every section of this influential report, is the "under-performance" of the American system of education as compared with the performance systems of our "major competitors." Hence in the process of assessing the dismal performance of public education in the United States, the report proposes solutions to what, at the time, were perceived as being *systemic failures* of such magnitude that the American system of education had deteriorated to levels inferior, in many instances, to what prevailed during the time of Sputnik and the National Defense Education Act of 1957. Notably missing in *A Nation At Risk* is any kind of sustained social and cultural analysis

regarding the context within which education takes place, and the moral content one might be able to achieve within that context. See *A Nation at Risk: The Imperative for Educational Reform*, A Report to the Nation and the Secretary of Education, United States Department of Education (Washington, DC: The National Commission on Excellence in Education, April 1983).

27. Randall Olson, "Paideia and Modern Educational Policy: The Conflict of Intent and Authority," in the *Proceedings of the Twentieth World Congress of Philosophy*, Boston, Massachusetts, 1998, http://www.bu.edu/wcp/Papers/Educ/EducOlso.htm (accessed January 28, 2005). Here one might also note that the "assessment" mandates of the "No Child Left Behind" policy of the Bush administration has been a windfall for the "testing" business; budgets have been tripled, and instruction in non-testable areas (for example, the Arts) have been cut.

28. The issues Arendt raises in "The Crisis of Education," are the same issues being discussed and, unfortunately, "resolved," in ways that she would find highly objectionable. By the early 1960s, Americans had entered into a world quite different than the one left behind—the defining mark of that difference being the emergence of mass popular culture being progressively controlled, manipulated and dumbed-down by the mass media.

29. On this topic, see David Steiner, *Philosophy and Education*, Vol. 3, Proceedings of the Twentieth World Congress of Philosophy (Philosophical Documentation Center, 2000) and, idem., *Rethinking Democratic Education: The Politics of Reform* (Baltimore, MD: Johns Hopkins University Press, 1994).

30. Cardinal Newman's lectures on *The Idea of a University* were delivered at Trinity in Dublin in 1852. See also the helpful schema contrasting Jaspers and Newman by Gregory Walters in *The Tasks of Truth*, edited by Walters, pp. 90–91.

31. References below are made to the Reiche and Vanderschmidt translation of the 1946 German edition of *The Idea of a University* (Boston, 1959; London, 1960). [Hereafter cited as IU, eds.]

32. IU, pp. 60–62.

33. IU, p. 138.

34. IU, p. 136.

35. IU, p. 139.

36. IU, p. 105.

37. IU, p. 46.

38. See *The Philosophy of Karl Jaspers*, The Library of Living Philosophers, edited by Paul Arthur Schilpp. Second, augmented ed. (LaSalle, IL: Open Court, 1981 [1957]), pp. 45–53, at 48.

39. IU, p. 136. Jaspers's conception is amazingly similar to that of Richard Tawney: "The business of the university is two-fold: to uphold an intellectual standard, and uphold a moral standard. The intellectual standard it upholds by maintaining a severe intellectual discipline. The moral standard it upholds by making that discipline accessible to all who will submit to it, by relaxing it for none merely because they are well to do or socially influential, by depriving none of it merely because they are poor or uncouth or socially

incompetent. It this way a University might become a center of moral authority. And it is precisely such moral authority which Englishmen need more than anything else at the present time. We require (a) to be taught the infinite difference between what is false and what is true, (b) think of knowledge, like religion, as transcending all differences of class and wealth, and (c) that in the eye of learning as in the eye of God, all men are equal, because they are infinitely small. To sell education for money is the next thing to selling the gifts of God for money." R. H. Tawney's *Commonplace Book*, edited J. M. Winter and D. M. Joslin (Cambridge: Cambridge University Press, 1972), p. 43. This passage called to my attention by Professor Adam B. Seligman, Boston University.

40. See C. P. Snow, *The Two Cultures and the Scientific Revolution* (New York: Cambridge University Press, 1959).

41. IU, p. 107.

42. IU, pp. 54–59.

43. See Kurt Salamun, "Jaspers's Concept of Liberality and His Idea of a University," in *The Tasks of Truth,* edited by Walters, pp. 39–53.

44. See also, Alan M. Olson, "Introduction: *Paideia* in Philosophy and Religion," in *Educating for Democracy: Paideia in an Age of Uncertainty*, edited by Alan M. Olson, David M. Steiner, and Irina S. Tuuli (Lanham, MD: Rowman & Littlefield Publishers, Inc., 2004), pp. 5–10.

45. Karl Jaspers, "Philosophical Autobiography," in *The Philosophy of Karl Jaspers*, edited by Paul Arthur Schilpp, Augmented Edition (La Salle, IL: Open Court Publishing Co., 1981 [1957]), p. 32. It is interesting to note that of all the philosophical problems and topics covered in the 1957 Schilpp edition, attention to the university-idea is missing.

KARL JASPERS'S AXIAL AGE THEORY

Its Relevance for Contemporary Cross-cultural Philosophy

Ram A. Mall

Karl Jaspers, particularly the later Jaspers, is one of the very few philosophers in and of the twentieth century to have projected and worked out the idea of a world philosophy in the sense of a new orientation and conception leading to a new historiography of philosophy. The main thesis proposed, discussed, and defended here is twofold. First, in the spirit of Jaspers's concern that philosophical reflection begins with our present historical situation, I situate this exposition and analysis within our current, global intercultural situation. In turn, I argue that the philosophy of Karl Jaspers, particularly his well-known and much discussed thesis of the axial age, his idea of "philosophic faith," and his theory of the "perennial philosophy" are rare and much needed contributions to the spirit of cross-cultural philosophy. Finally, I argue that the term "Cross-Cultural Philosophy" or "Intercultural Philosophy" is not the name of a particular philosophical discipline added to the already existing philosophical disciplines. It is, rather, the name of a basically new orientation in philosophy accompanying all our philosophical discourses and, thus, enabling us to discuss philosophical problems and issues in an intercultural philosophical perspective.

Philosophy and the Global Situation

The globally present intercultural context today has made one thing abundantly clear: The de facto intercultural hermeneutic situation has outgrown the Graeco-European and Jewish-Christian interpretation of culture, philosophy, and religion. It calls for a deconstruction of an exclusive relation between truth and tradition. Truth *of* the tradition and truth *in* the tradition are two different things and must not be confused with one another.

The fact that much of what we do in the name of intercultural studies takes place from the point of view of Western thought and shows signs of asymmetry and hegemony of the West is true, but one-sided. I do see the point of this remark, but feel that this one-sidedness is due to a historical contingency that made European thought the main paradigm of reference. Added to this is the prejudice of the orientalists of the earlier days that philosophy, culture, and religion are Western achievements. I have been trying to overcome this contingency, hoping to contribute to a common, global discourse and conversation of humankind beyond the narrow limits of the East-West dichotomy.

Chauvinism, whether religious, cultural, philosophical, national, or geographical must be given up for the sake of and in order to realize intercultural understanding. Western philosophy, according Mircea Eliade, cannot move within its own tradition without becoming provincial. This truth applies, *mutatis mutandis*, to all philosophical, cultural, and religious traditions, even more now than ever before.

In my attempt to answer the question concerning the conditions, possibilities, and limits of intercultural understanding I find myself caught up in a paradoxical situation, which I can neither avoid nor fully resolve; for I am an insider and outsider at the same time. Part of this exposition represents an impressionistic account of my constant effort at translating cultures into one another. I am, thereby, guided by the conviction that the two fictions of total translatability and commensurability, on the one hand, and of radical untranslatability and incommensurability among cultures, on the other, have to be given up in favour of a metonymic thesis of dynamically overlapping structures. Since no culture is a windowless monad, all cultures possess intercultural overlappings in varying degrees.

The metonymic figure of speech in its intuitive import stresses the fact of our indubitable consciousness of the difference between the name and the named. Since no philosophical reflection can fully overtake the reflected-upon, there is always an open possibility of multiple expressions. This is the bedrock for our practice of translating one culture into another. A closer look at the history of ideas in an intercultural perspective shows clearly that the practice of translation does not succeed, it rather precedes the question regarding the possibility of the same. Regarding the problem of translating cultures, Paul Ricoeur says that there is no absolute alienation and that there is always a genuine possibility of translation. One can understand without repeating, can imagine without experiencing, can transform oneself into the other and still remain the self one is.[1]

Whatever may be the merits and demerits of globalization, the universalistic bent of the European mind seems to be partly disillusioned because it is forced to realize now that the days are gone when Europe alone seemed to make world history. Europe today is one of the centers, and not the only one. According to Derrida, Europe often talks of "crisis" when its universality is in danger. The discovery of non-European cultures is mainly a European achievement leading to the unintended irony of relativizing the European culture itself. Many missionaries, for example, went out to convert others, but some of them got converted themselves.

The Axial Age Thesis and the Comparison of Cultures

Karl Jaspers, the former friend and later opponent of Heidegger, goes with Schopenhauer against Hegel in subscribing to the view that the spirit of philosophy knows no cultural boundaries, and it waves wherever it likes. This means philosophy is not only of Greek and European origin. The famous and quite revolutionary thesis of the axial age empirically fixes a period of time, between 800 to 200 BCE, that introduces a new chapter in world history and the history of ideas. It is the time when in China, India, and Greece human reason embarks upon asking and solving perennial philosophical questions from within its own bounds, without depending too heavily or exclusively on religion and mythology. In China, we have thinkers like Confucius, Lao Tzu, Chuang Tzu; in India the Upanishadic thinkers, Buddha and Mahavira; and, in Greece, Heraclitus, Parmenides, Socrates, Plato and Aristotle.

The project of a monumental universal "world history of philosophy"[2] that Jaspers worked on so hard in his later years of teaching and research is guided by his fundamental intention to find a way out of a fateful situation that jeopardizes all communication and understanding. Jaspers was fully and rightly convinced that no solution today can afford to be merely provincial because of cross-cultural bindings. Jaspers thinks that the fundamental categories developed in the axial age are of much help even today in an age of globalization, for they plead for unity without uniformity.[3]

In the spirit of the axial age, philosophy is to be considered as a universal human enterprise with its culture-bound and culture-independent aspects. Jaspers pleads for acquiescence in opposition to Heidegger who rather radically dichotomizes Europe and Asia and warns the former of the danger of losing itself in Asia.[4] Jaspers, who is fully aware of the narrowness of such an outlook, warns us against any hypostatization of the relationship between Europe and Asia because such a step may lead to a wrong type of ontology, which is not conducive to an intercultural communication and understanding.[5] Added to this, there is a danger of a self-fulfilling prophecy lurking in such a view. Jaspers is rightly of the opinion that no philosophical truth worth the name gives a privileged treatment to any one particular culture, philosophy, or religion. The axial age thesis is solid proof against the validity of the Heideggerian claim that European philosophy is a *tautolog* because philosophy is essentially and exclusively Greek and European. Jaspers makes it abundantly clear that the word "philosophy" is, no doubt, of Greek origin, but not the idea of philosophy. The concern of philosophy as a human enterprise is anthropologically anchored. Besides Europe, China and India are the other places in which philosophy originated.[6]

The axial age thesis of Jaspers rightly qualifies the Euro-Christian thesis of the one absolute axis of world history, which is Europe. Jaspers mentions Augustine and Hegel who explain world history as a movement from and to Christ. The birth of Christ is not the only axis of world history, and Christian faith is one faith among others, not the only faith for the whole of humanity. This is not only theoretically and ideologically true, but also empirically true.[7]

The axial age theory of Jaspers has been variously discussed and put to critical historical scrutiny. His thesis helps us to develop a conception of philosophy that is open and tolerant enough to enter into a discourse in the spirit of a reciprocal recognition. Jaspers further underlines the fact of a cultural, philosophical, and even religious axis that is common to the whole of humanity in spite of the illuminating differences that are there, and thereby enriches cultural and philosophical patterns of human thinking.

The critics of the axial age theory of Jaspers complain that it lacks empirical verification when we put it in the context of world history based on the recent historical and archeological findings. Added to this, the axial age thesis gives a privileged treatment only to the written traditions, neglects the powerful oral traditions, and thus betrays a narrow logo-centric tendency. While it is true that Jaspers did not discuss historical traditions of Africa and Latin America, the logo-centrism of Jaspers may be given up without denying the theoretical validity and practical applicability of his axial age hypothesis. The thesis provides us with a sound basis for doing intercultural studies and asks us to reject any kind of centrism, including the most historically powerful euro-centrism.

One may have certain reservations regarding the soundness of the axial age thesis when put to a severe test of a strict science of history.[8] But one should not forget that Jaspers really does not claim to have written his book on *The Origin and Goal of History* for students of the historical sciences. He has written this book from the point of view of a new historiography of philosophy, which should enable us to communicate with thinkers and philosophers like Confucius, Lao Tzu, Buddha, Shankara, Nagarjuna, Socrates, Plato, Augustine, Hegel, and Kant. The centrality of the perspective of the axial age should not be stretched too far, for it then becomes reductive and fails to do proper justice to the enormous richness of human written and oral history.[9]

Jaspers frankly admits to have been quite euro-centric in his earlier years, and to have thought of European rationality in too high terms. He singles out two fateful dates in this century, namely, 1914 and 1933, which awoke him from his euro-centric slumber. This also helped him give up the idea of any self-complacent universalism.[10] Jaspers was thoroughly disappointed by Europe and with European reason and humanity. In the years of his "inner immigration," when he was forced to live a secluded life, he became a serious student of Chinese and Indian philosophies. The reading of these philosophies convinced him that the idea of reason and the readiness to communication go hand in hand. Both together define our will to understand which, in turn, gives communication a primacy over consensus. The primary requisite for the will to communication is to abstain from exclusivist and absolutist claims. Human reason is the will to communicate.

Jaspers's Understanding of *Philosophia Perennis* and Cross-cultural Philosophy

Philosophia perennis was first introduced by Steuchus in 1540 where it meant the most fundamental truths of philosophy and religion that occupy the attention of all cultures, peoples, and philosophies. For quite a long time, the concept enjoyed a theological orientation and anchorage. Different philosophical traditions and systems have often claimed to have realized the *philosophia perennis*.

Jaspers criticizes such a claim to have realized the *philosophia perennis* exclusively in any one particular philosophical convention. His understanding of *philosophia perennis* is open-minded, tolerant and very conducive to a cross-cultural philosophical discourse. *Philosophia perennis* is nobody's possession all alone. *Philosophia perennis* is, of course, in need of expression, but it transcends bare linguisticality. It expresses itself in and through philosophical conventions, but is not exhausted by them. *Philosophia perennis* has no one single mother tongue, for it is polyphon in nature.

Jaspers was convinced that all philosophical traditions, Chinese, Indian, and European, possess *philosophia perennis* but only in its historical *Gestalt*.

Philosophia perennis, according to Jaspers, is the common ground "where the most distant cultures meet each other, the Chinese with the European, the thinkers of 2500 years ago with the thinkers of the modern time."[11] All philosophical traditions have posed cross-culturally valid philosophical questions and have tried to answer them from within their own cultural context. In asking questions, philosophers are nearer to each other than in their specific answers. This is why Jaspers maintains that philosophers belonging to different philosophical traditions meet to differ and differ to meet; and this they do in the spirit of one *philosophia perennis* that serves as a cipher.

PHILOSOPHIC FAITH/CONVICTION AND CROSS-CULTURAL UNDERSTANDING

The ultimate truth, in whatever field, bears the character of a cipher, which enables us to take *philosophia perennis* as an endless reservoir of interpretations without emptying it fully. No interpretation is *the* interpretation. Jaspers introduces his famous concept of "der philosophische Glaube" or (Philosophical Faith) in response to absolutist claims to possess the one absolute truth with a capital "T." It is quite difficult to find an exact equivalent expression for the German "*der philosophische Glaube*," for it is neither a "faith" in the sense of faith in a revealed religion, nor simply a philosophical belief. It is rather the name of a philosophical insight, of a philosophic conviction, which works both as a method and way of life, as well as a conviction.

The main imperative of Jaspers's philosophic faith/conviction is to abstain from any absolutistic claim for the simple but important reason that such a claim is not only reductive, but also violent and against all reciprocal understanding and communication. Philosophic faith/conviction is essentially committed to communication, and it is this commitment that relates it to reason, which is then defined as "an infinite will to communication." The voluntarist element is present in this concept. The idea of unity it aims at is analogous to the regulative idea of Kant. For Jaspers, "ideas of unity are quite deceptive if they want to be more than symbolic in nature."[12] Jaspers's theory of cipher goes hand in hand with his understanding of philosophic faith/conviction.

Jaspers has been often accused of underplaying the role of difference between cultures and philosophies. It is true that Jaspers does not very often refer to differences. But he neither neglects them nor underrates their force in human communication. As a philosopher committed, first and foremost, to communication, Jaspers defines truth as that which binds us—not as that which separates us.[13] That which binds us may be, at times, very meagre and consist just in our readiness to abstain from absolutistic claims in favor of our own standpoints. It is in the nature of such an abstention that we accept counterarguments as arguments even if they are contrary or contradictory to our own.

Jaspers's philosophic faith/conviction leads to an open hermeneutics of intercultural understanding. It allows us to read and let read, to interpret and let interpret, and to believe and let believe. Those who think such a hermeneutics of truth fails to take the idea of truth seriously seem to mistake earnestness with readiness to fight. The philosophical faith/conviction of Jaspers does not deny the evidence and unconditionality of one's own views, but only their exclusiveness, absolutism, and universal validity. Only the believers in the spirit of Jaspers's philosophic faith/conviction are able to enter into an intercultural dialogue and not those who are ready to use violence in defence of their intolerant exclusive claims.[14]

Cross-cultural philosophy and the philosophic faith/conviction of Jaspers are not so much against the idea of an absolute, unconditional, and primordial truth, be it in philosophy, religion, or politics. What is rejected is only the exclusive claim to possess the absolute truth. Absoluteness of truth is one thing, and our absolute claim to possess it is quite another. It is the second sort of claim, which makes intercultural communication rather impossible, and absoluteness of claims is a human invention.[15]

The philosophic faith/conviction of Jaspers is not so much a philosophical standpoint as it is the name of an attitude, which accompanies all standpoints, including one's own. It would hinder different standpoints from putting themselves in an absolute position, and helps us reject monistic temptations. Philosophic faith/conviction is also skeptical about the idea of an absolute, ultimate foundation, for, if it is in singular, it becomes reductive, and if plural, then it seems to defy itself. Added to this, there is no denying the fact that there is a plurality regarding ultimate principles.

From the Sunset of European Philosophy to the Dawn of World Philosophy

Jaspers's project of a monumental universal history of philosophy is inextricably connected to his axial age thesis, theory of *philosophia perennis*, as well as his concept of philosophic faith/conviction. Philosophy is no doubt of Greek and European origin, but not only and exclusively so, because philosophy has more than one birth place.[16] World philosophy is an *organon* of reason, which aims at communication between cultures, philosophies, and other kinds of *Weltanschau-*

ungen. Hans Saner, one of the best interpreters of Jaspers's philosophy, rightly speaks of a "poly-perspectival historiography of philosophy" in his introduction to Jaspers's *World History of Philosophy: Introduction.*[17]

Jaspers speaks of a "new world vision" (*Weltkunde*), which he arrives at after reading the philosophical and religious literature of China and India, receiving a renewed vision of philosophy in a global perspective.[18] It is this new vision, a new science of thought, which led Jaspers to think of more than one origin of philosophy. His philosophical reading of the comparison of cultures also convinced him that we are on the way "to a world philosophy from the sunset of European philosophy."[19] These words of Jaspers may appear a bit stilted, but any discussion of philosophy today must take account of the comparison of cultures, underlining the necessity of the idea of a world philosophy. There is no denying the fact that the days are gone when one particular philosophical tradition (mostly the European) could claim not only universal validity, but also universal acceptance.

The project of a world philosophy recognizes more than one birthplace of philosophy, and maintains that non-European philosophies are not merely duplicates of European philosophy. It is, no doubt, true that there is a fundamental similarity between the philosophical questions posed beyond cultural boundaries, even though their specific treatment may and does vary from culture to culture. Today our points of departure in dealing with world philosophies may be European, as well as non-European. Philosophical discourse between cultures is no more a one-way road.

The one-sided, historically contingent, paradigmatic (though wrong) Eurocentric approach is mainly responsible for a bundle of prejudices and clichés denying the very predicate "philosophy" to Indian, Chinese, and African philosophies. Jaspers was fully convinced that it is high time that professional European philosophers study non-European philosophies seriously, thereby aiding our teaching and research at different levels, broadening our philosophical outlook, and thereby enabling us to enter into philosophical, cultural, and religious discourses in the open spirit of cross-culturality.

INTERCULTURALITY AND CROSS-CULTURAL PHILOSOPHY

The term "interculturality" as used here is not a trendy expression. It is also not a romantic idea in an age of global technological transformation and world tourism. It must not be taken as compensation on the part of non-European cultures born out of some inferiority complex. It is also not just a makeshift ideology in face of the de facto encounters of world cultures today.

Far from being just a construct, an abstraction, or a syncretic idea, the concept of interculturality stands for the conviction or insight that no culture is the one culture for the whole of humankind. The fear that we may thereby deconstruct the general applicability of terms like philosophy, truth, culture, and religion is unfounded. What the concept of interculturality, nevertheless, does deconstruct is the monolithic, absolutistic, and exclusivistic use made of these terms. Intercultural thinking stands for an emancipatory process from all kinds of centrisms, be it Euro-, Sino-, or Afro-centrism. The spirit of interculturality approves of pluralism, diversity, and difference as values and does not take them as privations of unity and uniformity. An acceptance of diversity is what follows from the spirit of interculturality. It is wrong to view diversity as Aristotelian accidents. An intercultural horizon can very well envisage the "compossibility" (to use a Leibnizian term) of diverse cultural patterns striking a new note between total alterity and universality. The concept of order intercultural thinking implies is an order in, through, and with differences making room for a polyphony of different voices.

In order to delineate the concept of cross-cultural philosophy as clearly as possible, let me define what it is not, and then what it is.

(1) Philosophy in an intercultural orientation is not the universalization of a particular philosophical tradition, be it European, Chinese, Indian, African or Latin American.

(2) Cross-cultural philosophy is also not a syncretism of different philosophical traditions of the world.

(3) It is wrong to take cross-cultural philosophy as a mere construction forgetting the richness of concrete philosophical conventions.

(4) Cross-cultural philosophy is also not just a makeshift ideology in the face of, and under the pressure of, the de facto presence of a multiple philosophical cultures.

(5) It is wrong to identify cross-cultural philosophy with some form of a romantic and aesthetic reception of what is foreign to a particular culture. This has often been the case in the encounter of European philosophy with non-European philosophical traditions. Cross-cultural philosophy is, in other words, not a trendy expression.

(6) Cross-cultural philosophy is also not a compensatory move either, for it does not give any privileged treatment to one particular philosophical tradition. Such a privileged treatment of the tradition of European philosophy has given rise to the prejudice that philosophy proper is exclusively European. Great philosophers—like Hegel, Husserl, and Heidegger—contributed to such a prejudice.

We now turn to a positive description of what a cross-cultural philosophy is.

(1) Cross-cultural philosophy, properly understood, is *inter*cultural rather than *trans*cultural, and it locates the proper seat of philosophical activity in more than one culture, thereby enabling us to recognize the contributions of different philosophical traditions to philosophy proper. The prefix "trans-" is overloaded with speculative metaphysical and theological connotations, and it claims a stance over and above all cultures, philosophies, and religions.

(2) Cross-cultural philosophy is convinced that the idea of a perennial philosophy does not get exhausted in any one particular philosophical tradition, be it European or not. Different philosophical approaches—intracultural and intercultural—are different ways to deal with this idea, which, rightly understood, possesses a regulative character.

(3) As a result, cross-cultural philosophy accepts the plurality of different frameworks.

(4) Cross-cultural philosophy is the name of an emancipatory movement whereby it is an emancipation of non-European philosophies from the misunderstandings they suffered because of the self-ascribed and unfounded claim to singularity and universality of European philosophy.

(5) Cross-cultural philosophy implies an intercultural challenge of the necessity of a continuous deconstruction whereby what is de-constructed is not so much the idea of truth, reality, rationality, or philosophy, but only provincial claims to capitalize these ideas exclusively.

(6) As a consequence, cross-cultural philosophy entails the idea of developing a new type of historiography of philosophy. The universal philosophical idea of rationality is, no doubt, culture-bound but also transcends cultural limitations. It possesses some sort of a "situated unsituatedness" or "unsituated situatedness."

(7) Cross-cultural philosophy pleads, thus, for the regulative idea of unity without uniformity, and defines philosophy more with regard to philosophical questions than answers. There is some sort of an asymmetry between questions and answers, and philosophical questions outweigh philosophical answers both in quality and in quantity.

(8) Cross-cultural philosophy considers all monistic moves to be too narrow, reductionist, closed, exclusive, and intolerant.

(9) Cross-cultural philosophy is convinced that the idea of a total purity of a culture and philosophy is a fiction. It subscribes to the idea that there are fundamental similarities and illuminating differences between different cultures and philosophical traditions. Out of different reasons, we always find that there are overlappings, which are the *sine qua non* of philosophical discourse.

From what has been said above, we may well maintain that the idea of a cross-cultural philosophy is in fact a tautology, for it has ever been more or less intercultural.

The word "hermeneutics" is Greek and Western, but the idea and the practice of interpretation is an anthropological constant. Indian thought, for example, possesses a very rich hermeneutical tradition. The science of hermeneutics is an art of interpretation. Understanding undergoes a fundamental change in the global context of interculturality today, and experiences an unprecedented widening of horizon that does not necessarily go hand-in-hand with Gadamer's "fusing of horizon" (*Horizontverschmelzung*). For every hermeneutics has its own culturally sedimented roots and cannot claim a universal acceptance unconditionally. Any dialogue, most importantly of course the intercultural one, has to take this insight as a point of departure.

The Concept of an Analogous Intercultural Hermeneutics

The term "analogy" in the history of Graeco-Christian-European philosophy was appealed to in order to solve the perplexing problem arising from the Holy Scripture and the Hellenistic philosophy between the two paradoxical messages of the incommensurability of God with his creation, on the one hand, and of the possibility of a comparison between the creator and the created, on the other. Since God and his creation do not belong to the same species, analogy in theology and speculative metaphysics has always suffered from a tension between univocality and equivocation. Our use of the term "analogy" here relates to things and beings belonging to the same species, and we can very well use the means of analogy as a valid cause of the cognition of similarity. In the field of intercultural understanding, analogy first stands for a consciousness of non-identity; secondly, a consciousness of difference; third, a consciousness of not total difference; and, fourth, a consciousness of not total identity. It is defined here as a likeness of relation between unlike things.

The way the continents address each other today is of a different quality, one which takes place in a religious, cultural, and political atmosphere of an inevitable reciprocity. The *de facto* hermeneutic situation is characterized by the fact that for the last few decades the non-Europeans also think and write about Europe, explain it, and judge it. This has hardly been the case since the invasion of India by Alexander the Great or the discovery of America by Columbus. Our new hermeneutic situation further bears the label of a fourfold hermeneutic dialectics.

First of all, there is the way that Europeans understand themselves; second, there is the European understanding of the Non-Europeans; third, there is the way the non-Europeans understand themselves; and fourthly, there is the way non-Europeans draw a picture of the Europeans. Europe is, of course, surprised to see that she, too, is an object of interpretation in this situation.

The concept of "analogous hermeneutics" that does justice to such a *de facto* hermeneutic situation is neither the hermeneutics of total identity, which reduces the other to an echo of oneself and repeats its self-understanding in the name of understanding the other, nor is it that of radical difference, which makes the understanding of the other rather impossible. It does not put any one culture in an absolute position of generality or reduce all others to some form of the same. There is no one universal hermeneutic subject over and above the sedimented cultural, historical subject. Analogous hermeneutics is, rather, a reflexive-meditative attitude accompanying the different subjects with a warning not to reduce. Such a hermeneutic attitude helps us to overcome the feeling of our being hopelessly involved in the hermeneutic circle. It further frees us from our tendency to define truth in terms of one particular tradition and this one tradition in terms of truth. An excessive commitment to tradition and prejudices (Gadamer) endangers intercultural understanding. In this respect, Habermas is rightly critical of Gadamer's hermeneutics with its universalistic claim.

In the face of alternate traditions, cultures, and ethical pluralism, it is wrong to maintain that we are condemned only to our own tradition and that we can, at most, try to interpret and understand it. My moral intuition tells me that I can belong to my culture and can be, in some measure, a critic of it at the same time.

It is a wrong move in the field of intercultural understanding to reduce a theory of meaning to a theory of truth, and the latter to translatability. Davidson tends toward the thesis of a mutual untranslatability and speaks of radically different frameworks.[20] But cultures may be and are, in fact, meaningful if we abstain from claiming the best intuition of truth only for ourselves. Understanding cultures is a complex matter, and I assume the common sense view that there are degrees of understanding and degrees of misunderstanding both in the case of self-understanding and in the case of understanding of the other.

Since the encounter of cultures today no longer takes place on a one-way street, there is a mutual change of all the cultures involved in the process, e.g., in the field of medicine (Chinese acupuncture or the Indian ayurvedic medicine in Europe), in dance and music (from Africa and South America), etc.

With intercultural thinking as a goal, we cannot just insist on deciding problems of mutual understanding regarding the truth and falsity of a definite culture, religion, or philosophy in a metaphysical vein before undertaking steps at concrete mutual understanding. Any a priori, metaphysical, or ideological decision precludes the possibility of a genuine understanding. In spite of the great difficulties we face in our attempt to understand cultures other than our own, intercultural understanding is both theoretically and practically possible. Of course, we must not exclude intercultural understanding *per definitionem* by saying, for example, only a Buddhist can understand Buddhism, a Muslim Islam, a Christian Christianity, a Hegelian Hegel, a Taoist Taoism, and so on. This would be an understanding by identification.

Today we have to take into account that there is a double perspective a philosopher, theologian, and ethnologist can take. She can turn to herself and make her own culture an object of study. It is better to be diffident in one's truth claim. The philosophers may discuss the question of true knowledge in the best epistemological way, but ultimately it comes down to our preference for a particular set of arguments. All discourses deal with arguments for or against these preferences. Toward the goal of intercultural peace we expect all cultures to argue and to let argue. This is what an epistemologically oriented hermeneutics aims at. Those who talk about "the radical other" claim the truth for themselves and underrate the importance and virtue of a moderate relativism and pluralism.[21] The foreignness of the other is a phenomenon we are confronted with even in our own home culture. The question of making sense of a foreign culture possesses a constitutive reciprocity.

Even conceptual frameworks partly bear the signs of their being embedded in philosophical, cultural, and religious tradition. To put one particular framework in an absolute position is methodologically a wrong move. Intercultural philosophy favors an "analogous hermeneutics" of overlapping structures beyond the two fictions of total identity (commensurability) and radical difference (incommensurability). Such a hermeneutics also leads to a healthy concept of comparative philosophy,[22] which rejects the idea not only of an absolute text, but also that of an absolute interpretation. Comparative philosophy, worthy of the name, presupposes an intercultural orientation in philosophy.

The overlapping structures among cultures, philosophies, and religions, emphasized by our analogous hermeneutics may have their sources in the biological, anthropological, cultural, and social setup of human nature. There is, of course, a limit to every understanding if to understand means just to duplicate one's own way of understanding. An analogical apprehension of the other obtains between forms of understanding which may even be contrary. This is the reason why we concede that an antithesis is also a thesis. The concept of understanding characteristic of our analogous hermeneutics is more than simply a way of knowing, because it also implies a moral commitment and ethos.

TOWARD AN ETHOS OF INTERCULTURALITY

The true spirit of interculturality proclaims as its motto that the desire to understand and the desire to be understood are two sides of one and the same interculturally oriented hermeneutic coin. The mere desire to understand may turn out to be empty, and the total desire only to be understood may become blind. In the long period of colonization, whether in culture, religion, or politics, the desire to be understood was most powerful on the part of the colonizers. It is not always wrong to maintain that orientalists, missionaries, and ethnologists did play a conspiratorial role for quite a long time. They took great pains to learn foreign languages like Sanskrit, Chinese, and others in order not so much to understand others but to be understood by them.

Mircea Eliade* uses the term "the second renaissance" in the context of the discovery of Buddhism, the Upanishads, and the Sanskrit language in eighteenth- and nineteenth-century Europe. Although the hopes and promises of the European discovery of Asia were very high, it really was a failure.[23] The reason for this bankruptcy, in contrast to the grand success of the first renaissance, lies in the fact that it remained mainly a philologically oriented field of work and research for indologists, and was not taken seriously by philosophers, theologians, and historians. Even an indologist like Max Müller, to whom India owes so much, could not avoid his bias regarding the superiority of Western philosophy and Christian religion. He writes: "People do not yet see the full importance of the Veda in an historical study of religion. The bridge of thoughts . . . that spans the whole history of the Aryan world has the first arch in the Veda, its last in Kant's *Critique of Pure Reason.* While in the Veda we may study the childhood, we may study in Kant's *Critique* the perfect manhood of Aryan mind."[24] Müller's words remind us of Hegel who often used the metaphor of childhood, youth, and manhood in relation to cultures.

Indology is really a curious European invention with its academic institutionalization at universities. True, indologists deserve our praise for their solid philological, grammatical, and textual scholarship. Their main deficiency lies in their blindness to philosophical, historical, and religious contents of the text, and also in their prejudice to turn to original texts without taking the help of the rich hermeneutic tradition. Gadamer is here perfectly right in denying the legitimacy of such a hermeneutic move, for one cannot reach the original text or intuition

*Mircea Eliade (1907–86) was a Romanian historian and philosopher of comparative religion. Eliade studied Indian philosophy and Sanskrit at Calcutta University (1928–31). He lectured at the University of Bucharest (1933–39) on the history of religion and metaphysics. He served in the diplomatic service during World War II. He also taught at the Sorbonne (1946–48) and the University of Chicago (1957–85).

unless one goes through the interpretive history. It is a myth to believe in an absolute text and in an absolute interpretation.

In case we are on the verge of a third renaissance today, given global technological transformations (and it seems we are), we are all obliged to lead interculturality to success. This is possible only when we give up all centrisms and absolutistic truth claims. No culture, no religion, is only an exporter or importer. There is a give and take ethos at work in every reciprocal understanding.

An interculturally oriented philosopher is sometimes taken to face a dilemma: He or she cannot do good intercultural philosophy with centrism, but one can do no philosophy at all without having a center. I have thought over this paradox and have the following suggestion to offer: To have a center does not necessarily mean to be centrist. We must differentiate between strong and weak centrism. What we must avoid is centrism in the strong sense, for it is exclusive and discriminatory. But a weak sense of centrism allows us to be centrist without putting one's own center in an absolute position. It asks us to be very sensitive toward the problem of tolerance; it advises us to tolerate the tolerant and to fight back the different forms of intolerance, which if unchallenged lead to fundamentalist practices.

The study of cultures and religions from an intercultural perspective shows fundamental similarities and illuminating differences. This complex pattern of similarities and dissimilarities forms an important basis for intercultural dialogue. Interreligiosity is the name of an ethos connecting all religions as their overlapping center. In the absence of such an ethos, all interreligious dialogues are samples of no real value. Methodologically, and from the point of view of conviction, it belongs to the very essence of such an interreligious ethos that there are various ways to one and the same religious truth. The claim to absolute truth is not necessarily bad if it is just for the person or the group. But the moment it demands universal following it becomes absolutist in the fundamentalist sense.[25]

If the hermeneutic dilemma consists in the seemingly paradoxical situation that we cannot understand without having certain prejudices, and that we fail to understand if we have only prejudices, then the task of finding a way out is incumbent upon us. To say that we are caught in this hermeneutic circle does not help much. The way out seems to lie in the intercultural conviction of one truth under different names. Our concept of an analogous hermeneutics is guided by this conviction and bears ample resemblance to Wittgenstein's deepest insight about a family resemblance, which must not be taken to be an identity. If we reject the identity thesis because it makes no room for diversities, we also reject radical relativism because it heavily depends on a radical difference, which leaves no room for overlapping features among cultures.

ASIA VERSUS EUROPE, OR UNIVERSISM VERSUS UNIVERSALISM

It was the Dutch Sinologist J. J. M. de Groot who first coined the word "universism" (1918) for the Eastern (Chinese) view that humanity and nature form a continua and do not stand in a dichotomous relation, but rather one of reciprocal complementarity. That which sustains the great cosmic nature is more fundamental, pervasive, powerful, and binding than that which supports human history. Concepts such as impartiality, justice, and order that are embedded in the view of universism pose a challenge to the Western *Weltanschauung*, which seems to believe that the whole creation is exclusively for the sake of man.

From Herodotus to Heidegger there persists a thinking, which dichotomizes Asia and Europe far too heavily. Such a dichotomizing and ontologizing may take a conspiratorial form leading to a self-fulfilling prophecy. In his lecture entitled "Europe and the German Philosophy," which he gave in Rome in 1936, Heidegger speaks of the "protection of European peoples from all that is Asian" (*Bewahrung der europäischen Völker vor dem Asiatischen*).[26] Heidegger also maintains that the phrase "European philosophy" is a tautology because philosophy can simply only be European. Karl Jaspers, the former friend and later opponent of Heidegger, warns us against hypostatizing the Asian-European contrast.[27] Karl Löwith also rightly takes Heidegger to task for the latter's conviction that the question of Being (*Seinsfrage*) favors the occidental mind. The hermeneutic philosophy of the later Gadamer comes nearer the truth, for it seems to concede that the other could also be right.

We have discussed human encounters as cultural and religious encounters, and pleaded for the discovery and cultivation of the virtue of an overlapping consensus,[28] which enables us to live and to let live, to believe and to let believe, to interpret and to let interpret. There has always been a human encounter with nature. But the human encounter with nature in our postindustrial society of global pervasiveness is something qualitatively new because it is heavily destructive and only partly reconstructive and globally fateful. Humanity's encounter with nature mirrors the type of attitude we adopt in relation to nature. It is generally recognized that Asian attitudes toward nature are less anthropocentric than European perspectives. This is true in spite of the fact that, for all practical purposes, the ecological situation in Asian countries is not any better than in the Western countries.

In their search for an answer to the question regarding the special place of human beings in the cosmic household, the European anthropologists tend to place humans against nature. This is done by assigning human beings either a godly descendance, or a special faculty called reason, language, and knowledge. Even if we hesitatingly accept this and say: So far, so good, it is unjust to deduce from this the right of humans to control nature recklessly. The monotheistic bias of the revealed religions in combination with their anthropocentric and theocentic prejudices hardly allow us to develop a positive feeling of an essential relationship toward nature at large. Chuang Tzu helps us to enlarge our concept of analogous hermeneutics to nature at large, beyond the narrow limits of mainly anthropocentric-oriented hermeneutics.

Humanity and nature is a two-way road. This piece of knowledge is undoubtedly human, but the important insight is a joint product of humanity in its relation to nature. As against the anthropocentric universalistic tendency of declaring human beings as the *summum bonum* of all that is and degrading nature as an instrumental means to this end, leaving nature totally at the mercy of self-centered human nature, it is high time to learn from the Asian, especially from Chinese, wisdom of universism.[29] This comprehensive attitude of universism is convinced of a necessarily mutual complementarity between humanity and nature, assigns human beings a particular place in the cosmic scheme of things, and treats everything in this scheme equally.

As against the theocentric and anthropocentric models for human values, the ethos of universism pleads for the conviction of our embeddedness in the all-encompassing household of the cosmic nature. This means that we should strive for humanity *within* nature, not outside or without nature. There is much to learn from the impartiality that reigns supreme in nature. It is an irony of human history and culture that the so-called animistic *Weltanschauungen*, which were decried "primitive" by the so-called enlightened cultures and revealed religions, are today best seated to serve the cause of an ecological peace of which world peace in its various aspects is a part. Asian religiosity pleads for a positive attitude and essentially religious emotion not only toward human beings, but also toward all living creatures, nature, and even inanimate things. Chuang Tzu's famous discourse on the happiness of the fish substantiates the thesis of universism beyond doubt. This discourse is a masterpiece even from an epistemological standpoint. Here too obtains some form of analogical apprehension between the world of human beings and the cosmic nature at large.

The problem of ethics in its various ramifications—from the religious through the political to the ecological—is of central and global importance today. The love of and for nature is on everyone's lips, but one has the bad feeling that this love is rather an expression of an excessively self-centered anthropocentric ethos of humanity. It is humankind that worries about its future. We love nature and want to reconstruct it not so much because we love nature as such and in her own right, but because we love ourselves most. In the real spirit of an axiological deliberation we have to reorient ourselves and recognize the essentially interdependent relationship between humans and nature, leaving behind the classical models of anthropocentric and theocentric ethics.

The largest value system of which we human beings form a part demands from us not only our being committed to our fellow human beings but also to the whole ecosystem. Humans are cosmomorphic creatures (Scheler) and nothing entitles us to a singularly privileged rank in the democracy of all things in the organic cosmic nature. Oriental and occidental forms of ethos (over-) emphasizing nature and humanity respectively are badly in need of an adjustment, an adjustment which is double-faceted: Humans in their relation to society, and humans in their relation to nature.

The concept of an analogous intercultural hermeneutics in close contact with that of the ethos of interculturality leads to a fundamental change in our theoretical and practical attitude in teaching and research. It also implies a change in the ethnocentricity of historiography of all the humanities disciplines. Further, it is very critical of the deep-rooted tendency of modernity to subsumption and various forms of appropriation. In the name of understanding and overcoming the other, European thought from Hegel to Gadamer has been practicing some form of appropriation of the other. This appropriation was made easy by so many extra-philosophical factors like colonialism, missionarianism, and imperialism.

Whoever thinks of a universal logos, reason, culture, philosophy, and religion to be fully and exclusively realized in one particular tradition—whether European or non-European—does not accept the independent reality of the other and jeopardizes a cross-cultural understanding from the outset. Truth with a capital "T" is nobody's possession alone, and it does not favor any one particular *Weltanschauung* exclusively. The availability and nonavailability of one ultimate truth, if there is such, goes hand in hand and teaches us to be diffident in our claim of possessing the truth all alone.

CONCLUSION

The axial age theory of Karl Jaspers is fully in accord with the spirit of cross-cultural philosophy, and it substantiates the cross-cultural philosophical orientation by its vision and project of a coming world philosophy.[30] Jaspers's understanding of *philosophia perennis* is very liberal and open in a sense in which the classical European liberalism was not. Jaspers is not biased against other philosophical cultures and their values. He does not universalize the European philosophical convention. It is this cross-cultural liberalism of Jaspers's philosophy that leads him to the project of a new historiography of philosophy rejecting the provincial claims to superiority and exclusiveness.

Cross-cultural philosophy and Jaspers's axial age theory recognize the existence of overlappings between cultures, philosophies, and religions, and go hand-in-hand with illuminating differences among cultures and philosophies. Such a view leads us to an open and tolerant hermeneutics, which is characterized by two main factors: The desire to understand the other, and the desire to be understood by the other. A mere desire to understand the other is not a realistic hermeneutic move, for it does not recognize the validity of the "hermeneutic circle," which lets understanding follow a pre-understanding, pre-judgment, prejudice. The desire only to be understood by the other neglects the independent right of the other to be understood too. It is a hermeneutics that abstains from any reductive treatment of the other.

Some of the central ideas of Jaspers's philosophy, particularly his axial age theory, which we have sympathetically but also critically discussed in relation to the idea of a cross-cultural philosophy, represent the very preconditions for the possibility of an intercultural philosophical understanding. Such an attitude makes room for discourse even in the absence of consensus, for the presence of dissensus is not *eo ipso* the end of all communication.

In the renunciation of any absolutistic, exclusivistic, and universalistic claim to possess the truth with capital "T" all alone, we experience the richness, variety, and endless horizon of a manifold of cultural sedimentations. It is the regulative idea of a *philosophia perennis*, which triumphs here over all the unfounded and misguided claims to be in possession of the one truth all alone.

Cross-cultural philosophical orientation enables us to do real philosophy even in the absence of universalizing our own frameworks. Even conceptual frameworks show their own cultural sedimentations. Our acceptance of a plurality of frameworks rejects all monistic claims that stand in our way to a peaceful and fruitful philosophical and cultural encounter. The conception of philosophy entailed by such a cross-cultural philosophical orientation goes hand in hand with a hermeneutics that accepts the situatedness of different world philosophies along with the unsituatedness of the one *philosophia perennis*.

Jaspers was a responsible and committed thinker who took philosophy not only as a way of thought, but also as a way of life. Cross-cultural philosophy is also a committed philosophy, and it is committed, first and foremost, to reciprocal understanding and communication. It is further committed to reject all forms of absolutist and exclusivist claims, for such claims jeopardize cross-cultural understanding and communication. Monopolistic and hegemonic tendencies are a death-knell to cross-cultural understanding and must be fought back in theory as well as in practice. Raimon Panikkar, the famous theologian and philosopher committed to interculturality and interreligiosity, pleads for a non-universal approach and warns us against what he calls "a pars pro toto effect," meaning thereby that every universalization of a particular standpoint must be avoided in favor of a nonuniversal approach.[31]

Very much in the spirit of Chinese, Indian, and even Greek philosophy, Jaspers was fully convinced that philosophy *qua* philosophy can emancipate and liberate us. The truth that liberates us need not be necessarily theological. This is the central and most important message of Jaspers's understanding of "philosophic faith/conviction" in the face of the claims of revealed religions like Christianity. Philosophy is not against theology, nor an enemy of theology; but neither is it subservient to theology. It claims an autonomous position of its own and is quite critical, even suspicious, of our overconfidence in science and theology.

NOTES

1. Paul Ricoeur, *Geschichte und Wahrheit,* edited by Gert Hummel (Münich: List Verlag, 1974), pp. 290ff.

2. See the article by Hans Saner herein [eds.].

3. Ram Adhar Mall, "Unity Without Uniformity," in *Focus on Quality*, edited by Bernardine F. Nel, R. Singh, and W. M.Venter (Westville: University of Durban, 1985), pp. 22–47.

4. Martin Heidegger, "Europa und die deutsche Philosophie," in *Europa und die Philosophie*, edited by Hans-Helmut Gander (Frankfurt am Main: Klostermann, 1993), p. 31.

5. Karl Jaspers, *Vom Ursprung und Ziel der Geschichte* (Munich: R. Piper & Co., 1983), p. 96. [Hereafter, VUZG]

6. Karl Jaspers, *Provokationen. Gespräche und Interviews*, Hrsg. von Hans Saner (Munich: R. Piper & Co., 1969), pp. 21ff.

7. Jaspers, VUZG, p. 19.

8. Norbert Rigali, *Die Selbstkonstitution der Geschichte im Denken von Karl Jaspers* (Meisenheim am Glan: Hain, 1968), pp. 49ff.

9. Aleida Assmann, "Jaspers' Achsenzeit, oder vom Glück und Elend der Zentralperspektive in der Geschichte," in *Karl Jaspers. Denken zwischen Wissenschaft, Politik und Philosophie*, edited by H. Hardt (Stuttgart: J. B. Metzlersche Verlagsbuchhandlung, 1989), p. 190.

10. Jaspers, PGI, p. 141.

11. Karl Jaspers, *Weltgeschichte der Philosophie: Einleitung* (Munich: R. Piper & Co., 1984), p. 56.

12. VUZG, p. 326.

13 . Karl Jaspers, *Der philosophische Glaube* (Munich: R. Piper & Co., 1981), p. 40. ("Wahrheit ist, was uns verbindet—und in der Kommunikation hat Wahrheit ihren Ursprung"). [Hereafter cited as PG, eds.]

14. Jaspers, PG, pp. 134ff.

15. Ibid., p. 75.

16. Ram Adhar Mall and Heinz Hülsmann, *Die drei Geburtsorte der Philosophie. China, Indien, Europa* (Bonn: Bouvier, 1989); Ram Adhar Mall, *Philosophie im Vergleich der Kulturen. Interkulturelle Philosophie—eine neue Orientierung* (Darmstadt: Wiss. Buchgesellschaft, 1996); Ninian Smart, *World Philosophies* (London and New York: Routledge, 1999).

17. Hans Saner, edited by *Karl Jaspers. Weltgeschichte der Philosophie (*Munich: Piper, 1982), p. 6; Hans Saner, "Weltphilosophie und Globalkultur im interkulturellen Vergleich mit den Konzeptionen Weltmusik und Weltkunst," in *Karl Jaspers. Philosophy on the Way to "World Philosophy,"* edited by Leonard H. Ehrlich and Richard Wisser (Amsterdam: Rodolpi and Würzburg: Königshausen und Neumann,1998), pp. 241–55.

18. Richard Wisser, "Projekt und Vision einer Weltgeschichte der Philosophie und Weltphilosophie als Folgen der Grundverfassung von Karl Jaspers," in *Karl Jaspers: Philosophy on the Way to "World Philosophy,"* edited by Ehrlich and Wisser, pp. 61–70.

19. Karl Jaspers, *Philosophische Autobiographie* (Munich: R. Piper & Co., 1977), p. 122.

20. Donald Davidson, "On the Very Idea of a Conceptual Scheme," *Proceedings of the American Philosophical Association*, 17 (1973-74), pp. 5–20.

21. John Kekes, *The Morality of Pluralism* (Princeton, NJ: Princeton University Press, 1993).

22. Ram Adhar Mall, "Metonymic Reflections on Samkara's Concept of Brahman and Plato's Seventh Epistle," *Journal of Indian Council of Philosophical Research,* IX/2 (1992), pp. 89–102.

23. Mircea Eliade, *Die Sehnsucht nach dem Ursprung* (Wien: Europaverlag, 1973), pp. 75ff.

24. Krishna Roy, *Hermeneutics: East and West* (Calcutta: Allied Publishers in collaboration with Jadavpur University, 1993), p. 67.

25. Ram Adhar Mall, "Der Absolutheitsanspruch. Eine religionsphilosophische Meditation," *Loccumer Protokolle*, 7 (1991), pp. 39–53.

26. *Europa und die Philosophie*, Hrsg. Hans-Helmut Gander (Frankfurt am Main: Klostermann, 1993), p. 31.

27. VUZG, p. 97.

28. John Rawls, *A Theory of Justice* (Cambridge, MA: Harvard University Press, 1971), p. 388.

29. Joseph Needham, *History and Human Values: A Chinese Perspective for World Science and Technology*. The 1978 Inaugural Martin Wickramasinghe Lecture (Nawala: Martin Wickramasinghe Trust, 1979); Kah Kyung Cho, "Restauration of Universism: Toward an Ethics of Accord Beyond Human Society," in *The World Community in Post-Industrial Society* (Seoul: Wooseok Publishing Co., 1988), p. 5.

30. Hans Saner, "Jaspers' Idee einer kommenden Weltphilosophie," in *Philosophie der Freiheit*, Hrsg. von Rudolf Lengert and Peter Gottwald (Oldenburg: Holzberg Verlag, 1983), pp. 49–63.

31. Raimon Panikkar, "A Self-Critical Dialogue," in *The Intercultural Challenge of Raimon Panikkar*, edited by Joseph Prabhu (New York: Orbis Books, 1996), p. 45.

Part V
The Human Condition and the Meaning of Life

KARL JASPERS ON HUMAN SELF-REALIZATION

EXISTENZ IN BOUNDARY SITUATIONS AND COMMUNICATION

Kurt Salamun

The concepts of Existenz, boundary situations,[1] and communication are central elements of Jaspers's existentialism, as well as his idea of humanity and the overarching goal of his philosophizing. Because these concepts can only be understood within the context of his general philosophical anthropology, we begin with an exposition of his basic anthropological framework. Human beings are constantly involved in inescapable life situations, according to Jaspers, so I next identify Jaspers's understanding of the self's relation, as Existenz, to the "general" boundary situation of life, the "specific" boundary situations of death, suffering, struggle and guilt, and his extension of the concept of boundary situation to politics and political communication. Because the process of human self-realization as possible Existenz is an on-going cognitive and psycho-social development process tied to human language acquisition and communication, Existenz in Jaspers's philosophy of communication is next interpreted in terms of a threefold human relationality tied to the "objective" forms of the modes of being that we are (naïve vitality, consciousness as such, and spirit). Existential communication, as the most profound and authentic intersubjective communication between individuals, is the highest and most valuable form of communication according to Jaspers. What has not been emphasized enough in previous interpretations of Jaspers's philosophy of communication, however, is the fact that he also links communication to a set of moral attitudes that are needed for the realization or actualization of existential communication between persons. In turn, I identify these moral attitudes and argue that they are not only the necessary conditions for realizing existential communication with a communication partner—especially if we are to avoid the deficiencies and ruptures of human communication—but also serve as eminent normative principles that infuse Jaspers's liberal ethos of humanity.

THE BASIC ANTHROPOLOGICAL FRAMEWORK

Jaspers's anthropological framework consists of a conception of the human being as a dual self-realization project, an idea that bears obvious similarities to the philosophical anthropology of Immanuel Kant and Søren Kierkegaard. Both of these thinkers intensively influenced Jaspers's anthropology, as one may see from his early book *Psychologie der Weltanschauungen* (*Psychology of World-views*) published in 1919.[2] By a dual self-realization project, Jaspers understands the human being as both an empirical and nonempirical phenomenon. While the empirical dimension of the human being can be researched by the sciences (e.g., biology, psychology, and sociology), the nonempirical dimension of the human being cannot be described and explained by scientific terms alone. Already in this early work *Psychology of Worldviews*, Jaspers argues that the nonempirical dimension of humanity can only be elucidated by a hermeneutical approach drawing upon the best tools available in the field of psychology. In his later existential works, he argues that it is the task of transcending philosophizing to elucidate the nonempirical dimension of human existence or what he calls possible Existenz.

Jaspers's anthropological framework espouses the view that a human being realizes his or her self-actualization or unique potentialities in four dimensions or "modes" of being that constitute who we are as human animals with consciousness. In the context of his existentialism (Existenz-philosophy) as explicated especially in the three-volume *Philosophy*, Jaspers argues for an understanding of the empirical dimension of the human being from a "bottom-up" perspective wherein there is an explicit ranking of the modes of human self-realization from the lowest to the highest or most valuable stage. In his later conceptions of *Vernunftphilosophie* (philosophy of reason) and his philosophy of the Encompassing or "periechontology,"[3] the four dimensions or "horizons" of the modes of being that we are, are estimated as equal in stature and he points out the sophisticated mutual relations among each of the modes.[4]

Jaspers defines the first mode of our empirical being in terms of *naive vitality* or *vital existence*; that is, the biological and physical part of oneself, where physical conditions, spontaneous emotions, basic interests and instinctive impulses dominate. This most basic dimension of human existence or life, which he calls "*blosses Dasein*" (mere existence), is without self-reflection and self-consciousness. "Physically I am part of life," Jaspers writes, "a part whose form and function is the continuity of that ever-changing body of mine. I want this life; without it I do not exist. I am present in its vital functions, but these functions are not I. As nothing but life, I would be just a natural process."[5]

The second mode of our empirical being human, Jaspers calls "*Bewusstsein überhaupt*" or consciousness as such.[6] The human being as consciousness as such should be understood as analogous to Kant's epistemology: Our mind has a mere formal structure in virtue of the forms of perception (space and time) and the forms of conception (the categories of thought), which are *a priori* conditions for constituting knowledge in the human mind. By consciousness as such Jaspers refers to the dimension of logical thinking and rationality. Human beings have the intellectual capacity for reflecting according to the rules of logic and for constructing universal knowledge about the world in accordance with the formal categories of the understanding. In this way, consciousness as such is the universal medium of human consciousness for the attainment of generally valid and objectively compelling, cogent knowledge.

The third dimension of human being for Jaspers is the dimension of "*Geist*" (spirit). Although the human spirit is dependent upon correctness of understanding and thinking, the impulses of the spirit go beyond linear rationality. The specific capacity of the human spirit is *the production of ideas*, that allows one to see different phenomena or objects presented to consciousness as unities and parts of a meaningful whole. Such ideas are manifest in personal ideals, principles of religion, moral worldviews, political ideologies, and creative conceptions in the arts. The work of the spirit is illustrated by the fact that Jaspers, himself, often speaks of *the idea* of philosophy, democracy, freedom, etc., and in not one, but three monograph-length works, he creatively envisions the idea of the university in relation to the tasks and goals of university institutions.[7]

Now the three modes of being human as existence, consciousness as such, and spirit are, at the same time, loci or dimensions for human self-realization; and yet, they represent the human being only as an empirical phenomenon. All human beings, however, own the ability or possibility of a fourth and nonempirical dimension of being and human self-realization. From the viewpoint of Jaspers's existentialism, this fourth mode is the highest form of human self-realization, whereas the other three modes of being are merely the empirical mediums and necessary presuppositions for self-realization as Existenz. For Jaspers, human self-realization is the concrete realization of Existenz, that is, the authentic ground of human being, the intimate dimension of personal autonomy, existential freedom, undetermined moral decision, and the nonobjective actuality of self-being and true selfhood. No empirical studies, doctrines of ontology, or definitive ethical frameworks can give an adequate understanding of this fourth dimension of human subjectivity and our shared humanity. Such an understanding is possible only by means of actually realizing Existenz in one's own life and/or by "elucidating" Existenz by means of transcending philosophizing as the vehicle to human self-actualization.

Jaspers's methodological conception of elucidating Existenz and transcending philosophizing has strong affinities with Kierkegaard's understanding of subjective reflection.[8] Kierkegaard describes subjective reflection, in contrast to objective reflection, at length in his *Concluding Unscientific Postscript to the 'Philosophical Fragments.'*[9] Objective reflection dominates scientific thought and the individual gains knowledge of things in the world and of one's own objective (biological, psychological, sociological) nature. Subjective reflection, in contrast, directs the individual to the nonobjective and nonrational dimension of selfhood. Subjective reflection, which is genuine philosophical reflection, is not a "mere contemplation" of oneself, but a reflection upon oneself that constitutes a form of action in so far as self-reflection entails an act of self-conscious choosing of oneself. Human self-conscious choice regarding the self's own being also implies a moral act (and not simply a cognitive act) because in the act of choosing oneself an individual takes full responsibility for one's own lifestyle and its consequences. Jaspers holds a similar position with his conception of elucidating Existenz.

An urgent question arises in Jaspers's existentialism: How can one actually realize personal autonomy and Existenz? Jaspers's answer is that Existenz cannot be planned or managed at all because it is finally a gift from a nonobjectifiable being, which he calls "Transcendence."[10] Human self-realization *qua* possible Existenz is inextricably bound to an awareness of Transcendence. In the process of becoming Existenz, one feels that existential self-realization is not the result of rational planning or the product of self-management: Existenz is experienced as a gift from a transcendent source. Human self-realization as Existenz means the realization of self-autonomy (which is not to say that the self has no determinants), individual freedom, and personal authenticity. Crucial to this process of self-realization and development throughout the human life cycle, the human being becomes aware of fundamental limits to his or her human capacities. The individual recognizes that he or she *is not* the absolute ground or foundation of being. Transcendence cannot be known by rational categories, according to Jaspers, and every approach to rationalize or absolutize the radical "otherness" of Transcendence must necessarily founder in thought.

Indeed, if we closely exam Jaspers's conception of Existenz he makes it clear that the realization of Existenz, and thus human self-realization, is possible only in specific and rare moments of life. More specifically, such self-realization only occurs under two basic conditions of life: The first is the individual's unique experience of the boundary situations of death, suffering, guilt, and struggle. The second crucial condition is the unique and individual experience of mutual, existential communication with a communication partner.

Existenz and Personal Boundary Situations

Jaspers sees every human being as constantly involved in situations. To exist means to be in situations.

> Since existence means to be in situations, I can never get out of one without entering into another. Any understanding of situations means that I proceed toward ways of transforming them; it does not mean I might change my condition itself. There is nothing I can do about my being in situations. The consequence of whatever I do will confront me as a new situation which I have helped to bring about, and which is now given.[11]

Boundary situations confront all human beings in the process of living. Jaspers describes boundary situations in the second volume of his *Philosophy* in the following way:

> They never change, except in appearance. There is no way to survey them in existence, no way to see anything behind them. They are like a wall we run into, a wall on which we founder. We cannot modify them; all that we can do is to make them lucid, but without explaining or deducing them from something else. They go with existence itself.[12]

Boundary situations cannot be dealt with merely by using objective and rational knowledge such as we use to solve problems of everyday life. If we try to escape boundary situations by managing them with rationality and objective knowledge we necessarily founder with respect to their meaning for us. Instead, boundary situations require a radical change in our attitude and in our common ways of thinking about life and its meaning. Indeed, the only adequate way to react within boundary situations, "is not by planning and calculating to overcome them, but by the very different activity of becoming the Existenz we potentially are; we become ourselves by entering with open eyes into the boundary situations. We can know them only externally, and their reality can only be felt by Existenz. To experience boundary situations is the same as Existenz."[13]

Once again the affinities between Jaspers's philosophy of boundary situations and Kierkegaard's thinking are clearly evident. Jaspers insists, even more forcefully than Kierkegaard does in his conceptualization of subjective reflection, that becoming Existenz by experiencing boundary situations is necessarily bound to an intensive process of self-reflection, a nonempirical and nonobjective relationship to one's own self. The hard work and activity of self-reflection in the context of one's personal boundary situations, helps the self elucidate one's own existential possibilities. Self-reflection helps lead the self to an awareness of one's own possible Existenz and to an act of courage and self-acceptance when confronted by boundary situations. Boundary situations are evident in the inevitable fact that we are always in situations and cannot escape the *historicity* of existence. We cannot live without *struggle* and without pain and *suffering*. We cannot avoid *guilt*. We must all die and come to terms with our own *death*. The important point for Jaspers is that it is precisely as we stand within these specific boundary situations that we either open our being to the transcendent dimension of our humanity, or else we close ourselves off to the truth and authenticity of our Existenz.

Jaspers provides brilliant phenomenological descriptions of boundary situations in the *Psychology of Wordviews* and in volume two of the *Philosophy*, which present a remarkable range of deep psychological and hermeneutical insights into boundary situations. What Jaspers makes clear in both works is that many of our normal human reactions to boundary situations are often wrong when it comes to the ultimate life-goal of becoming the authentic self we potentially are. Because of the "antinomic structure" of all life and reality, human beings invariably have two basic options when confronted by boundary situations. First, we may decide to choose resignation, pessimism and nihilistic despair; or, second, we may decide to embrace a realistic, and yet, optimistic confidence in life and future activities and possibilities. The second, positive choice, to which Jaspers appeals as the correct option, is the direct consequence of a basic life attitude that dominates his philosophy from its very beginning. In his postwar philosophy, he begins to call this life attitude "philosophic faith" in contrast to any "revelational faith" grounded in a definitive revelation of God and as legitimated by the authorities of the church.

Jaspers makes a distinction between the "first" or "general" boundary situation of the human condition and "specific" boundary situations. The general boundary situation of humanity as a whole is the inevitable fact that in my existence I am always in a particular situation that I cannot suspend. I exist at a certain time in history, in certain social circumstances, and with specific parents that

I did not choose. I exist as a man or a woman. I am young or old. I have one mother tongue and not another. I exist in situations that are constantly being bombarded by various options and chances, as well as very real physical, psychological, economic, social and political constraints. "The unrest in this [general] boundary situation is that what is up to me lies still ahead; my freedom in it is to assume given facts, to make them my own as if they had been my will."[14]

As an adequate existential reaction to the general boundary situation of human existence, Jaspers advises that I take on the situation *as mine* in Nietzsche's use of the Greek expression *amor fati*:[15]

> Nietzsche uses the expression *amor fati* to refer to an affirmation of being that is at the same time an affirmation of my own conation [desire to perform an action]. When I am neither dissipated in a general affirmation of all being nor compressed within a single individual who clings anxiously to and wills nothing beyond himself, I have returned from both extremes to the present historicity of my existence in this actual world and am, precisely through this historicity, at one with being itself. . . . In *amor fati* the seemingly incompatible meet: intensified activity aiming at future fulfillments joins loving acceptance of whatever happens. But conceptual expression of this fusion is possible only through paradoxes. A merely rational distinction becomes specious, for it misses the point.[16]

The boundary situation of *death* as in the confrontation with the inevitable fact of awaiting one's own death or the death of a close friend or one's own child or parents, can be the source of fear and anxiety as well as nihilistic despair. But the dying process may also provide the occasion for the urgency of living authentically without postponement and self-deception. The confrontation with the inevitable presence of death can give a human being courage and integrity; it can give the individual an authentic perspective on the things that are most essential to life and relationship. Jaspers points out some of the authentic moral attitudes at stake for human beings confronted by death such as courage without self-deception, a profound serenity in spite of pain and suffering, the effort to attain peace in facing one's death with the calm knowledge that death is the final end, as well as approaching one's death with composure, patience, and dignity.

In connection with the boundary situation of *suffering*, Jaspers admits that no individual can survey the facticity of the various forms of suffering such as physical pain, diseases, impotent efforts that leave one exhausted yet disguise the real self, mental illnesses, pathological senility, destruction by the brute force of others, the "dependence" that causes suffering in all forms of "slavery, and the harsh reality of human starvation. In this context he distinguishes between "passive" and "active" suffering. In passive suffering, I confine myself to a de facto hedonist worldview: "On earth, though all is vanity and ends in suffering," Jaspers writes, "I can eat and drink and be merry as long as it lasts. All *meaning*, whether grasped or actively created, will be dispensed with."[17]

Jaspers's focus is on the attitude of "active" suffering, which is the exact opposite of resignation, and implies an effort to be happy despite suffering. Questions concerning the ultimate meaning and justice of suffering are viewed from the perspective of authentic Existenz as merely "idle" questions. For it is only in the active appropriation of one's own unique suffering that the individual is made aware of one's true self.

> He will not dodge it [suffering], will see it, will fight it to the best of his ability. Reduced to impotence, he will bear it until he perishes—until in going down he will keep his poise, at least, or will lose even that when the incomprehensible vortex drags him down to levels on which the strongest self-being finds itself relativized and subjected to unknown forces. . . . It is from its view of suffering, from this polarity of active and passive resignation, that possible Existenz soars in the boundary situation to the experience of knowing itself as one with its transcendence, in an *origin* which it conceives in the boundary situation of being.[18]

The boundary situation of *guilt* can give a human being the insight that one's acting or nonacting in several situations of life always has unforeseen and unintended consequences that make us guilty toward other persons. The point is that we inevitably discriminate against others as a consequence of our acting, or nonacting, as the case may be. The authentic moral attitude Jaspers correlates with the boundary situation of guilt is permanent readiness for taking personal responsibility for all our actions in the world.

> For Existenz in the boundary situation . . . I am myself, but guilt-laden. Now the only way I can live is the tension of seeking to lift myself up. It is not a matter of guiltlessness any more, but of really avoiding whatever guilt I can avoid, so as to come to the profound, intrinsic, unavoidable guilt—without coming to rest there either. Responsibility mounts to its existential pathos of accepting that inevitable guilt, which we usually shun only to be thoughtlessly and passively entangled in some paltry guilt. The benefits of exploitation will now impose obligations of performance. Impurity becomes a challenge to will only in the most lucid reality, to give a clear voice to original volition. The realization of Existenz in the One brings us to the true, inexculpable guilt of having spurned possibilities of Existenz.[19]

The boundary situation of inevitable *struggle* makes us conscious of the everlasting struggles of life. We practice it by enforcing our own interests and claims against others in many situations of everyday life, e.g., in the fight for material ends, social status, or prestige and power in every group and society. In this struggle my own success is necessarily accompanied by the defeat and suppression of the demands of others. Struggle may, of course, be extremely violent and coercive. But Jaspers contrasts the violent struggle for existence with an authentic moral attitude that he calls the "loving struggle" for Existenz.[20] The loving struggle is a nonviolent, noncoercive form of relation to another person whose dominant norm is solidarity.

> What Existenz and Existenz seek mutually, in this loving struggle . . . is the *source*. . . . In the struggle we aim at manifestation *by way of objectivities*. In the medium of accuracies we take up all that can be known, but our goal is not generally valid accuracy but truth in the present situation, the truth of the being which this communication makes real. . . . The fight stays wholly nonviolent. There is no victory or defeat for one side; both win or lose jointly. Victory is not won by my superiority but by our common achievement of manifestation. Nor does defeat indicate a lack of strength; defeat lies in evasion, in hiding, and is due to unpreparedness for the crisis of my own volition and the other's. The slightest use of force, including intellectual superiority, for instance, or the power of suggestion, brings the loving struggle to an end. . . . This [loving] struggle, this extreme jeopardizing of the other and of myself, is possible only on the basis of a *solidarity* which unquestioningly *presupposes* the possibility of Existenz in both of us.[21]

Summarizing Jaspers's phenomenological description of the boundary situations of death, suffering, guilt, and struggle, we may say that these existential phenomena ought to be accompanied by a radical change in one's own attitude and worldview. Jaspers links the challenge posed by boundary situations to a corresponding set of moral attitudes that are highly relevant for not only overcoming the disastrous implications and consequences of such situations, but also for individual authenticity and for the moral life of humanity as a whole.

The Extension of the Concept of Boundary Situation to Politics

Jaspers applies his concept of boundary situation both to concrete historical situations and to political states of affairs. Thus, his first political application of guilt as a boundary situation came with his analysis of the question of German culpability for the rise of Nazism. The phenomenon of guilt can enable a human being to become Existenz, but this is only possible if a radical change or "conversion" (*Umkehr*) takes place in one's attitude, worldview, and lifestyle concerning the question of responsibility. In a process of personal existential self-reflection that must avoid self-deception and dishonesty, one has to accept and prove one's own personal responsibility for the consequences of one's actions in the world. In *The Question of German Guilt* Jaspers argues that all German people who lived during the Nazi regime should accept this historical situation and reality in their lives as a boundary situation.[22] The Nazi crimes should provoke a deep shock to the moral and political identity of every German who lived under the regime, even those not guilty in a criminal sense of actually having committed crimes on behalf of the regime. Jaspers demands from the German people that each should faithfully prove to oneself how guilty one was in a moral and political sense during the Nazi reign of terror. Guilt arises in having made no efforts to prevent the rise of the Nazi movement, or as a result of having failed to conspire against the political establish of the Third Reich.

Serious moral and political self-reflection about one's own failings during the Nazi regime requires that every German accept the historical situation of Nazism in Germany as an existential phenomenon that touches directly his or her own personal dignity, freedom, and humanity. Only if this reality is acknowledged can the German people have a possible chance for redirecting their political attitudes and worldviews toward the development of a reasonable, "new politics."[23] The new politics of the Germans with a new democratic constitution and state ought to be free of narrow-minded nationalism, which had been so destructive in German history ever since the Bismarck government, and free of authoritarian leadership and the submissiveness of people to a few party leaders and political rulers.

It is not only the German people, however, who are confronted with a historical-political boundary situation. In *The Atom Bomb and the Future of Man* Jaspers applies the concept of a general boundary situation to the situation of humankind as a whole now confronted by two great dangers: First, there exists the possibility of annihilating all life on Earth with the atom bomb. The second danger, which is also a new historical phenomenon in its scope, is the possibility of a worldwide totalitarian regime. Although this second possibility may not be a reality in the short-term political horizon, it is a potential alternative for the future of humankind owing to the development of the techniques of mass communication and mass control. "The atom bomb," Jaspers writes, "as the problem of mankind's very existence, is equalled by only one other problem: the threat of totalitarian rule (not simply dictatorship, Marxism, or racial theory), with its terrorist structure that obliterates all liberty and human dignity. By one, we lose life; by the other, a life that is worth living."[24]

Jaspers wrote this passage in the 1950s at the height of the Cold War between the United States and the Soviet Union. In our present historical and technological situation, he would perhaps add a third (ecological) danger, and a perhaps even a fourth (biotechnological) danger for humankind as a whole, namely, the dangers of worldwide pollution and its consequence for global warming and of uncontrolled, worldwide manipulation of genes by genetic technologists. Such dangers for the future of humankind can only be overcome when as many individuals as possible recognize them and emotionally accept them as boundary situations. As situations of basic existential crisis, they require a radical change in worldview and moral and political behavior. The change entails, as its presupposition, a conversion to a new type of politics governed by reason and moral standards that overturn the usual power politics (*Realpolitik*) of the past, as well as the short-term political and economic policies based merely on vested interests.

Existenz and Communication

As many interpreters of Jaspers's philosophy have noted, communication is the basic intention of all his philosophizing. Jaspers stresses the vital importance of interpersonal relations and communication for human self-realization. By focusing on the relational aspect of human self-realization as possible Existenz, he underlines the nonstatic and unfinished character of the existential dimension of our being human. Human self-realization is a process, an unending self-effort through stages of becoming, and Jaspers's philosophy of communication interprets Existenz as a threefold relation: "Existenz is not everything and not for itself alone either, for its being depends on its relation to other *Existenz*[*en*] and to transcendence—the wholly Other that makes it aware of being not by itself alone."[25]

Jaspers distinguishes four types of communication that are correlative to the four modes of being and dimensions of self-realization that constitute his basic anthropological framework. In the dimension of *naive vitality* and spontaneous instinctive life, a human being lives in primitive communities with other human beings. Instinct tells them how to pursue their advantages. Persons use others only to reach vital ends such as the satisfaction of basic needs of sexuality, power, and desire. In the mode of existence or *Dasein*, the self's underlying communication motives are egocentric. Human beings use each other only as mere instruments and treat one another as controllable objects, not as independent subjects and autonomous personalities. In Kant's terms, persons are treated only as means to an end and not as an end in itself.

In the dimension of *consciousness as such* a type of communication is realized that is based on the capacity of rationality and its formal rules and categories such as intellectual discussions of scientific experts with the aim of solving a given technological or scientific problem. The participating experts can be replaced by other experts when their intellectual capacity for solving the problem is exhausted. The only aim of the communication is to get the best solution for the problem in question. Here it is not the irreplaceable individuality of a person that constitutes the interpersonal relation and communication, but rather the rational knowledge and technical ability for problem-solving.

In the dimension of *spirit*, human beings experience a mode of communication that goes beyond these other two modes. "Community in the idea of a whole—of this state, this society, this family, this university, this profession of mine—is what puts me for the first time into substantial communication. . . . Communication in the idea, and in its realization by Existenz, will move a man closer to his fellow man than will the intellect or a purpose, or primitive community."[26]

While communication as naïve vitality, consciousness as such, and spirit are objective forms of human interactions that may be described and explained by the special sciences, the highest and most valuable form of communication, whereby human beings realize Existenz, cannot be researched by the sciences or adequately described in an objectifying language. This type of communication Jaspers calls "existential communication," and it can only be elucidated by transcending philosophizing and be experienced in one's own life. Existential communication constitutes an intimate personal relationship between two human beings such as friends, lovers, a husband and wife, a father or mother and child, or a teacher and student. Once again, and in connection with this interpersonal relationality, Jaspers mentions a set of moral attitudes that are not only the necessary conditions of existential communication, but also eminent normative principles of humanity as well.

MORAL ATTITUDES IN EXISTENTIAL COMMUNICATION

The first moral attitude concerns the dignity of *solitude* or the willingness and ability to be in solitude. Solitude is not the same as social isolation, but is rather "a sense of readiness in possible Existenz. . . . I cannot enter into communication without being lonely. . . . "[27] For Jaspers it is an important feature of human dignity to dare to be lonely and to live in solitude as opposed to the desire to escape loneliness and social isolation at any price, even at the price of self-deception, humiliation, and personal degradation. Jaspers's concept of solitude shows an affinity to Kierkegaard's idea that the process of existential self-realization is grounded on permanent processes of self-reflection and self-contemplation. When Jaspers speaks of the necessary "will to solitude" and the "dignity of loneliness," he urges everyone to risk the adventure of self-contemplation and self-reflection, on their own, and without directives from others. The dignity of solitude in the process of self-reflection is also a norm closely connected with Jaspers's ideal of personal freedom. For his appeal to lonely self-reflection can arguably be interpreted as a "sign-post" of his opposition to the growing manipulative influences of persuasive clichés and stereotypes of human self-interpretation produced by new information technologies, mass media manipulation, and various forms of "self-help" books and industries.

A second moral attitude involves *open-mindedness* and *frankness*. These closely related attitudes enable a person to communicate with another person without prejudices or masked purposes. The only way to human self-realization in existential communication is to risk, as Jaspers says, the "empirical self"; that is, to risk a radical change in usual habits, opinions, and ways of life toward others with a new open-mindedness and candor.

A third moral attitude entails *a real intention to accept a communication partner in his or her own autonomy and individual possibility of self-realization*. This means not forcing one's own habits and standards of living on the other. In this context Jaspers appeals to the norm of *fidelity*, which demands "a level of complete equality" whereby the communication partners accept each other as completely equal in their personal freedom and chance of becoming Existenz, despite objective differences in social status, rank, fortune, age, sex, etc. Fidelity also, and necessarily, implies a nonegoistic intention to help a communication partner to realize his or her Existenz without using the other as a mere instrument for one's own purpose of self-realization. Jaspers speaks in this context of "existential solidarity" with a communication partner.

A fourth moral attitude concerns *intellectual integrity* and *truthfulness*, which allow an openness to criticize one's own failings and dogmatized opinions with the exact same force as one would critique the failings and dogmatized opinions of others. Jaspers calls this back-and-forth mutual critique and mutual support of communication partners a "communicative struggle" wherein all kinds of power and superiority, prejudice and calculating strategic reserve against the other are eliminated in favor of the "loving struggle" for Existenz.

COMMUNICATIVE SITUATIONS AND THE RUPTURE OF COMMUNICATION

In the context of his phenomenological and hermeneutical reflections concerning Existenz and communication, Jaspers also discusses deficiencies in communication and ruptures of communication that occur in a variety of communicative situations. His descriptions are rich, full of subtle psychological insights into different moods, feelings, attitudes, and emotional conditions that are relevant for constituting and preventing communication. In his reflections, Jaspers incorporates his former experience as a psychiatrist and psychologist directly into his existential philosophy.

Existential communication is embodied only in the medium of objective communication and arises always in the framework of psychological and social roles. Specific *communicative situations* include the master-servant relation, social intercourse, and public debate and political intercourse. In the master-servant relation, Jaspers argues that power in any form—whether physical, vital, intellectual, or authoritative—inevitably brings human beings into superior and subordinate relations to one another. Such power relations constitute the medium of communication on an unequal level whereby the relation may be determined by psychological forces on both sides. Thus, there exists communication with kindness to a subordinate and communication with humility toward a superior. There are mutual ties in loyal care and loyal service and in assuming responsibility for a servant and showing respect to the master. The crucial point is that this communicative situation can reveal an "objective" expression of two controversial possibilities. Both the servant and the master can use the communicative situation as a means for escaping solitude in a way that does not realize an encounter of self and self on the same level. The master may still act toward the servant in a dominating fashion, and the servant may find his self-being fulfilled in subordination and service to the master. Substantial communication can only be realized on an equal existential level, despite all the differences of comparable qualities. One has to accept the communication partner *as equal in rank at the level of a self-becoming Existenz*, and assess the other as a whole person.

Concerning the communicative situation of *social intercourse*, Jaspers argues that social relations and conventions are necessary conditions for our existence, and they function as a framework for existential communication. Nobody can communicate existentially with every person he or she encounters, and even persons who are existentially linked will also consort in a framework of merely formal relations quite often. Communications in the forum of public debate provide a good example of such a formal communicative situation. Debate can be a means of true communication when the disputants are really involved and none of them shifts the debate to monologues, sophisms, or a strict, rationally planned discourse in advance that destroys creative impulses to communicate.

Yet another example is the communicative situation entailed by *political intercourse*, which is usually dominated by the will to power and a wide range of psychological tricks to reach one's own goals in a permanent struggle with political opponents. Only if persons in self-reflecting processes become explicitly aware of the dominating tendencies in politics is there a chance for politicians and elected officials, as possible *Existenzen*, to realize authentic communication between each other and with a view to the reasonableness of proposal for the good of the human community as a whole.

Among the numerous types of *ruptures* and *deficiencies* that mark human communication, Jaspers mentions silence, indignity, fear of communication, the resistance of self-existence as "the opaque, autocratic, unreasoning, and uncommunicative will to be the way I am."[28] Even when one holds substantive philosophical positions, it is always necessary to avoid harmonizing worldviews and sophistry. In rejecting all sorts of philosophical dogmatisms as *anti-communicative*, Jaspers makes a statement that lends itselt to severe misunderstanding: "A thought is philosophically true to the extent to which its thinking promotes communication."[29] What does Jaspers mean by this statement? It does not have to be understood as a denial of every claim to an objective truth as understood, for example, in a correspondence theory of truth. Instead, Jaspers's intent is to prevent absolutist and unrevisable claims in the context of philosophical statements. Jaspers appeals to an open attitude that accepts statements as objectively true, but nonetheless always open to debate and revision. He articulates his objection to dogmatized philosophical positions, worldviews, and institutions in this way:

> For communication to be a vital source, man must not be definitively sheltered in self-less objectivities: in the authority of a state or a church; in an objective metaphysics; a prevailing, life-regulating ethics; an ontological knowledge of being. To me, being sheltered in such fashion may be a conditional form of the existence of my knowledge and my will; I may be living in such forms, but they will not remain unconditional and life-sustaining certainties until they take historic root in existential communication.[30]

COMMUNICATION AND THE LIBERAL ETHOS OF HUMANITY

The moral attitudes noted above link Jaspers's concepts of boundary situation and existential communication, but they are also highly relevant to a proper understanding of his moral philosophy, or what I call his *liberal ethos of humanity*.[31] Jaspers does not intend to postulate moral attitudes as explicit ethical norms and general ethical rules. He wants, rather, to stimulate the moral and ethical dimension of being human by his philosophy, and he appeals to every individual in an indirect way to accept these attitudes in their own lives and personal relations.

Jaspers's liberal ethos of humanity must be clearly distinguished from a Christian or a Socialist ethos of humanity. From the Christian viewpoint, the human being is a creature of God realizing his or her existence in communication with brothers and sisters in the revealed faith, within the institutional community of the church, and in missionary outreach to the world. The human being communicates with God in prayer and lives under the guidance of a specific body of divine and man-made postulates and moral commandments in the hope of salvation and the resurrection of the body for the life to come. The key concept of Christian humanism are God, revelation, sin, repentance, forgiveness, charity, divine grace, and salvation through Jesus Christ. From the Socialist viewpoint, a human being is mainly determined by socio-economic factors and human self-realization is only possible by eliminating self-alienation by means of the class struggle, a completely egalitarian social and economic community, and solidarity. Key concepts of socialist humanism are control over the ownership of the means and modes of production, abolition of capitalist profit-maximizing and its consequent human alienation, division of labor, unions, class interest, solidarity, and equality.

Jaspers's liberal ethos of humanity indicates the human potentialities of self-reflection, self-determination, and self-realization as possible Existenz, the existential and political freedom of the individual, personal autonomy and responsibility, the irreplaceable nature of every person in true human interaction, the absolute singularity of every human being, as well as the moral dimensions of human reasonableness. In contrast to some critics of Jaspers's liberalism, his ethos of humanity has nothing to do with "libertarianism" understood as favoring unrestricted capitalism that would reject redistributive taxation measures by the state (Nozick). It would also be wrong to identify Jaspers's liberal ethos with those versions of liberalism that have a strong tendency to reify individual freedom, or that are grounded on an atheistic denial of God. In Jaspers's view, human self-realization as Existenz and the experience of existential freedom are necessarily bound to the experience that individual freedom is not the product of an omnipotent self, but rather a gift from Transcendence (or God). The self has to accept the reality that its freedom is dependent upon a noncontrollable and nonmanageable dimension of being. In this context it is important to note that Jaspers does not view religious faith in atheistic terms; rather, he takes a critical position against any conception of "revelation" that would proffer objectively guaranteed proofs for the existence of God, or that is bound to rituals, churches, priests, and theologians who pretend to be the interpreters of God's will. Transcendence, absolute Being, or God—Jaspers uses these concepts or ciphers synonymously—is a dimension of being that is in a radical sense unknowable, but which still directs the self out of the horizon of the spirit. The danger is that religious creeds become illegitimate objectifications and anthropomorphizations of transcendent being. In their defensive and fundamentalist postures, they may turn aggressive and violent.

Jaspers's liberal ethos of humanity is indebted to the work of Max Weber, especially Weber's thesis concerning the "rationalization" of more and more dimensions of human life.[32] Jaspers rejects all rationalistic systems of philosophy and worldviews because a "system" implies, *a priori*, strong tendencies to dogmatization, indoctrination, and rigidity. Moreover, Jaspers intends no "doctrines" of philosophical anthropology, ontology, or ethics because they imply strong tendencies toward indoctrination, mass-unification, and the restriction of individual freedom and self-determined choices. For Jaspers, philosophic doctrines are illegitimate objectifications of the nuanced dimensions of subjectivity and privacy. Ethical or anthropological doctrines usually pretend to give information about human existence as a whole, when they can only really deal with the empirical dimension of humanity and not with the nonobjective, authentic ground of human being, i.e., with Existenz and freedom.

The task of philosophy—and this is a crucial aspect of Jaspers's conception of philosophy—is to appeal to every human being as possible Existenz to realize one's own existential possibilities and capacities. For the sake of this main task of philosophy it is necessary to make clear that human self-realization is an everlasting, dynamic and open process. It must not be dogmatized in a specific, generally valid conception of the nature of the human being or of what constitutes the true and good life. Philosophy has to struggle permanently against the dogmatizing tendencies of rationalist systems, doctrines, worldviews, and ideologies. To prevent dogmatization is the basic goal of his transcending philosophizing, a philosophy governed by reason (*Vernunft*) and not by mere rationality (*Verstand*).

Jaspers's methodological conception of existential elucidation and transcending philosophizing has been charged as constituting a form of philosophical mysticism. Consider, for example, his meta-reflections about transcending philosophizing where he proposes to introduce contradictory statements in order to accept such statements only as "sign-posts" or symbols pointing to a nonobjective dimension of being. Jaspers demands that we relativize all the descriptive meanings and informative contents of such statements. A similar problem arises in connection with the ladder-argument in Ludwig Wittgenstein's *Tractatus*.[33] If all the sentences of the *Tractatus* have the sole function of climbing the steps of a ladder and their cognitive and descriptive content is absolutely irrelevant, in other words, if they have only the therapeutic function of learning to see the world in the right perspective, then a discussion of the descriptive content of those sentences is of no purpose. They are not meant as objective propositions, but have only a therapeutic or "sign-post" function. Whether or not they can fulfill this function cannot be examined or proven because the dimension to which they point as sign-posts is nonobjective and cannot be verbally communicated.

As a consequence of this dilemma we must not follow Jaspers in his demand to transcend or relativize all the descriptive contents of his sentences; in that case, we would not be allowed to give any interpretation to his sentences at all. Every interpretation, however, presupposes a certain content that is open to hermeneutical approaches. If all content is *a priori* relativized we do not have anything that can be interpreted in this or that way or direction. Philosophy, as an activity of interpretation and argumentation, would have come to an end, and there would remain only silence and some intuitive awareness of a mystical or transcendental dimension of being about which we could neither know about nor communicate to others. This destructive consequence of Jaspers's conception of transcending philosophizing can be avoided only by not accepting his demands for transcending and relativizing the content of his philosophical sentences in a strict sense. The best way to interpret his methodology of "transcending" thinking is to interpret his demands as an appeal to an antidogmatic way of philosophizing and to a kind of open-mindedness that does not reduce all of being to objective determination.

NOTES

1. English translations of Jaspers's use of the German term "*Grenzsituation*" have been rendered in English by the use of "limit situation," "borderline situation," and "ultimate situation." We choose the expression "boundary situation" because E. B. Ashton uses it in his well-known English translation of Jaspers's three-volume *Philosophie*, and

the term "boundary situation" is still the most widely used term by Jaspers-researchers in the English-speaking world. See also, Edwin Latzel, "The Concept of 'Ultimate Situation' in Jaspers' Philosophy," in *The Philosophy of Karl Jaspers*, Augmented Edition, edited by Paul A. Schilpp (La Salle, IL: Open Court Publishing Co., 1981 [1957]), pp. 177–208.

2. See Jaspers, *Psychologie der Weltanschauungen*, 6. edited by Berlin 1971 (New Print Munich: Piper Verlag, 1985), pp. 109–14, 277–80, 448–52, 436–86.

3. See the article by George B. Pepper herein [eds.].

4. See Karl Jaspers, *Von der Wahrheit*, new edition (Munich: Piper Verlag, 1958), pp. 123–51; *Karl Jaspers. Basic Philosophical Writings*, edited, translated, and with introductions by Edith Ehrlich, Leonard H. Ehrlich, and George B. Pepper (Atlantic Highlands, NJ: Humanities Press, 1994), pp. 185–93. [Hereafter cited as BPW]; see also, Gerhard Knauss, "The Concept of the 'Encompassing' in Jaspers' Philosophy," in *The Philosophy of Karl Jaspers*, edited by Paul A. Schilpp (New York, Tudor Publishing Company, 1957), pp. 141–75.

5. Karl Jaspers, *Philosophy*, Vol. 2: Existential Elucidation, translated by E. B. Ashton (Chicago/London: The University of Chicago Press, 1970), pp. 28–29. [Hereafter cited as Ph 2 (eds.)].

6. The German expression "*Bewusstsein überhaupt*" has also been rendered in English translations of Jaspers's philosophy as "consciousness-in-general" or "consciousness at large." [eds.]

7. See Karl Jaspers, *The Idea of the University*, edited by Karl W. Deutsch, preface by Robert Ulich, translated by H. A. T. Reiche and H. F. Vanderschmidt (Boston: Becon Press, 1959).

8. For the influence of Kant, Kierkegaard, and Nietzsche on Jaspers's philosophy, see BPW, pp. 22–25, 37–53.

9. Søren Kierkegaard, *Concluding Unscientific Postscript to the 'Philosophical Fragments,'* in *Kierkegaard's Writings*, edited and translated by Howard V. Hong et al. (Princeton, NJ: Princeton University Press, 1978).

10. This concept and closely related conceptions as "cipher" and "philosophic faith" are analyzed and discussed in detail in Oswald O. Schrag, *Existence, Existenz, and Transcendence. An Introduction to the Philosophy of Karl Jaspers* (Pittsburgh, PA: Duquesne University Press, 1971), pp. 191–240; Leonard Ehrlich, *Karl Jaspers: Philosophy as Faith* (Amherst, MA: University of Massachusetts Press, 1975), pp. 117–56; and Alan M. Olson, *Transcendence and Hermeneutics. An Interpretation of the Philosophy of Karl Jaspers* (The Hague/Boston/London: Martinus Nijhoff publishers, 1979), pp. 30–41.

11. Ph 2, p. 178.

12. Ph 2, p. 178.

13. Ph 2, p. 179.

14. Ph 2, p. 184.

15. Ph 2, p. 192.

16. Cf., Karl Jaspers, *Nietzsche: An Introduction to the Understanding of His Philosophical Activity*, translated by Charles F. Wallraff and Frederick J. Schmitz (Baltimore and London: The Johns Hopkins University Press, 1997 [1965]), pp. 367–86.

17. Ph 2, p. 204 (italics added).

18. Ph 2, pp. 203–204.

19. Ph 2, pp. 217–18.

20. Ph 2, pp. 212–15.

21. Ph 2, pp. 212–13.

22. Karl Jaspers, *The Question of German Guilt*, translated by E. B. Ashton, 2nd ed. (New York: Capricorn Books, 1961).

23. See the article by Gregory J. Walters herein [eds.].

24. Karl Jaspers, *The Atom Bomb and the Future of Man*, translated by E. B. Ashton. (Chicago/London: The University of Chicago Press, 1963), pp. 4, and 160–73.

25. Ph 2, p. 4. See also, Fritz Kaufmann, "Karl Jaspers and a Philosophy of Communication," in in *The Philosophy of Karl Jaspers*, Augmented Edition, edited by Paul A. Schilpp (La Salle, IL: Open Court Publishing Co., 1981 [1957]), pp. 210–95; Indu Sarin, "Jaspers's Quest for Existential Communication," in *Karl Jaspers. Philosophy on the Way to "World Philosophy,"* edited by Leonard Ehrlich and Richard Wisser (Würzburg/Amsterdam/Atlanta: Königshausen & Neumann and Rodopi, 1998), pp. 205–10.

26. Ph 2, p. 49.

27. Ph 2, p. 56.

28. Ph 2, p. 75.

29. Ph 2, p. 97.

30. Ph 2, p. 94.

31. See Kurt Salamun, "The Concept of Liberality in Jaspers's Philosophy and the Idea of the University," in *The Tasks of Truth*, edited by Walters, 39–53, and, *idem.*, "The Ethos of Humanity in Karl Jaspers's Political Philosopy," *Man and World*, vol. 23 (1990), pp. 225–30. On the general moral implications of Jaspers's philosophy, see Leonard Ehrlich, "Tolerance and the Prospect of a World Philosophy," in *Karl Jaspers Today: Philosophy at the Threshold of the Future*, edited by Leonard H. Ehrlich and Richard Wisser (Washington, DC: University Press of America, 1988), pp. 93–100; also, Kurt Salamun, "Moral Implications of Karl Jaspers's Existentialism," *Philosophy and Phenomenological Research*, vol. 49 (1988), pp. 317–22.

32. Max Weber, *Economy and Society: An Outline of Interpretive Sociology*, edited by Guenther Roth and Claus Wittich (Berkeley/Los Angeles/London: University of California Press, 1978), pp. 63–74, 406, 426, 432–35, 1116–17.

33. Ludwig Wittgenstein, *Tractatus-logico philosophicus* translated by D. F. Pears & B. F. McGuinness, and with an Introduction by Bertrand Russell (London: Routledge Kegan Paul, 1961), p. 151.

THE ENCOMPASSING, FOUNDERING, AND THE TRAGIC INDIVIDUAL IN THE PHILOSOPHY OF KARL JASPERS

George B. Pepper

Karl Jaspers's analysis of the tragic individual is derived from the body of literature that literary theorists identify as tragedy.[1] His concern is not with literary theory however, although his work has had influence in this field. His interest, rather, is "existential," in what this body of literature reveals about the basic human condition. To obtain an appreciation of Jaspers's views on the tragic individual, and to avoid viewing it as an exercise in aesthetics, an examination is called for on how he identifies all the historically important individuals that are found in his writings. The importance of the tragic individual takes on its particular significance when viewed alongside other historically important individuals that Jaspers treats. A wide variety of such individuals can be found in Jaspers's writings including religious persons,[2] scientists,[3] eastern inspirational leaders,[4] and artists.[5] In these writings Jaspers employed the same principles of philosophical interpretation that he used in his exposition of the great philosophers. The suspicion can arise that Jaspers was forcing upon his subjects a philosophical framework that was alien to their work. Such a conclusion would be possible, however, only after the critic entered into the communicative criteria that Jaspers set for himself. These criteria involve a transformative experience of a personal nature, and are not of the generic type. Each dialogue Jaspers has with original religious personages, scientists, inspirational eastern leaders, and artists, therefore, would have to be evaluated one-by-one, and any critic is called upon to place his or her own serious concerns into the discussion. Behind any important work or text, strides the serious concerns of the author that a discerning reader or viewer can grasp. No matter whether the author dissimulates or even is unaware of such concerns, the alert reader/viewer can reach some recognition of the forces the author stood for or opposed.

In order to advance discussion on this facet of great figures and authors of important works, Jaspers coined the term "Existenz," i.e., the irreducible freedom within each person that resists any effort that seeks to explain the author in terms of antecedent inner or outer circumstances. Jaspers was confident that every person could recognize this awareness of selfhood, even though no purely sensible data can be identified to support its existence, since the reader's or viewer's own Existenz can be brought to bear on every reading. That is, within each person lies the awareness that he or she can make a difference in shaping the interplay of external and internal influences that are found in any human situation. Jaspers offers no rules for how one can read the serious concerns of the author. The text or work is a crucial datum, but even this criterion is not entirely sufficient. "May not similar positions held by philosophers," Jaspers writes, be only "surfaces that must be questioned as to what works through them?" And "may not apparently identical positions stand in the service of entirely different forces?"[6] Even when the reader/viewer shares agreement with the author's position, therefore, there still remains a more basic concern about what forces the author serves or opposes. Neither rules of method nor shared positions provide access to the author's serious concerns. How then is recognition available? The only resource I can recognize is empathy, a subject of philosophical hermeneutics whose epistemological contours deserve closer examination.[7] My focus, however, will be on the basic characteristics that Jaspers used in his selection of authors of works he found important enough to merit his attention, especially the tragic individual, and to offer a tentative defense of his position.

Jaspers's aim in treating the great authors and figures he found worthy of consideration is to show that philosophy is a calling that brings forth the highest efforts from the person who grapples with the major issues of the day. Past philosophers and other great figures may be regarded as eternal interlocutors because they provide examples of and challenges for what is possible for a person today. Reading the history of past accomplishments is not a detached exercise for viewing the errors and outmoded views of the past. It is, rather, a critical dialogue that requires placing oneself in the historic context of the author, the upshot of which can lead to "a transformation of consciousness that goes beyond objective understanding. [And] out of this transformation we arrive, be it in agreement or in opposition, at the truth which we ourselves are and with which we can therefore live."[8] Jaspers does not provide any generic criteria for carrying out the philosophical dialogue per se, but he does identify what I call "existential markers" for detecting authorial creativity. These existential markers are elucidated in Jaspers's various treatments of "periechontology," "boundary situations," and "foundering."[9] Besides identifying these markers and defending their appropriateness, the purpose of this paper is to locate the place of high importance that the tragic person held for Jaspers.

Periechontology: The Horizon-Encompassing Relation

The basic difference between "periechontology" and traditional "ontology" is that the former does not assert directly what "Being as such" is, but only how being appears for us in the subjective and objective modes of the Encompassing. "Horizon" and "encompassing" are notions that have a crucial place in Jaspers's writings, and they are given nuanced application in a number of issues that Jaspers explored in his long and eventful life. Since every human issue is situated within a given horizon, all available cognitive resources are to be used to make that horizon intelligible. Since the human person is always more than can be objectively known about him or her, existential elucidation is required to point to and make palpable what lies beyond each horizon and encompasses it. In this effort the ground is prepared for recognizing what each person is capable of doing in freedom's breakthrough out of the cognitively objective realm.

While Jaspers carefully explains the various modes of the encompassing, which he found capable of designating all aspects of human experience and thought, the inner linings of these demarcations have decisive differences that need attention.[10]

An example for envisioning cognitive horizons may be drawn from sight navigation. A particular horizon is selected for steering a ship. That horizon constantly recedes with new points arising until a destiny is reached. An assumption is made throughout the movement that conditions similar to the ones stretching before the ship will appear as the horizon recedes. The unexpected, however, can arise, for example, when weather conditions turn the sea into a nonnavigable cauldron. The point to bear in mind is that *there can be no horizon without an encompassing*. I shall call this the horizon-encompassing (H-E) relation, endeavor to explicate the specific character of the H-E nexuses in Jaspers's work, the relevance this has for his interpretation of the great writers and artists, as well as the tragic individual.

Six modes of encompassing are identified by Jaspers: existence, consciousness as such, spirit, Existenz, world, and transcendence. These modes are not the outcome of deduction from a philosophical principle, nor are they arbitrarily asserted. They are derived solely from experience and are heterogeneous in origin, even though one may be used to explaining all the others in reductionist terms. The purpose for identifying them is to achieve the greatest possible inclusiveness in philosophizing, which, for Jaspers, means "preparation and remembrance." Philosophy is not a self-sufficient activity, since it is always open to reality and is true only when conjoined with reality. A purely formal approach to philosophy, however, is not necessarily devoid of all importance. Philosophy may demonstrate in critical moments where the failure of thinking, at the limits of human cognition, is recognized by thinking itself, and thereby open up indeterminate realms of meaning, a movement of thinking that Jaspers found in the philosophy of Wittgenstein.[11]

The drive toward self-preservation and expansion that constitutes the necessary conditions for all other activities of a human being is identified as *existence*. The horizon of existence has a dual nature. Its positive side is the conscious satisfaction of an individual's unconscious functions. The negative side arises from the radical instability found in a life of pure self-interest: The boredom of repetition, the uncertainty of success, and the inevitability of biological death. The encompassing of existence is revealed in two ways that one can escape the dead end of the negative side. It comes into awareness when two individuals are involved in the boundary situation of "struggle," where they cannot find a truth both can share. Then force and cunning will decide the outcome. The two individuals, however, may also find in their confrontation resources of faith that enable them to relate without suppressing their differences. Hegel's description of the initial encounter between the master and the slave can be taken as an illustration. In this situation either freedom-at-all-costs or life-at-all-costs takes on supreme value to which the individual throws the whole weight of his existence. For it cannot be predicted in advance whether an individual would choose freedom or life as the imperative value. The choice taken in this situation takes on a transcendent significance for the individual. The other route open in this boundary situation can arise when both individuals, locked in mortal combat, find a source for agreement. Either an intellectual agreement of a contractual nature or the discovery of some spiritual bond both can share could offer a way out of the dead end of existence. However, only by having a faith in the validity of one's intellectual powers or in some kind of spiritual bond could this kind of resolution be sustained.

Besides being conscious of one's vital needs as existence, self-consciousness can arise in an individual. Jaspers does not explain how this comes about, but it is suggested that not only can two individuals find a common bond to share, they may come to see that all being has a common understanding. This dimension of the self is therefore called *consciousness as such*, the source of all logically valid thought and action. It is, in sum, "the self-consciousness in one's knowledge of oneself."[12] Since all of the modes of the encompassing are shaped by the historic circumstances in which the individual finds oneself, Jaspers turns to the contemporary sciences to locate the horizon and encompassing of consciousness as such.[13] Jaspers finds that while no one science can unify all the sciences, they share a similar intellectual climate, namely, that only a multi-perspectival approach—whose parts are constantly revisable by cogent evidence—can meet the demands of a scientific view of the world today.[14] Jaspers, however, following the lead of Dilthey and others, organizes the various sciences under two headings, the natural and cultural sciences. At the limits of these sciences, Jaspers locates the H-E nexus of consciousness as such. Both types of sciences share a common limit in that "*man is more than he will show of himself when he becomes an object of cognition.*"[15]

Two related limits are discernible in both the natural and cultural sciences, one on the external world's side, and the other on the knower's side. These limits, in turn, manifest a reality that cannot become an object for scientific understanding. On the world's side, the meta-scientific reality becomes evident in the antinomial character of two equally plausible, but incompatible, sets of categories used to explain the world. On the knower's side, the meta-scientific reality appears either in how the endlessness confronting the natural sciences is overcome through ideas that have a transcendent source, or how the content of the cultural sciences is appropriated existentially. The sciences, therefore, serve as negative indicators that direct a person to turn inward for the resources by which he or she can make commitments to basic choices about oneself and the world, including the choice to become a scientist. The encompassing as such (transcendence and Existenz) are the terms Jaspers uses to identify these two related realities. Their relationship is not beyond expression, but the language used can only be in ciphers, not in scientific categories. Jaspers, nonetheless, recognized that some philosophers have derived important philosophical positions from their work in science. He insisted, however, that such results can only have the form of "a speculative-metaphysical exegesis of ciphers";[16] and the works of C. S. Peirce and A. N. Whitehead come to mind as examples. Equally true would be scientists who pursued their work with such depth that they came to realize the presence of a transcendent source for their creative ideas, such as Einstein. Philosophical reasoning does not yield results that are cogent and universally valid. Rather, it "brings me to myself. Its consequences lie in the inner action I perform with it. It awakens the sources in me to which science itself owes its meaning."[17]

Spirit is as actual as existence and as inward as consciousness as such, but it springs from another source. Its basic characteristics are identified as action, presence, and effective wholeness. It *acts* in thought, feeling, and deed by holding together. It is *present* as guidance. It becomes *effective* through structure, measure, and the setting of limits. The posture of spirit is one of being jolted by ideas into activity, a jolting that can be realized as typical even though it cannot be defined. Such ideas produce wholes, which themselves are not objects, but serve as forces that penetrate everything and as goals that attract. While ideas can be crystallized into objective forms of configurations and patterns, they always have specific content for spirit and are never mere form. These contents arise from a source that is "infinite" and cannot be comprehended by any principle. Infinite here means that there is no end to the extent that these ideas can be embodied in life. They are "actual" in the obscurity of existence, awakened by Existenz, and find their illumination in consciousness as such.

The H-E nexus of spirit comes into clearer view when spirit is contrasted with Existenz. Jaspers identifies five basic differences that separate the two. The horizon of spirit can be characterized as (a) wholeness, (b) a tranquility of inclusiveness, (c) an understanding that can be thoroughly illuminated, (d) a historicity that is totally transparent, and (e) an immediacy of a burgeoning idea. The limits found in each of these characteristics reveal its encompassing. Specifically: (a') that any whole is inadequate to circumscribe the entire reach of reality open to Existenz, and that a breakthrough is an ever-present possibility; (b') that the certainty of spirit is never entirely beyond doubt; (c') that the understanding of spirit is surrounded by an incomprehensible other that admits of only limited clarity; (d') that the transparency of spirits historicity is always confronted by the possibility of ever new eruptions of eternity in time; and (e') the immediacy of the burgeoning idea in the clarity of its universality can always be confounded by an immediacy of faith whose certainty is beyond confirmation.

The movement of spirit, therefore, can involve a transition from totality to fragmentation, from certainty to uncertainty, from clarity to obscurity, from historic self-transparence to the incomprehensibility of eternity, and from the clarity of universality to the nonprovable eternity of faith. Creative individuals who achieved this breakthrough of spirit include Da Vinci, Strindberg, and Van Gogh in art; Dante, Shakespeare, Goethe, Hölderlin, and Dostoevsky in literature; and Jesus, Nicholas of Cusa, Confucius, Buddha, and Nagarjuna in the sphere of religion.

The encompassing to which *Existenz* is summoned is the encompassing that encompasses all other encompassings. For this reason it is called Transcendence, and the only definite statement that can be sounded about Existenz is that it stands before Transcendence. The relationship, however, is not devoid of expression. Existenz concerns the core of human freedom by which each person decides what is of utmost importance. Freedom is experienced as a gift that enables one to give of oneself in turn. Such decisions are always situated within historic circumstances, but always with an eye to what a person believes is of eternal importance. Some of these decisions concern boundary situations that can be found in every person's life such as struggle, suffering, guilt, and death. If these situations do not overwhelm a person's reasoning resources, they can provide an occasion for a person to decide what is eternally important for one's life.

Besides these intimate personal experiences, the H-E nexus of Existenz can also come into view in existence, consciousness as such, and spirit. When a decision is made that it is better to have lived than not at all, Existenz enters the domain of existence. When cognitive accomplishments of consciousness as such achieve compelling persuasiveness and become the basis of philosophical speculation, then they take on cipher-like importance for Existenz, as suggested by the works of Peirce, Whitehead, and Einstein. Or, again, when the unifying wholes of spirit in its active historic life take on momentous significance, they can become the medium of Existenz's transcendent commitment. The encompassing of Existenz, therefore, is transcendence. The horizons of Existenz, however, can be any of those found in the modes of the other encompassings heretofore discussed when these become momentous due to unique personal and historical circumstances.

The encompassings of existence, consciousness as such, and spirit altogether can be regarded as the collective encompassing of any person, or as Jaspers puts it, "the encompassing which we are." Once we recognize that Being cannot be exhausted by this encompassing, however, we enter into another encompassing that is decidedly not ourselves. It is the unknown. How can the unknown be recognized? It happens when the unknown overpowers us at the limits of our most extended consciousness. This can occur at two principal boundaries. The first one appears when we recognize that each fact that can be the object for the encompassing that we are, also possesses an "otherness," which exceeds our ability to totally appropriate it in knowledge or action. Now the totality of the otherness of facts Jaspers calls the *world*. The second boundary arises when we recognize that the encompassing we are cannot be comprehended out of itself, but points toward an "other" through which it is. This occurs when Existenz comes to know itself as given to itself, as standing before Transcendence through which it is.

The confluence of the otherness of facts in existence, consciousness as such, and spirit, therefore, constitute the world. The world cannot be captured in any theoretical or cognitive scheme. It is, rather, a regulative idea in the Kantian sense. It provides us with an ongoing perspective. We are derived from the world, are borne by the world, but we are finally defeated by the world. Even though the various ways the world can be designated fail to become definitive, they nevertheless indicate that the world can be transcended. They point to a source within our selves that is not derived from the world. The source of the world is ultimately beyond final comprehension, and concepts such as creation, emanation, or primal matter, however they may be explained, can function only as myth or symbol when applied to the world. However, since whatever designation is given to the world derives from the primal sources in consciousness as such or spirit, the world itself cannot be self-sufficient. The designations furnish the substantial background of all cognition. Reflection upon these designations, however, keeps us from getting bogged down in any one definitive designation. It also provides us with the calm of belonging to a ground that is never exhausted by what can only be recognized as appearance.[18] The world as such, therefore, is primarily an encompassing. The horizon that is related to this encompassing pertains to the encompassing that we are insofar as it consists of those facts that only in part can be appropriated in knowledge and action.

The otherness of the encompassing world becomes evident when any cognition of the world as a whole runs aground on the facts of research. Jaspers explains this cognitive shipwreck in several ways. Any total view of the world invariably gets entangled in antinomies. In these contradictions the world as object disappears. Such total views also fail because the reality constituting the world is fragmented. Physical events, biological events, consciousness, and spirit are four realities of which each latter one is tied to its prior reality, but not the reverse. A gap separates them that no theory of the natural sciences can successfully bridge with finality. The methods by which we observe and study the world are similarly fragmented, and no single cognition can entirely coincide with the object cognized by any theoretical framework.

The "bottomlessness" of the world, however, need not lead to skepticism about the reality of things. The appearances of the world are not illusions. Rather, this bottomlessness can lead to clarity about the world's reality and about the cognitions we have about the world. Jaspers draws three conclusions from this clarity. The first is that we are liberated for the world. The second is that we are liberated for ourselves in the world. And the third is that we are liberated for ourselves in relation to transcendence. That is, instead of clinging to one controlling theory or method, we are freed to entertain many theories and methods whose validity depends on their empirical fruitfulness. Instead of an ultimate framework of knowledge we are freed for a radical openness and a readiness for new experience in all modes of the encompassing. This explanation of the world provides

Jaspers with the critical basis for exposing every theoretical effort that seeks an exclusive explanation of either human nature or the world. It thus provides the basis for recognizing the breakthrough character of human accomplishments.

The three modes of existence, consciousness as such, and spirit each possesses an encompassing that is a kind of *transcendence*. But Jaspers calls them a universal transcendence and contrasts this with "authentic Transcendence," also called the "absolute Encompassing" or "the Encompassing of all that encompasses." For existence, consciousness as such, and spirit the encompassing transcendence is the world. For Existenz, in contrast, the encompassing transcendence is authentic Transcendence. Universal Transcendence and authentic Transcendence are radically different; the former is empty possibility, the unknown, while the authentic Transcendence of Existenz is the other in which it is anchored, and by which Existenz is given to itself in achieving authentic selfhood. Authentic Transcendence can take on various basic characteristics. Although it vanishes when turned into a thought; it implacably is. Even though it is easier to express what it *is not*, negative formulations also become questionable when taken as definite content. Only in an unending movement of thought that both expresses and revokes can the form of language about authentic Transcendence exist. Allegories are its expressions, and they can be endlessly accumulated. As thought, it has been called *Being*; as lived, *authentic Actuality*; as something governing, *Divinity*; and as personally encountered, *God*. No matter what clarity is achieved by these designations, authentic Transcendence remains hidden even as it sustains Existenz.

Jaspers identifies at least three distinguishable experiences that touch upon authentic Transcendence. One is called *formal transcending*, where the being of transcendence is ascertained by means of conceptually and methodically particular movements of thought. The second experience occurs in *existential relations* where the actuality of transcendence is brought to actual presence for Existenz in its self-transformation. The third experience arises when anything that becomes objective and a living experience to us is *read as cipher script*. When the transparency of things is experienced, these things can become comprehensible as a language of transcendence to the extent that we become existential and by virtue of our becoming authentic. The thread throughout these experiences is that everything in us is transformed when we address the encompassing that is Being as such, not only as the world but also as transcendence, and which appears to the basis of Jaspers's interpretation of Asian thinkers like Buddha and Nagarjuna, Lao-tzu and Confucius.[19]

Throughout the various encompassings so far discussed there is found a multiplicity of perspectives that are both diverse and fragmented. The intent behind Jaspers's delineation of these encompassings is to protect us from falling into any false closure on reality that may arise from errant willing, or a misguided craving for understanding by consciousness as such. In the encompassing we are, however, there lies a primal source for an unceasing drive toward unity. This drive is located in Existenz, one that resists diffuseness, and by which Existenz seeks to gain its own identity. But it is through *reason* that this drive becomes possible. Although the understanding in consciousness as such can illuminate the drives in existence and spirit, and thereby turn the contents of these two encompassings into scientific knowledge, the resulting cognitions remain disparate in both their connections and relative importance. There is another source of meaningfulness, however, which requires that none of these disparate cognitions be omitted or neglected. Reason seeks to find ways by which disparate cognitions can be related and unified. It is by reason that this is endeavored, and it is through the decisiveness of Existenz to be whole, that it springs. Reason, therefore, is the bond of all modes of the encompassing and of all their configurations. The illumination of the encompassing of reason is the main task of philosophical reflection.

The bonding character of reason is evident in various ways. Counter to the movement in the different encompassings we are to be dominant and exclusive, reason seeks to make manifest how anything can have importance for everything else. The concern of reason is to see that nothing of importance is lost. In the mode of consciousness as such, reason acts by seeking to go beyond every limit of a particular science, to identify contradictions, and to find relationships and complements. It functions as the idea of unity of all the sciences, but also seeks to relate this unity to the unity of all other encompassings. Even breaches of unity are the concern of reason. Thus reason also recognizes the "exception" to any universal validity, even as it also recognizes the "authority" that demands without being understood. But here, too, reason seeks to relate both exception and authority, because of their provisional nature, to an ultimate demanding one. Even the most alien attracts reason in that it strives to prevent every shattering of a unity from becoming a metaphysical breach of the true unity of being.

The fundamental attitude of reason, therefore, is the will to unity. It is active in all the modes of the encompassing we are. The unity reason seeks is the one that contains all truth. It acts as a force of attraction that overcomes all division. It therefore cannot be content with any unity derived from consciousness as such, for any unity coming from the sciences pales in significance when compared with the actuality of existence and spirit. Reason seeks to relate the importance of science to all the other truths that deserve recognition to the vital life of existence, the unifying wholes of spirit, and to exception and authority, and even to what is most alien in every rupture. Reason, therefore, may be viewed as the total will to communication in that it gives heed to everything that can be expressed in language and to everything there is, so that nothing is ignored and all is preserved. The horizon of reason therefore relates to every determinate boundary of knowledge. The encompassing of reason relates to the unlimited questioning that can be raised against every determinate boundary, and its encompassing is the One that attracts us to overcome all division.[20]

One key text that links boundary situations directly with the horizon-encompassing relationship previously noted comes from a memoir: "It is only in extreme [boundary] situations that man becomes aware of what he is."[21] These boundary situations have very different contexts in which limits are probed, such as the relationships between physician and patient,[22] the philosopher and the religionist,[23] the philosopher and the scientist,[24] and the citizen and the state.[25] It is in the tragic situation, however, that Jaspers finds the most extreme tension between knowledge and action. The method Jaspers used in exploring boundary situations combined phenomenological description, "scientific" analysis, and existential elucidation.

Boundary situations refer to those unavoidable circumstances that all persons meet at some time in their lives: "I cannot live without *struggling* and *suffering*; that I cannot avoid *guilt*; that I must *die*."[26] They cannot be modified, and all that can be done is to elucidate them. Any effort that seeks to explain them in other terms can only remove them from sight. It is not in explanation that we deal with them. A very different response is called for, an activity "of becoming the Existenz we potentially are."[27] In facing boundary situations a person's entire understanding and experience provides no guidance on how one should or can act. The action one takes, however, need not be merely impulsive. It can yield results that have decisive and lasting importance for the person's standing in his own eyes and the eyes of another. To account for such results, a person may receive the assurance that a transcendent source erupts into that person's life endowing the person with the ability to act freely. But what if no such transcendent source makes itself present? The outcome would be the loss of any valid or lasting meaning to one's life, what Jaspers terms "foundering."[28]

The Concept of Foundering

Foundering signifies the fruitlessness of all endeavors to reach, through consciousness as such or possible Existenz a satisfactory access to Being as such. Foundering is the ultimate realist worldview: Human existence is transitory and founders in death. Our cognition can lead to self-destruction as we attempt to comprehend absolute Being, and our actions founder when the final purposes for acting no longer retain a permanence. Foundering perceives clearly that all which is positive has its corresponding negative: There is no good without evil, no truth without falsehood, no life without death, all the while happiness comes with inevitable pain and efforts at human self-actualization founder on the shoals of risk and loss. As finite creatures human beings cannot arrive at the absolute, and foundering comes to represent the cipher that determines all other ciphers for Jaspers, what he calls "being in foundering," in its two main modes, i.e., foundering in existence and in Existenz.

> The human depth which gives voice to its transcendence is in reality tied to what is destructive, sick, or extravagant, but this bond in its unbounded variety is not unequivocally present. In all existence its antinomial structure is visible. . . . Thus the modes of foundering exist as objective actuality or as the inescapability of what can be thought, and hence signify, in some sense, a foundering in existence and as existence. The foundering of Existenz, however, lies on a different plane. When I come, in freedom, from existence to the certainty of Being, then I must experience, precisely in the clearest decisiveness of self-being within my acting, its foundering as well. For the impossibility to stand absolutely on one's own feet does not grow out of my being bound to existence, which is in fact destructive, but out of freedom itself. Through freedom I become guilty in every instance; I cannot become whole. Truth as genuine truth which I grasp because I am and live it lacks the possibility of being knowable as absolutely valid. What is absolutely valid could persist, timeless, in ever-changing existence; but authentic truth is precisely the truth that perishes."[29]

The evidence of foundering is omnipresent. Inanimate objects eventually decay. Death is the final destiny of all living organisms. Even humankind's greatest spiritual achievements can wither from indifference and forgetfulness. All existence and human cognition has its "antinomical structure."[30] The world founders as existence, the world remains incomprehensible as a whole, and human cognition cannot round itself into a whole. In logic, validity founders on relativity, and at the extreme limits of knowledge we encounter antinomies that finish the human mind's ability to think without contradictions. Thought founders and the "passion for the night" appears as the antithesis to reason, as passion for death, inhumanity, or cosmological dualism.

Foundering reveals the lack of compromise between the "law of the day" (the principle of order, clarity, and loyalty) and the "passion for the night" (the irrational urge to darkness, to ruin, and the end of all order). The "law of the day" (*Gesetz des Tages*) regulates our everyday existence, demands clarity, consistency, and loyalty, and binds us to reason and to "the idea," to "the One," and to "ourselves." It demands that the self actualize itself in the world, as a construction in time and development, ever reaching for the perfection of existence along a way that is ultimately "finite" in its historicity. The "passion for the night" (*Leidenschaft zur Nacht*) disrupts all orders. It "plunges us into the timeless abyss of nothingness," Jaspers writes, "dragging everything into its whirl. . . . No tasks, no goals speak for it; it is the urge to ruin myself in the world to gain perfection in the depth of worldlessness."[31]

Existenz founders, according to Jaspers, in the transcending movements of both existential elucidation and metaphysical speculations or cipher-reading. Existenz inevitably founders because it aspires to the infinite, and seeks to impose its unconditional absoluteness on the conditional world of existence. The important questions for Jaspers, however, are: Does foundering mean outright destruction? Or, does foundering reveal a being? Can foundering mean not merely foundering, but "eternalization" (*Verewigen*) as well? That is, can foundering in Existenz nonetheless be an access point to eternity? Jaspers's answer is that the individual can *appropriate* the reality of foundering. When this happens then my human foundering, as the decisive and ultimate cipher of transcendence, reveals *amor fati*: The daring or courage to take foundering upon oneself. We may indeed actually fail in this undertaking, but I nonetheless do all that is in my power to accept the foundering of existence and Existenz with a loving acceptance of whatever happens. This is why the foundering that comes to all human beings occurs for Jaspers on a different plane than all other situations. "It is precisely in the acts of my most lucid and forthright self-being that I must experience its [Existenz's] foundering."[32]

Foundering occurs when every assurance a person possesses is struck with default. Foundering may also come to defy its own interpretation as, for example, in the negativity that destroys in cases of mental illness or neurological disease that overpower human beings. We may founder by means of the habituated "denial of possibilities" which ruins human potentialities over time. Foundering occurs in the destruction that ends the chance of human continuity by means of burying all historical documents and traces in a "ruin of oblivion" as Jaspers witnessed during the Nazi period in Germany. While "nothingness" in its black and starkest form can confront a person, some individuals are still able to act with a willingness to take responsibility for outcome, and such is the arena in which the tragic individual appears in history.

FOUNDERING AS THE TEST OF ULTIMACY

Foundering, Jaspers maintains, can be taken as the ultimate test for ascertaining what is of utmost importance for human life. To live without transcending is to live in radical despair, but in view of foundering, it seems almost impossible to live. It is not nothingness, however, that is self-consciously present in boundary situations and the foundering that exists in existence, the sciences, arts, and social movements. For it is the "leap" from anguish to calm, from fear to serenity, that is the most enormous, difficult, and incomprehensible step human beings can succeed in making. The leap can only be experienced, and is neither definitively explained nor expressed in concepts, yet presupposes dread before the abyss of nothingness: "That he succeeds in it [the leap] must be due to a reason beyond the Existenz of his self-being. Undefinably, his faith ties him to transcendent being. . . . Active sufferance [*Dulden*] allows me to experience the foundering of all existence and yet to engage in realizations as long as an ounce of strength remains. In this tension I gain composure. Sufferance sustains the world of one who is receptive to reality and has become sensitive to transcendent being. In sufferance lies the not-knowing of the kind of faith that makes men active in the world without any need to believe in the possibility of a good and definitive world order . . . sufferance means that he will cling to being *in spite of* his foundering, where the cipher of foundering fails him. . . . That there is being suffices. Whatever we think we know about the deity is superstition; truth lies where a foundering Existenz can translate the ambiguous language of transcendence into the simplest certainty of being."[33]

THE PLACE OF TRAGEDY IN JASPERS'S THOUGHT

Jaspers's periechontology reveals how creative individuals respond to boundary situations and the ultimate cipher of "being in foundering," and provides the basis for comparing the tragic individual with the other historically important persons who are found in his writings. Before discussing the tragic individual, let us recall that the overall purpose of the preceding analyses has been to highlight Jaspers's intention to provide his readers with existential markers for recognizing the unique contributions that creative writers and artists make for all of us, as well as the uniqueness that each of us can find in ourselves, even when most of us never produce works that ever approach the recognition by others as being creative. Jaspers's intention is to awaken in his readers an awareness of what they are up against in this century, and to summon forth the free responses they can make. These concerns enabled and, indeed, motivated Jaspers to range widely in his treatment of writers and artists, and to undertake bold efforts to deal with figures in fields for which he did not possess the training that specialists in these fields possess. It opens him to the criticism mentioned earlier that he was imposing a philosophical framework that is alien to the writers and artists he examined. A partial answer to this criticism is now in order.

How to communicate across boundaries, both theoretical and cultural, was the issue that Jaspers found to be the most compelling one facing every serious and informed person today. The importance of this issue cannot be gainsaid. The influences that came in the wake of modern science and technology and the forces they have put into place reverberate throughout the world in the form of economic markets, communication media, and political organization. The world has become unified as never before. However, the ability to communicate about the important issues of human life and the shape of conditions on which human freedom is now called upon to address has not been advanced by these forces. The main direction of Jaspers's philosophizing has been to raise this issue in its starkest terms, namely, how are we to achieve meaningful mutuality in a world that is both culturally divided and instrumentally bound together by technological means? Others have also raised this question, but Jaspers also offered an intellectual basis for addressing it. His accomplishment no doubt has shortcomings and warrants criticism, yet it has merited the attention of scholars that demonstrates its fertility.[34] Since communication across cultural boundaries under present world conditions affects everyone, the answer to this question cannot be the sole responsibility of specialists. Not until specialists move out of their self-defined precincts and speak to the specifics on human freedom that different audiences can recognize will they earn a hearing. Jaspers's has given us one fruitful example for how this may be done in his notion of the Axial Age civilizations, a notion that merits continuing attention in our present historical situation.[35]

Jaspers looked to those individuals who were drawn to question the horizon of modernity out of depths they could find no home for in the world around them. At least three important writers provided him with guidance: Kierkegaard, Nietzsche, and Max Weber. Science and technology, with their socially embedded forms of production, commerce, and bureaucratically organized government, brought unprecedented gains in standards of living and population growth. Unlike the aspirations of the Enlightenment, which viewed the early stages of these developments as harbingers of a new age where human needs, class exploitation, and inevitable wars would no longer determine the shape of history, where the horizon of progress toward plenty and peace would henceforth govern human affairs, Kierkegaard, Nietzsche, and Max Weber, in their different historical situations, would raise questions about whether such a world would be fit to live in. As the vaunted promises of modernity gradually took over the ways the authorities in Western societies shaped their world, and now seem to shape the rest of the world, the downside of modernity became clearer.

Although Kierkegaard and Nietzsche did not live to see the downside of modernity, the questions they raised had prepared others to recognize that something very fundamental was amiss in the science-technology model of progress. For Kierkegaard, the anxiety of making choices about such basic human values as career and marriage becomes meaningless when we focus only on future developments. And the guilt that strikes a person who fails to live up to his or her own self-given commitments loses all significance in the bright light of a better future. Nietzsche's question has an equally haunting character. While no reasonable person would want to reject the upside of modernity with the better and longer life it brings, there is little argument available to defend the massive destruction and uprooted social conditions that came in modernity's wake. Nietzsche claimed with some persuasiveness that the great institutions of the West, to which the protection of basic human values were entrusted, were partially complicit in bringing about the ambiguous modernity that is so clear today.

In Max Weber, however, Jaspers found the person who would be his constant companion through out his philosophical career: "I did not philosophize without keeping him [Weber] in my mind, without asking my self what he would say. I made his basic position my own—not in the sense of continuing his sociology and furthering sociological research but in the sense of bringing his philosophizing to consciousness."[36] Weber was a historian and sociologist, a practitioner of the cultural sciences. It was because of his recognition of the limitless nature of scientific work and in the heroic stance he took toward it and toward the political conditions in Germany that Jaspers found him to be such an important guide for understanding modernity. The scientific enterprise draws on sources that derive from classical Greek philosophy. It was only in the twentieth century that people who reflected upon the nature of the scientific enterprise came to the realization that this undertaking has no necessary foundations in philosophy or theology. The inquiring mind of the scientist could focus on any object and proceed solely with the method of observation, theoretical and hypothetical thinking, and experimental testing, without any need to justify this activity with metaphysical principles or theological beliefs. Individual scientists could and do espouse philosophical and/or theological principles as justification for their work, but all such references could be shown not to be necessary for scientific inquiry.

What kind of person, it must be asked, is called to dedicate himself to such an undertaking that yields no lasting intellectual satisfaction of theoretical or personal wholeness? For Jaspers, Weber exemplified such a personality in his meticulous care of detail, attention to cogent reasoning, and historical research: "Weber was a man in whom the personal formation developing from cognition and original experience translated into such an interlocking knowledge that no more magnificent image of a contemporary philosopher can be imagined. For a philosopher is that human being who steadfastly thinks and cognizes by focusing on the ground of Existenz, always referring to an unspoken absolute while always expressing himself in the finite."[37]

Weber's ascetic commitment to the advancement of knowledge that is open to constant revision and advance gave him some satisfaction in following his will to know and to engage in a worthwhile career. But that satisfaction did not yield the formulation of a lasting theory that would memorialize his name forever or give him permanent well-being. The personal example of Weber's scholarship and life did not mean for Jaspers that science and philosophy were totally unrelated, only that no permanent bridges could be theoretically established.[38] As we have seen, for Jaspers any issue can become a vital necessity for an Existenz under specific historic circumstances, and in this sense Jaspers sees in every person a potential philosopher.[39] In the scientist's case, however, the vital necessity of scientific research forms a whole expressing an attitude toward life and a specific way of thinking. The scientists philosophical presence is not approached within his subject matter, but rather "by accepting or rejecting, by responding to states of mind, motivations, aspirations, and the measure of depth or superficiality in his relation to the actuality of human beings, the world, and transcendence."[40]

The preceding citation comes from an essay Jaspers wrote on Einstein. It equally applies to Weber, but for one exception. Einstein encountered in his work no force that was overwhelming for him in that "he replicates an ancient form of living, non-tragic, indeed, incapable of tragedy."[41] In contrast, Jaspers saw Weber to be the "heart of Europe." He embodied the widest and clearest consciousness of actual events, only to have his views ignored on how the horrific course of events that led to the catastrophe of World War I and the ensuing unstable peace could have been avoided. Jaspers does not apply the word "tragic" to Weber in either of his two treatments of Weber.

There are two reasons I want to offer for this omission. The first is that Jaspers was directly concerned with articulating the character of Weber's work as a scientist and political figure in as specific terms as possible. Only in this way could Jaspers set forth the extraordinary reach, as well as limits, in Weber's life and thought. And only in this way could Jaspers do justice to the personal depth he found in him. The term "tragedy" could have had a merely literary and diverting effect, thereby blunting Jaspers's aims. Jaspers's detailing of Weber's life and thought is of such intensity that it is unmatched in any other of Jaspers's personal studies. This prompts the second reason I offer for why Jaspers did not label Weber as tragic, and it comes from Jaspers: There is no general theory of tragedy, though there is a place of tragedy in Jaspers's thought since boundary situations and foundering are fundamental and inevitable in human life. Godfrey Carr states the situation about Weber clearly: "For Jaspers, and those who thought like him, the fragmentary output and the political failure reinforced their conviction that Weber's life and work were a unique mirror of the tragic situation of the age."[42]

Tragic knowledge relates to "original visions of reality."[43] All interpretations are inadequate, and it would be absurd to subsume all these visions under a single category. In the original vision of the tragic, Jaspers finds the essence of philosophy, namely, "movement, question, open-mindedness, emotion, wonder, truthfulness, lack of illusion."[44] Tragedy arises when there is disunity in the world and where consequences become visible. Tragedy is tied to the world and has no place in the realm of authentic transcendence, nor can it serve as the basis of Being. In being aware of what he knows and what he does not know, however, the genuine tragic person does not succumb to any one truth. Rather, such a person lives the meaning of truth in all the ways of being truthful. He/she stands fast in uncertainty and proves he/she is capable of unlimited love and hope, and thereby signifies a unity that stands for a destiny that is shaped by ever-changing historic circumstances.

> Tragic knowledge mounts in intensity through contradictions which it leaves unresolved but which it does not freeze as necessarily insoluble. Hence, tragic knowledge is all imperfection. . . . Tragedy arises wherever in the world there is disunity, and where its consequences become visible. . . . This failure to achieve unity underlies the ruin of all we see around us. Because unity fails in our temporal existence, it appears to us in the guise of the tragic. This is, however, tantamount to saying that tragedy is not absolute but belongs in the foreground. Tragedy belongs neither in the realm of transcendence nor in the Basis of all Being, but in the world of sense and time.[45]

Given Jaspers's interpretation of tragic knowledge in light of the encompassing-horizon nexuses, boundary situations and the foundering of existence and Existenz, another clarification is needed concerning the role of morality in the lives of creative persons. Although Jaspers has no exclusive work on ethics in the body of his writings, there are numerous references to ethics.[46] Moral behavior, however, is assigned the role of a necessary but not sufficient condition for identifying the great figures that Jaspers selected as original creators and tragic individuals. Jaspers explains the various aspects of Weber's moral concerns in his personal and professional life. To convey the utter importance that a commitment to a moral life held for Weber, Jaspers inserts an anecdote in his extended essay on Weber. A certain instructor had lied in public and was regarded as a disgrace to the teaching profession. Weber took the case to court, even though many others thought the incident should be ignored and found Weber's insistence to exceed the limits of common sense. After Weber won the case and the instructor was dismissed from the university, everyone found the proceedings perfectly sensible.[47] A moral life has equal importance for Jaspers, but it is subject to high tension inasmuch as there is no reasonable way to seek out and balance the various ultimate values that sway an individual, as the following statement conveys: "Reality is divided against itself, and so is truth. Truth opposes truth and must defend its own rightful claim not only against injustice, but also against the rightful claims of other truths. Tragedy is real because irreconcilable opposition is real: Every moral imperative is tainted by guilt, for it must destroy others equally moral and equally imperative."[48] The main problematic for Jaspers is the leveling forces that dominate in modernity, and his concern is with identifying the sources of originality and creativity that express human freedom. Since these expressions of freedom have their source in transcendence, he is led to seek out other expressions that can be found in other times and other cultures, inasmuch as these expressions have the potential to speak to all persons throughout time and across boundaries.

In Jaspers's description of the human condition there is a kind of tragic dimension in every person's life. But not everyone is challenged to embody tragedy in his or her historic situation. Some eras may provide cultural resources that enable many people to face their extreme boundary situations with equanimity based on a faith in the symbols and ciphers that are alive in their religious and other cultural institutions. And while every person is called to meet the challenge of a moral life, some persons are thrust into situations that call for something more than a moral response. In so responding they serve others, for "great historical figures show us what men can be; they open up to us the realm of the possible in which we live."[49]

The great historical figures, however, are not all tragic individuals. Artists in word, sound, or material substance; theoretically inspired religious visionaries; scientists who theorize out of the depths of their thinking; leaders who move their communities to higher levels of ethos; and, of course, philosophers of note—all these representatives from different realms are treated by Jaspers as great historical figures. All have responded to some kind of boundary situation and foundering in an original way, and in so doing they altered the ways of thinking and acting for others. It therefore becomes important to recognize the distinguishing marks of the tragic individual in Jaspers's view of great historical figures, keeping in mind that every person in the most ordinary circumstances of life is open to finding his and her own unique selfhood. Jaspers's writing on the tragic is unavoidable since he leads the reader through the great works of tragedy: Homer, the Edda and Icelandic sagas, heroic legends of all peoples; the early Greek tragedy of Aeschylus, Sophocles, and Euripides; the modern tragedy of Shakespeare, Calderón, and Racine; the German works of Lessing and Schiller; the Book of Job, Indic drama; as well as tragic knowledge in Kierkegaard, Dostoevsky, and Nietzsche. He does so, in order to help the reader realize the importance of being able to recognize one's own unique freedom and selfhood.

JASPERS'S INFLUENCE ON LITERARY THEORIES OF TRAGEDY

This paper has located the place of the tragic individual in the spectrum of great figures that can be found in Jaspers's writings, and the high importance he assigns to this individual. Some of Jaspers's comments on the nature and limits of tragic knowledge need attention in order to avoid confusion and leveling great figures to commonalties, a problem that arises in literary theory. Jaspers's views on tragedy have influenced some literary theorists dealing with the genre of tragedy, but their treatment often lacks the specificity that Jaspers connected with tragedy. Richard Sewall, for instance, seeks to incorporate Jaspers's perspective into his analysis of tragedy. The tragic vision is not a systematic explanation of a certain life and admits of wide variations and degrees, a perspective echoed in Jaspers. Sewall explains Jaspers's position as follows: "It [the tragic vision] impels the artist, in his fictions, towards what Jaspers calls 'boundary-situations,' Man at the limits of his sovereignty—Job on the ash-heap, Prometheus on the crag, Oedipus in his moment of self-discovery, Lear on the heath, Ahab on his lonely quarter-deck."[50] While the examples Sewall cites are genuine ones on any one's terms, his designation of "boundary-situation" is too general since not all such situations call for a tragic response.

Michelle Gellrich has a similar view of Jaspers, although her theoretical base for incorporating "boundary-situations" differs from Sewalls. Her lack of specificity leads her to advance a criticism against Jaspers's nuanced treatment of these situations that does not stand up. "I want to show," she writes, "that theories of Greek tragedy indebted, if only indirectly to the Kantian sublime [to which she links Jaspers] typically import into their arguments about heroic dignity an idea of personal autonomy or the will that is problematic in the interpretation of classical plays."[51] This criticism misses entirely the changing relationship Jaspers articulates between Existenz and world, and the differences he finds between Greek and modern tragedy.

Jaspers's position on tragedy is, of course, a philosophical theory.[52] As such, it "seeks to grasp the essential nature of the tragic not in pictures but in concepts. It attempts universal interpretations."[53]Jaspers insists, however, that when compared with the original visions of reality that tragic literature embodies, all interpretations are inadequate. Interpretations that claim universal truth either become too narrow, and fail to explain some genuine tragic works, or they miss the tragic altogether.[54] The universality in Jaspers's "theory" is akin to the open-ended character of his periechontology.

Jaspers identifies two levels to human tragedy. The first one constitutes the necessary basis of tragedy, namely, that all human life perishes and suffers "shipwreck" or foundering. It is only at the second level that genuine tragedy arises, when one comes to understand "that ruinous conflict is founded in the very nature of truth and goodness, and must inexorably claim its due."[55] Tragedy, therefore, is clearly distinct from all those horrific sufferings and miseries that visit all people, without meaning or justification, vastly more to some than to others. These misfortunes can become tragic only by virtue of a knowledge that renders them meaningful. This kind of knowledge, however, has distinct limits. "Tragic knowledge is open knowledge, well aware of its own ignorance."[56] When it is turned into absolute knowledge and subsumes all human experience into its grasp, it becomes a profound aberration. Within the limits of tragic knowledge lie the seeds of transcending it. Jaspers concludes that tragedy is found neither in the realm of transcendence nor as the basis of Being, but only in the world of sense and time. In the penetration of tragic knowledge with philosophic reflection lies "the vision of a great and noble life: to endure ambiguity in the movement of truth and to make light shine through it; to stand fast in uncertainty; to prove capable of unlimited love and hope."[57]

Jaspers's theory has a certain resonance with Hegel's view of tragedy. Hegel, in his overarching dialectics, however, "has so simplified its [tragedy's] meaning that he is well on the way to depriving it of the genuinely tragic. Indeed, the line that he sees exists, but it is valid only in its indissoluble unity with its opposite-un-reconciled assertion."[58] There is another difference between Hegel and Jaspers on tragedy. Unlike the logical demonstrations that Hegel draws out of the conflicts in natural, human, and historical phenomena, Jaspers's vision is grounded in the assurance that can come only from transcendence, but this calls for an act of philosophical faith.

The philosophic faith Jaspers advances is clearly distinguished from the faith that is offered in revealed religion. Philosophic faith is a position that has not received much attention from contemporary philosophers, and for some it may appear as a betrayal of philosophy.[59] That transcendence penetrates human experience is the reason why he claims that tragedy is tied to the world and has no basis in Being. Jaspers, however, provides no proof for transcendence. Although variously identified as Being, authentic Actuality, Divinity, or God, Jaspers's probing of these various views exposes the situation that rational argumentation cannot deliver either any conclusive or exclusive demonstration for transcendence. They remain ciphers that have genuine force only in specific historic situations for certain, given people. Many questions no doubt remain, but they will only enhance the importance for serious persons to find ways to communicate across boundaries, the key issue Jaspers has identified for today, as persons respect each others' freedom, experience the foundering of existence and Existenz, and endure through finitude, faith, and long-suffering the ambiguity of the movement of truth in time.[60]

NOTES

1. Karl Jaspers, *Von der Wahrheit: Philosophische Logik*, Part One, 3rd ed. (Munich: R. Piper, 1980), pp. 915–60; an abbreviated translation of the foregoing section of *Von der Wahrheit* appears in English as *Tragedy Is Not Enough*, translated by Harald A. T. Reiche, Harry T. Moore, and Karl W. Deutsch (Boston: Beacon Press, 1952). [Hereafter cited as TNE, eds.]

2. On Jesus, see Karl Jaspers, *The Great Philosophers*, Vol. I, translated by Ralph Manheim (New York: Harcourt, Brace and World, 1962), pp. 74–96. [Hereafter cited as GP 1, eds.] On Nicholas of Cusa, *The Great Philosophers*, Vol. II, translated by Ralph Manheim (New York: Harcourt, Brace and World, 1966), pp. 116–272. [Hereafter cited as GP 2, eds.] On Jakob Boehme, *The Great Philosophers 3: The Great philosophers: Xenophanes, Democritus, Empedocles, Bruno, Epicurus, Boehme, Schelling, Leibniz, Aristotle, Hegel,* edited by Michael Ermarth and Leonard H. Ehrlich, translated by Edith Ehrlich and Leonard H. Ehrlich (New York: Harcourt Brace, 1993), pp. 117–42. [Hereafter cited as GP 3, eds.] On Giordono Bruno, *Die grossen Philosophen: Nachlass 1: Darstellungen und Fragmente; Nachlass 2: Fragmente, Anmerkungen, Inventar.* Hrsg. von Hans Saner (Munich, Zurich: R. Piper, 1981), pp. 146–55. [Hereafter cited as GrPh/N1, eds.]

3. Max Weber is treated in Karl Jaspers, *Three Essays: Leonardo, Descartes, Max Weber*, translated by Ralph Manheim (New York: Harcourt, Brace and World, 1964), pp. 187–274. [Hereafter cited as TE, eds.] and *The Great Philosophers 4: The Disturbers: Descartes, Pascal, Lessing, Kierkegaard, Nietzsche—Philosophers in Other Realms: Ein-*

stein, Weber, Marx, edited by Michael Ermarth and Leonard H. Ehrlich, translated Edith Ehrlich and Leonard H. Ehrlich (New York, San Diego, London: Harcourt Brace, 1994), pp. 319–25 [Hereafter cited as GP 4, eds.] Freud and other psychologists are explained in *General Psychopathology*, translated by J. Hoenig and Marian W. Hamilton (Manchester, England: Manchester University Press, 1963). Jaspers's views of Einstein are found in Jaspers, GP 4, pp. 319–25.

4. On Buddha and Confucius, see GP 1, pp. 32–50, 51–73. On Lao-Tzu and Nagarjuna, see GP 2, pp. 388–434.

5. For Leonardo da Vinci, see TE, pp. 5–60. Jaspers devotes a monograph to *Strindberg and Van Gogh*, translated by O. Grunow and D. Woloshin (Tucson: University of Arizona Press, 1977). For Dante and Shakespeare, see GrPh/N1, pp. 616–33. For outlines of lectures Jaspers gave on Goethe, Hölderlin, Dostoevsky, Racine, Saint-Exupery, and T. S. Eliott, see *Die Grossen Philosophen: Nachlass 2: Fragmente, Anmerkungen, Inventar*. Hrsg. von Hans Saner (Munich, Zurich: R. Piper, 1981), pp. 1118–23. [Hereafter cited as GrPh/N2, eds.]

6. Karl Jaspers, "Reply to My Critics" in *The Philosophy of Karl Jaspers*, edited by Paul Arthur Schilpp, Augmented edition (La Salle, IL: Open Court Publishing Co., 1981 [1957]), pp. 749ff.

7. An early and still helpful analysis of the empathetic judgment can be found in Edith Stein, *On the Problem of Empathy*, translated Waltraut Stein, 2nd ed. (The Hague: Nijhof, 1960). For the development of the hermeneutic movement see Georgia Warnke, *Gadamer: Hermeneutics, Tradition, and Reason* (Stanford: Stanford University Press, 1987) and Paul Ricoeur, *Hermeneutics and the Human Sciences: Essays on Language, Action, and Interpretation*, translated John B. Thompson (Cambridge: Cambridge University Press, 1981).

8. Jaspers writes this about Hegel, but it applies to all of Jaspers's historical critiques. See GP 3, p. 295.

9. Jaspers's most detailed discussion of periechontology is in his *Von der Wahrheit: Philosophische Logik*. [This work is not translated into English in its entirety, eds.] Translations of passages from this work that are used in this paper are found in *Karl Jaspers: Basic Philosophical Writings, Selections*, edited, translated, and with introductions by Edith Ehrlich, Leonard H. Ehrlich, and George B. Pepper (Atlantic Highland, NJ: Humanities Press, 1994 [1986]. [Hereafter cited as BPW, eds.] On boundary situations, see Jaspers, *Philosophy*, Vol. 2, translated by E. B. Ashton (Chicago: University of Chicago Press, 1970), pp. 177–222. [Hereafter cited as Ph 2, eds.] On foundering, see Jaspers, *Philosophy*, Vol. 3, translated by E. B. Ashton (Chicago: University of Chicago Press, 1971), pp. 192–208. [Hereafter cited as Ph 3, eds.]

10. For an earlier, generic treatment, see Gerhard Knauss, "The Concept of the 'Encompassing' in Jaspers's Philosophy," in *The Philosophy of Karl Jaspers*, edited by augmented edition (La Salle, IL: Open Court Publishing Co., 1981 [1957]), pp. 141–76.

11. Jaspers, "A Reply to My Critics," *The Philosophy of Karl Jaspers*, edited by Schilpp, p. 804.

12. BPW, p. 147.

13. I have explored this subject in greater depth in George B. Pepper, "Karl Jaspers

on the Sciences: In Retrospect," in *Karl Jaspers Today,* edited by Leonard H. Ehrlich and Richard Wisser (Washington, DC: University Press of America, 1988), pp. 153–78.

14. Karl Jaspers, *The Origin and Goal of History*, translated by Michael Bullock (New Haven: Yale University Press, 1956), pp. 83–87.

15. Ph 1, p. 218.

16. Ph 1, p. 138.

17. Karl Jaspers, "Philosophical Memoir," in Karl Jaspers, *Philosophy and the World: Selected Essays*, translated by E. B. Ashton (Chicago: Gateway/Regnery, 1963), p. 233. [Hereafter cited as PW, eds.]

18. BPW, p. 165.

19. See the articles by Indu Sarin, Sawako Hanyu and Young-Do Chung herein [eds.].

20. See Amartya Sen, "East-West: The Reach of Reason," *The New York Review* (July 20, 2000), pp. 33–35, for a conception of reason that is similar to Jaspers's position.

21. Jaspers, "Philosophical Memoir," in PW, p. 299.

22. See Karl Jaspers, "The Idea of the Physician" and "Doctor and Patient" in PW, pp. 153–67, 168–92.

23. See Karl Jaspers, *Philosophical Faith and Revelation*, translated E. B. Ashton (New York: Harper and Row, 1967).

24. See Jaspers's treatment of Einstein in GP 4, pp. 319–25.

25. See Karl Jaspers, *The Future of Mankind*, translated by E. B. Ashton (Chicago: University of Chicago Press, 1961).

26. Ph 2, p. 178.

27. Ph 2, p. 179.

28. Jaspers treats the concept of "foundering" in Ph 3, pp. 192–208. See also Johannes Thyssen, "The Concept of Foundering," in *The Philosophy of Karl Jaspers*, edited by Schilpp, pp. 297–335.

29. BPW, p. 332.

30. Ph, 3, p. 194.

31. Ph 3, pp. 90–91.

32. Ph, 3, p. 194.

33. Ph 3, p. 207.

34. See Benjamin I. Schwartz, ed., "Wisdom, Revelation, and Doubt: Perspectives on the First Millennium B. C.," *Daedalus*, 104 (Spring 1975).

35. See S. N. Eisenstadt, ed., *The Origin and Diversity of Axial Age Civilizations*, (Albany: SUNY Press, 1986). The latter collection of essays and those edited by Benjamin Schwartz [note 34] utilize Jaspers's notion of the axial age as the focus of attention. [See also the article by Ram A. Mall herein, eds.]

36. GP 4, p. 323

37. GP 4, p. 321

38. GP 4, p. 330.

39. See Karl Jaspers, *Philosophy Is for Everyman: A Short Course in Philosophical Thinking*, translated by R. F. C. Hull and Grete Wels (London: Hutchinson, 1969).

40. GP 4, p. 323.

41. GP 4, p. 336.

42. Godfrey Carr, "Goethe or Jaspers?," *The English Goethe Society*, Vol. XLII (1972), p. 56.

43. TNE, p. 96.

44. TNE, p. 103.

45. TNE, pp. 102–103.

46. See Jaspers, "The Moral Claim," Ph 2, pp. 310–17. See also Kurt Salamun, "Moral Implications of Karl Jaspers's Existentialism," *Philosophy and Phenomenological Research*, Vol. XLIX, No.2 (December 1988), pp. 317–23, and his fuller treatment of Jaspers in *Karl Jaspers* (Wurzburg: Konigshausen and Neumann, 2005).

47. TNE, p. 264.

48. TNE, p. 95.

49. TNE, p. 193.

50. Richard Sewall, *The Vision of the Tragic* (New Haven: Yale University Press, 1959), p. 4.

51. Michelle Gellrich, *Tragedy and Theory: The Problem of Conflict Since Aristotle* (Princeton: Princeton University Press, 1988), p. 258.

52. One would expect Walter Kaufmann's work, *Tragedy and Philosophy* (Princeton: Princeton University Press, 1979), first published by Doubleday in 1968, to have treated Jaspers's views on tragedy, since both the German and English versions predated it. Such is not the case, but Kaufmann has important things to say about tragedy nonetheless.

53. TNE, p. 93.

54. TNE, p. 97.

55. TNE, p. 95.

56. TNE, p. 98.

57. TNE, p. 105.

58. TNE, p. 79.

59. Leonard H. Ehrlich, *Karl Jaspers: Philosophy as Faith* (Amherst: University of Massachusetts Press, 1975) has ably explored and defended Jaspers's notion of philosophic faith in his response to this problematic.

60. For an important study of tragedy in classical Greek writings, see Martha C. Nussbaum, *The Fragility of Goodness: Luck and Ethics in Greek Tragedy and Philosophy* (New York: Cambridge University Press, 1986). Although Jaspers is untreated, Nussbaum locates Aristotle's views on tragedy within his comprehensive treatment of the range and variety of philosophical knowledge.

Part VI

Communication with Asian Thought

KARL JASPERS AND ASIAN THOUGHT

BUDDHA AND NAGARJUNA

Indu Sarin

Karl Jaspers's philosophical voyages to historically distanced savants like Buddha and Nagarjuna represent authentic endeavors in the exploration of the human condition or *philosophia perennis*. He seeks existential contemporaneity with those great thinkers who would otherwise be lost in the bygone epochs and hazards of vanished cultures. Jaspers struggles with the texts of Buddha and Nagarjuna. His fresh reading of their philosophies still provides us today with the afterglow of their philosophical insights and gives a new echo to their philosophic voices. Jaspers's reconstructed philosophic reflections dig deep into the garden of their philosophical contents reactivating their evergreen insights for us today. Jaspers is not a mere archaeologist of philosophical doctrines; he is, rather, one who relives the living world of their thought as best as he can. In this essay I will identify key elements of Jaspers's humane renderings of Buddha and Nagarjuna. I begin with a presentation of the (1) similarities between Jaspers's philosophy and Buddhist philosophy, (2) and focus on Jaspers's interpretation of the doctrine of momentariness and the law of dependent origination. As numerous philosophers of Indian thought and history have noted, Buddhism reaches its climax with Nagarjuna's interpretation of Buddhism. (3) Jaspers's reads Nagarjuna's interpretation of Buddhism with emphasis upon his view of being and non-being, truth, momentariness, the law of dependent origination, suffering, silence, and emptiness, and the differing sects within Buddhism. Although there are many similarities between Jaspers's philosophizing and Buddhism, (4) there are also numerous dissimilarities related to distinctive views on suffering, detachment, the self, historicity, freedom, and communication. In the final section, (5) I offer a sympathetic, yet critical, analysis of Jaspers's more general comparison between Asian and Western philosophy.

SIMILARITIES BETWEEN JASPERS'S PHILOSOPHY AND BUDDHISM

Jaspers looks for the wisdom of Indian philosophers who show the way to "freedom grounded in transcendence" in a world where catastrophes of nuclear, chemical, and biological weapons threaten the existence of humankind. Jaspers is a philosopher with an open, cosmopolitan vision who not only reflects on Western philosophy, but also extends his vision to Indian philosophy, in particular, Buddhism. He wants to know the other philosophers, even those who are most "alien" to him, to understand their viewpoints, and to show their greatness and originality.

Jaspers maintains that the encounter with Buddha and Nagarjuna's thought helps us probe deeply into the existential problems faced by every human being, and their proposed solutions regarding the human quest of the metaphysical realm, which illuminates the life of the person and the meaning of existence. Jaspers is not doing scholarly work on the classical texts of the Indian philosophers in order to give us encyclopedic knowledge about them. He is interested, rather, in encountering the philosophers themselves as thinkers, but also as individuals who lived their lives and acted in the world. He seeks "to foster a personal encounter with the thinking of the great philosophers . . . [and to provide a] philosophical companion, a guide to [their] thought and self-reflection."[1]

Although all of the "great philosophers" that Jaspers interprets are separated by different ages and cultures, and hold differing viewpoints, they nonetheless share a close resemblance in their philosophical reflections on the perennial issues of human existence. Jaspers appreciates both the Buddha and Nagarjuna as "supra-historical" and eternal contemporaries who belong to a timeless era of "human kinship."[2] Jaspers's reading of the Buddha and Nagarjuna brings their voice and the relevance of Buddhist philosophy to a world marked by the reality of genocide, violence, and turmoil. He admirably internalizes the problems encountered by these two great Indian philosophers' enlightened reflections on the human condition. Buddhism reflects on the temporality of the human condition, on suffering, on the nonsubstantiality of self, and on the realms of freedom and transcendence. It shows the individual the way to be freed from the vicissitudes of time. The goal of release or enlightenment is not achieved through discursive reasoning, but through insight into Buddha's message of humanism. Jaspers appreciates Buddha's doctrine of ahimsa and the four modes of inner conduct, that is, "not to harm any living creature (*ahimsa*), and to observe the four modes of inner conduct: Loving kindness, Compassion, Sympathetic joy, and Equanimity toward the impure and evil. These four 'immeasurables' are raised to infinite heights by meditation."[3]

Jaspers highlights some of the most distinctive points about the life of the Buddha, whose powerful personality has created a tremendous influence in history, both in the East and the West. Buddha's mission is to show the path of salvation to others. His teachings have spread throughout the world and existentially transformed many individuals. In Buddha's philosophy there is no cleavage between philosophy and religion, between theory and praxis. To know is to be; knowledge is the path of liberation, redemption, and insight. Buddha does not teach a system of knowledge; he provides, rather, a "path for salvation."[4] The Buddha's doctrine must be understood by means of meditation; not through metaphysical speculation, which he shows to be futile. All metaphysical speculation merely clings to a rigid standpoint, which results in unending polemics and philosophical controversies. Propositions such as "the world is eternal" or "the world is not eternal," or "the world is finite" or "the world is not finite," do not play any role in overcoming real suffering in the world. Elaborating Buddha's view of metaphysical speculation, Jaspers notes that the "Buddha even regarded the theoretical treatment of metaphysical questions as harmful. It becomes a new fetter, because metaphysical thinking clings to the very form of thought from which a man must free himself if he is to find the way of salvation. . . . But the main reason for declining to answer metaphysical questions is that they do not advance us along the road to *Nirvana*."[5]

Buddha's life was released from all bonds as disclosed by the "nobility, sincerity and infinite gentleness" of his manner and way of being.[6] Self-conquest, or the negation of the self, is fundamental to Buddha's thought. The individual is not to be a victim either of one's own self, or of the world. Buddha does not believe in the caste system or the supreme power of the gods. The gods may be working at the worldly level, but from the highest level, their presence is of no significance. Moreover, Buddha emphasizes the equality of all beings. His message is not addressed to a particular community, but to the whole of humanity. Jaspers's ethos of humanity is informed by Buddhist thought:

> Thus for the first time in history the idea of humanity, of a religion for the whole world, became a reality. The barriers of caste, nationality, of all appurtenances to a historically grounded order of society were breached. What in India had been the carefully guarded secret of a privileged few became a truth to be divulged to all . . . he cared for not only men, but for all living things—the gods and the animals as well—salvation . . . was meant for them all.[7]

Buddha's heart beats in tune with the suffering and joy of all living beings. He refrains from all kinds of violence. In spite of the terrible things that have happened in Asia as everywhere else, an "aura of gentleness" lies over the people touched by Buddhism. It is "the one world religion that has known no violence, no persecution of heretics, no inquisitions, no witch trials, no crusades."[8]

Jaspers's philosophy comes close to Buddhist thought in so far as Jaspers reflects on the existential situation of the human being, rather than attempting to explain human nature or provide a thick description of "man" in abstract terms. Both the Buddha and Jaspers start with the concrete situation of life without any metaphysical presuppositions. They hold that human beings living in the flow of time are subject to suffering and ultimately, death, the final "boundary situation" of finitude. For Buddha, it is the tragic character of the human being that underlines the significance of life, while for Jaspers, tragedy taken alone does not capture it.[9] Both of them maintain that suffering shows a way to transcendence, for it is only through reflection on the temporal dimension of life that eternity can be realized. There is no pre-existing eternity. Eternity originates in time. Human beings, while living their uniquely transient historical existence or historicity, ascend to eternal truth.

The quest for freedom, critique of the faith in revelation, and emphasis on the spiritual dimension of the human being, without believing in an essentialist view of the soul, are all common to Jaspers's philosophy and Buddhist philosophy. Just as Jaspers delineates the conceptual limitations of idealism and materialism and awakens human beings to immense possibilities, Buddha also critiques the idealism of the *Upanishads* and the materialism of the *Carvakas.* Unlike the *Upanishads*, Buddha does not believe in the eternal essence of the human being; but unlike the *Carvakas*, he goes beyond the empirical realm as such. Buddha walks the middle path, which defies both worldly pleasures and ascetic denial and mortification of the flesh. In his very first sermon at Saranath, Buddha says,

> There are two extremes, O monks, from which he who leads a religious life must abstain. One is life of pleasure, devoted to desire and enjoyment: that is base, ignoble, unspiritual, unworthy, unreal. The other is life of mortification: it is gloomy, unworthy, unreal. The perfect one, O monks, is removed from both these extremes and has discovered the way which lies between them, the middle way which enlightens the eyes, enlightens the mind, which leads to rest, to knowledge, to enlightenment, to *Nirvana.*[10]

In *The Great Philosophers* Jaspers refers to Buddha as a "paradigmatic individual" who has exerted a historical influence of incomparable scope and depth. He is impressed by Buddha's search for enlightenment (*Erleuchtung*), which is to be attained through the individual's own efforts. Each individual is a lamp unto him or her self. You are to be "a light unto thyself." Knowledge and insight regarding enlightenment, Jaspers states, lie "within the power of the individual. It is won by his own insight, based on the power of his own moral conduct. No god bestows insight. . . ."[11] For the Buddha, human actions are not determined by the will of God. The individual is responsible for his or her own actions. No grace can help, and knowledge cannot be attained through the performance of religious rituals: "It is not prayer, not grace, and not sacrifice that brings redemption."[12]

The Buddhist way of life is called a *Shramana* way of life as contrasted with the Brahman's way of life. What later philosophers have elaborated through magic, *dhyana*, yogic practices, and adumbrated in various Buddhist cultures, happens to be another story, along with the Graeco-Roman and Chinese stories that emerged during the Axial Age (800-200 BCE),[13] spread over thousands of years of Buddhist civilizations in the Far East.

Momentariness and the Law of Dependent Origination

Buddhism holds that there are two levels of truth—empirical and absolute. On the empirical level of truth, the world is governed by time and by the various vicissitudes that produce suffering. On the absolute or transcendental level of truth, there is an eternal rest that brings liberation—*Nirvana*—for the individual. The core of Buddha's philosophy, however, is expressed in the doctrine of "momentariness," which holds that everything is momentary (*sarvam ksanikam*), everything is devoid of self (*sarvamanatman*), every thing is temporal (*sarvamanityam*), and things are dependent upon certain conditions without which they cannot come into being. Buddha believes that everything that exists is in time, and, consequently, is in the process of becoming. The very characteristic of time is that it is flowing, one moment succeeds the other. Momentariness is the play of time that gives rise to genesis, development, and death.

Moreover, for the Buddha, there is neither "being" (*sat*) nor "non-being" (*asat*), but only "becoming" (*bhu*). Since the individual is in a constant state of "flux" (*santana*), there is no abiding self. In fact, the person is actually the unity of five "aggregates" (*skandhas*), i.e., "corporeality" (*roop*), "sensation" (*samvedna*), "perception" (*sanjna*), "mental formation" (*samskara*) and "consciousness" (*vijnana*). The five elements are interdependent, and one originates the other in the developing "psychophysical organism" (*nama-rupa*) or ego.

Buddha's concepts of impermanence and selflessness imply the "law of dependent origination," which means continuity of cause and effect, and dependence of effect on the cause. The law of dependent origination revolves around the principle of *Arth-Kriya-Karitva*: any given cause has the capacity to produce its effect. More precisely, the law of dependent origination is a twelvefold sequence entailing primeval causes and their perceptible effects. The law starts from ignorance, grows to decay, and leads finally to death. The chain starts from the basic cause of ignorance, which produces, in turn, a subsequent chain of causes and effects in a series of dependent origination. The disappearance of cause is the appearance of effect, and the disappearance of effect is the appearance of cause, thus producing an unending cycle. The whole chain of dependent origination can only be broken with knowledge that overcomes ignorance, and thus eliminates the first cause of the chain.

The metaphor of the light persisting till such time as the oil and wick in the lamp lasts, reveals Buddha's extremely critical analysis of all mundane events and happenings, including the experience of human suffering. His explanation of the law of dependent origination is similar to earlier Western, mechanistic views of nature and of cause and effect. If a cause is known, then its effect can be removed. The twelve links of the causal "wheel of dependent origination" (*Dvadasanidana*) include:

1. Ignorance (*avidya*)
2. Impressions of karmic forces (*samskara*)
3. Internal consciousness of the embryo (*vijnana*)
4. Psychophysical organism (*nama-rupa*)
5. Sex sense-organs (*sadayatana*)
6. Sense-object-contact (*sparsha*)
7. Sense-experience (*vedana*)
8. Thirst for sense-enjoyment (*trsna*)
9. Clinging to this enjoyment (*upadana*)
10. Will to be born (*bhava*)
11. Birth and rebirth (*jati*)
12. Old age and death (*jara-marana*)

The world is a construction of consciousness, which through its ignorance gives birth to *trsna* or "thirst" for sense-enjoyment, which, in turn, creates a false ego-identity. The individual clings to different things around him, to the stuff of the material world, and becomes completely absorbed in them. When this happens, the individual regards the temporary world to be permanent, which has the causal result of ushering in more suffering for the individual.

The chief significance of Buddha's philosophy lies in the "Four Noble Truths" (*Arya Satyas*):

(1) There is suffering
(2) Suffering has a cause
(3) Desire for the Cessation of suffering; cessation of suffering is, in turn, effectuated by following
(4) The Eightfold Path.

It is his keen perception of the dynamics of suffering that turned Sidhartha into the Buddha. He analyzes the causes of suffering and shows us the way to transcend suffering. The problem of suffering and the law of dependent origination presuppose the concept of time. The doctrine that affirms the existence of things in the past, the present, and the future is explained by Buddhist sources as *kale asti*: The individual suffers because he is born, she grows old, and then dies. His or her "thirst" or "craving" (*trsna*) makes the individual hanker after one thing or another. Because of human finitude, however, the individual is never satisfied and never satiates what he or she desires.

The five *skandhas*, i.e., (1) corporeality, (2) sensation, (3) perception, (4) mental formation, and (5) consciousness, all produce suffering. The doctrine of dependent origination implies that things are relative, dependent, conditional, and finite. One moment arises because its preceding moment has vanished. The present is the effect of the past, as well as the cause of future life. The individual's rebirth is because of one's "actions" (*karmas*). Rebirth begins with ignorance and produces ignorance, and thus the whole cycle starts again.

The realization of *Nirvana* obtains with the final cessation of the cycle of rebirth and must be attained through knowledge. It must be noted that this kind of knowledge is not propositional, but rather insight into absolute or transcendental truth and enlightenment. Again, to quote Jaspers's reading of the Buddha, "it is only at the end that one attains clear knowledge of the Path one has travelled, Enlightenment. The circle closes, fulfillment is achieved. This Enlightenment is the step from endless coming-into-being and passing-away to eternity, from worldly existence to *Nirvana*."[14]

For Buddhism the realization of *Nirvana* is the realization of "non-self" (*Anatta*). When the flame of internal consciousness, *vijnana,* is blown out, there is no self. The "self" is merely an illusion formed because of past action or *karmas*. The empirical ego is merely an illusory continuity of different moments of consciousness. The analogy is given of a burning stick. When it is rotated in a circle, a fire circle appears to be there, but this is only an illusion. Since the moments in consciousness form a flowing stream, it appears as if there is a continuous self, but in reality the self is an illusion. As Buddha says, "'O, ye monks, the body is not the eternal ego, nor do feeling, perception, disposition and consciousness together constitute the eternal ego. He who holds that there is an eternal ego is a man with false notions.'"[15]

The whole effort of Buddha's teaching, therefore, is to blow out the false identity or "self," which is the ground of all suffering. Through knowledge and insight, the ego is dissolved and a state of "perfect wisdom" (*Sunyata*) is left. Buddha is silent about the metaphysical questions regarding the nature of *Sunyata*. He only says that there is no abiding self, but he does not discuss the state beyond the empirical realm or *Nirvana*:

> Two things only my disciples do I teach—misery and cessation of misery. Human existence is full of misery and pain. Our immediate duty, therefore, is to get rid of this misery and pain. If instead we bother about barren metaphysical speculation, we behave like that foolish person whose heart is pierced by a poisonous arrow and who, instead of taking it out, whiles away his time on idle speculation about the origin, the size, the metal, the maker, and shooter of the arrow.[16]

Those who engage in metaphysical speculations are like a man who gets wounded by an arrow "thickly smeared with poison."[17] Instead of seeking medical treatment, the person wastes time in inquiring about the caste, status, and whereabouts of the person who shot him. The wounded man will die before he gets knowledge about the latter if he does not seek treatment. Similarly, if a person aspiring to attain salvation keeps on inquiring about metaphysical speculations, he or she cannot attain salvation. Buddha, therefore, remains silent about any such metaphysical questions.

Now a key question for Buddhist philosophy is this: After attaining *Nirvana*, what is the relationship of the human being to the world? Is the relation a negative or a positive one? There are two sects—*Hinayana* and *Mahayana*—of Buddhism. The former holds that the human being's relationship to the world is negative. The Mahayanist school holds the human being's relation to the world in a positive light and even describes *Sunyata* in a positive sense. The Bodhisattva who has attained perfect wisdom is inspired by the love of all beings. Through his or her compassion the Bodhisattva helps others to achieve liberation from their suffering. For without the salvation of all persons and of all sentient life, individual salvation is incomplete and becomes mere selfishness.

Jaspers's interpretation maintains that the *Hinayana* school is actually closer to Buddha's teachings and that the *Mahayana* school transformed Buddha's philosophy of salvation into a religion. When this transformation was finally completed in history, the Buddha's teaching about faith in one's own powers disappeared. This, in turn, led to the deification of the Buddha, now widely worshipped as a god for centuries.

NAGARJUNA'S INTERPRETATION OF BUDDHISM

As has been noted by numerous philosophers of Indian thought and history, Buddhism reaches its climax with Nagarjuna's interpretation of Buddhism.[18] In the galaxy of Buddhist philosophers, Nagarjuna is the star that outshines all the others because of his distinctive contribution. Regarded by the Tibetans as an ornament of India's Southern Jambudvipa (*bharata*) region, he is one of the greatest thinkers that India has ever produced. He revolutionized Indian philosophy through his rigorous analyses and destructive dialectics. Though born into a Brahmin family where he renounced *Brahminism* in favor of Buddhism, Nagarjuna articulates the most penetrating critique of the world, the self, ultimate reality, and any final formulation of knowledge.

According to Jaspers, Nagarjuna contends that Buddha does not hold any metaphysical standpoint, that is, nothing exists ultimately or absolutely. Reality is ineffable because it is beyond conceptual categories. Nagarjuna is a propounder of *Sunyavada*. Although the concept of *Sunya* ("empty") was present before Nagarjuna, he is the first systematic expounder of *Sunyavada*. Nagarjuna maintains that reality is *Sunya*; things are momentary and without permanent essence and, therefore, interdependent. When the self, matter, motion, causality, time, space, the Four Noble Truths, *Nirvana,* and even Buddha, are held to be eternal objects, Nagarjuna believes we turn them into hypostatized relations. To be sure, on the empirical level of truth they are quite real, but not on the highest level of truth.[19]

"Enlightenment" (*prajna*) lies in a freedom that can be attained only through a type of philosophical thinking that is free from all objective determinations. Thought must commit suicide, as it were, thus leading to the dissolution of all representations and hypotheses. Nagarjuna rejects the entire logomachy of judgment, positing, and predication. Jaspers rightly notes that Nagarjuna does not devise a "system" in the sense of ontological constructions aspiring to encompass the whole of being in all its manifestations. Instead, Nagarjuna speaks of two kinds of truth—"worldly" (*samvritti*) truth, and the "highest" (*parmarthic*) truth that leads to the attainment of *Nirvana*. Worldly truth is only an appearance. *Samsara* ("world") and *Nirvana* are two sides of the same relative, worldly coin and hence unreal. When neither *Samsara* is destroyed, nor *Nirvana* is attained, why should *Samsara* and *Nirvana* be imagined at all?[20] Moreover, *Nirvana* is dependent upon *Samsara*. If there is no *Samsara*, the question of attaining *Nirvana* does not arise. The higher is in relation to the lower. One who does not understand the difference between these two levels of truth cannot understand the gravity of Buddha's teachings. Commenting on Nagarjuna's position, Jaspers writes, "there are two truths: the veiled worldly truth and the highest truth. . . . But the highest truth cannot be obtained independently of the veiled truth . . . this path can be travelled only with the help of enlightenment."[21]

Now the difference between the above-named twofold truths is realized only at the *parmarthic* (highest) level. At the level of worldly truth, existence is governed by cause; but at the *parmarthic* level, existence does not have a cause. At the *parmarthic* level, one accepts the appearance of the world, realizes its emptiness, but does not cling to it. Things do not exist permanently in themselves, and yet, at the same time, they are not no-thing. They exist in the realm of in-between being and nonbeing. Nagarjuna is, therefore, against both eternalism and nihilism. Eternalism takes the concepts of "existence," "is," "affirmation," and "Being" in the sense of absolute existence, whereas nihilism completely denies them. Those who maintain that the world exists are committing a great error because when we penetrate mundane reality more deeply, we find that the world and cosmos, with its manifold phenomena, is essentially relative and therefore ultimately unreal. Those who advocate nonexistence or nonbeing are also committing a great error because they deny the phenomenal reality of the world. Intellectual speculations that are essentially discursive, analytic, and relational, inevitably entail inner contradictions. All that can be grasped by instrumental rationality is relative.

Nagarjuna takes "the middle course" (*madhyama pratipad*) from whence his philosophical thinking gets the appellation as *Madhyamika*. The middle course is practically no position at all, but is, in fact, a rejection of all standpoints. It is beyond speech, just a review of things. For Nagarjuna, Buddhist philosophy is a critique of "dharma-nature" (*svabhava*), of the entities existing in the world. The existence of the world, which is constituted by various entities, as well as a person's consciousness that cognizes these entities, are in constant state of flux; therefore, they do not have any "substantial nature" (*svabhava*) of their own. The critique of dharma-nature in turn leads to the belief in *dharma-nairatmya* or the "unreality of all elements" including the existence of the self (*anatamvada*), which, like other entities of the world, is also in the process of endless becoming.

Jaspers points out that Nagarjuna interprets the doctrine of momentariness as a sort of "conditioned becoming." The world is not an established order or form, but is in the process of becoming. Every order must make way for another order, every form must make way for another form, known as "the doctrine of universal flux."[22] There is no absolute origin; instead, things come into being depending upon specific conditions. There is no perishing; one thing gives rise to another. There is no complete extinction; if things are completely destroyed, then new things cannot be born. Things come into being and pass away without absolute origin or destruction. There is a continuum that gives rise to the cycle of "birth and death" (*dharma cakra*).

The Buddhist theory of momentariness is internally linked with the law of dependent origination. Since there is no eternal essence or absolute origin, the origin is dependent upon antecedent conditions; therefore, there is the doctrine of dependent origination, which is regarded by Jaspers as one of the most "precious jewels" of Buddhist philosophy. The meaning of the doctrine has developed with the growth of Buddhist thought and various philosophical interpretations, but the doctrine generally means that, given the existence of one being or thing, a next being or thing follows. Although a previous moment is a condition of the subsequent moment in as much as the former does not impart any essence to the latter, the effect is not potentially contained in the cause. A previous or a subsequent entity has equal phenomenal reality; for this reason, there is no hierarchy, and the later dependent origination is in no way superior to the former. To be dependent upon another means that entities do not have a substantive nature of their own.

Nagarjuna maintains that the law of dependent origination reveals *Sunyata*, which is nothing other than the fact of dependent origination. Nagarjuna writes: "Whatever is the meaning of Dependent Origination, the same is the meaning of *Sunyata*."[23] Being dependent upon an antecedent object means that it has no essence of its own, it becomes intrinsically unreal or *Sunyata*. Nagarjuna proves the meaning of *Sunyata* through logic-disapproving conceptual categories. He demolishes logic through logic and argues against the possibility of holding any doctrine.

Jaspers highlights Nagarjuna's logic in terms of the "operations" that it seeks to carry out: All designations are meaningless.[24] Language fails to capture reality. There is always a gap between sign and *signatum*. When we predicate blue to the lotus, blue is neither identical with the subject, nor different from it. If they are identical, why are we using two words? If different, how can they be related? Jaspers elaborates Nagarjuna's viewpoint by stating that things and their designations are neither identical nor different. If they are identical, the word would burn when we say fire. They are not different because there is no designation without the thing designated, and no thing is designated without designation. The third way of saying this is that designation is only a mirror image of the thing. But in that case it is just a mirror image and, therefore, not real.[25] There is a gap between a name and its reference. No object, quality, or relation may be asserted by any name. All names and forms, judgments and theoretical constructs, fail to capture the truth. Commenting on Nagarjuna's philosophy in this context, Jaspers points out that since "designation and the thing designated can be neither one nor different, distinctions between things designated—such as coming and going, becoming and perishing—are also untenable. To live by signs is to live in illusion, far from Perfect Wisdom."[26]

The underlying idea, then, is that reality is indescribable. Nagarjuna describes reality only negatively, as "not destroyed," not produced, not dissolved, not eternal, not one, or not many. At the empirical level, the quest for reality is impossible because of universal flux. To say that "everything is, and at the same time it is not," implies that both eternity and destruction are untenable. If there is becoming, nothing is permanent or perishing. If anything is eternal, how can it come into being? If it gets destroyed, how can it become something else? The world is neither eternal nor perishable.

The above arguments suggest that there is neither eternalism nor nihilism. Nagarjuna refutes both being and nonbeing by rejecting the following steps:[27]

1. Independent Existence: The Buddhist doctrine of dependent origination proves that things do not exist independently because they come into being through causes and conditions, i.e., everything comes into being through something else. Therefore, things are interdependent. No thing can stand as an isolated entity apart from its predecessor and successor.

2. Otherness: If there is no independent existence, there is no otherness because otherness must have some source. Difference can be there only if there is sameness.

3. Things: Things can be there if there is being-as-such and being different.

4. Nonbeing: If there is no Being, how can there be nonbeing—because the latter is only the otherness of a being.

These four steps show that both being and nonbeing are equally impossible. Nagarjuna is critical of those Buddhist philosophers who interpret reality in terms of being or nonbeing, being-as-such, or being otherwise. When Buddha refutes being he asserts nonbeing; when he refutes nonbeing he asserts being. According to Nagarjuna, Buddha refutes both being and nonbeing, and Nagarjuna demonstrates through dialectical method that every possible statement can be refuted. Nagarjuna considers the following four possibilities (*catuskoti*), but rejects them all.

1. Something is (being)
2. It is not (nonbeing)
3. It both is and is not (both being and nonbeing)
4. It neither is, nor is not

Nagarjuna points out the inner contradiction implicit in the above examples. The views that if everything is interdependent there can be no being-as-such, and that if there is no independent existence then nonbeing is rejected, are logically contradictory. If something is already there, there is no need to prove it. If it does not exist, the attempt to prove it is meaningless. For Nagarjuna no doctrine is tenable and the attempt to prove the reality ends in failure. When man clings to *dharmas* (*svabhava* of entities) he does not visualize the emptiness, and the result is suffering. It is only through the realization of "conditioned becoming" in emptiness that suffering can be overcome. To hold the doctrine of conditioned becoming means that suffering is neither in the realm of being nor of nonbeing. If there is being, it will be interdependent. Consequently there will be no origin, no death, no things that exist permanently, and there is nothing more to be achieved. There would be no diversity and no suffering. If suffering is in the realm of being, it exists permanently and it cannot be destroyed. Suffering is due to the process of becoming through the cycle of birth and death, which is governed by causes and conditions. If there is no suffering (nonbeing), the question of its overcoming does not arise: There would be no Buddha, no doctrine of suffering and of the way to overcome it.[28] To quote Jaspers again, "those who see conditioned becoming, see suffering, its coming-into-being and the manner of its annihilation, that is, they see the way, just as a man endowed with eyes is enabled by the shining of a light to see the appearance of things."[29]

Suffering is overcome through nonattachment to *dharmas*. The freedom from the world of appearance is the attainment of *Nirvana*—the realization of the *parmarthic* truth (the highest truth). *Nirvana* is also empty (*Sunya*) as it is dependent upon the world (*Samsara*). At the level of worldly truth, thinking is fettered to the thought-content, the *dharmas*. The highest truth is attained through overturning of thought, which dissolves the thought-content destroying all kinds of fetters. Through this overturning of thought, one realizes freedom—the void (*Sunya*). This is a self-negating operation of thought. Realizing the *Sunyata* of the worldly truth, and regarding it only as an appearance, is to realize *Nirvana*. In case of the latter, there is no cause, no origination, no death, and, consequently, no suffering. It is the cessation of the cycle of becoming. Jaspers states that perfect wisdom is freedom from conflict: "Thoughts are made free, mastery over all thought is gained in the detached knowledge which masters itself . . . all coming and going have lost their meaning."[30] When the state of perfect wisdom is attained, one becomes a *Boddhisattva,* free from the fetters of *dharma*, and where *Dharma Cakra* loses its meaning.

Jaspers maintains that Nagarjuna believes that the highest truth cannot be achieved through "any knowable, logically determined content, but "'wakens suddenly to unexcelled perfect enlightenment.'"[31] The negative logic prepares the way not for a positive insight that can be logically justified, but for a silence that no logic can explain. Silence is realized by so-called *prajna–paramita* or indescribable transcendental highest wisdom. The silence is best illustrated by a number of anecdotes:[32]

1. The first disciple says that experience is unrelated to spoken words, though associated with them in instruction.
2. The experience is like a paradise but vanishes immediately and therefore cannot be expressed.
3. Since all existing things have only an illusory experience, the context of this experience, once expressed in words, would be mere illusion and emptiness.
4. Instead of answering, step before the master in an attitude of veneration and keep silence.

The last answer for Nagarjuna is the right one. Silence is neither in the realm of being nor nonbeing, but is instead free from all assertions and surrounded by emptiness and stillness. Critical of all metaphysical thinking and ontological questions, Nagarjuna champions the cause of salvation or *Nirvana* realized through meditation. Referring directly to Nagarjuna's writings, Jaspers writes,

> To the Bodhisattva all things are like an echo, he does not think them. . . . He lives in the world as in the "emptiness of a city of ghosts." The "illusory nature" of things, the fact that they are and are not . . . is compared with the materializations . . . of a magician: a magician at a crossroads conjures up a large crowd of people and makes them disappear again; so is the world. No one has been killed or destroyed by the magician; so without destroying them, the Bodhisattva makes multitudes of beings disappear.[33]

The third-person perspective so diligently spun by thoughts about words, acts, assertions, claims, counter-claims, their correlated objects, events, mental dispositions, and expressions, are as illusory as the images of the conjurer. The entire enterprise of "thatness" has to be sidestepped and seen as void. Sign is only a sign without carrying real meaning.

Jaspers argues that Nagarjuna's *Sunyata* does not imply skepticism, negativism, or nihilism. "This attitude is not what is ordinarily known as skepticism. For the operations of thought, which lead beyond the antinomy of true and false, that is, beyond thought, also carry it beyond . . . skepticism. To call it negativism is to fail to see that here the "no" as well as the "yes" has vanished. To call it nihilism is to forget that the alternative between being and nothingness has been dismissed."[34]

Emptiness is not a denial of being, but it is to be indifferent to being. It means detachment from the beings of the world. It is not to deny the world, but to change one's "perspective" *(dristi)* toward it—to see the world not as an ultimate truth and to realize the untruth of *dharmas* and of the language that describes them. In this way the path to the authentic or "highest truth" is shown. A monk, like a vigilant gatekeeper, bars access to the external stimulus so that he may not become a prisoner of the things around.[35]

Nagarjuna's anti-metaphysical philosophy is contrasted with the explicit metaphysical philosophy of *Vedanta*. The common point is that both Nagarjuna's philosophy and the *Vedanta* deny the reality of the world. *Vedantic* denial affirms the reality of Brahman (Being) whereas, for Nagarjuna, Buddhism does not assert anything: Buddhism dissolves any opinion, and leaves it with no specific standpoint that may be "grounded" by philosophical appeal. Buddhism shows the futility of even bare denials, which could be woven back into some architecture of claims about *Sunyata* or the unspeakable experience leading to the total silencing of reasoning.

There is no ontology of infinitude in Buddhism. No doubt, like Nagarjuna, the *Vedantist* shows the limitations of language. Being (*Brahman*) is ineffable (*neti neti*), but this ineffability is to be distinguished from Nagarjuna's *Sunyata*. Being is Atman in its purest form, it is "consciousness as such." In the case of Nagarjuna's *Sunyata*, there is no Atman as such.

Jaspers's interpretation surveys the differing sects of Buddhism. Common to all of them are the ideas of the knowledge of suffering, the insignificance of worldly reality, and the inevitable striving for redemption. But various sects differ in their viewpoints on the possibility of knowing reality. The "Sarvastivadins" hold that the world is ideal and can be known directly through perception. The "Sautrantikas" maintain that although the world is not perceived by the senses, its existence can be inferred through perceptions. The "Yogacaras" argue that only the inner world is real; the source of this certainty is consciousness itself.

Nagarjuna's conclusion about the nature of reality, by contrast, is negative. Neither inner nor outer world can be recognized as real, independent being, and there is no difference between subjective and objective reality as such. He denies the very possibility of knowledge, whether of the inner world or the outer world. Nagarjuna's philosophy is thus a scorching critique of ontology, epistemology, language, and any form of anthropocentrism. At the worldly level, there remains doctrine, language and the way of salvation. To be sure, the doctrine is like a ferryboat that carries the self to the other shore in order to enter a new country. After reaching the country, the boat becomes superfluous. The final step is to perceive the falsity of all signs, to see through conditioned becoming, *Sunyata* and silence.

In order to summarize the foregoing interpretations, it is helpful to note the association of the concept of *Sunyata* with the (1) world, (2) language, and (3) viewpoints.

The world, if viewed from the point of phenomena, will ultimately lead to *Sunyata,* i.e., the analysis of the world by the concept of dependent origination.

The language used in the philosophical enterprise is of little use for actually knowing the reality of objects.

Viewpoints generated by language are of no use because when subjected to critical examination they prove to be self-contradictory.

Sunyata is used in a double sense: It is both relative and a reality—*Samsara* and *Nirvana*. All "appearances" (*dharmas*) being "relative" (*pratityasamutpanna*) have no real origination and are therefore devoid of the "ultimate reality" (*svabhava Sunya*). But worldly appearances are not absolutely unreal; they must belong to reality. The real is constituted by a non-dual harmonious whole in which all plurality is "merged" (*prapanc Sunya*).

DISSIMILARITIES BETWEEN JASPERS'S PHILOSOPHY AND BUDDHIST PHILOSOPHY

The above interpretive sketch reveals that besides the similarities between Jaspers's philosophy and Buddhism there are also many dissimilarities. The civilizational differences seem to yawn between the two authentic reflections. Jaspers's cultural and political interests focus on the various modes of dehumanization that he witnessed in the twentieth century. He shows concern over the massive alienation of industrial society and the organization of the global political economy. The human being is increasingly reduced to a cog in a giant machine of mindless productivity.

Given Jaspers concern for the political and that no philosophy is without political implication, it is perhaps unsurprising that the worldviews of Jaspers and Buddha are quite different. The ideas of both philosophers are informed by the differences of their respective problematiques and differing historical contexts. The key difference between the two is not so much a function of their internally rational positions as it is their whole view of life and manner of thinking.

Both philosophers analyze the problem of suffering in different ways, and their views on the nature of liberation are also distinct. Buddha shares in the Asian belief that the world does not have an *ontic* status. The world, in other words, is the consequence of the malfunctioning of consciousness. The Buddha upholds the metempsychosis of moral continuity of psychic causation. Jaspers, on the other hand, accepts the reality of the world with all its pluralities and diversities. For him, suffering is not due to ignorance, but is instead an inevitable reality of life because of human finitude. Jaspers neither explains suffering through any causal chain, nor does he expound its solution through knowledge. "Detachment" for Jaspers comes by means of the heartfelt struggle to grapple with all of the "boundary situations"[36] of life by means of self-awareness and self-reflection:

> In all Western forms of detachment from the world, the essential is sought in something that is present in the world . . . in a self, which in historical immersion, in self-identification, takes upon itself the burden of being-given-to-oneself, but nevertheless illumines itself infinitely and achieves self-detachment in reflection.[37]

Enlightenment for Buddha is not any kind of sublimation of finitude of our historical nexus and dispositions. No, enlightenment is a radically complete cessation of suffering, which ends in the "void" (*Sunyata*). The individual comes to see the fall of fetters once and for all. Once enlightenment is attained, no more effort is needed. Enlightenment is final and there is no return to the state of suffering.

For Jaspers, by way of contrast, there is no eternal rest. The realization of eternity is "within time" and not outside of it. Buddhism, as a *way of life*, has a fixed goal that the individual has to achieve. It suggests the successful following of a definite "Eightfold Path" in order to attain *Nirvana*. For Jaspers there is no such permanent state, or even any direct path, to enlightenment or salvation. In contrast to the Buddha, Jaspers believes in an openness toward the Transcendence (or God) as a dimension of philosophic faith, and holds an optimistic attitude that enables the individual to overcome suffering and the foundering of existence by means of the Nietzschean appeal to *amor fati*.

For the Buddha the realization of *Nirvana* is the realization of "non-self" (*Anatta)*. Jaspers, on the contrary, holds that the reality of the self is not illusory. Freedom is to be attained through the self, which is always historical. He emphasizes the achievements of human beings as "exceptions" and is a great votary of individualism. He states that the fundamental attitude of the Buddhists and of Nagarjuna is an entirely different one from his own thinking: "the accent is on the impersonal; as the world becomes a matter of indifference, the self is extinguished. The detachment has its source not in my 'self,' but in a transcendent reality, which is not a self."[38]

Jaspers thus highlights the difference between Indian and Western forms of detachment. He holds that from the Indian perspective, freedom is attained through detachment from the world, as well as detachment from one's own self. The Indian philosophers reveal the meaninglessness of worldly pursuit. For Jaspers, Buddhism's position on the abandonment of the world, and even the renunciation of scientific knowledge, is fundamentally false. Moreover, Buddhism rejects action in shaping the world, which is not only futile but also holds us in a state of captivity and teaches men to liberate themselves from it and not to change it, as in the saying that "'as a lovely white lotus blossom is not stained by water, so I am not stained by the world.'"[39]

Jaspers argues that Buddha's insights concerning meditation as the way to enlightenment via indifference to the world is finally alien to the Western thought. It is the historicity of the individual that is all-important from the Western standpoint. Jaspers's emphasis is on the unique, irreplaceable, individual, whereas for Buddha the emphasis is on the dissolution of individuality. For Jaspers, *Existenz, the authentic self in relation to its transcendence,* is the focal point, the source of freedom and transcendence. As Jaspers says,

> the Buddhist Sage goes through the world like a duck; he no longer gets wet. He has transcended the world by dropping it. He seeks fulfillment in an unthinkable unworld. For Western man, however, reason finds its fulfilment, not in any absolute, but in the historicity of the world itself, which he gathers into his own Existenz. Only in historical realization, becoming identical with it, does he find his ground. He knows that this is the source of his freedom and of his relation to transcendence.[40]

Jaspers points out the multidimensionality of the human being. Apart from the psychophysical dimension, he highlights the spiritual dimension, which is the source of detachment and freedom, without equating this dimension with eternal essence. He takes an integral approach by synthesizing all the modes of our being, and by not rejecting any single mode of being that we are. Buddha explains the self in terms of a psychophysical dimension. The philosophical question remains, however, since *Nirvana*, which is a spiritual state of being, is to be attained not collectively, but by the individual himself: Can Buddha's "silence" be taken as complete extinction of consciousness? No, it can only be envisaged as a state of consciousness free from all positive attributions.

Buddhism has a type of metaphysics that goes beyond the world. The principle of *karma* admits the reality of the past and future life, i.e., birth and rebirth. There is no such belief in Jaspers's existentialism. He speaks only of one life for a human being whose time has a beginning and an end. And unlike the Buddha, he does not believe in the doctrines of karma, rebirth, and dependent origination.

CRITICAL EVALUATION

Although raised in European culture, Jaspers's interpretations successfully capture the spirit of Buddhism. Unlike other scholars who are more interested in the textual study of Buddhist scriptures, he tries to understand Buddhism through both the teachings and the life of Buddha. And yet Jaspers inevitably reads both Buddha and Nagarjuna from the horizon of Western, Christian moorings, and from his own unique historicity. Christian predilections of sin, the fall, guilt, recovery through faith in God, and historical apocalypse are absent in the world-dissolving meditations and ecstasies of Buddha. Serene detachment marks Buddha's timeless gaze. Asian mysticism reveals the absurdity of the very process of world-making as is done in the Occident. Buddhism dissolves time, history, self, world, and God. Jaspers, like many other Western thinkers, is awestruck by such radical detachment, but he remains open to all modes of the manifestation of being by virtue of his notion of the Encompassing.

Jaspers is primarily interested in the historicity of the individual. Human freedom is achieved in and through historicity, whereas the Buddhist concept of liberation is transcendent. If Jaspers had delved deeper into the existential aspects of the Buddhist lifestyle, he would have realized that this difference between Western historicity and so-called Eastern transcendence loses its significance. *Nirvana* is realized in and through one's unique historicity. By achieving *Nirvana*, the ego is dissolved and time is transcended. This kind of transcendence is not anti-historical, even as *Nirvana* is not achieved through rational speculation, but is a transcendence that is at the core of existence itself and which permeates historicity in the form of eternity and the uniqueness of every moment.

In this respect, I believe that the "existential freedom" to which Jaspers aspires can be seen as an early step of the freedom for which Buddha spent his whole life. While differences are real, the gulf between the Asian and Western philosophers is not an insurmountable hermeneutical chasm, but a difference in emphasis on the various dimensions of life. Western philosophers place more emphasis on the external world that is out there to be rationally analyzed and transformed by scientific and technological rationality. Asian thinkers like Buddha and Nagarjuna, on the other hand, are mostly inclined toward the inner core of one's being and find that human freedom cannot be achieved unless the various bindings of the self are discarded. In this context, Jaspers may well have appreciated Buddhism as the next step of the journey of one's existential quest that ultimately ends in the "foundering"[41] of existence (*Dasein*) and Existenz. Moreover, in Buddhism compassion plays a very significant ethical and spiritual role and reveals a positive attitude toward the other. In this respect, "perfect wisdom" and compassion go together.

Jaspers very aptly points out the destructive and constructive sides of Nagarjuna's dialectic and logic. He has not, however, explicitly elaborated the ethical implications of *Sunyata*. Buddha teaches *Sunyata* in order to enable us to overcome suffering and obtain *Nirvana*. As long as the duality of the subject and the object is not transcended, *Nirvana* cannot be realized. Ignorance is the real cause of duality. *Sunyata* is the antithesis of ignorance. It is pure knowledge (enlightenment) and removes all fears. The *prajnodaya*—realization of *prajna*—reveals compassion. The ethical implication of *Sunyata* is "compassion" (*karuna)*—the "highest truth" (*karunodaya*). There is no individuated self as distinguished from other beings, so there is no hierarchy of different beings in the world. As there is no knower, the subject-object duality dissolves. The distinction between others and my "self" disappears.

When the bondage of ignorance is shredded, the illumination fills *prajna* with deepest compassion toward the prisoners of nescience who rejoice in the fleeting shadows and stay in their crypts of unrelieved agonies. The seeker of *prajna-paramita* overflows with compassion (without any passionate attachment) for those who could have lit their own lamps to get illumination, but have failed to do so due to their ignorance.

A key point is that Jaspers argues that the culmination of Buddhism into the realm of mystical silence creates a serious problem for communication. In a real sense he is right: Silence cannot be communicated through words. But his view here is a twofold misunderstanding of Buddhism in my judgment. First, what is experienced at the peak of silence is something that is distinguishable from sheer nothingness. A mystic understands this difference. Buddhist thinkers have all clarified that the experience of mystical silence has a positive content, although the content is noncategorizable. Second, as far as the question of communication is concerned, language is only one mode of communication. One can understand ineffability of the deepest spiritual experience if one rises above the level of empirical truth. One does not lose contact with other human beings in this process, but, in fact, one's vision gets enlarged and expanded to encompass the larger reach of humanity and all other creatures. As a result, one develops very close communication with all sentient beings. Language sometimes creates more problems for inter-human communication than it does in facilitating communication.

It is only by means of dropping the superficial forms of communication that deeper, intersubjective (existential) communication grows. The entire paraphernalia of judgments, propositions, arguments, and co-related discourses prove in the end to be futile from a Buddhist worldview. Their emptiness does not lead to nullity, but to pregnant silence showing the limits of language, and perhaps even a "fusion of horizons" (Gadamer) between space, time, and the person. Through his silence, the Buddha has conveyed the deepest truth, which Jaspers himself acknowledges in his reading and interpretation of Buddhism. This pregnant silence is in many respects the glory of Buddhism, which reveals how human communication crosses the boundaries of verbal language and its forms of action may, in the end, have greater force than any determinant language games.

NOTES

1. Karl Jaspers, *The Great Philosophers 1: The Foundations*, translated by Ralph Manheim, edited by Hannah Arendt (New York: Harcourt, Brace & World, 1962), p. xiv. Hereafter cited as GP 1 [eds.].
2. GP 1, p. xi.
3. GP 1, p. 38.
4. GP 1, p. 36.
5. Ibid. p. 42.
6. GP 1, p. 44.
7. GP 1, p. 45.
8. GP 1, p. 49.
9. Karl Jaspers, *Tragedy Is Not Enough*, translated by Harald A. T. Reiche, Harry T. Moore, and Karl W. Deutsch (Boston: Beacon Press, 1952).
10. H. Oldenberg, *Buddha: His Life, Doctrine, Order* (Calcutta: The Book Company Ltd. 1927), p. 122.
11. GP 1, p. 47.
12. Ibid.
13. On the Axial Age theory, see the article by Ram A. Mall herein [eds.].
14. GP 1, p. 33.
15. Buddhaghosa, *Visuddimagga*, translated and edited by D. Kosambi (Bombay: Bhatiya-Vidya Bhavan, 1920), p. 8.
16. *Majjhimanikaya*, edited by R. Sankrtyayana (Nalanda: Nalanda Publication Board, 1958), p. 63.
17. GP 1, p. 42.
18. See Malcolm David Eckel, "Jaspers and Nāgārjuna," in *Karl Jaspers on Philosophy of History and History of Philosophy* edited by Joseph W. Koterski and Raymond J. Langley (Amherst, NY: Humanity Books, 2003), pp. 64–68.
19. Nagarjuna, *Madhyamika Karika* (Pretorsbourg: Editor Punse, St., 1903), p. xiv.
20. Nagarjuna, *Madhyamika Karika, Vritti Chandra Kirti* (Pretorsbourg: Editor Punse, St., 1903), p. xvi.
21. GP 1, p. 420.

22. GP 1, p. 417.

23. Nagarjuna, *Madhyamika Sastra*, edited by P. L. Vaidya, Buddhist Sanskrit Texts (Darbhanga: Mithila Vidyapeeth, 1960), p. 4.

24. Karl Jaspers, *The Great Philosophers 2: The Original Thinkers*, edited by Hannah Arendt, translated by Ralph Manheim (New York: Harcourt Brace & World, 1966), p. 417. [Hereafter cited as GP 2—eds.]

25. GP 2, p. 418.

26. Ibid.

27. Ibid.

28. GP 2, p. 421.

29. Ibid.

30. GP 2, p. 426.

31. GP 2, p. 422.

32. Ibid.

33. GP 2, p. 426.

34. Ibid.

35. GP 2, p. 429.

36. See the article by Kurt Salamun herein [eds.].

37. GP 2, p. 433.

38. Ibid.

39. GP 1, p. 49.

40. GP 2, p. 433.

41. See the article by George B. Pepper herein [eds.].

KARL JASPERS AND ASIAN THOUGHT

LAO-TZU AND CONFUCIUS

Young-Do Chung / Sawako Hanyu

1. JASPERS'S INTERPRETATION OF LAO-TZU

YOUNG-DO CHUNG

Jaspers regards the ideas of Confucius and Lao-tzu as "contrary poles" because Confucius's interest was directed toward order in society, while Lao-tzu's interest was in a sphere beyond the mundane world. Although Jaspers argues that Lao-tzu's philosophy deals with metaphysics, cosmogony, ethics, and politics, he comes to the conclusion that his focus is on one single, basic, and all-pervading metaphysical idea, i.e., the idea of the Tao. Jaspers summarizes Lao-tzu's philosophy in this way: "Tao is the origin and goal of the world and of all things, hence also of the thinker. The philosophy tells us first, what Tao is; second, how man lives in Tao, how he can lose it and regain it, both as an individual and in a political society."[1] It is not surprising that Jaspers's interpretation of Lao-tzu should be concentrated on his understanding of the Tao, which literally means "way," but also connotes a variety of other *metaphorical meanings*.

SIMILARITIES BETWEEN JASPERS'S METAPHYSICS AND LAO-TZU'S PHILOSOPHY

There are a range of remarkable similarities between Jaspers's conceptions of transcendence and the Encompassing, on the one hand, and Lao-tzu's conception of the Tao, on the other. Their similarities extend to both their positive and negative affirmations of being and the Tao, as well as Jaspers's interpretation of transcendence and the Tao as indicative of the essential unity of reality and the transcendent source of self-being.

Jaspers argues in his introductory book on philosophy titled *Way to Wisdom* that philosophy begins with the question: "What is?" At first sight, there are many kinds of being, the things in the world, the forms of animate and inanimate matter, and the infinite variety of things of the world that come and go. "But what is true being, that is, the being which holds everything together, lies at the base of everything, the being from which everything that is issues?"[2] According to Jaspers, the true being that holds everything together and that is the ground of all kinds of being in the world, is called transcendence or "the Encompassing of all Encompassings." Some genuine characteristics of this essential ground of all kinds of being are mentioned by Jaspers in *Von der Wahrheit* when he tries to distinguish "the Encompassing of all Encompassings" from the universal, inauthentic transcendence of each specific encompassing that obtains in relation to the modes of being that we are as existence, consciousness as such, spirit, and Existenz. In contrast to that "insufficient, never satisfactory actuality" of transcendence in the different modes of the encompassing, the authentic transcendence (or God) of "the Encompassing of all Encompassings" is described as follows:

> Authentic transcendence is not to be reached cognitively; it is only to be experienced existentially as something that offers itself gratuitously . . . the one and the sole transcendence is the authentic actuality in which tranquillity and grounding are to be found . . . it is not in need, but fulfils all need. . . . It is nothingness as well as Being. It is, simply, to be doubted, and then it is as if vanished. For transcendence, unlike other modes of the Encompassing, has no body signifying its presence and solely proper to it, but speaks only through those other modes, enclosing and penetrating them.[3]

TRANSCENDENCE AND THE TAO AS GENUINE AND AUTHENTIC BEING

From an epistemological perspective, Jaspers argues that transcendence has to be accepted as the nonobjectifiable Being as such, which encompasses the subject-object dichotomy. Transcendence is the source of all possible concrete being that we can constitute in our perceptions and cognitions. He associates analogous metaphysical ideas with the Tao as *essential Being* or as the source of all concrete being. Lao-tzu regards the Tao as the very basis of existence, a genuine and nonobjectifiable dimension of Being, which enhances all forms of objectifiable being. Those inauthentic forms of objective being are dependent upon the Tao as the basic ground or source of Being.

The *Tao Te Ching*, for example, starts with the passage: "Tao can be talked about, but not the Eternal Tao. Name can be named, but not the Eternal Name. As the origin of heaven-and-earth, it is nameless" (chapter 1).[4] The Tao that signifies Being as such or, the origin of all beings, is never recognized in words, forms, or anything perceivable. Thus, Lao-tzu appropriately characterizes the Tao negatively, using such words as "nameless," "empty," "fathomless" (chapter 4), or, as elsewhere, in phrases such as "Tao never makes any ado, and yet it does everything" (chapter 37). Conversely, Lao-tzu also speaks of the Tao affirmatively, as the source of every existence. It is said, "There was Something undefined and yet complete in itself, Born before Heaven and Earth . . . I do not know its name; I style it the 'Tao.'" (chapter 25). Jaspers recognizes well that the Tao is expressed paradoxically in many phrases such as: "All things in the world are born of the corporeal; [but] the corporeal is born of the Incorporeal" (chapter 40).

In turning directly to Jaspers's interpretation of the Tao as set forth in the chapter on Lao-tzu in *The Great Philosophers*, we read his summary characterization of the Tao:

> For us the multiplicity of things in the world results from separation and opposition. Tao is called empty, because it is undifferentiated, without object, without opposition, because it is not [the] world. In fulfilling itself, Tao posits objects, produces the world. But Tao is never filled in this way. If it could be filled by the created world, it would become one with it. In emptiness it remains—we are justified in interpreting—richer in potentiality than all mere reality in the world, in non-being it is more than being, in the undifferentiated ground greater than all determinate, objectively differentiated being. It [the Tao] remains the Encompassing.[5]

Transcendence and the Tao as Nonobjectifiable Being

In his metaphysical reflections, Jaspers emphasizes again and again that what he calls transcendence, absolute Being, infinite Being, authentic Being, Being as such, God, and the Encompassing of all Encompassings is in a radical sense unknowable and cannot be objectified in rational categories. "Transcendence is beyond all form," Jaspers writes, "I reject, as inapplicable to transcendence, whatever I can conceive. I must not define transcendence by any predicate, must not objectify it in any idea, must not conceive it by any inference."[6]

Another well-known statement of Jaspers's philosophy of religion, which reveals his roots in the Jewish and Christian traditions as well as in Greek philosophy, is found in his book *Philosophical Faith and Revelation* where he writes that "the rule of transcendence is 'Thou shalt not make unto thee any image or likeness.' This biblical commandment is ascribed to God but springs as well from philosophical insight."[7] Jaspers argues that even though transcendence cannot be known as an object, or reached by any thought, in any configuration, in any image, in any empirical reality, it is nonetheless present as the genuine Being for which all those thoughts, configurations, images, and realities can be allegories, symbols, or—in a specific sense—ciphers. All traditional symbols of God, the Transcendent, and the Absolute must be understood only as ciphers of transcendence, not as its direct embodiment. While everything in the world has the potential to become a cipher of transcendence, Jaspers explicitly names the perduring ciphers of nature, history, creations in the arts, metaphysical systems, myths, religions, and, most importantly, the cipher of man (the *humanum*).

Jaspers's metaphysics distinguishes three possible experiences by which the human being may have indirect contact, via ciphers, with transcendence. First, in formal transcending, the being of transcendence is ascertained by means of conceptually and methodologically particular foundering movements of thought. Second, in existential relations, the actuality of transcendence is brought to actual presence for human Existenz in the individual's own self-realization; and, third, we touch upon transcendence by reading the cipher-script in everything that becomes objective and a living experience for us. Such reading is the experience of the transparency of things so that they become comprehensible to us as a language of transcendence—we hear, but do not see, the ciphers of transcendence—by virtue of our becoming authentically existential.[8]

Ciphers must be interpreted as indirect "sign-posts" to the genuine Being that is unperceivable and unknowable by our senses and rational categories. Absolute, definitive cognitive content of metaphors and symbols must be relativized. By means of transcending, via the reading of the cipher-script, such sign-posts become authentic ciphers of transcendence. The key methodological step here is found in a type of *apophatic thinking*, or that methodological conceptualization of Jaspers, which Charles Wallraff affirms as having basic similarities to the *via negativa* of medieval theological reflection: "While Augustine could despise the world as the Devil's own realm, he could also enjoy it as the expressive creation of God. Consequently, it [the world] points to the Creator. It is a place of parables, images, traces. What cannot be said directly can be said indirectly."[9]

Jaspers's conception of transcendence and its manifold illumination in ciphers, then, is analogous to Lao-tzu's conception of the Tao. The Tao is not recognizable in the world by the capacity of our senses, perceptions, or cognitive abilities. "Look at it [the Tao] but you cannot see it! Its name is *Formless*. Listen to it but you cannot hear it! Its name is *Soundless*. Grasp it but you cannot get it! Its name is *Incorporeal*" (chapter 14). "We call it the formless Form, the imageless Image. We call it the indefinable and unimaginable. Confront it and you do not see its face! Follow it and you will not see its back!"

Now consider the language Jaspers uses to communicate Lao-tzu's thinking. Jaspers interprets the nonobjectifiable character of the Tao in this way:

> Insofar as being is what we see, hear, and grasp, insofar as it is image and form, Tao is nothing. Only in the Tao that is free from being is the source attained. This source is not no-thing in the sense of not-at-all, but in the sense of more-than-being. . . . If we name the Tao, grasp it, understand it, if we attempt to differentiate it in our thinking or to see distinctions in it, it vanishes: "It reverts to nothingness."[10]

According to Jaspers's interpretation, then, Lao-tzu is the unparalleled master of the "indirect method of transcending" in philosophical thinking. Lao-tzu clearly grasps, in Jaspers's reading of him, the method of *via negativa* as it must be applied to our human comprehension of the unobjectifiable ground of Being.

Transcendence and the Tao as the Essential Unity and Source of Self-Being

Both Jaspers and Lao-tzu refer to a metaphysical conception of "unity" in their philosophical reflections. In Jaspers's metaphysics, the idea of a transcendent "unity" is a basic cipher of Transcendence (God or Deity). In his book *Philosophical Faith and Revelation* Jaspers writes that

> the one Transcendence is fulfilled eternity. It excludes nothing, since there is nothing beside it, and all things are due to it. The cipher of "the One" aims beyond all other ciphers. It aims beyond the diversity of ciphers at their common ground, beyond their ambivalence at unquestioned unity. This "One—

> the great theme of philosophy since Plato—is not the One facing the Other, not one whole among other possible units, not the number One. Such ways of unity serve as guidelines for our conception of the cipher; but the transcendent "One" fades out if we identify it with them. As the number One, in particular, the cipher is not adequately conceived. It means a qualitative, not a quantitative, unity.[11]

It is significant that Jaspers's philosophy integrates this metaphysical idea of the unity of being into a conception of existential human self-realization in the unity of the self.

> The strength of unity brings me from distraction to myself. I want to be one with myself. The binding forces of my life grow in the same measure as my links with the source of unity. Unity, for me, is the one Transcendence as well as myself, the one guide to my historic realization. This infinitesimal, variable, temporal Existenz becomes the cipher of that unhistoric, immutable eternal One—which is another cipher. In so far as it is realized, the existential unit reflects the infinite one, so to speak, as any one of the innumerable drops of water reflects the one sun.[12]

By way of analogous comparison, we can also find the idea of a transcendent unity that is an essential "One" in the *Tao Te Ching*. This unity is a productive form of the Tao responsible for tendencies and activities that realize a higher or better stage of being.

> From of old there are not lacking things that have attained Oneness. The sky attained Oneness and became clear; the earth attained Oneness and became calm; the spirits attained the Oneness and became charged with mystical powers; the fountains attained Oneness and became full; the ten thousand creatures attained the Oneness and became reproductive; Barons and princes attained Oneness and became sovereign rulers of the world. All of them are what they are by virtue of Oneness. (chapter 39)

Jaspers's Description of the Tao's Components

In his interpretation of the *Tao Te Ching* Jaspers is confronted with the crucial problem of all metaphysics: How can we speak about a dimension of being that transcends our empirical experience and cognitive reflection? Jaspers argues that the intention of Lao-tzu is not to give us any positive or cognitive information about the Tao. It is rather necessary to transcend the descriptive content of all statements regarding the Tao. And yet, no interpretation of a written text is possible without making some descriptive statements about its content; even if one intends to clarify only the function of a text in a pragmatic context, it is unavoidable that the interpreter must construct some *positive* content and its relation to a verbal or pragmatic context. Given this unavoidable implication of any hermeneutical approach of texts, Jaspers is logically committed to reconstruct some positive content from the *Tao Te Ching*, as we see in the following statements:

> Tao is "boundless," standing alone without change, yet pervading all without fail. . . . It does not age . . . Tao is dependent on itself, while man, earth, heaven, and all things outside of the Tao are dependent on something else. . . . Tao is simple, it is silent, it is universal, it is undifferentiated, yet complete in itself. Tao moves, but in motion it is at the same time at rest. . . . The movement of the Tao consists in Returning. It moves, but not because it wishes to attain something that it is not and has not, for Tao is without need, "it makes no claims for itself" (chapters 34, 37).[13]

In a further interpretive approach, Jaspers formulates the paradoxical features of the Tao:

> The Tao is present as non-being, it acts though not acting, it is the source of the One within all oneness . . . all existence derives its being from Tao, Tao is beyond good and evil, but it is infinitely helpful. High virtue, authentic life, is unison with Tao; Tao implies acting through softness, Freedom from desire, Freedom from vanity, selflessness, Openness to all things, true self-knowledge. . . . "He who knows others, is wise; he who knows himself, is enlightened." (chapter 33)[14]

Jaspers's interpretation is also concerned with the *political* implications of the *Tao Te Ching*, including Lao-tzu's understanding of the true ruler, war, and punishment, and the most desirable political conditions and polity. The political order is intimately connected from the ruler to the common man. As Jaspers remarks, "in keeping with Chinese universalism Lao-tzu sees human existence as a single hierarchically ordered realm extending from the one ruler through states, communities, and families to the individual man."[15]

JASPERS'S CRITICAL EVALUATION OF LAO-TZU'S PHILOSOPHY

Jaspers appreciates the basic metaphysical intention and many components of Lao-tzu's philosophizing. He praises the "timeless character" of his metaphysical thinking and clearly affirms the *Tao Te Ching* as "one of the irreplaceable works of philosophy" and "the first great example of the indirect statement on which true philosophical thought always depends."[16] Although the reader of Lao-tzu cannot find an argumentative structure in the *Tao Te Ching,* but only aphoristic statements and repetition of the same idea in numerous modifications, the book gives a "magnificent" impression of consistency. The "power" of its paradoxical formulations, its "earnestness" and "unfathomable depth" make the book a profound philosophical reflection.

On the side of the interpretive coin, however, and despite these highly positive judgments about Lao-tzu´s philosophy in general, Jaspers also finds a severe lack or limitation in Lao-tzu´s philosophic thinking. Given the neo-Kantian background of Jaspers's conception of *the antinomic structure of reality*, as well as his own conception of an authentic, true, and, therefore, self-actualized life, Jaspers insists that Lao-tzu's reflection comes up short: Lao-tzu lacks the "intermediate stages" between the reality of human existence and the Tao. Lao-tzu lacks an awareness of the "finite things" in human life such as painful and boundless self-reflection, self-clarification and the "eternal process of dispelling the self-deceptions and mystifications and distortions which never cease to beset us."[17] In contrast to the unavoidable tensions and struggles in individual life affirmed by Jaspers, the life in the Tao and with the Tao means life in perfect peace and harmony. Finally, Jaspers insists that there is a basic difference between the Western mind and the Chinese mind that becomes quite apparent in Lao-tzu´s philosophy. At bottom, this difference is a radical difference in world-view:

> It is this deficiency that makes Chinese thought, for all its charm, seem so alien to us, as though here the abyss of horror had never opened in all its depth. The Chinese never developed an art of tragedy, and as their vision and experience of evil have been, the tragic has remained inaccessible to them. . . . For the Chinese mind the world is a natural process, living cycle, a tranquilly moving cosmos. All deviations from the Tao of the whole are incidental and temporary; they are always reabsorbed into the imperishable Tao itself. To us Westerners the world is not a self-contained whole; it is related to something that cannot be understood on the basis of the world as natural process. The world and our mind are engaged in the tension of struggle, with each other and with the other-

> worldly. . . . Lao-tzu does not know the symbol of the angry demanding God, the God who battles and desires battle. In the world, in time, in finiteness—in the area of intermediate stages—we need what is lacking in Lao-tzu: life in question and answer and new question, the weight of the alternative, of decision and resolution, the fundamental, paradoxical truth that the eternal is decided in time.[18]

2. Jaspers's Interpretation of Confucius

Sawako Hanyu

In Karl Jaspers's "Philosophical Autobiography" he states that he learned Chinese and Indian thought from his friend, the German indologist Heinrich Zimmer, who brought him literature and translations from the Chinese and Indian worlds. As Jaspers tells us, "spiritually I gladly tarried in China, feeling there a common origin of being-human as over against the barbarianism of my own surroundings. I turned in loving admiration toward Chinese humaneness."[19] For the twelve years of the Nazi regime from 1933 to 1945, Jaspers's social activities were strictly limited due to the war and political situation. Living underground with his Jewish wife, Gertrud, he worked on his philosophical logic and acquired extensive new knowledge of Asian thought, which triggered his philosophy to be developed in an even broader view point than before, one not limited to a European standpoint, but open to Chinese and Indian thought as well. Jaspers observes that "Asia only becomes essential to us . . . when we ask: What is it that, despite all of Europe's pre-eminence, has been lost to the West? What we lack and what vitally concerns us is to be found in Asia!"[20]

Confucius as "Great Philosopher"

The Asian influence on his thinking is obvious in his postwar development of "world philosophy" initially instantiated in the two books on *The Origin and Goal of History* and the four volumes of *The Great Philosophers*. In *The Origin and Goal of History* Jaspers refers to the period from 800 BCE to 200 BCE as the "Axial Age," an axial turning point in world history across three great ancient civilizations: the Graeco-Roman world, India, and China. During the Axial Age, humans came to identify themselves as humans, not only in Europe, but also in China and India. In the first volume of *The Great Philosophers* Jaspers discusses the philosophical "greatness" of European, Indian, and Chinese thinkers by his own standard and their unique thoughts. His concern is to see "the great philosophers as suprahistorical and therefore always actual, to look past the concrete details and individual types and perceive their depths. The way of their thinking and acting springs from a source which is the center and, at the same time, the encompassing Being of all particular things. It is here that we find what by its very nature binds us all together, when it speaks from the source, whose historical manifestation is always unique."[21]

In the Introduction Jaspers writes about "great men" and "greatness" in the following opening words:

> Great men have always been seen as images and myths, and have always found a following. Greatness is experienced in the heroism of the warrior, in the power of the lawgiver to establish and organize society, in the insights of the planner and inventor, in the revelations of the prophet, in the rapture and liberation conferred by the poet and the artist, in the illumination bestowed by the thinker. In the beginning all these were done or seen in one.
>
> Man has a history; greatness speaks to him from the past. His bond with the divine depths, his ethical resolution, the character of his perception of the world, the clarity of his knowledge, all have their source in great individuals. The rank of nations is determined by the way in which they make the great individuals their own, and the same will be true of mankind as a whole. Every present comes to itself; all present greatness finds its measure, in their image. They are forgotten and re-emerge. For a time they are seen clearly and then their aspect is veiled. Without them existence would be meaningless and without history.[22]

Philosophers who fall under the category of "greatness" are arranged in accordance with three main groupings consisting of, first, the "paradigmatic individuals:" Socrates, Buddha, Confucius, and Jesus. These individuals have done far more than any others to shape the foundations and trajectories of the history of human cultures and human self-understanding across the great axial civilizations. The second group contains "the great thinkers" of philosophical thought, especially Plato, St. Augustine, and Kant, but also including a group that Jaspers calls the "projective metaphysicians." The Asian philosophers Lao-tzu, Nagarjuna, Chuang Tzu, Mo Ti, and Mencius all fall into this second categorial grouping. And in his work *Die Großen Philosophen, Nachlass 2* we also find explicit references to Mo Ti and Chuang Tzu.[23] In this essay I will focus mainly on Jaspers's interpretation of Confucius and Chuang Tzu.[24]

Jaspers's hermeneutical method in approaching Confucius's philosophy is composed of a short description of his life, with emphasis placed upon Confucius's "basic idea" concerning the renewal of antiquity, his moral-political ethos, the basic wisdom, Confucius's awareness of limits, as well as the personality of Confucius, his adversaries, and the influence of Confucian thought as it has developed during the periods of Mencius (ca. 372-289 BCE) and Hsün Tzŭ (310–230), the Han dynasty (206 BCE—CE 220), as well as the Sung (960-1276) and Manchu (1644-1911) periods in history.

Confucius sought to save the disintegrating empire by way of knowledge of antiquity. His guiding questions were: "What is the old? How can we make it our own? How can we make it a reality?"[25] What Jaspers finds entirely *new* in Confucian thought is his critical appropriation of history with a view to its present actualization, with no mere nostalgic yearning for a putative golden past period. What Confucius advocates, therefore, is not "imitation" of the past, but rather repetition of the "eternally true," and in this framework he found a living solution to the problem of political "authority." Although the external form of Confucius's life is conservative and traditional, he nonetheless remains imbued by the spirit of a "liberal open-mindedness" that is critically attuned to distinguishing what was true and false in the past. One might say that the Confucian "idea" of education is about "learning" from the enduring traditions of the past, but with the ultimate "practical efficacy" in the flourishing of social and political life. A key text that unlocks the interpretive door to Confucius according to Jaspers is this:

> If a man can recite all three hundred pieces in the *Book of Odes* by heart and, entrusted with the government, is unable to perform (his duties) or if, sent abroad as an ambassador, he is incapable of replying on his own, where is the good of all his learning?
>
> But without learning, all other virtues are obscured as though by a fog and degenerate: without learning, frankness becomes vulgarity; bravery, disobedience; firmness, eccentricity; humanity, stupidity; wisdom, flightiness; sincerity, a plague.[26]

Confucius's new way of thinking, that is, a newness that expresses itself in the form of the perennial truths of antiquity or *philosophia perennis*, is manifest in three central ideas that lead Jaspers further in his interpretation of Confucian thought:

(1) Confucius's *moral-political ethos* that culminates in the ideal of the "superior man";

(2) Confucius's *basic wisdom* as related to the nature of man and human society; and

(3) his keen awareness of the limits of education, communicability, and knowledge as interpreted by Jaspers in light of his concept of the *Encompassing*.

Now in all three sections Jaspers argues that Confucius presupposed the primacy of *ethos* and authentic action in social and political affairs as the philosophic ground upon which he develops his essential ideas concerning the nature of human beings and their interaction with one another in society.

CONFUCIUS'S MORAL-POLITICAL ETHOS

Confucius's moral-political ethos is formed *relationally* through family ties and human association with and in government. Order in family, society, and the state is preserved by the "imperatives of conduct" or *li*. The *li* educate human beings into universal mental states such as earnestness, confidence, and respect; these become second nature over time. The concrete universal, embedded in the multifarious imperatives of conduct (interpersonal relations toward family, friends, authorities, subordinates, rites of sacrifice, marriage, birth, death, administration, as well as customs regarding work, war, the court, etc.) are experienced not as constraint, but rather as conditions of possibility for human self-actualization as expressed in individual fortitude, assurance, and freedom. The *li* is not absolute, but must be balanced against individual historicity in order to realize freedom.

In his discussion of Confucius's understanding of human (gendered) relationships, Jaspers is struck by his indifference toward women: "He has nothing to say of conduct in matrimony, speaks disparagingly of women, has only contempt for a pair of lovers who have committed suicide together, and frequently remarks that nothing is so hard to handle as a woman. The atmosphere around him is distinctly masculine."[27]

The moral and the political realms are intimately linked in Confucius, and ethical government, which must be directed by a good prince, is crucial to the maintenance of order and the imperatives of *li*. Jaspers also highlights Confucius's important distinction between *what must be made* and *what must grow*. Good governance cannot be fabricated like an object of technology, but must grow by virtue of appropriating the best of political tradition, right music, correct modes of social intercourse and good laws. Laws, however, while a necessary means of government, are nonetheless intrinsically harmful. Good human example is far better than law because

> where the laws govern, the people are shameless in evading punishment. But where example governs, the people have a sense of shame and improve. When an appeal is made to the laws, it means that something is not in order. When it comes to hearing complaints, I am no better than anyone else. What interests me is to see that no complaints arise.[28]

Confucius makes no distinction between the *li*, morality, and justice. The good prince resembles Plato's philosopher-king and the truly great statesman proves his mettle by restoring or reinforcing the moral-political ethos as a whole in accordance with two key principles:

> (1) A capable man must stand in the right place. If a man possesses the throne but lacks the necessary strength of mind, he should not venture to make cultural changes. Similarly, if he has strength of mind but not the highest authority, he should not venture to make cultural changes. (2) The political conditions must be such as to make effective action possible. Where the prevailing state of mind leaves no room for effective action, the true statesman remains in hiding. He waits.

Then Jaspers adds, in what may be interpreted as a comment from Existenz to Existenz: "Confucius spent his whole life looking for a prince to whom he might lend his intelligence. But in vain."[29]

THE "SUPERIOR MAN" (*CHÜN-TZŬ*)

Confucius's moral-political ethos culminates in the ideal of the "superior man" (*Chün-tzŭ*). While noble in birth and physical endowment, and realizing *li* and wisdom, the superior man realizes goodness, truth and beauty in existence by virtue of *self-discipline*. The superior man is essentially the man who seeks the truth, who is always *en route* to truth. "'To have the truth is the path of heaven, to seek the truth is the path of men. . . . But he who *seeks* the truth chooses the good and holds it fast. He investigates, he questions critically, ponders the truth and resolutely acts on it.'" Jaspers summarizes Confucius's conception of the superior man's character, cast of thought and gestures, in contrast to the inferior man:

> The superior man is concerned with justice, the inferior man with profit. The superior man is quiet and serene, the inferior man is always full of anxiety. The superior man is congenial, though never stooping to vulgarity; the inferior man is vulgar, without being congenial. The superior man is dignified, without arrogance; the inferior man is arrogant, without dignity. The superior man is steadfast in distress; the inferior man in distress loses all control of himself. The superior man goes searching in himself; the inferior man goes searching in others. The superior man strives upward; the inferior man strives downward. The superior man is independent. He can endure long misfortune as well as long prosperity, and he lives free from fear. He suffers from his own inability, not from others' failure to understand him. He avoids all competition, but if it must be, then only in archery. He is slow in words and quick in action. He is careful

> not to let his words outshine his deeds: first act, then speak accordingly. . . . The superior man does not waste himself on what is distant, on what is absent. He stands in the here and now, in the real situation.[30]

THE BASIC WISDOM AND *JÊN*

Jaspers interprets Confucius's "basic wisdom" primarily, though not exclusively, in relation to the nature of man and human society. He focuses on Confucius's concept of *jên*, which means *humanity and morality as one*. The Chinese ideogram means, literally, "man" and "two," a pictographic way of saying that to be human means to be in communication with others. Jaspers interprets *jên*, first, in terms of what the nature of humanity is and should be, and, then, in terms of the diversity of existence. All human beings share a common essence in *jên*, but differ according to habits, character, developmental life-stage, age, and knowledge. *Jên* is "all-embracing," and not merely one virtue among other virtues; it is an all-embracing source. By means of *jên* particular virtues become true in existence. Human action in accordance to *jên* flows from the "source of the absolute," but is untainted with expedience. The source is absolute, but the manifestations of acting in accordance with *jên* are not.

"To act according to *jên*," Jaspers writes further,

> is to follow not a definite law but what gives all definite laws their value and at the same time deprives them of any absolute character . . . *jên* . . . resides in what Confucius calls measure and mean. "Measure and mean are the summit of human nature." They operate from the inside out: "The state in which hope and anger, grief and joy, are not yet active is called the mean. The state in which they express themselves but always find the right rhythm is called measure."[31]

Confucius's concept of *Jên* retains a "mysterious" quality, but Jaspers notes how Confucius illuminates *Jên* by reference to the mean between two extremes. "To be magnanimous and mild in teaching and not to punish those who behave badly: that is the strength of the south. To sleep and die in the stable without having to: that is the strength of the north. But the superior man stands in the middle and bends to neither side."[32]

The main subject of *The Analects* is, of course, ethical thought,[33] and according to Confucius himself there is one major thread that runs through all of his doctrines, i.e., "conscientiousness and altruism (4:15)," concepts that Jaspers discusses in the context of the necessity of order and sense of "equality" (*shu*). For Confucius, conscientiousness and altruism maintain the social order of humanity. He identifies the fundamental meaning of *jên* as follows:

"Filial piety and brotherly respect are the root of humanity (*jên*) (1:2). Only the man of humanity knows how to love people and hate people (4:3). If you set your mind on humanity, you will be free from evil (4:4)." Confucius also argues that the human being of humanity (*jên*) differs from the human being of wisdom in his attitude. "The man of humanity has no worry; the man of wisdom has no perplexities, the man of courage has no fear (14:30)." While the human being of wisdom can get objective and fixed knowledge, the man of humanity *jên* may be at peace.[34]

The Encompassing and Confucius

Jaspers interprets Confucius's philosophy based on his own theory of the Encompassing and his transcending philosophizing methodology. For example, on Jaspers's interpretation the concepts of truth and reality in Confucius's ideas should not be given any fixed or dogmatic definition. But Jaspers also interprets the whole personality of Confucius in a similar fashion, that is, his openness to the world and thinking in according with spirit (*Geist*) in relation to the idea of the whole:

> Confucius did not turn away from the world to concentrate on himself. He devised no economic institutions, no legislation, no special form of government; he was passionately concerned with something that cannot be directly willed but only fostered indirectly, something on which everything else depends: *the spirit of the whole in the ethical-political state and the inner make-up of every individual man as a part of the whole*. He had no fundamental religious experience, no revelation; he achieved no inner rebirth, he was not a mystic. But neither was he a rationalist in his thinking; rather, he was guided by the idea of an encompassing community through which man becomes man. His passion was for beauty, order, truthfulness and happiness in the world. And all these are grounded in something that is not made meaningless by failure and death [i.e., "foundering"].[35]

Clearly, Jaspers interprets his own philosophic thoughts into those of Confucius who, like Jaspers himself, did not depend upon a faith in revelation, the primacy of mystical experience, or rationalistic thinking. Given Jaspers's own writings on the idea of the university, it is easy to understand why he appreciates Confucius's keen awareness of the limits of education, communicability, and knowledge. Jaspers draws a direct parallel between Confucius and Plato with respect to the limits of knowing when Confucius asserts that "to represent what you know as knowledge and what you do not know as ignorance: that is knowledge."[36]

Confucius was keenly aware of evil in the world, but evil results from the failure of human beings, not from a dualistic ontology of the world as evil. Confucius never writes about eschatology (the end of history) or makes any direct statement regarding metaphysical questions. Jaspers comments perceptively that "though such an attitude may be put down as agnosticism, it does not signify indifference to the unknowable, but rather a reverence which is unwilling to transform intimation into pseudo-knowledge or lose it in words."[37]

Confucius ultimately affirms, however, that ultimate truth cannot be captured in language.

> A disciple of Confucius asks: "If you do not say anything, what can we little disciples ever learn to pass on to others?" And Confucius answers, "Does Heaven (*T'ien*, Nature) say anything? The four seasons run their course and all things are produced. Does Heaven say anything? (17:19). As nature silently changes its appearance, each season and the origin of all beings also never reveals itself to us."[38]

Now in *The Analects* of Confucius we see the idea that nature is presupposed as the source of every existence and social order. By having this base in nature, human beings can live in society and maintain peace. There is no need to worry if humans can live in accordance with the harmony of nature.

Jaspers is of course interested in drawing parallels between Confucian ideas and his own philosophical point of view. On the question concerning a parallel between his idea of the Encompassing and Confucius's thought, Jaspers is aware of a crucial difference. For Confucius, he writes, "the Encompassing is a background, not a theme to work with; it is the limit and foundation to be considered with awe, not the immediate task."[39]

The crucial difference that separates Jaspers's idea of the Encompassing from Confucius's philosophy (especially his conceptions of "basic wisdom" and *Jên*) is a natural one as long as his hermeneutical approach stresses the moral and ethical dimensions of Confucian thought. For Confucius, a secure society is a key presupposition of his theory, but Jaspers also interprets this fundamental point of departure as a Confucian "background."

CHUANG TZU'S PHILOSOPHY AND CIPHERS

In addition to Confucius and his thinking, Jaspers also pays attention to a successor of Lao-tzu, i.e., Chuang Tzu. Here I want merely to note, briefly, the homeomorphic similarities between the idea of the Tao in *The Chuang Tzu* and the idea of ciphers in Jaspers's philosophy,[40] in which the cipher (or an open-ended signum) of transcendence is characterized as "immanent" transcendence or as "the language of" transcendence. "We call the metaphysical objectivity a cipher," Jaspers explains, "because it is the language of transcendence, not transcendence itself. It is not a language to be understood or even heard in consciousness at large. This kind of language and the manner in which it accosts us are for possible Existenz alone."[41] The cipher is only "heard" by possible Existenz; ciphers enable the self as possible Existenz to hear the language of and to cognize the otherness of transcendence. Indeed, for Jaspers, "every phenomenon may turn into a cipher."[42]

In *Philosophical Faith and Revelation* and in the context of his theory of ciphers of transcendence, Jaspers refers to the Tao of Chinese thought as "all-embracing" and cites a passage from Chuang Tzu's writings: "Man sees his father in heaven and loves him personally. How much more must we love that which is higher than heaven," and Chuang Tzu adds, "namely, the Tao."[43]

Chuang Tzu characterizes the unique thought of the Tao in *The Chuang Tzu*. The Tao has unique characteristics, since the Tao, itself, is never grasped in any restricted word or concept. In section II of *The Chuang Tzu* entitled, "The Equality of Things," we find many phrases that illustrate that there is no ground to grasp the world in any restricted word. "There is nothing that is not the 'that' and there is nothing that is not the 'this.' Things do not know that they are the 'that' of other things; they only know what they themselves know. Therefore I say that the 'that' is produced by the 'this' and the 'this' is also caused by the 'that.'" The 'that' or the 'this' is only a provisional and relative distinction. And every being in itself is beyond such restriction. In this way, the distinction of being—nonbeing or reality-nonreality must be dissolved. Besides, in *The Chuang Tzu* even the distinction between the subject and the object is transcended in so far as the "universe and I exist together, and all things and I are one." According to *The Chuang Tzu,* any judgment is a temporary judgment at that time, and any concept is only a mark or a sign of the Tao. That is to say, the mark is the cipher of the Tao. When this is understood, it may be said that a cipher mediates between immanence and transcendence. We can never get Being as such by consciousness as such or rationalist thinking, but we realize that we must try to transcend all knowledge expressed in any words or concepts. In Jaspers's words, "all that appears in the world is able to become cipher," and every sign or every "thing" may become the language or the cipher of being or transcendence. In *The Chuang Tzu,* as well as in Jaspers's philosophy, Being as such never has any distinction. In order to pursue such Being, we have to recognize first these distinctions and then transcend these limits. This recognition leads us to the way of the Tao, and by considering Jaspers's philosophy of the process of thought we are able to understand the Encompassing and the cipher as the language of transcendence.

In *The Analects of Confucius* Jaspers interprets the thought of Confucius through the word *jên*. In order to recognize *jên* it was necessary for Confucius to think in his particular way. He was not satisfied with acquiring fixed metaphysical knowledge, but tried instead to live a harmonious human life. Both Jaspers and Confucius take interest in the basis of existence that is never perceived, nor expressed in words. Both try to think of "Being as such" (Jaspers's term) throughout these existences and words, and are aware of their limits. However, Jaspers strongly points out the difference of his viewpoint from Confucius's. Whereas he philosophically pursues the question concerning being systematically in "world orientation," "existential elucidation," and "metaphysics," Confucius presupposes being and, in turn, argues for the primacy of the human ethos and the ethical dimension of human life.

Differing from Confucius, Chuang Tzu is interested in a sphere beyond human society. He advocates the Tao that is expressed only *negatively* or *paradoxically*. Chuang Tzu, like Lao Tzu, thinks of the Tao in terms of being, negates intellectual knowledge (consciousness as such), and expresses the Tao as an unrestricted concept in a fashion similar to Jaspers's "basic philosophical operation" and conceptualization and idea of the nonforeclosable "Encompassing" of all being. Jaspers's keen ability to pass over, as it were, conceptually, to obtain such a foothold (not without errors, of course) into Asian thought, especially Confucian philosophy, reveals why I prefer to speak of Jaspers's *communication with* Chinese thought: His hermeneutical work illustrates a de-centering of Eurocentric philosophy on its way toward a coming "history of world philosophy" and "world philosophy."[44]

Nevertheless, we must pay attention to the fact that there is a clear distinction between Jaspers's philosophical thinking and Asian thought, which turns on their respective attitudes toward the existent world. Jaspers's philosophy is *existential* philosophy; he regards action in the world as vitally important for self-being and one's unique historicity therein. In contrast, Lao Tzu knew the advantage of taking no action, and for Chuang Tzu, it is more important to transcend the world than to live in it. These are decisive points of difference that must not go unheeded in any comparative philosophical analysis of Jaspers and Asian thought.

RECEPTION OF JASPERS'S PHILOSOPHY IN JAPAN

Ever since the "Jaspers Society of Japan" was founded in 1951 there has been an on-going and in-depth relationship between Jaspers's philosophy and the

Japanese.[45] Jaspers quest for "world philosophy" after the Second World War made it possible for him to approach Asian thought with a fresh attitude, and, at the same time, to be received, in turn, by way of reciprocal existential communication on the part of Asian philosophers and scholars. I also believe that there has been a conceptual philosophical ground for the reception of Jaspers's philosophy in Japan that is based, at least partially, in the Japanese concept of "*kokoro*." In the Japanese language, *kokoro* implies an idea that is very close to what Jaspers envisions with his idea of the subject-object poles of "the Encompassing." As Hideo Mineshima notes, the Japanese *kokoro* means, etymologically, "cohesion" or "condensation" or, respectively, "focus" or "center."[46] A Chinese ideogram for this concept copies the form of the human heart, and includes the various meanings of the mind, intellect, emotion or feeling, mood, heart, will (or volition), and spirit (in a religious sense).

Kokoro typically means the true nature of Human Being. Or, in its broader sense, *kokoro* may also mean the true nature or essence of things. The term is polysemic, and thus implies a wide range of meanings, including, mind, intellect, feeling, mood, heart, will, and spirit in English. Even if we succeeded in analyzing *kokoro* psychologically, medically or biologically, it would only throw light on certain aspects of *kokoro* that can be observed as phenomena. *Kokoro*, itself, can never be directly probed as an object.

Furthermore, in Japanese Buddhism *kokoro* is even defined as "non-existence of *kokoro*" (*mushin*), which is a state of "unification with universal being by [means of] eliminating personal *kokoro*."[47] This resonates with the statement by Toru Sagara that "*kokoro* in the state of *mushin* is resolved in nature."[48] The concept can also be applied to nature as well as to individuals. In the former case, it refers to what makes nature *emerge as the way it is*, and *it is what stays unchanged* within transitory phenomenon. *Kokoro* also connotes temporal feelings, will and intellect as expressed and observed in the world, and implies the true (and authentic) mode of human being and of the nature of all existing beings.

Whether in reference to nature or to the self, *kokoro* cannot be grasped as an "object" of cognition. Thus, there can be no direct answer to the question: What is *kokoro*? We can only explore its whatness, which leads to further questions: In what modes is *kokoro* assumed to exist? How can we achieve the true mode of *kokoro*? But it is agreed that we may only examine the modes of *kokoro*'s appearing, and not *kokoro* as such. The concept of *kokoro* is close to Jaspers's idea of the Encompassing in so far as it represents both: (1) all beings and (2) the source or ground (Being as such, in Jaspers's terminology) of all beings, at the same time. In other words, we too as Japanese thinkers must adopt an analogous way of "transcending" philosophizing, as Jaspers does in illuminating the meaning of "the encompassing of the modes of being that we are" and "the Encompassing of all Encompassings" that refers to— but never breaks through to completely in time owing to human historicity— Being as such.

The Japanese cultural ethos that has been typically represented by the concept of *kokoro* would seem, then, to have contributed in no small way, to the broad acceptance, reception, and early interaction with Jaspers's philosophy in Japan.[49]

Jaspers's theory of existential communication and reorientation to world philosophy enabled him to accept Asian thought. This communication was made possible only when his philosophy had attained broadness and depth not limited to the transfer of information or confined to the narrowness of a specific and individualized sphere of existence. In this communication, what is important is that different aspects of truth can interact with each other, which is what Jaspers actually achieved in his philosophical thinking and action.

His theory of the Encompassing enables him to interpret Asian thought originally. It was made possible as he eliminated all fixed or closed definitions of the concept of Being in his theory of the Encompassing. For existence grasped in any one mode of understanding is regarded as only one mode of Being as such, and all standpoints asserting particular ideas with any absolute value are rejected. This way of thinking was a prerequisite for Jaspers to be able to understand Asian thought developed through thousands of years of thinking based on concepts different from those in Western, European culture.

Communication between truths is achieved only upon the basis of thinking through "reason" just as the theory of the Encompassing requires it. Reason is the glue that holds together the modes of the encompassing that we are as subjects. Jaspers's philosophy rejects any fixed mode of knowledge and continues to perform dynamic thinking in pursuit of infinite clarification. This is an operational way of thinking that continues to pursue broader and clearer knowledge, while discarding knowledge already obtained as it becomes dogmatic or reified. This function of reason is what brings about the full-fledged function of the communication Jaspers advocates. Jaspers's concepts of communication, the Encompassing, and reason are key concepts that have brought about broad validity and great significance to Jaspers's philosophy in Asia. Jaspers unique interpretation of these concepts has made it possible for him to interact with Asian thought, and furthermore, to open the door to the "world philosophy" that he attempted to establish. In his "Philosophical Autobiography,"[50] Jaspers writes that "we are on the road from the evening-glow of European philosophy to the dawn of world philosophy."[51] Jaspers's philosophy was broadened and enriched through the communication he made with Asian thought, and is really on the road to the dawn of a world philosophy in an age of globalization.

Notes

1. Karl Jaspers, *The Great Philosophers 2: The Original Thinkers*, edited by Hannah Arendt, translated by Ralph Manheim (New York: Harcourt, Brace & World, 1966), p. 389. [Hereafter cited as GP 2, eds.]

2. Karl Jaspers, *Way to Wisdom: An Introduction to Philosophy*, translated by Ralph Manheim (New Haven, London: Yale University Press, 1973), p. 28.

3. Cited from *Karl Jaspers, Basic Philosophical Writings, Selections*, edited, translated, and with introductions by Leonard H. Ehrlich, Edith Ehrlich, and George B. Pepper (Athens, OH and London: Ohio University Press, 1986), p. 176. [Hereafter cited as BPW, eds.]

4. This and all other passages from the *Tao Te Ching* are cited from the following edition: *Lao Tzu, Tao Te Ching*, translated by John C. H. Wu (Boston, London: Shambhala Publications, 1990).

5. GP 2, p. 391.

6. Karl Jaspers, *Philosophy*, Vol. 3, translated by E. B. Ashton (Chicago, London: The University of Chicago Press, 1971), p. 35.

7. Karl Jaspers, *Philosophical Faith and Revelation*, translated by E. B. Ashton (New York: Harper & Row, 1967), p. 136. [Hereafter cited as PFR, eds.]

8. BPW, p. 176.

9. Charles F. Wallraff, *Karl Jaspers: An Introduction to His Philosophy*, (Princeton, NJ: Princeton University Press, 1970), p. 183.

10. GP 2, p. 390.

11. PFR, p. 137.

12. Ibid.

13. GP 2, p. 391.

14. GP 2, p. 393.

15. GP 2, p. 408.

16. Ibid.

17. GP 2, p. 415.

18. Ibid.

19. Karl Jaspers, "Philosophical Autobiography," in *The Philosophy of Karl Jaspers*. The Library of Living Philosophers, edited by Paul Arthur Schilpp (New York: Tudor Publishing Company, 1957), p. 82.

20. Karl Jaspers, *The Origin and Goal of History* (New York and London: Yale University Press, 1953), p. 69.

21. *The Great Philosophers 1: The Foundations*, edited by Hannah Arendt, translated by Ralph Manheim (New York: Harcourt, Brace & World, 1962), p. 3. [Hereafter cited as GP 1, eds.]

22. GP 1, p. 3.

23. Cf. Karl Jaspers, *Die Großen Philosophen. Nachlass 2: Fragmente, Anmerkungen, Inventar.* Hrsg. von Hans Saner, Unter Mitarbeit von Raphael Bielander (Munich, Zürich: Piper & Co., 1981), pp. 1136 ff., 1138 ff. [Hereafter cited as GrPh/N2, eds.]

24. See Shozo Shida, ["The Problem of Comparative Philosophy in Jaspers] *Jaspers Niokeru Hikakutetugaku No Mondai*, in *Risou Tokyo*, No. 425 (Tokyo: Risousha, 1968), pp. 31–39; *idem.*, ["Jaspers and Oriental Thought"] *Jaspers To Touyoushisou, Jituzonshugi* (*Journal of the Society of Existentialism*), No. 48 (Tokyo: Risousha, 1969), pp. 64–75.

25. GP 1, p. 53.

26. GP 1, p. 54.

27. GP 1, p. 57.

28. Ibid.

29. GP 1, p. 58.

30. GP 1, pp. 58-59.

31. GP 1, p. 60.

32. Ibid.

33. For *The Analects*, *Lao Tzu*, and the *Chuang Tzu* I refer to *The Sacred Books of China*, translated by James Legge, in *The Sacred Books of the East*, edited by Max Muller, vols. 39-40 (Oxford: Oxford University Press, 1891; Delhi: Motilal Banarsidass, 1968). *A Source Book in Chinese Philosophy*, translated and compiled by Wing-Tsit Chan (Princeton, NJ: Princeton University Press, 1963). *Confucius, The Analects*, translated by D.C. Lau (Penguin Books, 1979). *Lao Tzu, Tao Te Ching*, translated by D. C. Lau (Penguin Books, 1963); *Chuang Tzu*, translated by Burton Watson (New York: Columbia University Press, 1996).

34. GP 1, pp. 60ff.

35. GP 1, p. 67 (italics emphasis). On the concept of "foundering" in Jaspers's philosophy, see the article by George Pepper herein [eds.]

36. GP 1, p. 63.

37. Ibid.

38. GP 1, p. 64.

39. GrPh/N2, pp. 410ff.

40. GrPh/N2, p. 181.

41. Cf., GrPh/N2, p. 412ff.

42. Jaspers, *Philosophy*, vol. 3, p. 112.

43. Karl Jaspers, *Philosophical Faith and Revelation*, translated by E. B. Ashton (London and Glasgow: Collins Clear-Type Press, 1967), p. 95.

44. Karl Jaspers, *Der philosophische Glaube angesichts der Offenbarung* (Munich: Piper & Co., 1962), pp. 393–94 [translation by the editors].

45. See the article by Hans Saner herein [eds.].

46. For an earlier historical review of Jaspers research trends in Japan, see Denzaburo Yoshizawa, "The Reception of Jaspers in Japan," in *Karl Jaspers Today*, edited by Leonard H. Ehrlich and Richard Wisser (Washington, DC: University Press of America, 1988), pp. 395–400.

Subsequent Jaspers publications include, among others,Yukio Masubushi, *A Study of Educational Philosophy in Jaspers* [*Jaspers No Kyouikutetugaku Kenkyuu*] (Tokyo: Ibunsha, 1989); Hironobu Terawaki, *Existenz and Political Thought in Jaspers* [*Jaspers*

No Jitsuzon To Seijishisou] (Tokyo: Hokujyu Shuppan, 1991); Sawako Hanyu, *The Ontology of Karl Jaspers From the Viewpoint of Comparative Philosophy* [*Jaspers No Sonzairon*] (Tokyo: Hokujyu Shuppan, 1996); Hiroshi Ban, *Kant To Jaspers* (Tokyo: Hokujyu Shuppan, 1999). Recent Japanese translations of Jaspers's works include *Martin Heidegger / Karl Jaspers, Briefwechsel 1920-1963*, edited by Walter Biemel and Hans Saner, (Munich, Zürich: Piper & Co., Frankfurt am Main: Vittorio Klostermann, 1990), translated by Jiro Watanabe (Nagoya: Nagoya University Press, 1994); *Von der Wahrheit*, Vol. 4, translated by Tadashi Kozuma and Shinichiro Morinaga (Tokyo: Risoshya, 1997); *Psychologie der Weltanchauungen*, translated by Hideo Shigeta (Tokyo: Risoshya, 1997); *Der Philosophische Glaube*, translated by Shinji Hayashida (Tokyo: Risoshya, 1998); *Die Schuldfrage*, translated by Fumio Hashimoto (Tokyo: Heibonshya, 1998); *Die Idee der Universität*, translated by Kazuteru Fukui (Tokyo: Risoshya, 1999).

47. See Hideo Mineshima, "The 21st Century: The Role of Philosophy," in *L'esprit d'aujourd'hui*, edited by Yukio Masubuchi, No. 352 (Tokyo: Shibundo, 1996).

48. Ibid.

49. Toru Sagara, *Japanese Thought* [*Nihon No Shisou*] (Tokyo: Pelican, 1998), p. 169; see also, *idem., Japanese Kokoro* [*Nihonjinn No Kokoro Sagara*] (Tokyo: Tokyo University Press, 1996).

50. Karl Jaspers's philosophy of the Encompassing has the potential to be developed further in relation to contemporary Japanese philosophies of mind, but also, and especially, holds its greater potential for appropriation and actualization in the direction of Jaspers's unfinished efforts toward a "world philosophy."

51. Jaspers, "Philosophical Autobiography," *The Philosophy of Karl Jaspers*, edited by Paul Arthur Schilpp, pp. 83–84.

BIBLIOGRAPHY

1. Bibliographies

Karl Jaspers. Eine Bibliographie. Bd. I. *Die Primärbibliographie.* Bearbeitet von Gisela Gefken und Karl Kunert. Oldenburg, 1978.

Primärbibliographie der Schriften Karl Jaspers'. Im Auftrag der Karl Jaspers Stiftung auf der Grundlage der Bibliographie von Gisela Gefken und Karl Kunert völlig neu bearbeitet und herausgegeben von Christian Rabanus. Tübingen und Basel: Francke, 2000.

The Philosophy of Karl Jaspers. Edited by Paul Arthur Schilpp, 2nd augmented edition with section on Heidegger [75/1–75/16]. Lasalle: Open Court, 1981, pp. 871–904. [Bibliography of the writings of Karl Jaspers to 1957, compiled by Kurt Rossmann, revised and continued from 1958 to 1973 by Gisela Gefken.]

2. Works of Karl Jaspers

(German editions in chronological order, with English translation edition)

Allgemeine Psychopathologie. Ein Leitfaden für Studierende, Ärzte und Psychologen. Berlin: Springer, 1913.—4. völlig neu bearb. Aufl. Berlin, Heidelberg: Springer, 1964.

General Psychopathology. Translated from the German 7th Edition by Julius Hoenig and Marian W. Hamilton. Manchester: Manchester University Press, 1962. Toronto: University of Toronto Press, 1963. Chicago: University of Chicago Press, 1968. Baltimore: Johns Hopkins University Press, 1997.

Psychologie der Weltanschauungen. Berlin: Springer, 1919.—6. Aufl. Berlin, Heidelberg, New York: Springer 1971. Paperback-Ausgaben nach der 6. Aufl. München, Zürich: Piper, 1990 und 1994.

Max Weber. Gedenkrede. Tübingen: J. C.B. Mohr, 1921.—2. Aufl. 1926.

Strindberg und van Gogh. Versuch einer pathologischen Analyse unter vergleichender Heranziehung von Swedenborg und Hölderlin. Bern: Bircher, 1922—4. Aufl. München: Piper, 1977.

Strindberg and Van Gogh. An Attempt of a Pathographic Analysis. With References to Parallel Cases of Swedenborg and Hölderlin. Translated by Oskar Grunow and David Woloshin. Tucson: University of Arizona Press, 1977.

Die Idee der Universität. Berlin: Springer, 1923.—Neufassung 1946 und (mit Kurt Rossmann) 1961. Berlin, Göttingen, Heidelberg: Springer, 1961.

The Idea of the University. Edited by Karl W. Deutsch. Preface by Robert Ulich. Translated by Harold A. T. Reiche and H. F. Vanderschmidt. Boston: Beacon Press, 1959.

Die geistige Situation der Zeit. Berlin: de Gruyter, 1931.—13. Aufl. 1979.

Man in the Modern Age. Translated by Eden and Cedar Paul. New York: Henry Holt & Co., and London: Routledge & Kegan Paul, 1933; New edition Routledge & Kegan Paul, 1959 and 1966.

Philosophie. 3 Bde. (Bd. I: *Philosophische Weltorientierung*. Bd. II: *Existenzerhellung*. Bd. III: *Metaphysik*.) Berlin 1932.—4. Aufl. 1973.

Philosophy. 3 vols. Translated by E. B. Ashton. Vol. 1: *Introduction to Philosophy/Philosophical World Orientation*, 1969, vol. 2: *Existential Elucidation*, 1970, vol. 3: *Metaphysics*, 1971. Chicago and London: University of Chicago Press, 1969-1971.

Max Weber. Deutsches Wesen im politischen Denken, im Forschen und Philosophieren. Oldenburg: Stalling, 1932.—2. Aufl. unter dem Titel: *Max Weber. Politiker, Forscher, Philosoph*. Bremen: Storm, 1946.

"Max Weber as Politician, Scientist, Philosopher." Translated by Ralph Manheim. In: *Karl Jaspers: Three Essays. Leonardo, Descartes, Max Weber*. New York: Harcourt, Brace & World, 1964, 187-274; "Max Weber: Politician, Scientist, Philosopher (1932)." Translated from the German by Robert J. Whelan. In: *On Max Weber*. New York: Paragon House, 1989, 29-135.

Vernunft und Existenz. Fünf Vorlesungen. Groningen: Wolters, 1935.—5. Aufl. und Neuausgabe München: Piper, 1973.

Reason and Existenz. Translated with an introduction by William Earle. London, Toronto, and New York: Noonday Press, 1955, Routledge & Kegan Paul, 1956.

Nietzsche. Einführung in das Verständnis seines Philosophierens. Berlin, Leipzig: de Gruyter, 1936.—4. Aufl. Berlin, New York 1981.

Nietzsche: An Introduction to the Understanding of His Philosophical Activity. Translated by Charles F. Wallraff and Frederick J. Schmitz. Tucson: University of Arizona Press, 1965.

Existenzphilosophie. Drei Vorlesungen. Berlin, Leipzig: de Gruyter, 1938.—4. Aufl. Berlin, New York 1974.

Philosophy of Existence. Translated and with an Introduction by Richard F. Grabau. (Editor's note: John R. Silver). Philadelphia: University of Pennsylvania Press, Oxford: Blackwell, 1971.

Vom europäischen Geist. München: Piper, 1947.

The European Spirit. Translated with an Introduction by Ronald Gregor Smith. London: SCM Press, New York: Macmillan, 1949.

Nietzsche und das Christentum. Hameln: Seifert, 1946.

Nietzsche and Christianity. Translated by E. B. Ashton. Chicago: Henry Regnery Co., 1961.

Die Schuldfrage. Heidelberg: Schneider, Zürich: Artemis, 1946.—Neuausgabe München, Zürich: Piper, 1987.

The Question of German Guilt. Translated by E. B. Ashton. New York: Dial Press, 1947, Westport: Greenwood Press, 1978.

Von der Wahrheit. Philosophische Logik. Erster Band. München: Piper, 1947.—4. Aufl. Neuausgabe München, Zürich: Piper, 1991.

Tragedy Is Not Enough. Translated by Harold A. T. Reiche, Harry T. Moore, and Karl W. Deutsch. The Bibliography, Notes and Index were prepared by Harold A. T. Reiche. Boston: Beacon Press, 1952 and London: Gollancz, 1953.

Truth and Symbol. From *Von der Wahrheit*. Translated with an Introduction by Jean T. Wilde, William Kluback and William Kimmel. New York: Twayne Publishers, and London: Vision Press, 1959.

Der philosophische Glaube. Zürich: Artemis, 1948.—6. Aufl. Neuausgabe München: Piper, 1974.

The Perennial Scope of Philosophy. Translated by Ralph Manheim. New York: Philosophical Library, 1949 and London: Routledge & Kegan Paul, 1950.

Vom Ursprung und Ziel der Geschichte. Zürich: Artemis, und München: Piper, 1949.—8. Aufl. Neuausgabe München: Piper, 1983.

The Origin and Goal of History. Translated from the German by Michael Bullock. New Haven: Yale University Press, and London: Routledge and Kegan Paul, 1953.

Einführung in die Philosophie. Zwölf Radiovorträge. Zürich: Artemis, 1950.—München: Piper, 1953. Neuausgabe München: Piper, 1971.

Way to Wisdom. Translated by Ralph Manheim. London: Gollancz, and New Haven: Yale University Press, 1951.

Vernunft und Widervernunft in unserer Zeit. Drei Gastvorlesungen. München: Piper, 1950.—3. Aufl. Neuausgabe München: Piper, 1990.

Reason and Anti-Reason in our Time. Translated by Stanley Goodman. London: SCM Press, and New Haven: Yale University Press, 1952.

Rechenschaft und Ausblick. Reden und Aufsätze. München: Piper, 1951.—2. Aufl. 1958.

Existentialism and Humanism. Three Essays. Edited, with introduction, and biographical details by Hanns E. Fischer. Translated by E. B. Ashton. New York: Moore, 1952.

Lionardo als Philosoph. Bern: Francke, 1953.

"Leonardo as Philosopher." Translated by Ralph Manheim. In: Karl Jaspers: *Three Essays. Leonardo, Descartes, Max Weber*. New York: Harcourt, Brace & World, 1964, pp. 1-58.

Die Frage der Entmythologisierung. Karl Jaspers, Rudolf Bultmann. München: Piper, 1954.—Neuausgabe mit einer Einführung von Heinrich Ott, München, Zürich: Piper, 1981.

Myth and Christianity: An Inquiry into the Possibility of Religion without Myth. Karl Jaspers, Rudolf Bultmann. Translated by Norbert Guterman. New York: Noonday Press, 1958.

Schelling. Größe und Verhängnis. München: Piper, 1955. Neuausgabe München, Zürich: Piper, 1986.

"Philosophische Autobiographie." In: *Karl Jaspers*. Hg. Paul A. Schilpp, Stuttgart: Kohlhammer, 1957, pp. 1–80.

"Philosophical Autobiography." From the original German manuscript translated by Paul

Arthur Schilpp and Ludwig B. Lefebre. In: *The Philosophy of Karl Jaspers*. Augmented Edition with New Section on Martin Heidegger. Edited by Paul Arthur Schillpp/La Salle, IL: Open Court Publishing Company, 1981, pp. 1–94.

"Antwort." In: *Karl Jaspers*. Hg. Paul A. Schilpp, Stuttgart: Kohlhammer, 1957, S. pp. 750–853.

"Reply to my Critics." Translated from the original German by Paul Arthur Schilpp and Ludwig B. Lefebre. In: *The Philosophy of Karl Jaspers*, pp. 747–869.

Die großen Philosophen. Erster Band. München: Piper, 1957. Neuausgabe München, Zürich: Piper, 1988. [Selected chapters of these two volumes are also published as: *Anaximander, Heraclitus, Parmenides, Plotinus, Lao-tzu, Nagarjuna*. New York: Harcourt, Brace, Jovanovich, 1974; *Anselm and Nicholas of Cusa*. New York: Harcourt, Brace, Jovanovich, 1974; *Kant*. New York: Harcourt, Brace and World, 1962; *Plato and Augustine*. New York: Harcourt, Brace & World, 1962; *Socrates, Buddha, Confucius, Jesus*. New York: Harcourt, Brace, Jovanovich, 1990; *Spinoza*. New York: Harcourt, Brace, Jovanovich, 1974.]

Die Atombombe und die Zukunft des Menschen. Politisches Bewußtsein in unserer Zeit. München: Piper, 1958.—6. Aufl. Neuausgabe München, Zürich: Piper, 1982.

The Future of Mankind. Translated by E. B. Ashton. Chicago: The University of Chicago Press, 1961.

The Future of Man. Translated by E. B. Ashton. Chicago: The University of Chicago Press, 1963.

Philosophie und Welt. Reden und Aufsätze. München: Piper, 1958.

Philosophy and The World: Selected Essays and Lectures. Translated by E. B. Ashton. Chicago: Henry Regnery Co., 1963, Reprint 1989.

Freiheit und Wiedervereinigung. Über Aufgaben deutscher Politik. München: Piper, 1960.

Über die Bedingungen und Möglichkeiten eines neuen Humanismus. Drei Vorträge. Mit einem Nachwort von Kurt Rossmann. Stuttgart: Reclam, 1962.

Der philosophische Glaube angesichts der Offenbarung. München: Piper, 1962.—3. Aufl. München, Zürich: Piper, 1984.

Philosophical Faith and Revelation. Translated by E. B. Ashton. New York: Harper & Row, and London: Collins, 1967.

Gesammelte Schriften zur Psychopathologie. Berlin, Göttingen, Heidelberg: Springer, 1963. Neuauflage 1990.

Lebensfragen der deutschen Politik. München: DTV-Verlag, 1963.

Philosophie und Offenbarungsglaube. Ein Zwiegespräch. Karl Jaspers, Heinz Zahrnt. Hamburg: Furche, 1963.

Nicolaus Cusanus. München: Piper, 1964.

Hoffnung und Sorge. Schriften zur deutschen Politik 1945-1965. München: Piper, 1965.

Kleine Schule des philosophischen Denkens. Philosophische Aufsätze. München: Piper, 1965.

Philosophy is for Everyman: A Short Course in Philosophical Thinking. Translated by Richard F. C. Hull and Grete Wels. New York: Harcourt, Brace & World, 1967.

Wohin treibt die Bundesrepublik? Tatsachen, Gefahren, Chancen. München: Piper, 1966.

The Future of Germany. Selection. Translated by E. B. Ashton, Foreword by Hannah Arendt. Chicago, London: University of Chicago Press, 1967.

Antwort. Zur Kritik meiner Schrift "Wohin treibt die Bundesrepublik?" München: Piper, 1967.

Schicksal und Wille. Autobiographische Schriften. Hg. und mit einem Vorwort versehen von Hans Saner. München: Piper, 1967.

Aneignung und Polemik. Gesammelte Reden und Aufsätze zur Geschichte der Philosophie. Hg. Hans Saner. München: Piper, 1968.

Provokationen. Gespräche und Interviews. Hg. Hans Saner. München: Piper, 1969.

Chiffren der Transzendenz. Hg. Hans Saner. München: Piper, 1970. 4. Aufl. München, Zürich: Piper, 1984.

Was ist Philosophie? Ein Lesebuch. Textauswahl und Zusammenstellung von Hans Saner. München: Piper, 1976.

Philosophische Autobiographie. Erw. Neuausgabe (erstmals mit dem Kapitel über Martin Heidegger). München: Piper, 1977.

Was ist Erziehung? Ein Lesebuch. Textauswahl und Zusammenstellung von Hermann Horn. München, Zürich: Piper, 1977. Neuausgabe 1992.

Notizen zu Martin Heidegger. Hg. Hans Saner. München, Zürich: Piper, 1978. 3. Aufl. 1989.

Die großen Philosophen. Nachlaß 1: Darstellungen und Fragmente. Hg. Hans Saner. Unter Mitarbeit von Raphael Bielander. München, Zürich: Piper, 1981.

Die grossen Philosophen. Nachlass 2: Fragmente, Anmerkungen, Inventar. Hg. Hans Saner. München, Zürich: Piper, 1981.

The Great Philosophers. Volume 3: *Xenophanes, Democritus, Empedocles, Bruno, Epicurus, Boehme, Schelling, Leibniz, Aristotle, Hegel.* Edited by Michael Ermarth and Leonard H. Ehrlich. Translated by Edith Ehrlich and Leonard H. Ehrlich. Foreword by Michael Ermarth. New York, San Diego, London: Harcourt Brace & Company, 1993.

The Great Philosophers. Volume 4: *The Disturbers. Descartes, Pascal, Lessing, Kierkegaard, Nietzsche. Philosophers on Other Realms. Einstein, Weber, Marx.* Edited by Michael Ermarth and Leonard H. Ehrlich. Foreword by Michael Ermarth. New York, San Diego, London: Harcourt Brace & Company, 1994.

Weltgeschichte der Philosophie. Einleitung. Aus dem Nachlaß hg. von Hans Saner. München, Zürich: Piper, 1982.

Hannah Arendt/Karl Jaspers: Briefwechsel 1926-1969. Hg. Lotte Köhler und Hans Saner. München, Zürich: Piper, 1985.

Hannah Arendt, Karl Jaspers. Correspondence 1926-1969. Edited by Lotte Köhler and Hans Saner. Translated from the German by Robert and Rita Kimber. New York, San Diego, London: Harcourt, Brace, Jovanovich, 1993.

Erneuerung der Universität. Reden und Schriften 1945/46. Nachwort und hg. von Renato de Rosa. Heidelberg: Schneider, 1986.

Der Arzt im technischen Zeitalter. München, Zürich: Piper, 1986.

Briefwechsel Karl Jaspers–Oskar Hammelsbeck 1919–1969. Hg. und erläutert von Hermann Horn. Frankfurt/M.: Peter Lang, 1986.

Max Weber. Gesammelte Schriften. Mit einer Einführung von Dieter Henrich. Zusammenstellung der Texte: Hans Saner. München, Zürich: Piper, 1988.

On Max Weber. Edited with Introduction and Notes: John Dreijmanis. Translated from the German by Robert J. Whelan. New York: Paragon House, 1989.

Martin Heidegger/Karl Jaspers: Briefwechsel 1920-1963. Hg. Walter Biemel und Hans Saner. München, Zürich: Piper, 1990.

The Heidegger-Jaspers Correspondence (1920-1963). Edited by Walter Biemel and Hans Saner, translated by Gary E. Aylesworth. Amherst, New York: Humanity Books, 2003.

Nachlaß zur Philosophischen Logik. Hg. Hans Saner und Marc Hänggi. München, Zürich: Piper, 1991.

Das Wagnis der Freiheit. Gesammelte Aufsätze zur Philosophie. Hg. und mit einer Vorbemerkung versehen von Hans Saner. München, Zürich: Piper, 1996.

Was ist der Mensch? Philosophisches Denken für Alle. Ausgewählt und mit einleitenden Kommentaren versehen von Hans Saner. München, Zürich: Piper, 2000.

3. Secondary Sources

3.1 Books in English and German

(Authors in alphabetical order)

Allen, E. L. *The Self and Its Hazards: A Guide to the Thought of Karl Jaspers.* New York: Philosophical Library, 1951.

Böversen, F., Hg. *Philosophie der Politik.* Wuppertal, 1984.

Buri, F. *Albert Schweitzer und Karl Jaspers.* Zürich: Artemis, 1950.

Burkard, F.-P. *Ethische Existenz bei Karl Jaspers.* Würzburg: Königshausen & Neumann, 1982.

Carr, G. R. *Karl Jaspers as an Intellectual Critic: The Political Dimension of His Thought.* Frankfurt/M.: Peter Lang, 1983.

Di Cesare, D. *Die Sprache in der Philosophie von Karl Jaspers.* Tübingen, Basel: Francke, 1996.

Ehrlich, L. H. *Karl Jaspers: Philosophy as Faith.* Amherst: University of Massachusetts Press, 1975.

Ehrlich, L. H./Wisser, R., eds. *Karl Jaspers Today. Philosophy at the Threshold of the Future.* Lanham: University Press of America, 1988.

Ehrlich, L. H./Wisser, R., eds. *Karl Jaspers. Philosophy on the Way to "World Philosophy."* Würzburg: Königshausen & Neumann, and Amsterdam, Atlanta: Rodopi, 1998.

Fukui, K. *Wege zur Vernunft.* Basel: Schwabe, 1995.

Gerlach, A. M. *Existenzphilosophie–Karl Jaspers.* Berlin: Akademie, 1987.

Harth, D., Hg. *Karl Jaspers. Denken zwischen Wissenschaft, Politik und Philosophie.* Stuttgart: Metzler, 1989.

Hersch, J. *Karl Jaspers: Eine Einführung in sein Werk.* München, Zürich: Piper, 1980.

Hersch, J./Lochman, J. M./Wiehl, R., Hg. *Karl Jaspers. Philosoph, Arzt, politischer Denker.* München, Zürich: Piper, 1986.

Horn, H. *Karl Jaspers: Was ist Erziehung?* München: Piper, 1977. 2. Aufl. 1992.

Howey, R. L. *Heidegger and Jaspers on Nietzsche.* The Hague: Nijhoff, 1973.

Kane, J. F. *Pluralism and Truth in Religion: Karl Jaspers on Existentialist Truth.* Chico, CA: Scholars Press, 1981.

Kirkbright, S. *Karl Jaspers, A Biography: Navigations in Truth.* New Haven, Conn: Yale University Press, 2004.

Koterski, J. W. and R. Langley, eds. *Karl Jaspers: On Philosophy of History and History of Philosophy.* Amherst, New York: Humanity Books, 2003.

Lengert, R. *Philosophie der Freiheit. Karl Jaspers. 23. Februar 1883–26. Februar 1969.* Oldenburg: Holzberg, 1983.

Lichtigfeld, A. *Jaspers' Metaphysics.* London: Colibri Press, 1954.

Long, E. T. *Jaspers and Bultmann: A Dialogue Between Philosophy and Theology in the Existentialist Tradition.* Durham, N.C.: Duke University Press, 1968.

O'Connor, B. F. *A Dialogue between Philosophy and Religion: The Perspective of Karl Jaspers.* Lanham, Md.: University Press of America, 1988.

Olson, A. M. *Transcendence and Hermeneutics: An Interpretation of Karl Jaspers.* The Hague: Nijhoff, 1979.

_____. edited by *Heidegger and Jaspers.* Philadelphia: Temple University Press, 1994.

Piper, K., Hg. *Karl Jaspers: Werk und Wirkung. Zum 80. Geburtstag von Jaspers.* München: Piper, 1963.

Piper, K. and Saner, H., Hg. *Erinnerungen an Karl Jaspers.* München: Piper, 1974.

Salamun, K. *Karl Jaspers.* München: C. H. Beck, 1985; 2. erweiterte Aufl. Würzburg: Königshausen & Neumann, 2006.

_____. Hg. *Karl Jaspers: Zur Aktualität seines Denkens.* München, Zürich: Piper, 1991.

_____. Hg. *Philosophie—Erziehung—Universität. Zu Karl Jaspers' Bildungs- und Erziehungsphilosophie.* Frankfurt/M.: Peter Lang, 1995.

Samay, S. *Reason Revisited.* Notre Dame, Ind.: University of Notre Dame Press, 1971.

Saner, H. *Karl Jaspers in Selbstzeugnissen und Bilddokumenten.* Reinbek: Rowohlt, 1970. 12. Aufl. 2005.

_____. *Einsamkeit und Kommunikation.* Basel: Lenos, 1994.

_____. Hg. *Karl Jaspers in der Diskussion.* München: Piper, 1973.

Schilpp, P. A., ed. *The Philosophy of Karl Jaspers.* The Library of Living Philosophers. 2nd Augmented Edition with section on Heidegger [75/1–75/16]. Lasalle: Open Court, 1981.

Schneiders, W. *Karl Jaspers in der Kritik.* Bonn: Bouvier, 1965.

Schrag, O. O. *Existence, Existenz, and Transcendence.* Pittsburgh: Duquesne University Press, 1971.

Simon, Gabriel, SS.CC. *Die Achse der Weltgeschichte nach Karl Jaspers. Analecta Gregoriana* 147, Series Facultatis Philosophicae. Roma: Libreria Editrice dell'Universita Gregoriana, 1965.

Thornhill, C. *Karl Jaspers: Politics and Metaphysics*. London and New York: Routledge, 2002.
Wallraff, C. F. *Karl Jaspers: An Introduction to His Philosophy*. Princeton: Princeton University Press, 1970.
Walters, G. J. *Karl Jaspers and the Role of 'Conversion' in the Nuclear Age*. Lanham and London: University Press of America, 1988.
_____. ed. *The Tasks of Truth: Essays on Karl Jaspers's Idea of the University*. Frankfurt/M. and New York: Peter Lang, 1996.
Weidmann, Bernd, Hg. *Existenz in Kommunikation. Zur philosophischen Ethik von Karl Jaspers*. Würzburg: Königshausen & Neumann, 2005.
Wisser, R. *Karl Jaspers: Philosophie in der Bewährung. Vorträge und Aufsätze*. Würzburg: Königshausen & Neumann, 1995.
Wisser, R. and L. H. Ehrlich, eds. *Karl Jaspers. Philosopher among Philosophers*. Würzburg: Königshausen & Neumann, and Amsterdam, Atlanta: Rodopi, 1993.
Yearbook of the Austrian Karl Jaspers Society (*Jahrbuch der Österreichischen Karl Jaspers-Gesellschaft*): Vols. 1–20. Edited by Elisabeth Salamun-Hybasek and Kurt Salamun. Vienna and Innsbruck: Studien Verlag, 1988–2007.
Wiehl, R. and Kaegi, D., Hg. *Karl Jaspers—Philosophie und Politik*. Heidelberg: C. Winter, 1999.
Young-Bruehl, E. *Freedom and Karl Jaspers's Philosophy*. New Haven: Yale University Press, 1981.

3.2 Selected Articles in English

Akerma, K. "The End and the Permanence of Mankind in Karl Jaspers's Philosophy." *Yearbook of the Austrian Karl Jaspers Society* 12 (1999): 83–103.
Arendt, H. "Jaspers as Citizen of the World." In *The Philosophy of Karl Jaspers*, edited by P. A. Schilpp, pp. 539–49. La Salle, IL: Open Court, 1982.
_____. "What Is Existenzphilosophie?" *Partisan Review,* 13 (1946): 34–56.
Baumgarten, E. "The 'Radical Evil' in Jaspers' Philosophy." In *The Philosophy of Karl Jaspers*, edited by P. A. Schilpp, pp. 337–67. La Salle, IL: Open Court, 1982.
Beatty, J. "The Scope of Philosophizing in Jaspers." *Journal of the British Society for Phenomenology* 8 (1977): 110–18.
Bennet, J. "Karl Jaspers and Scientific Philosophy." *Journal of the History of Philosophy of Existentialism* 6 (1965): 59–68.
Blattner, W. D. "Heidegger's Debt to Jaspers's Concept of the Limit-Situation." In *Heidegger and Jaspers*, edited by Alan Olson, pp. 153–65. Philadelphia, PA: Temple University Press, 1994.
Brinkmann, K. "Heidegger and Jaspers on Plato's Idea of the Good." In *Heidegger and Jaspers*, edited by Alan Olson, pp. 111–25. Philadelphia, PA: Temple University Press, 1994.
_____. "Jaspers and Arendt on Communication and Politics." *Yearbook of the Austrian Karl Jaspers Society* 11 (1998): 44–57.

Buczynska-Garewicz, H. "Jaspers and University Self-Governance." In *The Tasks of Truth: Essays on Karl Jaspers's Idea of the University*, edited by G. J. Walters, pp. 117–28.

_____. "Jaspers's Defense of the University." *Yearbook of the Austrian Karl Jaspers Society* 7/8 (1994/95): 149–58.

Buri, Fritz. "Concerning the Relationship of Philosophical Faith and Christian Faith." *Journal of the American Academy of Religion* 40 (1972): 454–57.

Cathcart, A. J. "Existenz and the Knight of Faith: Jaspers on the Existential Significance of Pascal and Kierkegaard." *Yearbook of the Austrian Karl Jaspers Society* 14 (2001): 81–104.

Chatterjee, M. "Karl Jaspers—Physician of Culture." In *Karl Jaspers Today: Philosophy at the Threshold of the Future*, edited by L. H. Ehrlich and R. Wisser, pp. 101–108. Washington, DC: Center for Advanced Research in Phenomenology & University Press of America, 1988.

Cho, J. "A Cosmopolitan Faith in Karl Jaspers: Decoupling Commitment and Narrowness." *Journal of Ecumenical Studies*, 37 (2000): 46–65.

Clark, Mark W. "A Prophet without Honour: Karl Jaspers in Germany, 1945-48." *Journal of Contemporary History*, 37 (2002): 197–222.

Coffin, P. R. "Philosophical Method and the Existenz-Philosophy of Karl Jaspers." *Personalist* 53 (1972): 141–49.

Collins, J. "An Approach to Karl Jaspers." *Thought* 20 (1945): 657–91.

_____. "Jaspers on Science and Philosophy." In *The Philosophy of Karl Jaspers*, edited by P. A. Schilpp, pp. 115–40. La Salle, IL: Open Court, 1982.

Corrington, R. S. "From World Exegesis to Transcendence. Jaspers's Critique of Nietzsche." In *Karl Jaspers. Philosopher Among Philosophers*, edited by Wisser and Ehrlich, pp. 77–87.

Courtney, C. "*Existenz*, the University, and Moral Education." In Walters, ed. *The Tasks of Truth: Essays on Karl Jaspers's Idea of the University*, pp. 69–75.

Durfee, H. A. "Karl Jaspers as a Metaphysician of Tolerance." *International Journal for Philosophy of Religion* 1 (1970): 201–10.

_____. "Philosophic Faith and Foundationalism." In Ehrlich/Wisser, eds., *Karl Jaspers Today*, pp. 213–20.

Earle, W. "Jaspers and Existential Analysis." *Journal of Existentialism* 1 (1960): 166-175.

_____. "Jaspers' Philosophical Anthropology." In Schilpp, ed. *The Philosophy of Karl Jaspers*, pp. 523–38.

Ehrlich, L. H. "Philosophical Faith and Mysticism: Karl Jaspers." *Bucknell Review* 17 (1969): 1–21.

_____. "Truth and Its Unity in Jaspers." *Revue internationale de philosophie* 147 (1983): 423–39.

_____. "Tolerance and the Prospect of a World Philosophy." In Ehrlich/Wisser, eds., *Karl Jaspers Today*, pp. 93–100.

_____. "Being and Truth. Heidegger vis à vis Jaspers." In Wisser/Ehrlich, eds., *Karl Jaspers. Philosopher Among Philosophers*, pp. 121–38.

Erickson, S. A. "The University and the Spirit." In Walters, ed. *The Tasks of Truth: Essays on Karl Jaspers's Idea of the University*, pp. 141–54.

_____. "The Space of Transcendence in Jaspers and Heidegger." In Olson, ed., *Heidegger and Jaspers*, pp. 126–38.

Fuller, T. "The University and the Experience of Tanscendence." In Walters, ed. *The Tasks of Truth: Essays on Karl Jaspers's Idea of the University*, pp. 129–39.

Gorniak-Kocikowska, K. "The Concept of Freedom in Jaspers and Heidegger." In Olson, ed., *Heidegger and Jaspers*, pp. 139–52.

_____. "Freedom and Responsibility in Jaspers and Nietzsche." In Wisser/Ehrlich, eds., *Karl Jaspers. Philosopher Among Philosophers*, pp. 88–98.

Grieder, A. "Karl Jaspers and the Quest for Philosophic Truth." *The Journal of the British Society for Phenomenology* 17 (1986): 17–35.

_____. "Karl Jaspers on Medical Therapy." *Yearbook of the Austrian Karl Jaspers Society* 5 (1992): 103–119.

Habermas, J. "Karl Jaspers: The Figures of Truth." In Habermas, *Philosophical-Political Profiles*, translated by Frederick G. Lawrence, Cambridge: MIT Press, 1983, pp. 45–52.

Hanyu, S. "The Concept of the 'Encompassing' in World Philosophy." In Ehrlich/Wisser, eds., *Karl Jaspers. Philosophy on the Way to "World Philosophy,"* pp. 45–50.

_____. "Jaspers and Cross-Cultural Philosophy—Jaspers's Philosophy and Japanese Thought." *Yearbook of the Austrian Karl Jaspers Society* 14 (2001): 71–80.

Harries, K. "Shame, Guilt, Responsibility." In Olson, ed., *Heidegger and Jaspers*, pp. 49–64.

Hartt, J. H. "God, Transcendence and Freedom in the Philosophy of Karl Jaspers." *Review of Metaphysics* 4 (1950): 247–58.

Hayashida, S. "The Ethical Significance of Jaspers's Philosophy." In Wisser/Ehrlich, eds., *Karl Jaspers. Philosopher Among Philosophers*, pp. 235–41.

Hersch, J. "The Central Gesture of Jaspers' Philosophy." *The Journal of the British Society for Phenomenology* 17 (1986): 3–8.

_____. "Jaspers' Conception of Tradition." In Schilpp, ed., *The Philosophy of Karl Jaspers*, pp. 593–610.

Henning, J. "Karl Jaspers' Attitude Towards History." In Schilpp, ed., *The Philosophy of Karl Jaspers*, pp. 565–91.

Hersch, J. "Jaspers' Conception of Tradition." In Schilpp, ed., *The Philosophy of Karl Jaspers*, pp. 593–610.

Hoffman, K. "The Basic Concepts of Jaspers' Philosophy." In Schilpp, ed., *The Philosophy of Karl Jaspers*, pp. 95–113.

Holm, S. "Jaspers' Philosophy of Religion." In Schilpp, ed., *The Philosophy of Karl Jaspers*, pp. 667–92.

Hossfeld, P. "Karl Jaspers and Religion." *Philosophy Today* 3 (1959): 277–280.

Howe, L. T. "Karl Jaspers on History: An Appreciation." *Personalist* 52 (1971): 691–716.

Howey, R. L. "Jaspers's Nietzsche: The Lonely Iconoclast." In Wisser/Ehrlich, eds., *Karl Jaspers. Philosopher Among Philosophers*, pp. 65–76.

Junghy, C. "Confucianism and Existentialism: Intersubjectivity as the Way of Man." *Philosophy and Phenomenological Research* 30 (1969): 186–202.

Kanakappaly, B. "'Faith' and 'Communication' in the Philosophy of Karl Jaspers." *Studies in Interreligious Dialogue* 10 (2000): 77–95.

Katasonov, V. "The Gadfly, Stinging the Sluggish Horse: The Socratic Mission of Jaspers's Philosophy." In Ehrlich/Wisser, eds., *Karl Jaspers. Philosophy on the Way to "World Philosophy,"* pp. 109–14.

_____. "Karl Jaspers: The Origins of Philosophy and Its Place in Culture." *Yearbook of the Austrian Karl Jaspers Society* 3/4 (1990/01): 34–45.

Kaufmann, F. "Karl Jaspers and A Philosophy of Communication." In Schilpp, ed., *The Philosophy of Karl Jaspers*, pp. 210–96.

Kaufmann, W. "Jaspers' Relation to Nietzsche." In Schilpp, ed., *The Philosophy of Karl Jaspers*, pp. 407–36.

Kelemen, J. "The 'Thing-in-itself' and the 'Encompassing'." In Wisser/Ehrlich, eds., *Karl Jaspers. Philosopher Among Philosophers*, pp. 18–21.

Kennedy, A. L. "The University as a Constituting Agent of Culture." In Walters, ed. *The Tasks of Truth: Essays on Karl Jaspers's Idea of the University*, pp. 97–115.

_____. "Existenz and Dialectic: Reflections of Jaspers' Philosophical Foundations." *Yearbook of the Austrian Karl Jaspers Society* 5 (1992): 84–102.

Kluback, W. "Karl Jaspers and Schmuel Hugo Bergman. Believing Philosophers." In Wisser/Ehrlich, eds., *Karl Jaspers. Philosopher Among Philosophers*, pp. 173–85.

_____. "Philosophy's Discordant Voice: Heidegger and Jaspers." *Yearbook of the Austrian Karl Jaspers Society* 3/4 (1990/91): 204–16.

Knauss, G. "The Concept of the 'Encompassing' in Jaspers' Philosophy." In Schilpp, ed., *The Philosophy of Karl Jaspers*, pp. 141–76.

Knudsen, R. D. "Transcendental Motives in Karl Jaspers' Philosophy." *Philosophia Reformata* 34 (1969): 122–33.

Koenker, E. "God and the Ambiguities of Freedom in the thought of Karl Jaspers." *Proceedings of the American Catholic Philosophical Association* 50 (1976): 90–98.

Kolle, K. "Jaspers as Psychopathologist." In Schilpp, ed., *The Philosophy of Karl Jaspers*, pp. 437–66.

Koterski, J. W. "Jaspers on Freedom and Truth in Science." In Ehrlich/Wisser, eds., *Karl Jaspers Today*, pp. 133–52.

_____. "Jaspers on Realism and Idealism." *Yearbook of the Austrian Karl Jaspers Society* 11 (1998): 58–69.

Kornmüller, H. "Karl Jaspers' Philosophy of History." *Modern Schoolman* 42 (1965): 129–52.

Krell, D. F. "The Heidegger-Jaspers Relationship." *Journal of the British Society for Phenomenology* 9 (1978): 126–29.

Kunz, H. "Critique of Jaspers' Concept of Transcendence." In Schilpp, ed., *The Philosophy of Karl Jaspers*, pp. 499–522.

Langley, R. "Jaspers's Three Critiques of the University." In Walters, ed. *The Tasks of Truth: Essays on Karl Jaspers's Idea of the University*, pp. 23–38.

Latzel, E. "The Concept of 'Ultimate Situation' in Jaspers' Philosophy." In Schilpp, ed., *The Philosophy of Karl Jaspers*, pp. 177–209.

Lefebre, L. B. "The Psychology of Karl Jaspers." In Schilpp, ed., *The Philosophy of Karl Jaspers*, pp. 467–98.

Lichtigfeld, A. "Jaspers in English: A Failure Not of Communication But Rather of Interpretation." *Philosophy and Phenomenological Research* 41 (1980/81): 216–22.

_____. "The God-Concept in Jaspers' Philosophy." In Schilpp, ed., *The Philosophy of Karl Jaspers*, pp. 693–702.

_____. "Jaspers's Cipher and Levinas's Trace." In Wisser/Ehrlich, eds., *Karl Jaspers. Philosopher Among Philosophers*, pp. 186–89.

Loewenstein, J. "Judaism in Jaspers' Thought." In Schilpp, ed., *The Philosophy of Karl Jaspers*, pp. 643–66.

Long, E. T. "Jaspers' Philosophy of Existence as a Model for theological Reflection." *International Journal for Philosophy of Religion* 3 (1972): 35–43.

Malhotra, M. K. "The Existence-Thought Disjunction." *The Southern Journal of Philosophy* 8 (1970): 15–23.

Manasse, E. M. "Jaspers' Philosophy of Existence and His Attitude Toward Psychoanalysis." *Journal of Existentialism*. 6 (1965): 59–68.

_____. "Max Weber's Influence on Jaspers." In Schilpp, ed., *The Philosophy of Karl Jaspers*, pp. 369–92.

McInerney, R. M. "Metaphysics and subjectivity: An approach to Karl Jaspers." *Proceedings of the American Catholic Philosophical Association* 32 (1958): 172–83.

McLachlan, M. "Jaspers' 'General Psychopathology' as a Synthesis of Empirical Science with Transcending Philosophy." *Yearbook of the Austrian Karl Jaspers Society* 15 (2002): 115–29.

Mann, G. "Freedom and the Social Sciences in Jaspers' Thought." In Schilpp, ed., *The Philosophy of Karl Jaspers*, pp. 551–64.

Marcel, G. "The Fundamental and the Ultimate Situation in Karl Jaspers." In *Creative Fidelity*, translated by Robert Rosthal. New York: Noonday, 1964, pp. 222–55.

Margolis, J. "On the Responsibility of Intellectuals: Reflections on Heidegger and Jaspers." In Olson, A., ed., *Heidegger and Jaspers*, pp. 77–91.

Mercier, A. "Some Thoughts on Jaspers and Heidegger, their Distance and Relationship." In Wisser/Ehrlich, eds., *Karl Jaspers. Philosopher Among Philosophers*, pp. 107–12.

Michaelides, C. "Plotinus and Jaspers: Their Conception and Contemplation of the Supreme One." *Diotima* 4, (1976): 37–46.

Miyang Cho, J. "A New Frontier in German Universal History: Continuity and Mutuality in Karl Jaspers." *Yearbook of the Austrian Karl Jaspers Society* 12 (1999): 59–81.

Nelson, E. S. "Faith and Knowledge. Karl Jaspers on Communication and the Encompassing." *Societas Philosophia Classica* XIII (2003): 207–18.

Nystrand, S. "A Struggle at the Borders of Life and World. The Philosophies of Jaspers and Wittgenstein." *Yearbook of the Austrian Karl Jaspers Society* 3/4 (1990/91): 217–31.

Oliver, H. H. "Karl Jaspers and Modern Physics." In Ehrlich/Wisser, eds., *Karl Jaspers Today*, pp. 111–31.

_____ "The Psychological Dimension in Jaspers's Relationship with Heidegger." In Olson, ed., *Heidegger and Jaspers*, pp. 65–76.

Olson, A. M. "Jaspers, Heidegger, and 'The Phantom of Existentialism.'" *Human Studies* 7 (1984): 387–95.

_____. "Jaspers's Critique of Mysticism." *Journal of the American Academy of Religion* 51 (1983): 251–66.

_____. "Jaspers' Critique of Modernity: A Postmodern Reflection." In Ehrlich/Wisser, eds., *Karl Jaspers Today*, pp. 363–80.

_____. "Hegel and Jaspers on the Comparative Philosophy of Religion." In Wisser/Ehrlich, eds., *Karl Jaspers. Philosopher Among Philosophers*, pp. 41–56.

_____. "Glasnost and Enlightenment. Karl Jaspers and Eastern Europe." *Yearbook of the Austrian Karl Jaspers Society* 3/4 (1990/91): 101–17.

Pepper, G. B. "Karl Jaspers on the Sciences: In Retrospect." In Ehrlich/Wisser, eds., *Karl Jaspers Today*, pp. 153–78.

_____. "Jaspers's Response to Modernity: Critical Reflections on Communication, Science, and Education." In Walters, ed. *The Tasks of Truth: Essays on Karl Jaspers's Idea of the University*, pp. 55–68.

Pfeiffer, J. "On Karl Jaspers' Interpretation of Art." In Schilpp, ed., *The Philosophy of Karl Jaspers*, pp. 703–18.

Rabinbach, A. "The German as Pariah: *Karl Jaspers's* The Question of German Guilt." In *In the Shadow of Catastrophe: German Intellectuals between Apocalypse and Enlightenment*. Berkeley, Los Angeles, London: University of California Press, 1997, pp. 129–65.

Rauche, G. "The Paradox of '*Das Scheitern*' as a World Formula." In Ehrlich/Wisser, eds., *Karl Jaspers. Philosophy on the Way to "World Philosophy,"* pp. 257–64.

Rehder, H. "Literary Criticism and the Existentialism of Jaspers." In Schilpp, ed., *The Philosophy of Karl Jaspers*, pp. 719–47.

Ricci Sindoni, P. "Teleology and Philosophical Historiography: Husserl and Jaspers." *Analecta Husserliana* 9 (1979): 281–99.

Rickman, H. P. "The Philosophic Basis of Psychiatry: Jaspers and Dilthey." *Philosophy of the Social Sciences* 17 (1987): 173–96.

Ricoeur, P. "The Relation of Jaspers' Philosophy to Religion." In Schilpp, ed., *The Philosophy of Karl Jaspers*, pp. 611–43.

Riesterer, B. "Karl Jaspers's New View of Philosophy." *Metaphilosophy* 17 (1986): 318–28.

_____. "Existenz and Transcendence. Karl Jaspers and the Crisis of Contemporary Liberalism." In Wisser/Ehrlich, eds., *Karl Jaspers. Philosopher Among Philosophers*, pp. 228–34.

_____. "Karl Jaspers and the Reassessment of the Self by contemporary Philosophers and Physicists." *Yearbook of the Austrian Karl Jaspers Society* 3/4 (1990/91): 232–44.

Rigali, N. J. "A New Axis: Karl Jaspers' Philosophy of History." *International Philosophical Quarterly* 10 (1970): 441–57.

Riordan, T. M. "Karl Jaspers: An Existentialist Looks at University Education." *Educational Theory* 26 (1976): 113–20.

Rockmore, T. "Jaspers and Heidegger: Philosophy and Politics." In Olson, ed., *Heidegger and Jaspers*, pp. 92–110.

Sablone, G. M. "Man Before God in the Philosophy of Karl Jaspers." *Philosophy Today* 11 (1967): 155–65.

Salamun, K. "The Concept of Liberality in Jaspers's Philosophy and the Idea of the University." In Walters, ed. *The Tasks of Truth: Essays on Karl Jaspers's Idea of the University*, pp. 39–53.

_____. "The Ethos of Humanity in Karl Jaspers's Political Philosophy." *Man and World* 23 (1990): 225–30.

_____. "Moral Implications of Karl Jaspers's Existentialism." *Philosophy and Phenomenological Research* 49 (1988): 317–22.

Saner, H. "Jaspers's 'Theses' on the Question of University Rejuvenation. A Critical Comparison with Heidegger's 'Rectorial Address'." In Wisser/Ehrlich, eds., *Karl Jaspers. Philosopher Among Philosophers*, pp. 139–52.

Sarin, I. "Jaspers's Quest for Existential Communication." In Ehrlich/Wisser, eds., *Karl Jaspers. Philosophy on the Way to "World Philosophy,"* pp. 205–10.

_____. "Jaspers' Analysis of Existenz and Human Solidarity: New Vista of Communication." *Yearbook of the Austrian Karl Jaspers Society* 7/8 (1994/95): 58–69.

_____. "Existential Problematic of Temporality and Transcendence: Jaspers and Buddha." *Yearbook of the Austrian Karl Jaspers Society* 13 (2000): 57–67.

_____. "Jaspers on Scientism, Historicity and the Quest for Values." *Yearbook of the Austrian Karl Jaspers Society* 15 (2002): 105–13.

_____. "Freedom and Reason. Jaspers and Kant." In Wisser/Ehrlich, eds., *Karl Jaspers. Philosopher Among Philosophers*, pp. 29–40.

Smith, R. G. "Karl Jaspers on Theology and Philosophy." *The Hibbert Journal* 49 1951): 62–66.

Schacht, R. L. "On Existentialism, Existenz-Philosophy and Philosophical Anthropology." *American Philosophical Quarterly* 11 (1974): 291–305.

Schmitt, W. "Karl Jaspers' Influence on Psychiatry." *Journal of the British Society for Phenomenology* 17 (1986): 36–51.

Schrag O. O. "Jaspers: Beyond Traditional Metaphysics and Ontology." *International Philosophical Quarterly* 5 (1965): 163–82.

_____. "Jaspers and Heidegger. Hermeneutics of Religion." In Wisser/Ehrlich, eds., *Karl Jaspers. Philosopher Among Philosophers*, pp. 113–20.

_____. "Existence, Existenz, and Social Organization." In Ehrlich/Wisser, eds., *Karl Jaspers. Philosophy on the Way to "World Philosophy,"* pp. 101–108.

Tillich, P. "Heidegger and Jaspers." In Olson, ed., *Heidegger and Jaspers*, 16–28.

Thyssen, J. "The Concept of 'Foundering' in Jaspers' Philosophy." In Schilpp, ed., *The Philosophy of Karl Jaspers*, pp. 297–336.

Wahl, J. "Notes on Some Relations of Jaspers to Kierkegaard and Heidegger." In Schilpp, ed., *The Philosophy of Karl Jaspers*, pp. 393–406.

Walker, C. "Karl Jaspers and Edmund Husserl, I: The Perceived Convergence, II: The Divergence, in Philosophy." *Philosophy, Psychiatry and Psychology* 1 (1994): 117–34 and 245-262.

_____. "Karl Jaspers and Edmund Husserl, III: Jaspers as a Kantian Phenomenologist, IV: Phenomenology as Emphatic Understanding." *Philosophy, Psychiatry and Psychology* 2 (1995): 65–82 and 319–43.

Wallraff, C. F. "Jaspers in English: A Failure in Communication." *Philosophy and Phenomenological Research* 37 (1977): 537–48.

Walters, G. J. "Karl Jaspers and the Role of 'Conversion' (*Umkehr*) in the Nuclear Age: Moral-Political Dimension in the Thought of Karl Jaspers." *Yearbook of the Austrian Karl Jaspers Society* 2 (1989): 88–106.

_____. "Human Rights, World Philosophy, and the Quest for Global Solidarity: Jaspers's Abiding Contribution." *Yearbook of the Austrian Karl Jaspers Society* 10 (1997): 127–50.

_____. "Academic Freedom and the University Idea: Jaspers and Newman Compared." In Walters, ed. *The Tasks of Truth: Essays on Karl Jaspers's Idea of the University*, pp. 77–96.

_____. "Jaspers's Philosophical Faith and Revelational Faith Today. Can the Two Faiths Meet in the Struggle for Human Liberation?" In Wisser/Ehrlich, eds., *Karl Jaspers. Philosopher Among Philosophers*, pp. 217–27.

_____. "Technology, Transcendence, and Modernity: Marcel and Jaspers." In *Visual Information Processing*. Edited by Sal Soraci Jr. and Kimiyo Murata-Soraci. Westport, Connecticut, London: Praeger Publishers, 2003, pp. 261–85.

Weldhen, M. "The Existentialists and Problems of Moral and Religious Education: Tillich and Jaspers." *Journal of Moral Education* 1 (1972): 97–101.

Wiggins, O. P., and Schwartz, M. A. "Edmund Husserl's Influence on Karl Jaspers's Phenomenology." *Philosophy, Psychiatry and Psychology* 4 (1997): 15–36.

Wisser, R. "Jaspers, Heidegger, and the Struggle of Existenz-Philosophy for the Existence of Philosophy." *International Philosophical Quarterly* 24 (1984): 143–55.

Yoshizawa, D. "Jaspers's Concern with Nietzsches Philological Psychology." In Wisser/Ehrlich, eds., *Karl Jaspers. Philosopher Among Philosophers*, pp. 99–106.

Young-Bruehl, E. "'Cosmopolitan History'." *Revue Internationale de Philosophie* 147 (1983): 440–59.

ABOUT THE CONTRIBUTORS

ANDREAS CESANA is professor of philosophy and head of the *Studium generale* (Department for Interdisciplinary Studies) at the University of Mainz, having previously taught at the University of Basle. He has published several studies on Karl Jaspers. His books include *Geschichte als Entwicklung? Zur Kritik des geschichtsphilosophischen Entwicklungsdenkens* and *Johann Jakob Bachofens Geschichtsdeutung*. He is chief editor, *Jacob Burckhardt Werke: Kritische Gesamtausgabe*, XXVII Vols., and president of the International Association of Jaspers Societies.

YOUNG-DO CHUNG, Professor Emeritus of philosophy at Dong-A University, Busan, South Korea. He was president of the Korean Nietzsche Society, head of the Busan Forum, and president of the New Korean Philosophical Association. He has translated more than thirty books on German philosophy. His major works include *Nietzsche as Antichrist* (1964), *Ortega's Philosophy of Vital Reason* (1979), *Marxism and Neo-Marxism* (1982), the *Contemporary Philosophy of Europe* (1985), *The Acceptance and Understanding of Nietzsche's Philosophy* (1998), *Principal Problems of Jaspers's Philosophy* (2000), *Thought and Culture* (2001), and an *Introduction to Philosophy* (2001).

EDITH EHRLICH did graduate study at Basel with Karl Jaspers, Karl Barth, and Edgar Salin, and completed her M.A. in philosophy at Yale University. At the University of Massachusetts (Amherst), where she taught for twelve years, she received her doctorate in German literature with a dissertation on *Suffering in Nietzsche: Motive and Mask*. Dr. Ehrlich is co-editor and/or translator of Jaspers's *The Great Philosophers*, Vols. 3 and 4 (1993 and 1994) and *Karl Jaspers: Basic Philosophical Writings, Selections* (2nd ed., 1995) She is translator of numerous articles about, and original selections by Jaspers published in scholarly journals and collections.

S. NASSIR GHAEMI, MD, is associate professor of psychiatry and public health, Emory University, where he directs the Bipolar Disorder Research Program. He is a member of the executive council of the Association of Philosophy and Psychiatry (AAPP), co-founder of the Boston AAPP Chapter. He was co-recipient of the Karl Jaspers prize of the AAPP for his essay, "Mind/Brain Theories and Their Discontents," *Integrative Psychiatry*, 10 (1994): 52-57. He is editor of *Polypharmacy in Psychiatry* (2002), and has published extensively in psychopharmacology, psychiatric phenomenology, and philosophical aspects of psychiatry. His most recent book is *Concepts of*

Psychiatry: A Pluralistic Approach to the Mind and Mental Illness. Baltimore, MD: Johns Hopkins University Press, 2007.

SAWAKO HANYU is professor of philosophy at Ochanomizu University, Tokyo, Japan. She is the author of *Jaspers no Sonzairon* (*The Ontology of Karl Jaspers*, 1996), *Tetugakue* (*An Introduction to Philosophy*, 1996), as well as of numerous articles on Jaspers's philosophy and comparative philosophy written in Japanese, English and German. She is editor-in-chief of *Kommunikation*, the journal of the Jaspers Society of Japan, and the Asian International Delegate for the Sixth International Jaspers Conference, Seoul, South Korea (2009).

JOSEPH W. KOTERSKI, is professor of philosophy, Fordham University, director of the Masters Program in Philosophical Resources, and editor-in-chief of the *International Philosophical Quarterly*. He is the editor of ten books, and has published articles in natural law ethics, Thomistic metaphysics, the history of medieval philosophy, and has served for many years as an executive member of the Karl Jaspers Society of North America. He is also author of the articles "Jaspers on Freedom and Truth in Science" (1988) and "Jaspers on Realism and Idealism" (1998).

GERHARD KNAUSS, Emeritus Professor of philosophy, University of Saarbruecken, Germany. He studied with Karl Jaspers in Heidelberg and Basel, and taught philosophy at Tohoku-University in Sendai, and Komaba University in Tokyo. He is the author of *Gegenstand und Umgreifendes*, as well as numerous articles on Jaspers´s philosophy, including "The Concept of the 'Encompassing' in Jaspers's Philosophy," in P. A. Schilpp, *The Philosophy of Karl Jaspers* (2nd. Rev. ed., 1982).

RAM ADHAR MALL is president of the International Society for Intercultural Philosophy, and co-editor of the series *Studies in Intercultural Philosophy*. He is author of *Hume's Concept of Man: An Essay in Philosophical Anthropology* (1967); *Experience and Reason: The Phenomenology of Husserl and its Relation to Hume's Philosophy* (1973); *Naturalism and Criticism* (1975); *Der Hinduismus: Seine Stellung in der Vielfalt der Religionen* (1997); *Intercultural Philosophy* (2000); and *Essays zur interkulturellen Philosophie* (2003).

ALAN OLSON is professor of philosophy of religion, at Boston University; executive director and editor, *Proceedings of the Twentieth World Congress of Philosophy* (12 Vols.,1998); chairman, Committee on International Cooperation, American Philosophical Association; and director, Paideia Project, Boston University. He is author of *Transcendence and Hermeneutics* (1979), *Video Icons and Values* (1990) and *Hegel and the Spirit: Philosophy as Pneumatology* (1992); he is editor of *Jaspers and Heidegger* (1994) and *The Quest for Paideia in an Age of Uncertainty* (2004).

GEORGE B. PEPPER is Emeritus Professor of philosophy, Iona College. In 1980 he and Leonard H. Ehrlich founded the Karl Jaspers Society of North America. He, together with Edith Ehrlich and Leonard H. Ehrlich, edited *Karl Jaspers: Basic Philosophical Writings* (1996, 2nd ed., 1995). He is author of "Karl Jaspers on the Sciences: In Retrospect" (1988) and "Die Relevanz von Jaspers' Achsenzeit für interkulturelle Studien" (1991).

KURT SALAMUN is professor i. R. at the Department of Philosophy, University of Graz, Austria and president of the Austrian Karl Jaspers Society. He is the author of *Karl Jaspers* (1985, and three translations), editor of *Karl Jaspers—Zur Aktualität seines Denkens* (1991), *Philosophie-Erziehung-Universität. Zu Karl Jaspers' Bildungs- und Erziehungsphilosophie* (1995), and co-editor of The *Yearbook of the Austrian Karl Jaspers-Society*. He also edits the *Series in the Philosophy of Karl R. Popper and Critical Rationalism.*

HANS SANER is lecturer for philosophy of culture at the Academy of Music Basel, and was the last personal assistant of Karl Jaspers. He is author of *Karl Jaspers: Mit Selbstzeugnissen und Bilddokumenten* (1970, 12th ed. 2005), *Einsamkeit und Kommunikation* (1994), and *Kant's Political Thought*, translated by E. B. Ashton (1973). He is editor of Jaspers's *Nachlass* (1991) and co-editor of Jaspers´s correspondence with both Hannah Arendt and Martin Heidegger.

INDU SARIN is professor, Department of Philosophy, Panjab University, Chandigarh, India. She is author of *Kierkegaard: A Turning Point* (1996), "Freedom and Reason: Jaspers and Kant" (1993), "The Problematic of Temporality and Transcendence: Jaspers and Buddha" (2000), "Scientism, Historicity and the Quest for Values" (2002), and the book *Man in the World and Beyond: Jaspers's Vision* (forthcoming).

GREGORY J. WALTERS is professor of philosophy, Saint Paul University / Université Saint-Paul, Ottawa, Canada. He is the author of *Karl Jaspers and the Role of 'Conversion' in the Nuclear Age* (1987) and *Human Rights in an Information Age: A Philosophical Analysis* (2002), and editor of *The Tasks of Truth: Essays on Karl Jaspers's Idea of the University* (1996).

INDEX